NEW PRACTITIONER'S GUIDE TO INTELLECTUAL PROPERTY

David R. Gerk
John M. Fleming

Section of Intellectual Property Law
AMERICAN BAR ASSOCIATION

Cover design by ABA Publishing

Printed in the United States of America.

16 15 14 13 12   5 4 3 2 1

Library of Congress Cataloging-in-Publication Data

New practitioner's guide to intellectual property / David R. Gerk and John M. Fleming.

p. cm.

1. Intellectual property—United States. 2. Trademarks—Law and legislation—United States. 3. Competition, Unfair—United States. 4. Patent laws and legislation—United States. 5. Trade secrets—Law and legislation—United States. 6. Copyright—United States. I. Fleming, John M. II. Title.

KF2979.G47 2012

346.7304'8—dc23   2012012370

ISBN: 978-1-61438-476-2

Contents

About the Authors

David R. Gerk is an attorney in the Office of Policy and External Affairs (OPEA) at the U.S. Patent and Trademark Office (USPTO) where he advises the Under Secretary of Commerce for Intellectual Property and Director of the U.S. Patent and Trademark Office on domestic and international IP issues as well as on United States treaty obligations and helps to formulate U.S. domestic and international policy regarding protection and enforcement of intellectual property rights. In his role at the OPEA, he also helps promote development of intellectual property systems nationally and internationally, consults with foreign governments and other U.S. Government agencies on substantive intellectual property rights laws and legal and judicial regimes, and provides and participates in technical assistance and capacity-building programs and conferences with foreign governments seeking to develop or improve their intellectual property laws and regulations.

Prior to joining the USPTO, David was a shareholder in Banner & Witcoff's Washington, D.C., office where he practiced intellectual property law with a focus on counseling, prosecution, and litigation of utility and design patent matters, principally in the mechanical, electrical, and computer arts. He also prosecuted and counseled in copyright, trademark, and trade dress matters. He is experienced representing client interests, including large corporations, small and medium-size businesses, and individual inventors in technologies ranging from manufacturing processes and consumer products to Internet and cellular communications to biomedical devices and nutraceuticals and various other technologies.

David is a co-founder of the *Patent Law Option* at The George Washington University School of Engineering and Applied Science (SEAS), where he serves as a part-time professor. He regularly publishes and lectures on a wide array of intellectual property issues. David also served in committee leadership for both the ABA and AIPLA, regularly meeting with attorneys, organizations, business leaders, and the USPTO and international IP officials regarding intellectual property legislation, legal decisions, and U.S. and foreign IP practice and procedures. He received an Honors B.S. in mechanical engineering from Marquette University and a J.D. from The George Washington University Law School.

John M. Fleming is a principal shareholder at the law firm of Banner & Witcoff, Ltd., specializing in all forms of intellectual property protection, where he concentrates on preparing and prosecuting utility and design patent applications in a variety of technical fields while participating in litigation matters, client counseling, and a wide spectrum of opinion work. John's technical areas include telecommunications, Internet-related and private network technology, semiconductors, e-commerce, digital/electronic handwriting, color management, graphical user interface systems, financial security and authentication, application programming interfaces, and computer-relation technologies involving hardware, software, and firmware. In addition, he has design prosecution experience and development, including various hardware, computer interfaces, and icons. John has filed and prosecuted hundreds of design applications from initial prototypes to commercially available products. With a practical-based background in electrical engineering, he has experience in all phases of writing and prosecuting complex patent applications in a variety of technical fields.

John co-serves as an associate professorial lecturer in the Mechanical and Aerospace Engineering Department (MAE) at The George Washington University teaching patent law for engineers with David R. Gerk. John earned his B.S. degree in electrical engineering from Clemson University with concentrations in circuit design and configurations and fiber-optic technologies. He earned his J.D. from The Catholic University of America Columbus School of Law in 2002.

Acknowledgments

People are like dirt. They can either nourish you and help you grow as a person or they can stunt your growth and make you wilt and die.

—Plato

No matter how independent we all like to believe we are, very few of life's accomplishments are possible without help from others, whether directly or indirectly. Along those lines we would like to acknowledge not only those who directly made this book possible, but those who nourished our growth as people and professionals and helped us to even be in a position to turn this book into a reality. First we would like to thank a few of the people in our careers who have given us opportunities or trusted in our abilities when it perhaps would have been just as easy, if not easier, to not give us a chance. Thanks to Paul Raptis, Roger Schechter, Beth Stein, Robert Katz, Bob Altherr, Joseph Potenza, Gary Fedorochko, Ross Dannenberg, Michael K. Myers, Michael W. Plesniak, and Mary Critharis. We would also like to thank the ABA and the ABA Section of Intellectual Property Law especially, including Jeffrey Salyards, Amy Mandel, and Amelia Stone. Additionally, thanks goes to our colleagues, partners, and friends at the law firm of Banner & Witcoff, Ltd., for their support, insight, and patience. Thanks also to Helene Liwinski for her insightful input on trademarks. A very special thanks goes to our families—Ron Gerk, Barb Gerk, Dana Gerk, Madeline Saban, Mack Fleming, Libby Fleming, and Katie Carmona—for all the ways they have helped and supported us through the years. Last, but certainly not least, we would like to thank our wives, Katie Sharpee and Candace Fleming, and John's children, Colton and Cooper, for their seemingly endless patience, understanding, and support as we worked late into the night, weekends, and in between various obligations. Without their gentle reminders to continue forging ahead and their willingness to let us write when we should have been helping them on many of life's tasks, we could have never finished this book.

Section 1

Introduction

Those who dare to fail miserably can achieve greatly.
— John F. Kennedy
35th President of the United States

Perhaps no area of law evolves at the pace with which intellectual property law evolves. Like the inventors, businesses, artists, and writers that rely upon intellectual property law to provide protections for their work and value to their toils, intellectual property law continues to revise and update itself to keep pace. While human ingenuity and creativity continues to prove we as a human race will seemingly never cease innovating, creating, and evolving, the magnitude of our creations sometimes make us wonder what could be left to create? It is rumored that in 1899 the Commissioner of the U.S. Office of Patents stated, "everything that can be invented has been invented." Since then the airplanes took flight (1903), assembly line manufacturing took shape (1913), insulin (1921) was extracted and prepared resulting in its availability for diabetics, and lasers were fired (1958). More recently smart phones, electric cars, the human genome project, Google,® Facebook,® and Twitter®—concepts that were even a stretch for science fiction novels—have become realities.

It has been several decades now since intellectual property issues were merely matters of interest to a small number of attorney specialists practicing law in obscurity. Intellectual property rights today are front-page news. Intellectual property (IP) is subject matter that touches everyone's life regardless of profession, socio-economic standing, or nationality and whether or not it is recognized. From an economic and business perspective, *The Economist* has reported that up to 75 percent of the value of a U.S. publicly traded company is based solely upon the company's intellectual property. For start-ups or companies in certain tech sectors, the entire value of a company may be tied to its IP. National and international intellectual property policies and agreements stand as pillars of government supporting the ability of nations to do business in globalized markets and provide assurances for economic investment in jurisdictions across the globe. Absent IP protections, global economic development cannot happen and economic opportunity for all would be lost.

IP and IP rights not only influence economies and the business world, they play a strong role in virtually every aspect of our modern life. Patent rights or lack of rights may dictate functionality incorporated into new devices. Trademark rights influence what products or services we purchase and copyright law protects musicians and moviemakers from rapid unauthorized duplication of their works and the resulting loss of financial benefits and credit. IP and the technologies enabled under IP rights systems also affect world events. Recently, online social media sites have become so intertwined in world events that the sites have played a significant role in social and political movements—including revolutions—around the world. For those that view life with a less global view, IP rights are still critical to their daily life. Any action involving an iPhone® or a movie rental involves intertwined IP rights, even if few realize it.

Despite the prominence and importance of intellectual property and the immense value to individuals that grasp even IP basics, there seems to be a gap in comprehensive educational materials for individuals who are not already experts in intellectual property matters. Significant volumes have been written for experienced IP attorneys and others who have already acquired both a theoretical understanding of legal principles in their law school studies and further legal knowledge through years of practical experiences in law firms, governmental work, or other IP occupations. Likewise, case law books written in the traditional casebook format for use in law school IP courses often focus on one particular type or aspect of IP. These materials have a wealth of knowledge and serve their purpose, but they typically are not very helpful to those with a thirst for practical and comprehensive experience-based information on intellectual property law and IP practice in the United States.

We have set out in the *New Practitioner's Guide to Intellectual Property* (*NPG*) to provide a resource distinct from any in existence. As such, we believe the *NPG* provides for the first time a comprehensive, practical, frequency- and occurrence-based guide to intellectual property and intellectual property law that is suited for new intellectual property practitioners (including new patent, trademark and copyright attorneys); general counsels; students and individuals studying and working in the sciences; non-IP attorneys who wish to get up to speed on IP issues; and institutions of higher learning offering courses on intellectual property practice. Therefore, the *NPG*, in contrast to other resources, provides general understanding of all the major areas of U.S. intellectual property law but also provides an understanding of the acquisition/prosecution process, as well as the enforcement/litigation process of all the major areas of intellectual property.

The *NPG* is intended to be not just a reference but also a cover-to-cover readable reference book. In particular, the *NPG* discusses in detail prosecution before the United States Patent and Trademark Office and the U.S. Copyright Office for those matters that are most regularly encountered by IP practitioners and entities securing IP rights in the United States. Likewise, common litigation actions and matters are also covered as they occur in patent, trademark, and copyright cases. The *NPG* is aimed to be the "senior IP associate" or "partner" that you can ask for guidance as you begin your intellectual property career or start working with matters that relate to or involve intellectual property. But again, the *NPG* is certainly not aimed just at new IP lawyers. For thousands of engineers and scientists who enter the work force each year, information about IP issues and how they are likely to be handled can be critical to professional success. Similarly, entrepreneurs, businessmen, and businesswomen of all walks of life can gain greatly from basic IP knowledge. We hope and believe the *NPG* can assist in those endeavors through its simple and enjoyable presentation of IP information that includes just the right amount of detail, providing readers with knowledge to understand and utilize the IP tools that are available in the United States. As one of America's best known and earliest inventors, Benjamin Franklin, once said, "an investment in knowledge pays the best interest." We hope and believe you will find the *New Practitioner's Guide to Intellectual Property* to be educational, agreeable, and worth your time as a reader.

Section 2

Patents

PART 1

Patent Groundwork

Next came the Patent laws. These began in England in 1624; and, in this country, with the adoption of our constitution. Before then, any man might instantly use what another had invented; so that the inventor had no special advantage from his own invention. The patent system changed this; secured to the inventor, for a limited time, the exclusive use of his invention; and thereby added the fuel of interest to the fire of genius, in the discovery and production of new and useful things.

—Abraham Lincoln,[1]
16th President of the United States,
inventor of U.S. Pat. No. 6,469 (1849) for a "manner of buoying vessels."

I. HISTORY

Perhaps the most useful background information to keep in mind when analyzing patents, patent law, and the patent system is the purpose and motivation behind the patent system. While virtually all countries have a

1. Abraham Lincoln, second lecture on discoveries and inventions, delivered to the Phi Alpha Society of Illinois College at Jacksonville, Ill., Feb. 11, 1859, as cited by *The Collected Works of Abraham Lincoln*, ed. Roy P. Basler, vol. 3, p. 357. Abraham Lincoln is the only U.S. President to be named as an inventor on a U.S. patent.

patent system, the prevailing purposes and motivations of each system are varied.

At the heart of the U.S. patent system is the desire to promote progress and development in areas we today loosely refer to as science and technology. Encouragement of continued progress and development of science and technology is set forth in the United States Constitution in Article I, Section 8, Clause 8, and this single clause has served as the backbone for the U.S. Patent System for several hundred years. The drafting of Article I, Section 8, Clause 8 was not the initiation of the concept of a patent system, and one certainly cannot claim that the Founding Fathers invented a patent system in the broad sense.

The term patent originates from the Latin phrase *patere,* which means "to lie open." *Patere* is a shortened form of the phrase *lettre patere,* or "open letter or document for some authority."[2] While the origins of the concept of a patent system are claimed by a variety of nations, U.S. patent law arises from a multicultural heritage that may not be properly assigned to a single source. The Venetians are among the first to have patent laws. Their laws provided a dual right that included (1) the exclusionary right that later became the sole "right to exclude" of U.S. patent law, as well as (2) a privilege to operate the patented invention free from interference by the guild's monopoly in the particular area of technology.[3] The concepts that underlie our current U.S. patent system are also apparent in varying degree in early English and Continental systems that developed in the wake of the Venetian system.[4] While American patent law extends back at least to the Act of 1790, patent legislation in the individual states stretches back as far as 1641 to Massachusetts.[5] Early American patent laws in at least nine of the original thirteen colonies granted rewards to inventors, but not all of them were necessarily "patents" in the sense of providing rights to exclude others.[6]

As patent law and its application attempt to keep up with the pace of innovation, the U.S. patent system is sometimes criticized. In particular, when patents are issued for inventions deemed by the public not

2. Collins English Dictionary—Complete & Unabridged 10th Edition, Wm. Collins Sons & Co. Ltd. (2009).

3. Martin J. Adelman, Randall R. Rader, John R. Thomas, Harold C. Wagner, Cases and Materials on Patent Law, American Casebook Series, West Group, St, Paul, Minn. (1998), at p. 9.

4. *Id.* at pp. 10–11.

5. *Id.*

6. *Id.*

to be sufficiently innovative or to be overly broad in their coverage such that they appear to stifle further innovation, the patent system can get called into question. However, the historical purpose and motivation of most patent systems, including the U.S. patent system, are clearly the promotion of progress and innovation in the "useful arts" (science and technology).

A. Purpose and Motivation

The majority of patent practitioners prosecute, litigate, opine, and advise on the *application* of the patent laws and regulations in relation to *facts* of extreme interest to their clients. To effectively advocate or opine regarding scenarios of interests, it is beneficial to understand the purpose and motivation behind the laws, statutes, and regulations. Equity and justice may be a pivotal distinction between two scenarios and two distinct outcomes in similar or even related factual scenarios. Practitioners may effectively use an understanding of both the broad purpose(s) of the patent system and the more narrowly focused purpose(s) of individual laws and regulations to advocate on behalf of a client, to predict a likely outcome before a judicial or quasi-judicial official, and sometimes even to invoke a change in the application of a law or regulation itself through either the legislative process or judicial review.

While patent systems across the globe continue to become increasingly similar and related under the provisions of various intellectual property and trade treaties, individuality continues to exist among countries in relation to their individual patent systems. Regardless, the impetus behind intellectual property rights often can be understood as promoting an incentive theory.

Similar to the U.S. Constitution's explicit authorization of Congress "to promote progress,"[7] patent systems (and intellectual property systems generally) are structured to encourage behavior or actions. Manifestation of an incentive theory in U.S. patent law is the *quid pro quo* of the patent system. In exchange for you, Mr./Ms. Inventor, publicly describing the fully developed version (best mode) of your invention in a manner sufficient to enable one skilled in the art (perhaps another engineer, computer scientist, chemist, or the like) to re-create your invention, the government will grant you a right to exclude others from making, using, selling, offering for sale, or importing your claimed invention for a limited

7. U.S. CONST. art. I, §8, cl. 8.

period of time. As such, inventors are encouraged or incentivized to publicly disclose their inventions through government publication (patents and patent applications) so that the invention can be further used by the public. Other inventors who learn of these developments theoretically will be able to build on the previous inventors' work in a more expeditious manner than had discoveries been kept secret. Just as researchers and developers often work in teams to improve the efficiency, reliability, and success of the innovation, it may be argued that the patent system enlists all the patentees and applicants, and the public itself, as an enormous research and development team pushing innovation ever forward.

However, realists recognize that human and business self-interest most often drives the efforts of mankind; therefore, a sufficient carrot or reward must be dangled to entice innovators to publicly disclose their innovation and developments in a manner to benefit society. This carrot has taken the form of a right to exclude others from certain activity relating to the invention. This right to exclude, depending on its particulars, may be extremely worthwhile to people and business. Biotechnology and pharmaceutical sectors often are cited for some of the more extreme examples of the value of patent protection. It is not unheard of for a single day of patent protection (exclusivity) in these areas to be valued at or result in millions of dollars in further revenue for the owner of those rights. However, these figures may seem less extreme upon consideration that it may take the same owner months or years of research, significant capital expenditures, and several unsuccessful attempts at a new biotechnology product before a successful product is produced, much less makes it to the public marketplace. Additionally, significant amounts of money may be expended in obtaining a patent to protect the innovation.

Beyond the specific quid pro quo of the patent system, significant investments of time and money in research and development are encouraged with a view to the "pot of gold" if a successful innovation is the result. Of course, individuals and entities may choose not to utilize the patent system, thereby hoping to keep their innovations secret[8] and avoid the time limitation of protection afforded by a patent or the costs of governmental and representative fees. While choosing not to pursue patent protection has proven successful for such products as the secret formula for Coca-Cola or the secret recipe for Kentucky Fried Chicken,[9] the risk

8. See *Trade Secret Section.*

9. These are well-known historical examples of successful and highly valued "trade secrets."

of unforeseen disclosure, reverse engineering, and copycats make pursuit of patent protection an attractive option in many instances.

B. Opposing Views—The Good, the Bad, and the Ugly

The incentive theories behind the U.S. patent system in particular are clear as evidenced by explicit recitation in the U.S. Constitution. However, practical effects and implementation are often less clear and not agreed upon. As patents have moved from a niche topic to a mainstream item on the front page of newspapers and websites, varied opinions exist regarding the good, bad, and perhaps even ugly effects of the system.

The Good—As intended by the Framers, the patent system provides a strong incentive for the devotion of resources toward innovation with the prospect of future compensation, reward and accolade, and personal praise for successful innovation. From a business and economic perspective, the patent system provides business protection for those doing innovative work to develop new and useful products or services without being undercut in the marketplace by a copycat that can offer the same product or service at a cheaper price because it was able to spend comparatively little or no money in development. The United States Patent and Trademark Office (USPTO) is a neutral governmental agency, and the process of obtaining a patent from the USPTO is structured to be a fair and objective process regardless of who the applicant or inventor is and regardless of the type of technology.[10] Further, patent prosecution is a non-adversarial process which entitles applicants to receive a patent unless certain circumstances[11] exist that prevent the USPTO in its governmental role from issuing a patent. On the litigation side, some comfort can be drawn from the appeal process. Since 1982, the U.S. Court of Appeals for the Federal Circuit (Federal Circuit) has had exclusive jurisdiction for cases arising under the patent laws. Accordingly, the judges who sit on this court have acquired significant expertise in patent law and many of the technologies involved in patent cases.

The Bad—The devil is in the details. While implementation of a patent system in the United States primarily provides incentive for innovation, errors in implementation do happen and may undermine the very goals of the patent system with varying effect and magnitude. For example, patent applications may involve complex technologies, and pat-

10. Certain unique exceptions apply. For example, small entities and applicants over 65 may receive expedited handling and/or reduced fees.

11. *E.g.*, *see* 35 U.S.C. §§101, 102, 103, 112, etc.

entability may be a complex issues. However, the USPTO can allocate only limited man-hours and resources to examination of each patent application. Examiners have varied amounts of experience and, as in any profession, vary in their skills and abilities. As a result, some patent applications issue each year that should not have been allowed, while others are rejected that should have proceeded on to issuance. Likewise, patent litigations may be imperfect forums for justice. Juries with few or no technical skills are tasked with understanding cutting-edge technology and the terminology used to describe it, and come to decisions on abstract and nuanced issues such as infringement, obviousness, and the knowledge and understanding of "one skilled in the art."

The Ugly—Obtaining a patent can be an expensive endeavor, especially if the applicant is represented by counsel.[12] The USPTO governmental fee schedule does provide reduced "small entity fees" for small companies and individual inventors. Regardless, the requisite fees require a significant capital investment for any entity pursuing a patent application. Applicants also are extremely eager to obtain patent protection; however, there continues to be a backlog of applications awaiting even a first action by the USPTO (and in other international patent offices). On the litigation side, patent litigations are typically among the most costly types of litigations. Costs do vary depending on the particulars, including the number of patents and claims involved, complexity of the technology, amount of damages or size of market involved, importance of the technology covered by the patent(s), and the amount and type of discovery required. However, in most patent litigations, each side will be required to retain expensive technical expert witnesses, perform significant discovery relating to the patent(s) and products at issue, and hold claim construction hearings and other costly components of a patent litigation.[13] Further, the business operations of litigants may be significantly burdened by their involvement in the discovery process. Patent litigation may be especially fierce between direct competitors that may have a long history of competition and sometimes even previous personal ties that have gone bad.

---

12. It is strongly recommended that anyone interested in pursuing a patent seek legal representation prior to pursuing one or more patent applications with the USPTO.

13. The "average" patent litigation is estimated to cost about $3 million—to $5 million with appeal—and these figures continue to rise. *See U.S —Litigation: Cost and duration of patent litigation*, MANAGING INTELLECTUAL PROPERTY (February 2009).

Winston Churchill once referred to democracy as "the worst form of government except all the others that have been tried." Some might take a similar view of the U.S. patent system. As a practitioner, it is important to understand the strengths and weaknesses and, perhaps more importantly, the certainties and uncertainties to help clients "manage their risks" when utilizing the patent system.

II. UNITED STATES FRAMEWORK

The United States patent system can be characterized as an interwoven network of authorities and decision makers implementing the authority derived from the U.S. Constitution. The legislative, executive, and judicial branches each play a pivotal role in the U.S. patent system. In the U.S. patent system, the legislative branch[14] passes U.S. patent laws. In order to execute or implement these laws on a daily basis, Congress delegated powers such as review of patent applications and issue of patents to an administrative body (USPTO) in the executive branch within the Department of Commerce. Lastly, when disputes arise under these federal patent laws, federal courts in the judiciary branch consider these matters.

A. Article I, Section 8, Clause 8, the Patent Act, and the Hierarchy of Authority

The U.S. Constitution is the highest authority of law in the land. As such, all patent laws must be consistent with the provisions of the Constitution. Further, no executive branch action or judicial decision regarding patents or patent laws may violate the Constitution. Article I, Section 8, Clause 8, is well known as the Constitutional source of the framework for U.S. patents laws, but also for U.S. copyright laws.

> "The Congress shall have Power . . .To promote the Progress of Science and useful Arts, by securing for limited Times to Authors and Inventors the exclusive Right to their respective Writings and Discoveries."
>
> *U.S. Constitution*, Article I, Section 8, Clause 8

While a quick read of Art. I, §8, cl.8 and our modern vernacular with regard to technologies, patents, and copyrights might suggest terms such as "Science" relate to patents and "Arts" relate to copyright, this, in

14. The U.S. House of Representatives and the U.S. Senate.

fact, is not the case. It is understood that when the Framers drafted this provision of the Constitution, the terms in bold below relate to what we now refer to as patents, and the words underlined below relate to what we now refer to as copyrights.

> "The Congress shall have Power...To promote the Progress of <u>Science</u> and **useful Arts**, by securing for limited Times to <u>Authors</u> and **Inventors** the exclusive Right to their respective <u>Writings</u> and **Discoveries**" *U.S. Constitution*, Article I, Section 8, clause 8 (Emphasis added).

Interestingly, trademark law does not find its constitutional basis in Art. I, §8, cl. 8, but instead is rooted in Congress's broad powers under the Commerce Clause—Article I, Section 8, Clause 3.[15] The Commerce Clause is described further in the *Trademark & Trade Dress Sections.*

Patents are exclusively federal subject matter. Using the authority granted to it by the Framers in the Constitution, Congress over time has passed a series of laws to establish the U.S. patent system. These laws were not passed at one time and can and will be added to, revised, or otherwise tweaked as Congress deems proper "to promote progress in the useful arts." Today's patent system draws its roots back to the Framers and notable figures from U.S. history, such as George Washington, John Quincy Adams, Thomas Jefferson, and Henry Clay laying pen to the early patents, as some of the highest ranking officers of the new U.S. government were tasked with review and issuance of early patents.[16] The most recent large overhaul of the U.S patent system, prior to the recently enacted America Invents Act (AIA), occurred in 1952 as part of the U.S.

---

15. "[The Congress shall have Power] To regulate Commerce with foreign Nations, and among the several States, and with the Indian Tribes." U.S. CONST. art. I, §8, cl. 3.

16. The first U.S. patent was granted on July 31, 1790, to Samuel Hopkins and was directed to improved "making of Pot ash and Pearl ash by a new Apparatus and Process." Among the notable signatories were the Secretary of State (Thomas Jefferson), Secretary of War (Henry Knox), and Attorney General (Edmund Randolph). This group of officers given the duty of determining if an invention was sufficiently useful and important to merit the grant of a patent called themselves the "Commissioners for the Promotion of Useful Arts" or "Board of Arts," while others referred to them as the Patent Commission or Patent Board. Frederico, P.J., *Operation of the Patent Act of 1790*, JPOS 18:237–51 (April 1936).

Patent Act of 1952. Practitioners today will recognize changes as a result of what is commonly referred to as the "Patent Laws" or Title 35 of the United States Code.

Consistent with the laws of Title 35,[17] the USPTO issued 167,349 utility patents, 23,116 design patents, and 1,009 plant patents in 2009.[18] In order to carry out its delegated administrative authority of granting patents on behalf of the United States of America, the USPTO sets forth a series of "Patent Rules," which are found in Chapter 37 of the Code of Federal Regulations.[19] These Patent Rules govern the implementation of the Patent Laws by the USPTO and include provisions relating to submission of information disclosure statements,[20] reissue applications,[21] and payment of fees,[22] to name a few illustrative examples. Some of the more common and more important Patent Rules for practitioners are discussed further in the *Patent Prosecution Section.*

With Congress and the USPTO issuing laws, rules, and regulations, there have been and may be again occasions in which provisions may be in conflict. As such, certain courts, including the U.S. Court of Appeals for the Federal Circuit and the U.S. Supreme Court may be asked to review certain provisions for their appropriateness and constitutionality in the framework set forth by the Framers in the Constitution and further specified by Congress in the Patent Laws. It may be helpful to remember the hierarchy of patent provisions should a conflict arise. First and foremost, the U.S. Constitution (e.g., Art. I, §8, cl. 8) sits atop the hierarchy and must be complied with in all instances. Any law, rule, or provision contrary to the Constitution will be stricken as unconstitutional. Below the Constitution sit federal statutes enacted by Congress and international treaties ratified by the Senate. Below these sit the administrative laws of the Code of Federal Regulations.[23]

B. Patent Enforcement in the United States

If an owner believes his or her patent is being infringed, he or she may bring a suit in federal court to enforce the patent against one or more of

17. 35 U.S.C. §§1 *et seq.*
18. http://www.uspto.gov/web/offices/ac/ido/oeip/taf/us_stat.htm.
19. 37 C.F.R. §§1 *et seq.*
20. 37 C.F.R. §1.56.
21. *Id.*
22. *Id.*
23. 37 C.F.R.

the accused infringers. While the particulars of patent infringement are discussed in more detail herein, there are several case paths available to owners of patent rights for enforcing their rights.

The majority of patent infringement cases are initiated in one of the many federal districts in the United States. Not all federal districts are equal in size or case load, especially in regard to the number of patent cases. For example, the state of Illinois has three districts, the Northern (N.D. Ill.), Central (C.D. Ill.), and Southern Districts (S.D. Ill.). Among those districts, the N.D. Ill. (which includes Chicago) is among the more popular districts for patent litigation cases. In contrast, the entire state of Wyoming falls within a single district (D. Wyo.) and has few patent litigation cases.[24] The district courts in which patent litigations are most often pursued include some of the larger and more tech-focused metropolitan areas, but also include perhaps some surprising venues to those not familiar with patent litigation, such as the Eastern District of Virginia (E.D. Va.) and the Eastern District of Texas (E.D. Tex.). Both of these district courts are historically attractive to patent owners since they are currently known to have very aggressive and expedited case schedules. As a result, trials, decisions, and final determinations regarding infringement are arrived at more quickly, typically much to the preference of the case filer—often the patentee.[25]

The International Trade Commission (ITC) is another venue or case path those alleging patent infringement may pursue according to 19 U.S.C. §1337.[26] ITC litigation is described in more detail herein. However, its existence as a case path option should be noted. The ITC is an independent federal agency—not a traditional court—that determines import injuries to U.S. industries and can direct actions against unfair trade practices involving patent, trademark, and copyright infringement.[27] The ITC also investigates unfair trade practices wholly unrelated to IP, however, it has become an increasingly popular venue for patent owners to bring cases. The ITC differs generally from federal district courts in that the ITC exercises "in rem jurisdiction" (jurisdiction over the alleged infringing article). Also, cases are heard before an administrative law judge and no

---

24. *See, e.g., Patent Infringement Cases: Selecting the Right Venue Can Be Critical*, Metro. Corp. Counsel (July 2007).

25. *See id.*

26. Intellectual property infringement investigations brought under 19 U.S.C. §1337 before the International Trade Commission are commonly referred to as 337 investigations.

27. http://www.usitc.gov/.

money damages can be awarded as a remedy, only as an exclusion order. Additionally, the ITC has an extremely fast case schedule once an investigation is initiated—often concluding in about 12 months time. This expedited adjudication of a claim of patent infringement is an attractive aspect to many patent rights owners, compared to many federal district courts before which the case may not reach trial for several years. An ITC action may be sought since the rights of a patent owner include the right to prevent others form importing the invention covered in the patent.

Just as patent right owners can bring suit in a federal district court to obtain an infringement ruling, in certain circumstances a party that believes it is going to be sued for infringement may initiate a suit requesting a ruling on the issues of non-infringement and/or invalidity and other issues typically raised in patent infringement litigations.[28] One might logically wonder why a party that has yet to be sued for infringement would instigate a declaratory judgment action that might raise issues for which the party could be liable. In certain instances, the threat of suit, if allowed to linger for an extended period of time, may have detrimental consequences on continued business. Further, preemptively filing a declaratory judgment action may have strategic advantages, such as venue selection—especially when the probability of suit, whether or not a declaratory judgment action is filed, is high.

Regardless of which federal district court serves as the trial court for a patent case, appeals that "arise under" the U.S. patent laws are heard before the U.S. Court of Appeals for the Federal Circuit.[29] The Federal Circuit, as it is commonly called, was created in 1982 and sits in Washington, D.C. This specialized appellate court has exclusive jurisdiction over cases that are based in whole or part on U.S. patent law issues. However, the Federal Circuit also has jurisdiction over a variety of other cases, including government contracts, money claims against the U.S. government and veterans benefits. The Federal Circuit also hears appeals of decisions by the Board of Patent Appeals and Interferences (BPAI)[30] and the International Trade Commission (ITC).

---

28. *See, e.g.*, SanDisk Corp. v. STMicroelectronics, Inc., 480 F.3d 1372 (Fed. Cir. 2007). Under the Declaratory Judgment Act, jurisdiction for a Declaratory Judgment Action may be found "where a patentee asserts rights under a patent based on certain identified ongoing or planned activity of another party, and where that party contends that it has the right to engage in the accused activity without license."

29. *See* 28 U.S.C. §§1295(a) and 1338.

30. The Federal Circuit will hear appeals of the decisions of the Patent Trial and Appeal Board (PTAB) under the AIA.

The U.S. Supreme Court also *may* choose to hear patent cases from time to time at the Court's discretion. It is uncommon for the Supreme Court to grant certiorari and hear more than one or two patent cases a year and patent practitioners should consider decisions by the Federal Circuit to be dispositive unless the case raises a Constitutional issue regarding implementation of the patent laws or conflicting precedents by the Federal Circuit. Even so, successful appeal of a patent case to the Supreme Court is rare.

Figure 1-1

Diagram of Illustrative Patent Litigation and Appeal Forums

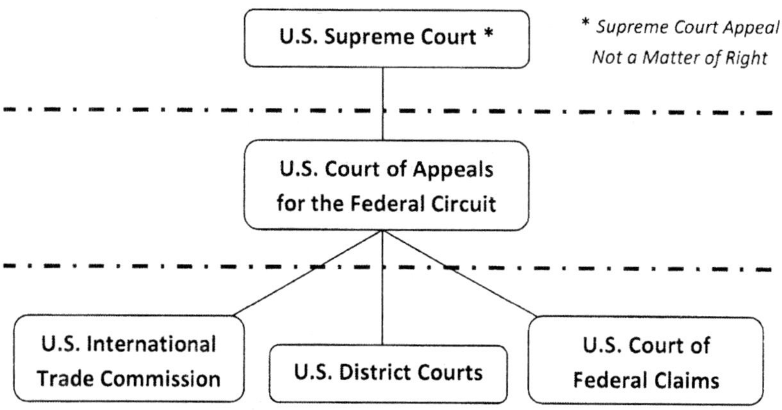

III. U.S. PATENT TYPES AND ANATOMY

What is a patent? A patent is a grant by the government (e.g., U.S.) of a *right to exclude* others from practicing (i.e., making, using, selling, offering to sell, and importing) a particular invention for a set period of time. Patent rights, like other property rights—e.g., personal property—can be assigned, sold, given away, inherited, mortgaged, and licensed. Just as you can sell, trade, assign, or donate your car, so too can you do the same with intellectual property rights, including patent rights. Further, patent rights also can be licensed away in portions or subparts, in nonexclusive or exclusive licenses or in a specific market, because licenses are merely contracts in which the parties generally may structure in any way they desire.

One of the most common misconceptions regarding patentees (a party receiving a patent) is the belief that a patent gives you the right to practice the invention you claimed in your patent. This is unequivocally false. A patent only *gives you the right to exclude others from practicing* an invention, but *it does not give you the right to practice* your invention. A simple example that illustrates this concept involves support devices (a chair and a stool).

Assume for a moment that no *support devices exist* in the world. Inventor A comes along and creates a three-legged support device and receives a valid patent on "a support device comprising three (3) legs." Inventor B creates a support device that has a back rest that makes your device much more comfortable than any device out there. Additionally, Inventor B *adds* another leg to provide for a more stable support device. Inventor B applies for and receives a patent on "a support device comprising four (4) legs wherein the support device includes a backrest."

Figure 2
Support Devices

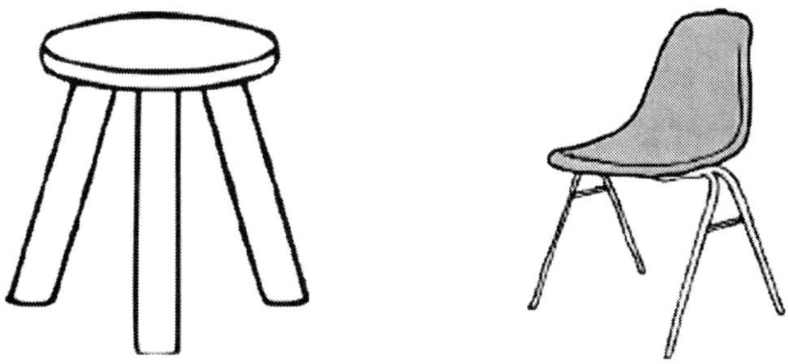

3 legged support device ("stool")

4 legged support device with backrest ("chair")

Can Inventor B legally make, use, sell, or offer for sale her new four-legged support device with a backrest? No! If Inventor B does, she will infringe Inventor A's patent. Can Inventor B exclude others from making, using, selling, or offering for sale a four-legged support device with a backrest? Yes. In this instance, Inventor B will be able to exclude all others from practicing a four-legged support device with a backrest in light of the claim in the patent. What happens now, especially if the four-legged support device with a backrest is better functioning or more desirable? In theory, Inventor A could continue making his three-legged support device and could prevent Inventor B from making or selling her improved chair. However, Inventor A cannot make the four-legged chair with a backrest. The logical next question is how then does technology progress since an early patent might be broad enough to cover patentably distinct improvements? In short, how does the four-legged chair with backrest make it to the public? Answer: Licensing. If the four-legged chair with a backrest will be a commercially viable product and it is of value as a product, Inventors A and B will enter into a license agreement. Inventor B may license or purchase Inventor A's patent so she can sell the four-legged chair with backrest as well as a three-legged support device. Alternatively, Inventor A may be an excellent manufacturer of support devices and may license his patent to Inventor B if he is made the "sole manufacturer" of support devices that Inventor B sells. In another scenario, Inventor B may sell her patent rights to Inventor A for a lump sum without making a single four-legged support device with a backrest. Many scenarios can and do occur in these instances.

Knowing some of the rights associated with patents, a review of the different types of patents is warranted. In the United States, there are three types of patents—utility patents, design patents, and plant patents. Most countries also have similar patent types that cover similar types of subject matter. However, the patent types may be arranged differently or have varied degrees of review or examination.[31]

A. Utility Patents

Utility patents are the most common patent type and protect utilitarian inventions, both animate and inanimate, and have a term of life of 20 years[32] from the date of filing with the USPTO.

31. For example, in some countries a registration system is used in lieu of a design patent system. Design registration systems often differ from the U.S. design patent system in that designs are not reviewed for patentability—novelty and non-obviousness—as they are done in the United States. Instead, registrations are merely reviewed for compliance with the submission requirements, and issues of validity are left to be handled during enforcement.

In France there are two different types of protection for functional inventions: (1) the patent of invention and (2) the utility certificate. These protections vary in their term of life (20 years v. 6 years) and requirements for obtaining the protection, including the requirement or absence of a requirement for a search report.

32. For applications filed on or after June 8, 1995, the patent term is 20 years from the filing date of the earliest U.S. application to which priority is claimed (excluding provisional applications). For applications that were pending on and for patents that were still in force on June 8, 1995, the patent term

Utility patents include the following:

- *Cover page*—Provides the most often searched information at the front of the patent. Information included on the cover page includes the Patent Number, Issue Date, Filing Date, Inventor(s), Assignee(s) at time of issuance, Priority Data, Cited References, Abstract, and an Illustrative Figure.
- *Abstract*—A 150-word or less general description of the invention for future searching that ultimately appears on the cover page. In filing patent applications, the abstract is provided alone on its own page.
- *Drawings*—Drawings are used to further show or illustrate features described in the application. Typically "figure labels" or numbers are used to label the parts or aspects of that shown in the figures. Often, arrows or lines are used, along with the numbers to clearly convey the components, steps, and features of that shown in the figures. While a patent need not include a drawing(s), the USPTO can require applicants to include one or more drawings to facilitate understanding of the described invention. Applicants should typically consider including one or more figures when filing patent applications. While "rough sketches" can be submitted and later supplemented with "formal drawings," care should be taken such that all features are included in the originally filed drawings or else they will be rejected later for including "new matter."
- *Field of the invention*—The field of the invention briefly and broadly describes the general area of technology of the patent. Typically the field of the invention is only about two sentences long and very general. It often states that the present invention

is either 17 years from the issue date or 20 years from the filing date of the earliest U.S. or international (PCT) application to which priority is claimed (excluding provisional applications), the longer term applying. *See* GATT Uruguay Round implementing legislation (P.L. 103-465), signed by then President Clinton on December 8, 1994. The term lengths identified assume all maintenance fees are paid. The term of a patent may also be adjusted in certain instances if there are delays during prosecution at the USPTO. Delays by the USPTO in acting on a patent application beyond proscribed time periods may result in these time periods being added onto the end of the life of the patent. Added time is reduced by applicant delays during prosecution. *See* 35 U.S.C. §154 (also known as the Patent Term Adjustment Act).

"relates" to a certain area of technology. This is not a requirement for an application.

- *Background*—The background may vary from patent to patent. In some instances, applicants provide a brief statement to provide general background information to facilitate an understanding of the invention disclosed in the application. Applicants may describe related art, such as some of the more relevant references that also may be identified in an information disclosure statement. Such a description of related art may be utilized in an instance where the technology for patenting is an improvement over the known art and the applicants wish to identify explicitly distinctions over the identified art. These distinctions also may be referenced generally and/or placed in the summary or detailed description to reduce the risk of a litigant asserting features the applicant intended to be attributable to the invention claimed in the patent are associated with the prior art. This is not a requirement for an application.
- *Summary*—This is a general description of the invention disclosed in the patent application. The summary section provides a brief description of various arrangements of the invention that is described in more detail in the detailed description. Patent practitioners may take care to ensure statements made in the summary cannot be used to unnecessarily limit the breadth of the invention.
- *Brief description of the drawings*—A brief listing of the drawings or "figures" is included in the patent application. A single sentence is typically provided for each figure and describes what is shown in the figure. For example, the brief description of the drawings might state language such as, "Figure 1 is an illustrative perspective view of an umbrella attachment device in an in use position in accordance with at least one aspect of the present invention."
- *Detailed description*—The detailed description typically forms the largest portion of the body of a patent application and resulting patent. In the detailed description, the features of the invention are described in detail that includes the features shown in the figures, as well as various contemplated aspects, even if not explicitly shown in the figure. Practitioners typically prepare the detailed description to describe the configurations and ar-

rangements of the invention in an organized fashion to facilitate understanding of the invention, uses and related aspects.

- *Claims*—The claims of a patent define the scope of the invention covered in the patent. Similar to a deed for a plot of land, the claims of a patent set forth the "metes and bounds" of that which the patentee or patent owner is entitled to exclude others from practicing. Each claim is a single sentence that has a preamble, a transitional phrase, and a body. The preamble generally sets forth whether the invention is a process, machine, manufacture, or composition. Transitional phrases may be "open" language, such as "comprising" or "including," closed language, such as "consisting of," or partially closed language, such as "consisting essentially of." Each claim is a single sentence and must be written with proper "antecedent basis."[33] Each claim is also characterized as

33. The indefinite articles "a" or "an" are used when first describing features in a patent claim. Once the features have been identified, they may be referenced using the definite articles "the" or "said." A further description of proper antecedent basis and claim usage can be referenced in the MPEP. MPEP §2173.05(e) ("A claim is indefinite when it contains words or phrases whose meaning is unclear. The lack of clarity could arise where a claim refers to "said lever" or "the lever," where the claim contains no earlier recitation or limitation of a lever and where it would be unclear as to what element the limitation was making reference. Similarly, if two different levers are recited earlier in the claim, the recitation of "said lever" in the same or subsequent claim would be unclear where it is uncertain which of the two levers was intended. A claim which refers to "said aluminum lever" but recites only "a lever" earlier in the claim is indefinite because it is uncertain as to the lever to which reference is made. Obviously, however, the failure to provide explicit antecedent basis for terms does not always render a claim indefinite. If the scope of a claim would be reasonably ascertainable by those skilled in the art, then the claim is not indefinite. Energizer Holdings Inc. v. Int'l Trade Comm'n, 435 F.3d 1366, 77 USPQ2d 1625 (Fed. Cir. 2006) (holding that "anode gel" provided by implication the antecedent basis for "zinc anode"); *Ex parte* Porter, 25 USPQ2d 1144, 1145 (Bd. Pat. App. & Inter. 1992) ("controlled stream of fluid" provided reasonable antecedent basis for "the controlled fluid"). Inherent components of elements recited have antecedent basis in the recitation of the components themselves. For example, the limitation "the outer surface of said sphere" would not require an antecedent recitation that the sphere has an outer surface. *See* Bose Corp. v. JBL, Inc., 274 F.3d 1354, 1359, 61 USPQ2d 1216, 1218–19 (Fed. Cir. 2001) (holding that recitation of "an ellipse" provided antecedent basis for "an ellipse having a major diameter" because "[t]here can be no dispute that mathematically an inherent characteristic of an ellipse is a major diameter").

being independent (standing alone) or as being dependent (depends on a previous claim or claims). Dependent claims include all the features of the claims upon which they depend. For example, if a hypothetical independent claim 1 in a patent recites:

> *A vehicle comprising: four wheels, an engine, intermittent windshield wipers and a pair of headlights.*
>
> A dependent claim 2 may recite:
>
> *The vehicle of claim 1, further comprising a pair of red taillights.*
>
> As such claim 2 in effect actually is directed to:
>
> *A vehicle comprising: four wheels, an engine, intermittent windshield wipers, a pair of headlights, and a pair of red taillights.*

A portion of illustrative utility patent, U.S. Pat. No. 6,302,230 ('230 Patent), is shown in Figure 1-3. The '230 Patent is understood to be one of a number of patents that relate to Segway® Personal Transporters. Dean Kamen, a founder of Segway, is listed as the first named inventor on the patent.

Figure 1-3

Illustrative utility patent ('230 Patent)

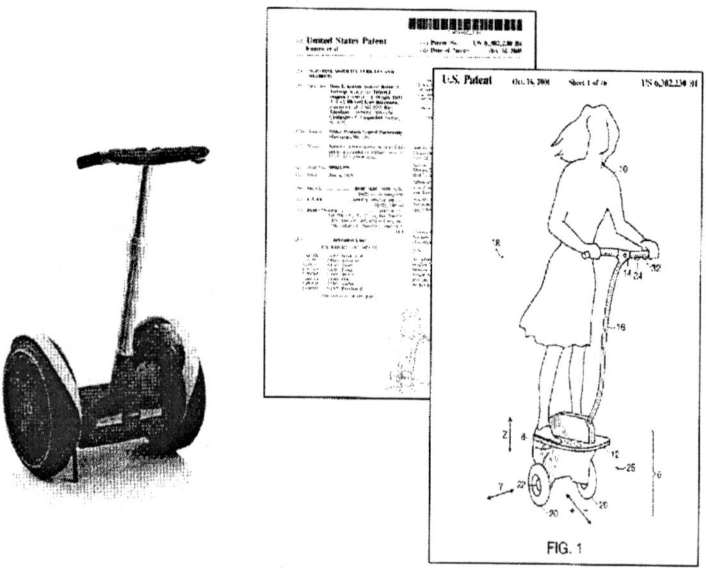

B. Design Patents

Design patents protect the ornamental features of new and original designs[34] for articles of manufacture[35] and have a term of life of 14 years from issuance.[36] Design patents and design patent applications must have one or more drawings that depict the scope of protection for the design. For design patents, the "claim" of the patent is what is shown in the one or more drawings. Design patents also must have *only a single claim*[37] and thus are directed to a single design. If more than one patentably distinct design is claimed (i.e. shown in the drawings) in a design application, the USPTO will issue a restriction requirement and the applicant must select one of the designs to pursue in the application unless the restriction requirement is traversed. As discussed herein, the claimed design is defined by that which is shown in the drawings. Applicants may claim only a portion of article of manufacture by depicting only a portion of the article in solid lines, while depicting any unclaimed portions by showing them in broken lines. While it is not surprising to most that consumer products—athletic shoes, cellular telephones, home appliances, and automobiles—are common subject matter for design patent protection, it may be somewhat surprising to learn that icons and graphical user interfaces for computer programs are also proper subject matter for design patent protection in the United States. As such, design patents can be utilized to provide protection for misappropriation of the ornamental appearance of most designs.

34. 35 U.S.C. §171.

35. Design patents generally protect aesthetic features of manufactured goods. However, computer icons, font, graphical user interfaces, and other subject matter not immediately thought of as manufactured goods are also protectable subject matter of U.S. design patents.

36. 35 U.S.C. §173.

37. 37 C.F.R. §1.154 (b)(6).

Figure 1-4 contain two illustrative design patents that may be familiar to fans of "Star Wars"—U.S. Des. Pat. Nos. D251,627 and D251,628, may be recognized as being similar in appearance to C-3PO and R2-D2 from the well-known Star Wars® movies.

Figure 1-4
Illustrative robot design patents

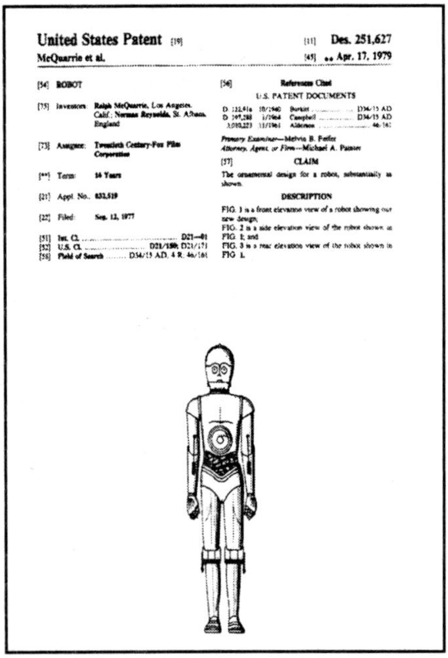
United States Patent [19] [11] **Des. 251,627**
McQuarrie et al. [45] ** **Apr. 17, 1979**

[54] **ROBOT**
[75] Inventors: **Ralph McQuarrie**, Los Angeles, Calif.; **Norman Reynolds**, St. Albans, England
[73] Assignee: **Twentieth Century-Fox Film Corporation**
[**] Term: **14 Years**
[21] Appl. No.: **832,519**
[22] Filed: **Sep. 12, 1977**
[51] **Int. Cl.** .... D21—01
[52] **U.S. Cl.** D21/150; D21/171
[58] **Field of Search** .... D34/15 AD, 4 R; 46/161

[56] **References Cited**
U.S. PATENT DOCUMENTS
D [illegible] 10/1940 Burkitt .... D34/15 AD
D [illegible] 1/1964 Campbell .... D34/15 AD
3,010,223 11/1961 Alderson 46/161

Primary Examiner—Melvin B. Feifer
Attorney, Agent, or Firm—Michael A. Painter

[57] **CLAIM**
The ornamental design for a robot, substantially as shown.

DESCRIPTION
FIG. 1 is a front elevation view of a robot showing our new design;
FIG. 2 is a side elevation view of the robot shown in FIG. 1; and
FIG. 3 is a rear elevation view of the robot shown in FIG. 1.

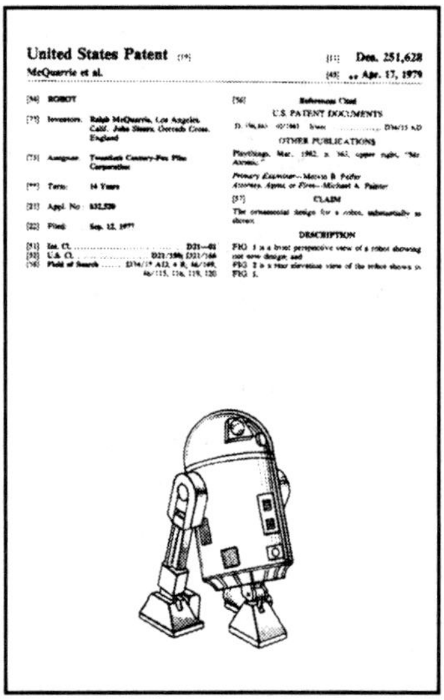
United States Patent [19] [11] **Des. 251,628**
McQuarrie et al. [45] ** **Apr. 17, 1979**

[54] **ROBOT**
[75] Inventors: **Ralph McQuarrie**, Los Angeles, Calif.; **John Stears**, [illegible], England
[73] Assignee: **Twentieth Century-Fox Film Corporation**
[**] Term: **14 Years**
[21] Appl. No.: **832,520**
[22] Filed: **Sep. 12, 1977**
[51] **Int. Cl.** .... D21—01
[52] **U.S. Cl.** D21/150; D21/166
[58] **Field of Search** .... D34/15 AD, 4 R; 46/149, 46/115, 116, 119, 120

[56] **References Cited**
U.S. PATENT DOCUMENTS
D [illegible] .... D34/15 AD
OTHER PUBLICATIONS
[illegible]

Primary Examiner—Melvin B. Feifer
Attorney, Agent, or Firm—Michael A. Painter

[57] **CLAIM**
The ornamental design for a robot, substantially as shown.

DESCRIPTION
FIG. 1 is a front perspective view of a robot showing our new design; and
FIG. 2 is a rear elevation view of the robot shown in FIG. 1.

C. Plant Patents

Plant patents are typically the least common patent type encountered and are granted to "whoever invents or discovers and asexually reproduces any distinct and new variety of plant, including cultivated sports, mutants, hybrids, and newly found seedlings, other than a tuber propagated plant or a plant found in an uncultivated state."[38] The grant of a plant patent provides the inventor the "right to exclude others from asexually reproducing, using, offering for sale, or selling the plant so reproduced, or any of its parts, throughout the United States, or from importing the plant so reproduced, or any parts thereof, into the United States."[39] The

38. 35 U.S.C. §161.
39. 35 U.S.C. §163.

specification of a plant patent may describe typical traits and features and will include a picture of the plant. Interestingly, no plant patent shall be declared invalid for noncompliance with section 112 if the description is "as complete as is reasonably possible."[40] Plant patents will often have a claim that reads similarly to the illustrative plant patent claim below:

> "A new and distinct variety of the rose plant of the Hybrid Tea class, substantially as herein shown and described"—*See, e.g.*, Plant Patent No. 11,062, shown in Figures 1-5, 1-5B, and 1-5C.[41]

Figure 1-5A

Plant Patent No. 11,062

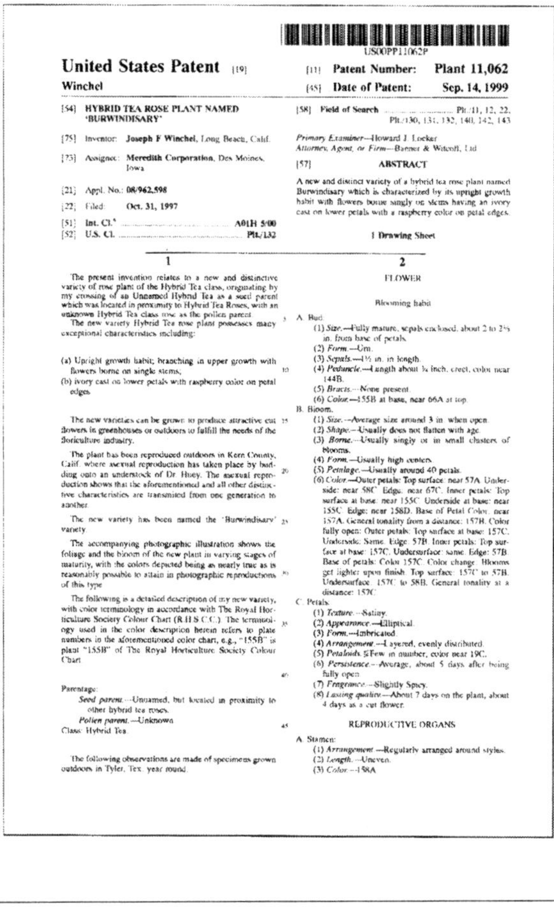

US00PP11062P

United States Patent [19] **Winchel**

[11] **Patent Number: Plant 11,062**

[45] **Date of Patent: Sep. 14, 1999**

[54] **HYBRID TEA ROSE PLANT NAMED 'BURWINDISARY'**

[75] Inventor: **Joseph F Winchel**, Long Beach, Calif.

[73] Assignee: **Meredith Corporation**, Des Moines, Iowa

[21] Appl. No.: **08/962,598**

[22] Filed: **Oct. 31, 1997**

[51] **Int. Cl.**[6] **A01H 5/00**

[52] **U.S. Cl.** **Plt./132**

[58] **Field of Search** Plt./11, 12, 22, Plt./130, 131, 132, 140, 142, 143

Primary Examiner—Howard J. Locker

Attorney, Agent, or Firm—Banner & Witcoff, Ltd

[57] **ABSTRACT**

A new and distinct variety of a hybrid tea rose plant named Burwindisary which is characterized by its upright growth habit with flowers borne singly on stems having an ivory cast on lower petals with a raspberry color on petal edges.

1 Drawing Sheet

1

The present invention relates to a new and distinctive variety of rose plant of the Hybrid Tea class, originating by my crossing of an Unnamed Hybrid Tea as a seed parent which was located in proximity to Hybrid Tea Roses, with an unknown Hybrid Tea class rose as the pollen parent.

The new variety Hybrid Tea rose plant possesses many exceptional characteristics including:

(a) Upright growth habit; branching in upper growth with flowers borne on single stems;

(b) ivory cast on lower petals with raspberry color on petal edges.

The new varieties can be grown to produce attractive cut flowers in greenhouses or outdoors to fulfill the needs of the floriculture industry.

The plant has been reproduced outdoors in Kern County, Calif. where asexual reproduction has taken place by budding onto an understock of Dr. Huey. The asexual reproduction shows that the aforementioned and all other distinctive characteristics are transmited from one generation to another.

The new variety has been named the 'Burwindisary' variety.

The accompanying photographic illustration shows the foliage and the bloom of the new plant in varying stages of maturity, with the colors depicted being as nearly true as is reasonably possible to attain in photographic reproductions of this type.

The following is a detailed description of my new variety, with color terminology in accordance with The Royal Horticulture Society Colour Chart (R.H.S.C.C.). The terminology used in the color description herein refers to plate numbers in the aforementioned color chart, e.g., "155B" is plant "155B" of The Royal Horticulture Society Colour Chart.

Parentage:

Seed parent.—Unnamed, but located in proximity to other hybrid tea roses.

Pollen parent.—Unknown.

Class: Hybrid Tea.

The following observations are made of specimens grown outdoors in Tyler, Tex. year round.

2

FLOWER

Blooming habit

A. Bud:
- (1) *Size.*—Fully mature, sepals enclosed, about 2 to 2⅓ in. from base of petals.
- (2) *Form.*—Urn.
- (3) *Sepals.*—1½ in. in length.
- (4) *Peduncle.*—Length about ¼ inch, erect, color near 144B.
- (5) *Bracts.*—None present.
- (6) *Color.*—155B at base, near 66A at top.

B. Bloom.
- (1) *Size.*—Average size around 3 in. when open.
- (2) *Shape.*—Usually does not flatten with age.
- (3) *Borne.*—Usually singly or in small clusters of blooms.
- (4) *Form.*—Usually high centers.
- (5) *Petalage.*—Usually around 40 petals.
- (6) *Color.*—Outer petals: Top surface: near 57A. Underside: near 58C. Edge: near 67C. Inner petals: Top surface at base: near 155C. Underside at base: near 155C. Edge: near 158D. Base of Petal Color: near 157A. General tonality from a distance: 157B. Color fully open: Outer petals: Top surface at base: 157C. Underside: Same. Edge: 57B. Inner petals: Top surface at base: 157C. Undersurface: same. Edge: 57B. Base of petals: Color 157C. Color change: Blooms get lighter upon finish. Top surface: 157C to 57B. Undersurface: 157C to 58B. General tonality at a distance: 157C.

C. Petals.
- (1) *Texture.*—Satiny.
- (2) *Appearance.*—Elliptical.
- (3) *Form.*—Imbricated.
- (4) *Arrangement.*—Layered, evenly distributed.
- (5) *Petaloids.*—Few in number, color near 19C.
- (6) *Persistence.*—Average, about 5 days after being fully open.
- (7) *Fragrance.*—Slightly Spicy.
- (8) *Lasting quality.*—About 7 days on the plant, about 4 days as a cut flower.

REPRODUCTIVE ORGANS

A. Stamen:
- (1) *Arrangement.*—Regularly arranged around styles.
- (2) *Length.*—Uneven.
- (3) *Color.*—158A

40. 35 U.S.C. §162.

41. At least the highlighted sections will vary from plant patent to plant patent.

Figure 1-5B
Plant Patent No. 11,062

Plant 11,062

3

(4) *Filaments.*—Color — 157C.
(5) *Annthers.*—Color — 157D.
(6) *Pollen.*—Color — 10C.

B. Pistil:
(1) *Stigma.*—Color 41B.
(2) *Ovary.*—Shape — orbicular; average diameter 0.5 in.; average height 0.75 in.

Hips:
(1) *Shape.*—Globular.
(2) *Size.*—Average one in.
(3) *Color.*—31B.
(4) *Seeds.*—None protruding.

PLANT

A. Form: Upright with uniform branching.
B. Growth: Moderate.
Height.—4' at maturity.
C. Stem: Length about 8 inches under average conditions.
D. Foliage: Compound of 5 leaflets, medium size, abundant quantity
(1) *Mature size.*—3 leaflet leaf 1.5 to 2.5 in., measured from base of stipule to terminal leaflet tip.

4

(2) *Color.*—New foliage upper side 183C; underside 148C. Mature foliage upper side 147A; underside 147C.
(3) *Shape.*—Elliptic.
(4) *Texture.*—Smooth.
(5) *Petiole.*—Color 158C.
(6) *Stipule.*—Color near 161B.
(7) *Edge.*—Serrated with regular symmetry.

Wood:
New wood.—Color 148B with smooth bark.
Old wood.—Color 147B with rough bark.

F. Thorns:
Color.—165A. Ordinarily thin with slight down curve and medium length; spaced at about 12 nodes.

G. Prickles: Color near 185B.

I claim:

1. A new and distinct variety of the rose plant of the Hybrid Tea class, substantially as herein shown and described.

* * * * *

Figure 1-5C
Plant Patent No. 11,062

U.S. Patent Sep. 14, 1999 **Plant 11,062**

IV. PATENT ACT—TITLE 35 OF THE UNITED STATES CODE

A. More Than Just Patentability

1. §101—Patentability

Whoever invents or discovers any new and useful process, machine, manufacture, or composition of matter, or any new and useful improvement thereof, may obtain a patent therefor, subject to the conditions and requirements of this title. 35 U.S.C. §101

As described in *Diamond v. Chakrabarty*[42] in 1980, virtually "anything under the sun" constitutes potentially patentable subject matter as long as it is new and useful—with a few caveats. These caveats include abstract ideas, laws of nature, and natural phenomena.[43] Recently, computer-related method claims have received attention as the Federal Circuit and U.S. Supreme Court have opined on the proper analysis as to whether these types of claims satisfy §101 and constitute patentable subject matter.[44] Innovations in the biotechnology or chemical arts also are known to sometimes raise §101 patentability issues.[45]

The "new" requirement is self explanatory and aligned with the granting of "the right to exclude" in exchange for public disclosure and explanation of "new" inventions. The "useful" requirement of §101 does not require the invention to work better or be more useful—e.g., better than current technology—just that it possesses functionality. Outside of these caveats, patentability is not a particularly high hurdle for patent applicants to overcome.

2. §102—Novelty

35 U.S.C. §102 begins by stating "a person shall be entitled to a patent unless," following which are seven sections (a-g) delineating "novelty destroying events" that can prevent an invention from receiving U.S. patent protection. These novelty-destroying events can be categorized as: (1) events prior to invention—§§102(a), 102(e), 102(g); (2) time-barring events that occur before filing a patent application in the U.S—

42. 447 U.S. 303, 308–09, 206 USPQ 193, 197 (1980).

43. MPEP §2106.

44. Bilksi v. Kappos, 561 U.S. ___ (2010).

45. Mayo Collaborative Services v. Prometheus Labs. Inc., 132 S. Ct. 1289 (2012).

§§102(b) and 102 (d); and (3) events not tied to when they occur—§§102(c), 102(f).

- *Events prior to invention*: *102(a)*—An invention is not patentable in the U.S. if the claimed invention is publicly known by another or used by others in the U.S. or patented or described in a printed publication by another in the U.S. or any foreign country.[46] It is noteworthy that actions by the same inventor(s) cannot form the basis for a 102(a) novelty- destroying event.[47] *102(e)*—A published U.S. application (or PCT application designating the U.S. and in English) by another that was filed before invention destroys novelty of the invention. Similarly, a U.S. patent by another filed before invention also destroys novelty.[48] *102(g)*— If the priority of another is established in an interference before the USPTO or before a U.S. court based upon inventive acts in any NAFTA or WTO country, novelty is destroyed. 102(g)(1) Also, if it is made by another in the U.S. before invention and it is not purposely abandoned, suppressed, or concealed, novelty is destroyed. 102(g)(2).[49] 102(g) rejections or novelty-destroying events

46. 35 U.S.C. §102(a)—"[t]he invention was known or used by others in this country, or patented or described in a printed publication in this or a foreign country, before the invention thereof by the applicant for patent."

47. However, the same actions if certain time has passed (e.g., 1 year) can prevent patentability under a statutory barring event such as a §102(b) event.

48. 35 U.S.C. §102(e)—"[t]he invention was described in—(1) an application for patent, published under section 122(b), by another filed in the United States before the invention by the applicant for patent or (2) a patent granted on an application for patent by another filed in the United States before the invention by the applicant for patent, except that an international application filed under the treaty defined in section 351(a) shall have the effects for the purposes of this subsection of an application filed in the United States only if the international application designated the United States and was published under Article 21(2) of such treaty in the English language."

49. 35 U.S.C. §102(g)—"(1) during the course of an interference conducted under section 135 or section 291, another inventor involved therein establishes, to the extent permitted in section 104, that before such person's invention thereof the invention was made by such other inventor and not abandoned, suppressed, or concealed, or (2) before such person's invention thereof, the invention was made in this country by another inventor who had not abandoned, suppressed, or concealed it. In determining priority of invention under this subsection, there shall be considered not only the respective dates of conception and reduction to practice of the invention, but also the reasonable diligence of one who was first to conceive and last to reduce to practice, from a time prior to conception by the other."

occur less frequently than 102(a) or 102(e) events and patent applicants infrequently receive rejections based upon 102(g).

- *Time-barring events*: *102(b)*—Public use, sale, patenting or printing of a publication by anyone *more than 1 year before the filing date* of an application will destroy novelty of the invention. Unlike 102(a) events, actions by the inventor can result in a bar from patentability if more than a year passes before the filing date of an application. *102(d)*—A foreign patent, issuing before an application on the same invention is filed in the U.S., destroys the novelty of the U.S. application if the foreign application was filed by an inventor (or inventor's assignee or representative) more than 1 year before the filing date of the U.S. application.[50] This critical time period of 1 year with regard to 102(d) events is reduced to only 6 months in relation to design patents.[51]
- *Events not tied to when they occur*: Abandonment of the invention under 102(c)[52] and instances in which the applicant derived the invention from someone else 102(f)[53] are less common novelty destroying events and are more likely to be raised as novelty defeating events in litigation or in an interference than sua sponte by the USPTO during prosecution since they are likely to arise based upon a detailed understanding of the facts and circumstances surrounding the conception and reduction to practice of the invention as this would typically be flushed out in the discovery phase of litigation. The USPTO typically would not have access to that information or the resources or ability to uncover these facts and circumstances.

50. 102(d))—"[t]he invention was first patented or caused to be patented, or was the subject of an inventor's certificate, by the applicant or his legal representatives or assigns in a foreign country prior to the date of the application for patent in this country on an application for patent or inventor's certificate filed more than twelve months before the filing of the application in the United States."

51. 35 U.S.C. §172 ("The right of priority provided for by subsections (a) through (d) of section 119 of this title and the time specified in section 102(d) shall be six months in the case of designs. The right of priority provided for by section 119(e) of this title shall not apply to designs.")

52. 35 U.S.C. §102(c)—"[h]e has abandoned the invention."

53. 35 U.S.C. §102(f)—"[h]e did not himself invent the subject matter sought to be patented."

Actual abandonment under 35 U.S.C. 102(c) requires that the inventor intended to abandon the invention, and intent can be implied from the inventor's conduct with respect to the invention.[54] Practically speaking, abandonment under 102(c) requires a clear showing, as the intent to abandon the invention will not be imputed, and every reasonable doubt is resolved in favor of the inventor.[55] Time delay alone will not bar a patent because of abandonment.[56]

Logically, as set forth in 102(f), if the alleged inventor(s) did not invent that which is claimed in their patent or application, they are not entitled to a patent on that invention. Most, if not all, 102(f) determinations involve a question of whether one party derived or misappropriated an invention from another.[57] Derivation requires complete conception by another and communication of that conception by any means to the party charged with derivation prior to any date on which it can be shown that the one charged with derivation possessed knowledge of the invention.[58]

3. §103—Obviousness

While a new invention may be novel and not prevented from patentability under 35 U.S.C. §102, it may still be prevented from patenting in the United States if it is deemed to be "obvious" under 35 U.S.C. §103. 35 U.S.C. §103(a) states:

> A patent may not be obtained though the invention is not identically disclosed or described as set forth in section 102 of this title, if the differences between the subject matter sought to be patented and the prior art are such that the subject matter as a whole ***would have been obvious at the time the invention was made to a person having ordinary skill in the art to which said subject matter pertains.*** Patentability shall not be negatived by the manner in which the invention was made. (Emphasis added)

Not surprisingly, application of §103(a) and the concept of what is "obvious" is one of the most frequently contested and debated concepts

54. *In re* Gibbs, 437 F.2d 486, 168 USPQ 578 (CCPA 1971).
55. *Ex parte* Dunne, 20 USPQ2d 1479 (Bd. Pat. App. & Inter. 1991).
56. MPEP §2134.
57. MPEP §2137, *quoting Ex parte* Kusko, 215 USPQ 972, 974 (Bd. App. 1981).
58. Kilbey v. Thiele, 199 USPQ 290, 294 (Bd. Pat. Inter. 1978).

in patent law both generally and on a case-by-case basis. As the statute explicitly states, obviousness is determined (1) "at the time the invention was made" and (2) "to a person having ordinary skill in the art to which said subject matter pertains." Different entities often have varied arguments and beliefs as to "time of invention" and/or the hypothetical person of "ordinary skill in the art." Numerous patent litigations have been decided based on the court's ruling on the issue of obviousness.

While a significant body of case law, including Federal Circuit and Supreme Court jurisprudence, helps guide the analysis, obviousness is a concept with inherent subjectivity.

In *Graham v John Deere*,[59] the Supreme Court set forth the basic factual inquiries to be made under §103(a):

1. the level of ordinary skill in the prior art;
2. the scope and content of the prior art; and
3. the differences between the claimed invention and the prior art.

In addition, the Supreme Court in *Graham v. John Deere* set forth "secondary considerations" that may serve as evidence of nonobviousness. These secondary considerations include showings of *commercial success*, *long felt but unsolved needs*, and *failure of others*. The Supreme Court recently reaffirmed the case-by-case obviousness determination in light of the above consideration in *KSR v. Teleflex*.[60]

4. §112—Written Description, Enablement and Best Mode

35 U.S.C. §112 has six paragraphs setting forth several of the substantive requirements for what applicants may and must include in patents and applications. Paragraph one[61] sets forth what is commonly referred to as the "written description," "enablement," and "best mode" requirements.

59. 383 U.S. 1 (1966).

60. 550 U.S. 398 (2007).

61. 35 U.S.C. §112, para. 1 ("The specification shall contain a written description of the invention, and of the manner and process of making and using it, in such full, clear, concise, and exact terms as to enable any person skilled in the art to which it pertains, or with which it is most nearly connected, to make and use the same, and shall set forth the best mode contemplated by the inventor of carrying out his invention.").

Paragraph two[62] sets forth that the specification concludes with one or more claims particularly pointing out and distinctly claiming the subject matter the applicant regards as his invention. Paragraphs three through six describe further details regarding claims in a patent. Paragraph three[63] states that claims may be in independent, dependent, or multiple dependent form. Paragraph four[64] states that dependent claims contain a reference to a claim previously set forth and that the dependent claim is construed to contain all the limitations of the claim to which it refers. Paragraph five[65] provides for use of multiple dependent claims, which contain a reference in the alternative to more than one claim previously set forth and then specifies a further limitation of the subject matter claimed. Much like a regular dependent claim, multiple dependent claims are construed to contain all the limitations of the particular claim to which it is being referenced. Last, paragraph six[66] sets forth that a claim may recite one or more features of a claim in what is commonly referred to as a "means-plus-function" language, which will be construed, if properly drafted, to cover the corresponding structure, material, or steps described in the specification and equivalents thereof.

B. Timing, Priority, and Provisional Rights

Patent practice is a time-sensitive practice, as patent rights in the United States and internationally require procurement actions within specified time periods or by certain due dates. Patent procurement is extremely time-sensitive, and most law firms that have patent procurement or prosecution practices have docketing departments dedicated to tracking and monitoring large numbers of patent applications and files. To facilitate the docketing departments and the practitioners they support, various computer and software systems can be utilized to ensure that action is taken at appropriate time periods to avoid inadvertent abandonment or forfeiture of rights. As these computer- and software-related tools continue to develop, many are becoming integrated with the USPTO's electronic databases to ensure data integrity and redundancy, as well as real-time updates.

62. 35 U.S.C. §112, para. 2.
63. 35 U.S.C. §112, para. 3.
64. 35 U.S.C. §112, para. 4.
65. 35 U.S.C. §112, para. 5.
66. 35 U.S.C. §112, para. 6.

United States and international law recognizes the pursuit of patent rights on inventions is not an instantaneous event and requires some time even for the most diligent of applicants and their respective advisors, counselors, and attorneys or agents. Through international treaties and domestic laws and statutes, patent systems utilize priority claims, grace periods, and provisional patent applications to facilitate the ability of the inventor(s) or applicant(s) to pursue protection nationally and internationally. Several key domestic provisions from Title 35 of the U.S. Code relating to timing and patent rights are highlighted below.

1. §119—Foreign Priority

Section 119(a) generally sets forth that, among other things, an application filed in the United States will receive the benefit of a corresponding application previously filed in another country if the U.S. application was filed within 12 months from the earliest application on which the foreign application was filed. The foreign application must either be filed in another country that affords similar privileges to applications filed in the U.S. or to U.S. citizens, or in a World Trade Organization (WTO) member country. However, a foreign priority claim under §119 will not salvage a U.S. application that would not be patentable because the U.S. filing is more than one year before a §102(b) novelty destroying event.[67] Section 119(b) sets forth further particulars relating to requirements for perfecting a proper claim for foreign priority, including identification of the foreign application by application number, country, or international authority for which it was filed and filing date of the application. Section 119(b) also authorizes the director of the USPTO to consider failure to make a timely claim for priority a "waiver of any such claim"[68] and to require submission of a certified copy of the original foreign application on which it is based.[69] Agreements between the USPTO and certain jurisdictions, such as the European Union (EU) and Japan, have reduced this burden on applicants, as the USPTO will obtain priority documents from certain countries via the Patent Document Exchange

67. 35 U.S.C. §119(a) ("but no patent shall be granted on any application for patent for an invention which had been patented or described in a printed publication in any country more than one year before the date of the actual filing of the application in this country, or which had been in public use or on sale in this country more than one year prior to such filing.").

68. 35 U.S.C. §119(b)(2).

69. 35 U.S.C. §119(b)(3).

(PDX) program such that the applicant no longer may need to provide a certified copy of the foreign priority application to the USPTO.[70] Additionally, the USPTO has reached agreement with other countries to expedite or fast-track applications through the Patent Prosecution Highway (PPH). Through the Patent Prosecution Highway (PPH), an applicant receiving a ruling from the Office of First Filing (OFF) that at least one claim in an application filed in the OFF is patentable may request that the Office of Second Filing (OSF) fast-track the examination of corresponding claims in corresponding applications filed in the OSF.[71] Thus if the Office of First Filing, such as the USPTO, finds a claim allowable, the Office of Second Filing, such as the Japan Patent Office, may be requested by the applicant to fast-track the same claims.

2. §120—Domestic Priority

A later-filed U.S. patent application may be entitled to the benefit of an earlier-filed U.S. patent application by making specific reference to the earlier-filed application in the later-filed application. In order to receive the benefit of the earlier filing date, the later-filed application must be by an inventor or inventors named in the previously filed application; the earlier-filed application must contain a sufficient disclosure to satisfy the written description, enablement, and best mode requirements of 35 U.S.C. §112, first paragraph, with regard to that claimed in the later-filed application; and the earlier-filed application must still be pending before the USPTO. These requirements may be referred to as a *continuity in inventorship, continuity in disclosure,* and *continuity in prosecution*, respectively.

3. §121—Divisional Application

If two or more independent and distinct inventions are claimed in one application, the director of the USPTO may require the application to be restricted to one of the inventions. If the non-elected invention is made the subject of a divisional application complying with the requirements of §120, the divisional application shall be entitled to the benefit of the original application. It is fairly common for applicants to receive a restriction requirement requiring election or selection of claims to be pursued in a patent application as the result of an Office Action containing a

70. http://www.uspto.gov/patents/announce/prioritydocexch.jsp.
71. http://www.uspto.gov/patents/init_events/pph/index.jsp.

restriction requirement. At any point during pendency of the original application, a divisional patent application may be pursued regarding the non-elected claims. In some instances, the USPTO may provide a restriction that restricts the claims in more than two patentably distinct groups. Further divisional applications may be required to pursue all of the originally filed claims to issuance. See the *Patent Prosecution Section* for further discussion of restriction requirements and divisional patent applications.

4. §154—Contents and Term of Patent; Provisional Rights

Subject to payment of maintenance fees, the term of grant of a utility patent is 20 years[72] from the date of filing in the United States.[73] Additionally, §154(b) sets forth provisions for adjusting the above 20-year term from filing based upon time delays due to the USPTO during prosecution. For example, the USPTO is tasked with examining the application and taking action on the application within certain time frames including, but not limited to, examining the application and issuing a first Office Action within 14 months of filing and responding to replies to Office Actions by the applicant within four months of filing of the response by the applicant. Prosecution is also to be concluded within three years of filing. If these conditions and others set forth in §154 are not satisfied, the issued patent may be entitled to a term of patent extension beyond 20 years from filing. This patent term extension will be one additional day for each day of delay attributed to the USPTO. However, certain delays by the applicant, such as time extensions in responding to Office Actions, will offset delays attributed to USPTO for purpose of calculating patent term extension.[74]

While an applicant cannot enforce a patent until it has issued, §154(d) sets forth that a patent owner may be entitled to a reasonable royalty for any person who makes, uses, offers for sale, or sells in the U.S. the claimed invention, or imports the invention into the U.S., during the

72. The term of a design patent is 14 years from the date of grant rather than 20 years from filing. 35 U.S.C. §173. Maintenance fees do not apply to design patents. Also, if a terminal disclaimer is filed in a patent application, the term of life may be reduced as further described in the Patent Prosecution section.

73. 35 U.S.C. §154(a)(2).

74. 35 U.S.C. §154(b)(2)(C); *See also, Section II, Patent Prosecution.*

period between publication of the patent application and the date the patent issued.[75] The alleged infringer must have had actual notice of the published patent application,[76] and an action must be brought no later than six years after the patent issued.[77] The right to obtain a reasonable royalty will not be available unless the invention as claimed in the patent is "substantially identical" to the invention as claimed in the published patent application.[78]

V. FOREIGN PATENTS AND PATENT LAWS

U.S. practitioners are unlikely to ever "directly practice" in a jurisdiction outside of the United States. However, an understanding of foreign patent law and systems is beneficial in developing and managing patent portfolios on behalf of clients. An understanding of patent principles and practice before foreign patent offices will facilitate advising foreign associates (foreign lawyers) tasked with representing clients in a particular foreign jurisdiction. For example, if an attorney represents a client in the cellular telephone industry, the client may wish to protect the new cellular telephone technology in various jurisdictions across the globe where it is anticipated the telephone will be sold, manufactured, and/or copied. An illustrative, but by no means exhaustive, list of foreign jurisdictions that regularly may be of interest to companies pursuing patent protection beyond the United States may include the EU, Japan, China, Canada, Mexico, Brazil, Korea, Hong Kong, and/or Australia. The goal of most patent systems, like that of the patent system in the United States, is to promote progress and innovation in science and technology. As such, many of the core principles in the patent systems across the globe have related provisions. Many jurisdictions have patent principles akin to those of the U.S. patent system, but each system also has varied nuances and implementation of a system to promote progress. Prosecution of patent applications before these jurisdictions involves filing a patent application, responding to Office Actions, and addressing issues presented by the patent office, including novelty or obviousness and certain formality issues. However, the time periods, manner of response, and particulars vary from jurisdiction to jurisdiction.

75. 35 U.S.C. §154(d)(1)(A).
76. 35 U.S.C. §154(d)(1)(B).
77. 35 U.S.C. §154(d)(3).
78. 35 U.S.C. §154(d)(2).

The United States also varies from many foreign jurisdictions as well. Most countries are *first-to-file* systems where the first person or company to file an application with the patent office is deemed to be the first inventor of the invention if two or more people or entities claim the same invention. The U.S. instead is actually (or was until recently) a *first-to-invent* system in which a patent application filing date is initial proof of first invention.[79] However, applicants are able to prove an earlier invention date by showing proof of an earlier conception and reduction to practice. In the U.S., the proverbial race to the patent office will not always be dispositive of first invention.[80] Some, but certainly not all, jurisdictions differ from the U.S., as some are absolute novelty countries in which an inventor can be barred from receiving a patent if the invention is publicly disclosed. Examples of absolute novelty destroying public disclosure include such events as an invention being sold or shown or described in a publication prior to the inventor filing a patent application. Such a public disclosure will not prohibit the ability to receive a U.S. patent on the invention as applicants have a one-year grace period within which to file a patent application before losing their right to receive a patent on the invention.[81]

A. Prosecution Considerations

Whether pursuing patent protection in the United States, internationally, or both, certain considerations shape the number, location, type, and focus of patent applications. Among the considerations that may be important in the decision making:

- *Who are the competitors?* Typically one of the main reasons patent applicants pursue patent protection is to prevent competitors from appropriating the technology and from competing with the inventor or patent owner for customers. Are competitors U.S.-based companies with only U.S. customers? Is there a single large global competitor with markets in many countries on continents across the globe? Do competitors wait for others to innovate and then make a similar product trying to compete primarily on price? Who are the competitors, where do they do business,

79. The U.S. will move from a first-to-invent system to a first-inventor-to-file system when certain provisions of the AIA go into effect. See *America Invents Act (AIA)* subpart of this section.

80. *See also Patent Prosecution Section.*

81. *See also Patent Prosecution Section.*

and how might they exploit technology if left unprotected by patent coverage may be significant factors in determining whether patent protection is pursued in any of numerous countries or just in the United States.

- *Who is likely to copy or infringe?* Direct competitors are usually the entities of first concern. However, in many instances infringers can be small "copycats" or makers of "knockoffs" rather than more sophisticated direct competitors, especially if the products are regularly protected by patents. As such, an important consideration in choosing how to protect an innovation is determining who is most likely to copy or infringe. Knowing this information may dictate which countries to pursue protection in, as well as the scope or breadth of coverage in those countries. If the infringers are likely to be pure copycats in a variety of countries, it may be cost effective to get narrow coverage on the commercial embodiments they are likely to copy without the expenditures to pursue broader coverage that may require lengthier and more expensive prosecution. However, if the likely infringers are those that also are developing their own products in certain industries, a broad range of protection may be more desirable even if the broad coverage is in key markets to protect the core customer bases or clientele.
- *Where are the infringing products made? How are they distributed or imported?* If "copycats" or "knockoff artists" are based in a foreign country, it may be desirable to pursue patent protection in the foreign jurisdiction where the knockoffs are being made. It is not uncommon for molds used in foreign manufacturing to disappear or be copied and the appearance of knockoffs to be quick and prevalent. If there is a single source of manufacturing that supplies a large number of much smaller entities for distribution into the United States, it may be impractical to stop each of these small distributors and easier to stop the infringing activity at the source. Of course, U.S. patents will not be able to shut down purely foreign manufacturing, therefore patent protection in the country of infringing manufacture would be desirable and could be used to stop infringing activity at the source rather than pursuing various down stream distributors.
- *What is your budget? What intellectual property is the most important to protect?* If costs and budgets were of no concern, pro-

tection of intellectual property could be exhaustive with every morsel of protectable subject matter being pursued and protected. Obviously that is unrealistic. As such, an important quasi-business/quasi-law consideration is the prioritization of intellectual property protection in light of corporate business goals. Skilled patent practitioners, when provided clear patent protection goals and priorities regarding a business or certain products, can develop cost-effective strategies. For example, if a client has an important line of products that are similar in their core traits but vary with regard to a certain subset of features, a skilled patent practitioner is likely to be able to pursue cost-effective coverage that covers the broad common functionality and/or design. Further coverage can be pursued with a focus on the varied subset of features to the extent there is a sufficient budget remaining and based upon order of importance to the client.

B. Foreign Filing Mechanisms

Those new to IP are quick to inquire, logically so, as to whether there is a global or international patent. The question quickly can be answered—there is no single international *patent* that can be enforced across the globe. The absence of a global patent makes sense when one considers the diverse laws and sovereign rights of each country. Absent a specific agreement otherwise, a company in the United States cannot enforce rights given to it by the U.S. government against a company located in France, without locations in the United States. That company is outside the reach of U.S. law. However, through various worldwide treaties among member countries of the World Trade Organization (WTO), the World Intellectual Property Organization (WIPO), and others like it, certain mechanisms are in place to help patent applicants desiring protection in various countries to more efficiently pursue patent rights in those countries.

1. Patent Cooperation Treaty

While there is no "international patent application," the Patent Cooperation Treaty (PCT) provides for a unified procedure for filing patent applications to protect the inventions in those applications in each of the contract states of the treaty. An applicant can file an application with one of several designated receiving offices in one language. This application is then searched by an international searching authority and an international search report and a written opinion regarding patentability of the subject application is provided. An applicant may request a further examination performed by the international preliminary examining authority for additional fees, although many applicants forego this option. The applicant has 30 months from the priority date of the PCT application in which to enter the national stage of the countries of their choice by designating (checking a box for) these countries.[82] It is possible to select all of the 142 of the countries shown in Figure 1-6.[83] However, it must be remembered that designation of these 142 countries (of the approximately 195 countries worldwide[84]) merely results in the application beginning the "national stage" in those countries. As such, 142 national stage applications will need to be prosecuted to issuance, including payment of all requisite associated governmental fees before patent rights accrue in all of those countries. It is uncommon for applicants to designate all countries available for designation as the fees are significant and prohibitive. Typically, applicants choose a few of the countries, the most commonly selected being those with the most significant economic markets, unless there are unique markets or attributes for the technology.

82. For example, if the PCT application claims priority to another application (the "priority application"), the 30 months begin running from the filing date of the priority application, *not* from the filing date of the PCT application. Therefore, in an instance like this, the applicant may have less than 30 months from the filing date of the PCT application in which to enter the national/regional stage.

83. http://www.wipo.int/export/sites/www/pct/en/list_states.pdf (list current as of November 2010). (PCT member countries are shaded in dark.)

84. While the exact number varies based on the counter, there are likely 195 countries in the world. This count includes Vatican City, Kosovo, and Taiwan. The U.S. government officially lists 194 countries. The U.S. does not recognize Taiwan as a country, although many suggest it satisfies the criteria that define a "country." (List current as of November 2010.).

Figure 1-6
Map of PCT Contracting Countries

2. National Stage

Pursuant to the PCT, the international phase of the international application typically ends 30 months from the priority date of the application. As such, an application properly filed through the PCT and pursued in a national stage application in a designated country as described above will have the priority date of the PCT application, typically the filing date of the PCT application, if the PCT application does not claim further priority to another application. Additionally, certain countries or regions may set forth a delayed national entry—a period longer than 30 months[85]—during which an application may pursue a national phase application off of a PCT application. As such, in those certain countries, applicants have longer than 30 months in which to enter the national or regional stage. Once the application enters the national stage, it is pursued as if the applicant had filed an application directly in that jurisdiction subject to that jurisdiction's patent procedures, rules, protocols, and regulations. As such, it should be apparent that a PCT application will not issue and no rights will be granted from the PCT application itself. Instead, rights can

85. For a listing of time limits for entering national/regional phase under PCT chapters I and II, see the WIPO website, http://www.wipo.int/pct/en/texts/time_limits.html.

be obtained using a PCT application as an entry mechanism into the desired jurisdiction(s).

3. Regional Phase

Applicants also may designate a region, perhaps the most well known of which is the European Union, as a jurisdiction in which they wish to pursue patent protection based on a properly filed PCT application. An applicant may designate "EP," which is the code for the European Patent Office (EPO), to enter the "regional phase" based off a PCT application.[86] Thus entering the "regional phase" is akin to entering the national phase but for a region rather than a single jurisdiction.

4. Foreign National Applications

Instead of filing a PCT application and then pursuing protection in designated states based on the PCT application, applicants may file applications directly in the jurisdiction(s) in which they wish to obtain protection. Typically, this is done using an attorney or agent in the country or jurisdiction in question that is licensed to practice before that jurisdiction's patent office. As such, the "foreign associate," as they may commonly be labeled, is knowledgeable regarding practice in the jurisdiction in question and may help advise regarding the nuances of the jurisdiction in question. While U.S. practitioners can file PCT applications without assistance from foreign associates, especially since the USPTO is an international receiving office and English is an official filing language, a representative in the designated state or region may need to be identified when filing national or regional phase applications. Accordingly, it is common for foreign associates and USPTO practitioners to develop reciprocal business relationships in which each utilizes the other for foreign filings in their representative countries. A foreign-filed application typically may claim priority to an earlier-filed application in the United States within a one- year grace period under the Paris Convention for the Protection of Industrial Property[87] and may receive the benefit of the filing date of the earlier-filed U.S. patent application. The converse is true. An application that is foreign-filed may serve as a priority basis for a U.S. application filed within one year that claims priority to the foreign-filed application.

---

86. http://www.wipo.int/export/sites/www/standards/en/pdf/03-03-01.pdf#country_codes.

87. http://www.wipo.int/treaties/en/ip/paris/trtdocs_wo020.html.

5. Benefits of PCT Applications

It should be apparent from the above description that a PCT application is a mechanism that may be utilized for deferring the national or regional procedures and the respective fees and translation costs. Additionally, PCT applications provide a unified filing procedure that can reduce the work required and time spent to preserve an early filing date. This deferral of costs and decisions may prove beneficial to applicants, as they may have a better understanding as to whether the inventive technology will be desirable in the marketplace and worth further expenditures in pursuing patent protection in various jurisdictions.

C. Foreign Enforcement Considerations

Having obtained patent rights in various countries, the focus now may turn to enforcement of these acquired patent rights. Enforcement considerations can and should play an important part in a practitioner's prosecution analysis as an unenforceable patent or difficult patent may have little value. As described in the *Patent Litigation Section* herein, effective patent enforcement in the U.S. often involves important decisions of where and when to file the litigation in addition to the most effective arguments to make before the court and jury. Each federal district court may have varied patent litigation procedures, rules, and tendencies that may aid or hinder patent owners or defendants. Foreign jurisdictions also may vary in their procedures, rules, and tendencies. Further contributing to the varied enforcement practices and success rate is that the underlying patent law or rules, and sometimes even the type of court, can vary from country to country, something not true of the varied U.S. jurisdictions. As such, international enforcement of patent rights can be extremely speculative, and U.S. practitioners often look to foreign practitioners experienced in the local courts and in dealing with local judges and officials for practical guidance in helping to assess the merits and likelihood of success in potential enforcement proceedings. In particular, despite the Agreement on Trade-Related Aspects of Intellectual Property Rights (TRIPS) under the General Agreement of Tariffs and Trade (GATT), there is still a pervasive belief among U.S. practitioners that certain jurisdictions may be less friendly or open to enforcement of local patent laws by foreign corporations against domestic companies. For example, many U.S. companies remain skeptical of enforcing their patent rights in China, as China's courts have a reputation for infrequently finding for U.S. companies bringing suit on their acquired Chinese patent rights against Chinese companies.[88] As such, patent case outcomes may be affected by the larger international relations and posturing of the countries that may trickle into the legal system of that country and create a certain posture of the courts which makes enforcement more difficult in foreign jurisdictions.

Patent owners and practitioners also should be aware that related international cases in a portfolio should be monitored and may need to be prosecuted with an understanding that their actions or arguments in a foreign jurisdiction *could* affect their rights in a related case in the United States. The Federal Circuit has repeatedly indicated that it is "jurisprudentially inappropriate to disregard any relevant evidence on any issue in any case."[89] However, U.S. courts have been reluctant to base decisions on statements contained in a foreign prosecution history. In a number of cases in which a foreign prosecution history was raised, the courts have either declined to address the issue or have cautioned against placing too much weight on the foreign prosecution history.[90] Arguments in a foreign case as to claim construction are considered extrinsic evidence and, as such, will only be considered if the intrinsic evidence regarding the claim construction in the U.S. is ambiguous. Statements in the prosecution history of foreign cases also may be relevant to the issue of prosecution history estoppel and the doctrine of equivalents in a U.S. counterpart application; however, again U.S. courts are generally reluctant to place too much weight on statements made during foreign prosecution.[91] Claim construction, prosecution history estoppel, and the doctrine of equivalents are issues in which a U.S. case may theoretically be affected by actions in a foreign counterpart application but typically are not affected

88. There may be many reasons for this perceived reputation regarding enforcement of patent laws in China and other countries by U.S. practitioners. For example, some U.S. practitioners may suggest a bias against the U.S. and other foreign entities suing local companies in the jurisdiction. However, low success rates may also be explained at least in part by less than effective representation of the U.S. companies in the foreign courts, poorly prosecuted patents, lack of appreciation of Chinese patent laws, or many other factors not directly tied to a bias against foreign entities.

89. Stratoflex, Inc. v. Aeroquip Corp., 713 F.2d 1530, 1538, 218 U.S.P.Q.2d 871, 879 (Fed. Cir. 1983).

90. Tung T. Nguyen, The Rules of Foreign Prosecution History in Patent Infringement Actions (http://www.aipla.org/Content/ContentGroups/Speaker_Papers/Road_Show_Papers/200512/Patent_Prosecution/NguyenPaper.pdf).

91. *Id.*

in practice. In contrast, the prosecution history of foreign cases will be relevant for purposes of satisfying the USPTO's duty of disclosure under 37 C.F.R. §1.56 to disclose "all information known to that individual to be material to patentability." Thus, prior art cited during prosecution of a foreign counterpart application for the same, similar, or related inventions may be deemed material to patentability. The *Manual of Patent Examining Procedure* further states that there is a strong inference that prior art used in rejecting the same or similar claims or that has been identified in some manner in a foreign application is material to patentability of the U.S. claims and should be brought to the attention of the USPTO.[92] Therefore, many practitioners create status charts or other monitoring devices to ensure that potentially material information from foreign cases is disclosed to the USPTO in the related U.S. case.

VI. AMERICA INVENTS ACT (AIA)

On September 16, 2011, President Barack Obama signed into law the Leahy-Smith America Invents Act (AIA).[93] It is not a stretch to characterize the changes to the U.S. patent laws in the AIA as the most significant changes in more than 50 years. Among the most notable changes is the switch of the U.S. patent system from a "first-to-invent" system to a "first-inventor-to-file" system. Other changes that have received attention and undoubtedly will help shape the U.S. patent system moving forward include the new post-grant review mechanisms, modifications to what constitutes prior art under 35 U.S.C. §102, and the prior user right defense. While some of the changes to U.S. patent law ushered in by the AIA became effective immediately upon the date of enactment of the law (September 16, 2011), many of the most substantive changes do not go into effect until 12 months (September 16, 2012) or 18 months (March 16, 2013) after the AIA became law. As such, the U.S. continues to operate under its current laws until these trigger dates are reached. In anticipation of these laws taking effect, a preview of some of the more noteworthy provisions are described in more detail below.

92. MPEP §2001.06(a) ("Applicants . . . have a duty to bring to the attention of the Office any material prior art or other information cited or brought to their attention in any related foreign application. The inference that such prior art or other information is material is especially strong where it has been used in rejecting the same or similar claims in the foreign application or where it has been identified in some manner as particularly relevant.").

93. Pub. L. No. 112-29, 125 Stat. 284 (2011).

A. General Changes and Timelines

1. Timeline

Certain provisions of the AIA are already in effect having taken effect upon passage of the bill into law. Below is a high level listing of selected sections of the AIA that went into effect upon enactment of the AIA.

Table 1-1	
Notable Provisions Effective Upon Enactment (September 16, 2011)	
Sec. 5 –	Prior User Rights Defense
Sec. 6(c) –	Inter Parte Reexam Threshold Modified
Sec. 6(h) –	District Court appeal of ex parte reexamination eliminated
Sec. 7(e) –	Appeals go to Federal Circuit
Sec. 9 –	Suits against USPTO to be brought in E.D.Va (Venue)
Sec. 14 –	Tax strategy already deemed in prior art
Sec. 15 –	Best Mode cannot be used to challenge validity
Sec. 16 –	Marking (including virtual marking and false marking)
Sec. 19 –	Jurisdiction clarification and limitation on joinder
Sec. 33 –	No patents claiming or directed to "human organisms"
Sec. 37 –	Calculation of patent term extension (*Medco*)

Additionally, certain provisions of the AIA take effect 12 months or 18 months after enactment respectfully. Below are two illustrative charts identifying sections of the AIA that go into effect progressively rather than immediately upon the passage of the law.

Table 1-2	
Notable Provisions Effective 12 Months After Enactment (September 16, 2012)	
Sec. 4 –	Inventor's Oath and Declaration
Sec. 6(a) and (d) –	Inter Partes Review & Post-Grant Review
Sec. 7 –	Patent Trial and Appeal Board (PTAB)
Sec. 8 –	Third Party Submissions
Sec. 12 –	Supplemental Examination
Sec. 17 –	Advice of Counsel
Sec. 18 –	Transition Program for Business Method Patents

Table 1-3	
Notable Provisions Effective 18 Months After Enactment (March 16, 2013)	
Sec. 3(b)(1) –	First to File (§102)
Sec. 3(c) –	Modified Obviousness Standard (§103)
Sec. 3(i) –	Derivation Proceedings Established (§135)
Sec. 3 (e)(1) –	Statutory Invention Registration (SIR) Repealed (§157)

2. Structure of the USPTO and Fees

Aside from the substantive law provisions, the AIA also provides some structural and authoritative changes that relate to the USPTO. Sec. 7 of the AIA establishes a new Patent Trial and Appeal Board (PTAB) which will effectively replace the current Board of Patent Appeals and Interferences (BPAI).[94] The AIA also authorizes three or more USPTO satellite offices within three years, the first of which opens in Detroit, Michigan, in 2012. Sec. 22 of the AIA also establishes the "Patent and Trademark Fee Reserve Fund" effective October 1, 2011, which is responsive to calls from some to guarantee the USPTO is able to retain any money from fees collected from users in excess to what Congress budgeted for it to use rather than having to return to the general treasury. Now any excess money from fees will go into the new reserve fund but Congress still must authorize USPTO use of the funds—a somewhat middle ground approach between the previous mechanism in place and Congress fully relinquishing its control of the monies collected and expended by the USPTO.[95]

94. §7, 125 Stat. at 313 (to be codified at 35 U.S.C. §6) (effective 1 year after the enactment date of the AIA).

95. The USPTO, from a practical perspective, is self funding with fees it collects for action by the Office such as filing fees and examination fees for patent and trademark applications. However, Congress is responsible for authorizing and overseeing the USPTO budget as part of the budgetary process. The issue of "fee diversion" by which some of the moneys collected from users of the USPTO is contributed by Congress to the general budget rather than remaining with the USPTO to provide funding for USPTO operation including efforts to hire and train examiners to reduce backlogs was an important issue discussed during consideration of the AIA.

B. Prosecution

1. First to File

Among the more notable changes the AIA makes to U.S. patent law is a transition from a a first-to-invent system to a first-inventor-to-file system effective 18 months after the date of enactment of the AIA (March 16, 2013). This change in the system will apply to applications with effective filing dates on or after March 16, 2013 and applications that ever include any claims with effective dates after that date. Prior to this change, the U.S. stood as a lone system and a change to a first-inventor-to-file moves the U.S. closer to harmonization with the patent systems of the rest of the world. This change to U.S. patent law results in the first date of invention no longer being available to establish inventive priority as it theoretically has been in the past. Additionally, interferences before the USPTO are replaced with derivation proceedings. Also, the grace period for filing a patent application before activity by the inventor becomes a novelty destroying event will be tweaked but still provides inventors a one-year grace period from certain actions in which to file a patent application.

2. §102 Prior Art

Title 35 continues to set forth conditions for novelty in §102 but with revised provisions after the AIA.[96]

---

96. (a) NOVELTY; PRIOR ART—A person shall be entitled to a patent unless—

(1) the claimed invention was patented, described in a printed publication, or in public use, on sale, or otherwise available to the public before the effective filing date of the claimed invention; or.

(2) the claimed invention was described in a patent issued under section 151, or in an application for patent published or deemed published under section 122(b), in which the patent or application, as the case may be, names another inventor and was effectively filed before the effective filing date of the claimed invention.

(b) EXCEPTIONS—

(1) DISCLOSURES MADE 1 YEAR OR LESS BEFORE THE EFFECTIVE FILING DATE OF THE CLAIMED INVENTION—A disclosure made 1 year or less before the effective filing date of a claimed invention shall not be prior art to the claimed invention under subsection (a)(1) if—

(A) the disclosure was made by the inventor or joint inventor or by another who obtained the subject matter disclosed directly or indirectly from the inventor or a joint inventor; or.

Pursuant to 35 U.S.C. §102(a)(1) novelty will be destroyed if before the effective filing date the patented or claimed invention as patented, was described in a printed publication, in public use, on sale, or

---

(B) the subject matter disclosed had, before such disclosure, been publicly disclosed by the inventor or a joint inventor or another who obtained the subject matter disclosed directly or indirectly from the inventor or a joint inventor.

(2) DISCLOSURES APPEARING IN APPLICATIONS AND PATENTS—A disclosure shall not be prior art to a claimed invention under subsection (a)(2) if—

(A) the subject matter disclosed was obtained directly or indirectly from the inventor or a joint inventor;

(B) the subject matter disclosed had, before such subject matter was effectively filed under subsection (a)(2), been publicly disclosed by the inventor or a joint inventor or another who obtained the subject matter disclosed directly or indirectly from the inventor or a joint inventor; or.

(C) the subject matter disclosed and the claimed invention, not later than the effective filing date of the claimed invention, were owned by the same person or subject to an obligation of assignment to the same person.

(c) COMMON OWNERSHIP UNDER JOINT RESEARCH AGREEMENTS—Subject matter disclosed and a claimed invention shall be deemed to have been owned by the same person or subject to an obligation of assignment to the same person in applying the provisions of subsection (b)(2)(C) if—

(1) the subject matter disclosed was developed and the claimed invention was made by, or on behalf of, 1 or more parties to a joint research agreement that was in effect on or before the effective filing date of the claimed invention;

(2) the claimed invention was made as a result of activities undertaken within the scope of the joint research agreement; and

(3) the application for patent for the claimed invention discloses or is amended to disclose the names of the parties to the joint research agreement.

(d) PATENTS AND PUBLISHED APPLICATIONS EFFECTIVE AS PRIOR ART—For purposes of determining whether a patent or application for patent is prior art to a claimed invention under subsection (a)(2), such patent or application shall be considered to have been effectively filed, with respect to any subject matter described in the patent or application—

(1) if paragraph (2) does not apply, as of the actual filing date of the patent or the application for patent; or

(2) if the patent or application for patent is entitled to claim a right of priority under section 119, 365(a), or 365(b), or to claim the benefit of an earlier filing date under section 120, 121, or 365(c), based upon 1 or more prior filed applications for patent, as of the filing date of the earliest such application that describes the subject matter.

otherwise available to the public. Novelty also will be destroyed under 35 U.S.C. §102(a)(2) if the claimed invention was described in an issued patent or a published application filed before the applicant's effective filing date and names another inventor. A geographic limitation—requiring that certain actions take place within the United States—no longer exists with respect to certain novelty defeating actions.

The AIA provides for certain exceptions to novelty destroying events. 35 U.S.C. §102(b)(1) provides that a disclosure less than one year before the effective filing date does not count as prior art under §102(a)(1) if the disclosure was made by the inventor, joint inventor or another who obtained the subject matter from the inventor or joint inventor. 35 U.S.C. §102(b)(2) provides that a disclosure in a patent or application is not considered prior art under §102(a)(2) if the subject matter was obtained from the inventor or a joint inventor; if before the effective filing date of the subject matter of the disclosure the subject matter had been disclosed by the inventor, joint inventor or another who had obtained the subject matter disclosed directly or indirectly from the inventor; or if the subject matter disclosed and the subject matter claimed were owned by the same person or under an obligation of assignment to the same person. Effectively these exemptions create what has been described as a "first to publish" priority date for the inventor by which the inventor must file within one year after publication. Additionally, the AIA also abolishes what was referred to in patent circles as the *Hilmer Doctrine*,[97] that a foreign-priority patent or application is considered to be prior art only as far back as its U.S. filing date (not its foreign-priority date.) Patents and applications may now be considered prior art as of the filing date or priority date.

3. §103 Prior Art

Under §103 as modified by the AIA, obviousness is a determination made as of *the effective filing date of the claimed invention* rather than *at the time the invention was made*.[98] Obviousness is still a determination made by the hypothetical "person having ordinary skill in the art." As amended, §103 of Title 35 reads:

> "A patent for a claimed invention may not be obtained, notwithstanding that the claimed invention is not identically disclosed as

97. *In re* Hilmer, 359 F.2d 859 (CCPA 1966).

98. Effectively in practice, these two dates are often the same. As such, this change may be more of a clarifying change than a shift in policy.

set forth in section 102, if the differences between the claimed invention and the prior art are such that the claimed invention as a whole would have been obvious before *the effective filing date of the claimed invention* to a person having ordinary skill in the art to which the claimed invention pertains. Patentability shall not be negated by the manner in which the invention was made." (emphasis added)

While the point in time of reference may have been modified as a result of the AIA, the analysis performed in making determinations with respect to obviousness is not expected to change significantly.

4. Inventor's Oath or Declaration

Historically, patent applications in the U.S. could only be filed by (in the name of) inventor(s). Pursuant to sec. 4 of the AIA,[99] assignees or those to whom there is an obligation for the inventor to assign, may make an application for a patent.[100] Patent applications that are filed under this provision, should they issue as a patent, will be granted to the real party in interest. The AIA has also removed the requirement for the oath or declaration to contain a statement of "lack of deceptive intent."[101] Sec. 4 also simplifies difficulties encountered in filing oaths or declarations if the inventor is deceased, under legal incapacity or cannot be found or reached after diligent effort, or if the inventor(s) is under an obligation to assign the invention but has refused to make the oath or declaration, providing for the filing of a "substitute statement" in these instances.[102] The changes provided for in sec. 4 further harmonizes U.S. law with those elsewhere in the world.

5. Preissuance Submissions by Third Parties

Sec. 8 of the AIA provides for prior issuance submissions by third parties.[103] Any third party may submit for consideration and inclusion in the record of a patent application any patent, published patent application, or other printed publication of potential relevance to the examination of the

99. Effective one year after the enactment date of the AIA.
100. §4, 125 Stat. at 296-29 (to be codified at 35 U.S.C. §118).
101. §4, 125 Stat. at 293-296 (to be codified at 35 U.S.C. §115).
102. *Id.*
103. §8, 125 Stat. at 315-316 (to be codified at 35 U.S.C.§122(e)).

application. Any such submission must be before an allowance has issued or the later of six months after publication or the date of the first rejection. Submissions must include a concise description of the asserted relevance of each submitted document, the requisite fee, and a statement by the person making the submission affirming that the submission was made in compliance with this section.

6. Derivation Proceedings

Under the AIA, "interferences" before the USPTO have been eliminated[104] giving way to derivation proceedings.[105] As such, interference proceedings as a mechanism to antedate prior art by establishing an earlier date of invention are gone. Rather, for derivation proceedings, an applicant may file a petition to institute a derivation proceeding alleging that another derived a claimed invention from the applicant. Petitions to institute a derivation proceeding must be filed within one year of the first publication of a claim to an invention that is the same or substantially the same and set forth with particularity the basis for finding that an inventor named in an earlier application derived the claimed invention from an invention named in the petitioner's application. The Director of the USPTO determines whether the petition satisfies the standard and may institute a derivation proceeding upon such a determination. The Director's determination is "final and nonappealable."[106]

Derivation hearings are heard by the PTAB. The PTAB is empowered to make a determination whether an inventor named in the earlier application derived the claimed invention from an inventor named in the petitioner's application.[107] The PTAB may defer action on a petition for a derivation proceeding until three months after the issue date of a patent that includes the claimed invention that is subject of the petition or may defer or stay the proceeding after it has been instituted until the determination of an ex parte reexamination, inter partes review or post-grant review proceeding involving the patent of the earlier applicant.[108] If the final decision of the PTAB is adverse to claims in an application, the decision will be considered a final refusal by the Office on those claims. If the final decision of the PTAB is adverse to claims in a patent, and no

104. §3(j), 125 Stat. at 290.
105. §3(i), 125 Stat. at 289-290.
106. §3(i), 125 Stat. at 289 (to be codified at 35 U.S.C. §135(a)).
107. §3(i), 125 Stat. at 289 (to be codified at 35 U.S.C. §135(b)).
108. §3(i), 125 Stat. at 289 (to be codified as 35 U.S.C. §135(c)).

appeal or other review of the decision can be taken or had, the decision constitutes cancellation of those claims.[109] Derivation proceedings can be terminated by settlement agreement between the parties, with a written statement reflecting the agreement of the parties as to the correct inventors of the claimed invention in dispute being filed with the Director. Settlement agreements may be treated as "business confidential information," kept separate from the files of the application(s) and/or patent(s) at issue, and made available only to government agencies on written request, or to any person on a showing of good cause.[110] Parties may utilize arbitration to determine the entire contest or any aspect thereof.[111]

7. Tax Strategies and Human Organisms

The AIA includes some subject matter specific carve outs with respect to patentability of certain specific technologies. Pursuant to Sec. 8, any "strategy for reducing, avoiding or deferring tax liability" shall be "deemed insufficient to differentiate a claimed invention from the prior art." By making such technologies statutorily unable to distinguish from the prior art—these tax liability strategy inventions are no longer patentable subject matter. This carve out went into effect upon enactment of the AIA and applies to any patent application pending or filed on or after the date of enactment of the AIA.

In a similar fashion, sec. 33 of the AIA sets forth that "[n]o patent may issue on a claim directed to or encompassing a human organism." This carve out applies to any application pending or filed on or after the date of enactment of the AIA, but does not apply retroactively to previously issued patents. Some have already raised questions as to what constitutes a "human organism" and what are the bounds of the "directed to" language. Litigation under the AIA will likely provided further insight as the USPTO and the courts interpret these terms.

C. Post-Grant Proceedings

The AIA will significantly change the landscape one year after enactment of the AIA with respect to post-grant proceedings. For example, interferences (priority contests as to who the first inventor and rightful owner of an invention being claimed by two distinct inventive entities)

109. §3(i), 125 Stat. at 289-290 (to be codified as 35 U.S.C. §135(d)).
110. §3(i), 125 Stat. at 290 (to be codified as 35 U.S.C. §135(e)).
111. §3(i), 125 Stat. at 290 (to be codified as 35 U.S.C. §135(f)).

no longer exist and have given way to revised post-grant proceedings and mechanisms.

1. Ex parte reexamination

While the AIA modifies the appellate process for ex parte reexamination (appeals go to the U.S. Court of Appeals for the Federal Circuit),[112] the remainder of ex parte reexamination is left unchanged by the AIA.

2. Inter partes review[113]

Inter partes reexamination will effectively be replaced with "inter partes review." Inter partes review proceedings cannot be initiated until after nine months from the issue date (or after the termination date of any post-grant review proceedings). Only novelty and obviousness challenges may be made and these challenges are to be based only on patents or printed publications. Inter partes review may be initiated against any patent (including reissued patents) and the new Patent Trial and Appcal Board (PTAB) will conduct inter partes review proceedings which are to be completed within one year of the USPTO's ordering of the review with a six month extension available for "good cause."[114] The USPTO must make a determination as to whether or not to initiate a proceeding within three months of the patent owner's response to the petition to initiate the proceeding (or the expiration of the period to file such a response). The standard for the USPTO to grant the review is "reasonable likelihood that the petitioner would prevail with respect to at least 1 of the claims challenged,"[115] which is a stricter standard than the "substantial new question of patentability" standard that was previously in place for inter partes reexamination. Intervening rights are provided for any new or amended claims.

Inter partes review may not be initiated by a petitioner that has filed a civil action contesting the validity of the patent in question and no inter partes review can be filed more than one year after the petitioner has been served with a complaint for a patent infringement. There appears to

---

112. §6(h)(2)(A), 125 Stat. at 312 (to be codified as 35 U.S.C. §306).

113. §6(a), 125 Stat. at 299-305 (to be codified as 35 U.S.C. §§311-319).

114. The AIA grants the USPTO the authority to limit the number of inter parte review proceedings during the first four years.

115. §6(a), 125 Stat. at 300 (to be codified as 35 U.S.C. §314(a)).

be some risk for parties in initiating an inter partes review as a petitioner will be estopped from raising any ground of invalidity that was "raised or reasonably could have raised" in the inter partes review proceeding in a lawsuit, ITC proceeding, or another USPTO proceeding. Like appeals of ex parte reexaminations under the AIA, inter partes reviews can be appealed directly to the U.S. Court of Appeals for the Federal Circuit.[116] The change from inter partes reexamination to inter partes review may be considered somewhat of a "graduated implementation" with the Director of the USPTO being empowered to impose a limit on the number of inter partes reviews that may be instituted. Also there are three varied inter partes reexamination or review mechanisms co-existing depending upon when the inter partes reexamination or review was filed.[117]

3. Post-grant review[118]

The AIA provides for post-grant review of patents. Post-grant review under the AIA is akin to what are typically called "oppositions" in many other countries. A post-grant review petition is to be filed within nine months after issuance of the patent and challenges may be brought based upon any patentability ground with the exception of "best mode" or based upon any "novel or unsettled legal question that is important to other patents or patent applications." The threshold for grant of a request for post-grant review proceedings is that it is "more likely than not" that at least one of the claims is not patentable and evidence is to be submitted that supports the challenge to each of the claims.[119]

Post-grant review is held before the PTAB, with many of the provisions governing post-grant review and its process being governed by

116. §6(a), 125 Stat. at 304 (to be codified as 35 U.S.C. §319)).

117. Reexamination requests filed before the date of enactment (September 16, 2011) will be handled pursuant to the previous inter partes reexamination provisions. Reexamination requests filed on or after September 16, 2011 but before September 16, 2012 will operate in a "transition" period in which the standard is changed to the new "reasonable likelihood that the requester would prevail" standard but the estoppel and other provisions remain unchanged. Inter partes reexamination/reviews filed on or after September 16, 2012 will be handled as inter partes reviews falling under the full AIA provisions for the new inter partes review mechanism.

118. §6(d), 125 Stat. at 305-311 (codified as 35 U.S.C. §§321-329).

119. §6(d), 125 Stat. at 306 (codified as 35 U.S.C. §322).

substantially similar provisions as those regarding inter partes review.[120] For example, post-grant review proceedings are to be completed by the PTAB within one year with a six month extension available for good cause. Intervening rights are provided for new and amended claims, and the estoppel standard for post-grant review is "raised or reasonably could have been raised."

4. Transitional program for business method patents[121]

Sec. 8 of the AIA provides that the Director of the USPTO no later than one year after enactment of the AIA shall issue regulations establishing and implementing a transitional post-grant review proceeding for review of the validity of covered business method patents. This transitional post-grant review proceeding with respect to business method patents is to employ the same standards and procedures of a post-grant review with some exceptions including the requirement that the petitioner, or the petitioner's real party in interest, "has been sued for infringement of the patent or has been charged with infringement under that patent." Patents that are covered under this provision include those that claim a method or corresponding apparatus for performing data processing operations utilized in the practice, administration, or management of a financial product or service. However, patents for "technical inventions" are not covered, with the Director of the USPTO being charged with issuing regulations for determining whether a patent is for a "technical invention" under this provision.

5. Supplemental examination[122]

The AIA establishes a process for patent owner to request supplemental examination of a patent to consider, reconsider, or correct information believed to be relevant to the patent. Within three months after receiving

120. Just as with inter partes review, the AIA permits the USPTO has the authority to limit the number of post grant review proceedings during the first four years.

121. Sec. 8 also sets forth an ATM exception providing that in actions for infringement an automated teller machine shall not be deemed to be a regular and established place of business for purposes of venue. §8, 125 Stat. at 331.

122. Supplemental examination provisions become effective after expiration of a one-year period after the date of enactment of the AIA and apply to any patent issued before, on, or after the effective date. §12, 125 Stat. at 325–27.

a proper request the Director is to conduct a supplemental examination to determine whether a "substantial new question of patentability" has been raised. If it has, the Director will order ex parte reexamination of the patent. A patent shall not be held unenforceable on the basis of conduct relating to information that had not been considered, was inadequately considered, or was incorrect in a prior examination of the patent if the information was considered, reconsidered or corrected during supplemental examination of the patent. However, this prohibition on challenging enforceability based on information in a supplemental examination does not apply if the enforceability of a patent was challenged before a request for supplemental examination. A patentee cannot use supplemental examination to inoculate itself from an inequitable conduct allegation after litigation has begun. Also, if the Director becomes aware of material fraud during the supplemental examination, the Director may take appropriate action and must refer the matter to the Attorney General.

D. Litigation

1. Joinder

Sec. 19(d)(1) of the AIA clarifies federal court jurisdiction over patent and copyright cases and establishes requirements for joinder of accused infringers in patent litigations commenced on or after the date of enactment of the AIA. Merely alleging that a group of defendants infringe a patent or patents in suit is not sufficient alone to join the defendants in one action. In order to join defendants in patent cases the right to relief must relate to or arise out of the same transaction, occurrence or series of transactions or occurrences; must relate to the making, using, importing into the U.S., offering for sale or selling the same accused product or process; and the questions of fact that will arise must be common to all defendants or counterclaims defendants.[123]

2. Prior User Rights

Since 1999, the United States has recognized a limited defense to infringement for a "method of doing or conducting business" that was reduced to practice at least one year before the effective date of the patent being asserted and that was commercially used before the effective filing date of the patent.[124] As of September 16, 2011, eligibility for

123. §19(d)(1), 125 Stat. at 332 (codified at 35 U.S.C. §299).
124. 35 U.S.C. §273.

the prior use defense is no longer limited to a "method of doing or conducting business;" instead, it is available to any patentable subject matter and technology type.[125]

In order to be eligible, the accused infringing subject matter must have been used commercially in the United States, "either in connection with an internal commercial use or an actual arm's length sale or other arm's length commercial transfer of a useful end result of such commercial use."[126] This commercial use must also have occurred at least one year before the earlier of either: "(A) the effective filing date of the claimed invention; or (B) the date on which the claimed invention was disclosed to the public in a manner that qualified for the exemption from the prior art under section 102(b)." Additionally, if the commercial use is "abandoned," activities performed before the date of abandonment cannot be relied on to establish a prior user defense with respect to actions taken on or after the date of abandonment.[127]

The statute also affirmatively sets forth several scenarios in which subject matter is explicitly considered as being "commercially used" and thus eligible for the prior user rights defense. Section 273(c)(1) provides that subject matter for which "commercial marketing or use is subject to a premarketing regulatory review period during which safety or efficacy is established" shall be deemed to be commercially used for purposes of the prior user right defense during the regulatory review period. Additionally, section 273(c)(2) provides that use of the subject matter by a "nonprofit research laboratory or other nonprofit entity, such as a university or hospital, for which the public is the intended beneficiary" will be considered a "commercial use" for purposes of the prior user right defense.

Finally, the AIA provides that doctrine of exhaustion applies to "the sale or other disposition of a useful end result by a person entitled to assert a defense under this section in connection with a patent . . . to the extent that such rights would have been exhausted had such sale or other disposition been made by the patent owner."[128] If an action such as a sale would have exhausted the patent rights in certain goods, then that same action such as a sale exhausts the patent rights when the action is performed by an entity with prior user rights. Thus, customers that purchase or acquire goods and the like from an entity that acquired prior user

125. §5, 125 Stat. at 297 (codified at 35 U.S.C. §273(a)).
126. *Id.* (codified at 35 U.S.C. §273(a)(1)).
127. *Id.* at 298 (to be codified at 35 U.S.C. §273(e)(4)).
128. *Id.* at 297-298 (to be codified at 35 U.S.C. §273(d)).

rights are beyond the reach of the patent rights as the patentee's patent rights are exhausted by the sale of the goods or the like to the same extent that exhaustion would have prevented the entities from liability if they had acquired them in the same fashion from the patentee. This provision prevents the prior user right defense from being eroded with creation of a "catch-22" of being protected by the prior user rights defense but not being able to sell your products because the liability for infringement was merely passed down the chain to the customers.

The AIA provides that only commercial use in the United States may provide the basis for a prior use defense. In particular, the subject matter must have been commercially used "in the United States, either in connection with an internal commercial use or an arm's length sale or other arm's length commercial transfer of a useful end result of such commercial use."[129] As such, activity performed wholly outside the United States will not give rise to a prior user rights based upon the geographic location of the activity.

According to the AIA, "good faith" is an explicit qualification for the prior user right defense.[130] Derivation may not be utilized to establish the defense as the AIA also sets forth that a prior use defense may not be asserted if the subject matter forming the basis for the defense was "derived from the patentee or persons in privity with the patentee."[131]

Pursuant to the AIA, the prior use defense is a personal right and may not generally be transferred. The defense may only be asserted by "the person who performed or directed performance of the commercial use . . . or by an entity that controls, is controlled by, or is under common control with such person."[132] Further, except for any transfer to the patent owner, the right to assert a prior user defense cannot be "licensed or assigned or transferred to another person except as an ancillary and subordinate part of a good-faith assignment or transfer for other reasons of the entire enterprise or line of business to which the defense relates."[133]

As previously mentioned, the AIA has expanded the technology or subject matter eligible for the prior use defense to include any subject matter consisting of "a process, or consisting of a machine, manufac-

---

129. *Id.* at 297 (to be codified at 35 U.S.C. §273(a)(1)).
130. *Id.*
131. *Id.* at 298 (to be codified at 35 U.S.C. §273(e)).
132. *Id.*
133. *Id.*

ture, or composition of matter. . . ."[134] The listing of subject matter eligible for the prior user right defense tracks the listing of subject matter eligible for patentability under 35 U.S.C. §101.[135] As such, the prior user right defense to infringement will be available for any patentable subject matter, assuming the other requirements are also met.

The main exception explicitly provided for in the AIA is the "university exception," which disqualifies a person from asserting the prior user defense if the claimed invention was "owned or subject to an obligation of assignment to either an institution of higher education . . . or a technology transfer organization whose primary purpose is to facilitate the commercialization of technologies develop by one or more such institutions of higher education."[136] Thus technology owned, assigned or developed by universities and other like institutions will not be subject to the prior user rights defense.

Concurrent with the enactment of the AIA and the newly amended section 273, Congress mandated the USPTO to produce a report on the operation on prior user rights in industrialized countries in order to explore the implications of a prior use defense in the United States.[137] In January 2012, responsive to Congress's mandate, the USPTO provided its Report on the Prior User Rights Defense which sets forth among other findings that the new prior user right provisions has generally moved U.S. patent law towards harmonization with prior user rights regimes in other countries.[138] The new U.S. prior user rights provisions now notably deviate from many of the regimes across the globe with respect to only a few provisions. While the new U.S. prior user right provisions still vary from those common in many international regimes with respect to the "university exception," the one year "look back" period for acquiring rights, and the requirement of commercialization rather than merely "substantial preparations to commercialize," the U.S. prior user rights system now generally aligns with most prior user rights systems abroad.

134. *Id.* at 297 (to be codified at 35 U.S.C. §273(a)).

135. 35 U.S.C.§101 (2006) ("Whoever invents or discovers any new and useful process, machine manufacture, or composition of matter, or an new and useful improvement thereof, subject to the conditions and requirements of this title.").

136. §5, 125 Stat. at 298 (to be codified at 35 U.S.C. §273(e)(5)).

137. §3(m), 125 Stat. at 292.

138. Report on the Prior User Rights Defense prepared by the USPTO (January 2012) (http://www.uspto.gov/aia_implementation/20120113-pur_report.pdf).

3. Best Mode

Sec. 15 of the AIA eliminated as a defense in infringement actions the failure to disclose the best mode for carrying out the subject invention. However, the best mode requirement itself has not been eliminated.

4. Virtual Marking

Sec. 16(a) of the AIA amends Title 35 to permit virtual marking to satisfy the marking requirements. In particular, virtual marking can be done by "fixing thereon the word 'patent' or the abbreviation 'pat.' together with an address of a posting on the Internet, accessible to the public without charge for accessing the address that associates the patented article with the number of the patent. . . ."[139]

5. False Marking

Under the AIA, only the U.S. government may bring suit for statutory damages for false marking claims.[140] Entities other than the U.S. government may still bring suits for competitive injuries for false marking with damages being limited to "damages adequate to compensate for the injury." The changes to the false marking provisions under the AIA apply to all proceedings pending or commenced on or after the date of enactment of the AIA.

6. Jurisdiction

The AIA clarifies, to the extent jurisdiction was questioned, the exclusive federal jurisdiction for patents, plant variety protection, and copyright.[141]

7. Advice of Counsel

The failure of an infringer to obtain advice of counsel with respect to any allegedly infringed patent, or to present such advice of counsel to the court or jury, may not be used to prove that the accused infringer willfully infringed the patent or intended to induce infringement of the patent.[142]

139. §16(a), 125 Stat. at 328-329 (to be codified as 35 U.S.C. §297(a)).
140. §16(b), 125 Stat. at 329 (to be codified as 35 U.S.C. §292(a)) .
141. §19, 125 Stat. at 331-333.
142. §17(a), 125 Stat. at 329 (to be codified as 35 U.S.C. §298).

PART 2

Patent Prosecution

> *That reminds me to remark, in passing, that the very first official thing I did, in my administration—and it was on the first day of it, too—was to start a patent office; for I knew that a country without a patent office and good patent laws was just a crab, and couldn't travel any way but sideways or backways.*
>
> — Mark Twain,
> *A Connecticut Yankee in King Arthur's Court* (1889)

While the prosecution of patent applications differs in many ways from the prosecution of trademark applications, there are also many similarities, or at least synergies, with the prosecution of trademark applications, particularly with respect to some of the formalities and the handling of examination and procedural matters. The similarities in some of the procedural operations and processing may not be overly surprising given that the same bureau of the United States Government, the U.S. Patent and Trademark Office (USPTO), is charged with the authority and responsibility to handle these administrative agency matters. Also, in many instances, the particulars about office procedure may have distinct nuances, but the concepts and general handling will be the same. Applicants and representatives should reference the *Manual of Patent Examining Procedure* (MPEP) as well as the relevant provisions of the United States Code and Code of Federal Regulations when practicing before the USPTO. While there are an almost infinite number of factual circumstances and considerations practitioners could encounter or consider during the procurement process, this section will provide insight regarding many of the more regularly encountered matters relating to patent prosecution.

I. ASPECTS OF PATENT PROSECUTION PRIOR TO FILING

A. How Does the Process Usually Start?

A number of manners exist for identifying subject matter that may be patented. Most commonly for practitioners, an inventor and/or a company create some form of disclosure document that describes the invention's subject matter in some detail. The goal of a practitioner is to wade through the documentation and materials to identify and optimize potentially patentable subject matter. Whether the end result is a patent to protect a commercial embodiment and/or to prevent others from implementing a feature, a practitioner is charged with a number of tasks that must be investigated before a patent application is even prepared.

B. Inventorship

One task for a practitioner when receiving and reviewing disclosure documents is identifying inventorship and ownership. Understanding the difference between these two concepts is important under U.S. patent law practice. Under U.S. law, for any type of patent—whether it is a utility patent, a plant patent, or a design patent—inventorship is defined solely by the claims. An entire team of individuals might have worked in some capacity on a project. The team may include designers, code writers, individual managers, project managers, and testers, and the disclosure materials provided may include input from each of these individuals. Yet, the claims of an application for a patent will define the inventors.

As a rule, an inventor is one who: (1) conceives of at least one portion of at least one claim of the patent application, and (2) reduces that claim to practice. These two concepts together define who should and should not be identified as an inventor. Understanding these concepts will help ensure that a patent issued on the subject matter will not subsequently be vulnerable to an invalidity argument for failure to identify proper inventorship.

Conception represents the inventor formulation of the definite and permanent idea for solving a problem in such a way that a person skilled in the relevant art could practice the invention by following the inventor's conception. In other words, conception is the idea of the invention. It may be considered the "eureka" moment. Who helped think up the features of the invention? Did the project manager actually contribute to the conception of the invention or did she merely oversee the entire project?

To complete an invention, there must be "a reduction to practice," a term of art meaning that the invention must have been applied and tested. This may be an "actual" reduction to practice, which is when the invention is made and tested to determine that it works. However, reduction to practice does not require the invention to be made. An invention can be "constructively" reduced to practice by filing a patent application, whether in the U.S. Patent & Trademark Office or another recognized foreign patent office, claiming the invention. For purposes of invention, a constructive reduction to practice is considered to be equivalent to an actual reduction to practice.

By knowing what defines an inventor, proper identification of inventorship may be accomplished. There may be only one inventor, which occurs when one person has conceived of the entire invention, i.e., each and every claim in the patent application. When more than one person contributes to the conception of an invention, each person is considered to be a joint inventor. Joint inventors do not have to have physically worked together on the invention. However, there must have been some collaboration, and each of the inventors must have worked on the same subject matter and must have made some contribution to the conception of the invention as it is claimed in the patent application. All of the joint inventors do not have to be inventors of every claim, since conception and reduction to practice are required of only one feature of at least one claim. As such, even if an individual contributes a conception and reduction to practice to only one claim in a patent application, that individual is still a joint inventor of the entire patent application.

C. Problem to Be Solved

A second task for a practitioner in receiving and reviewing disclosure documents is to understand the problem to be solved. A practitioner should be analyzing the materials to appreciate how the inventors got from a first point (the problem at hand and the prior manners for handling) to a resulting point—(the invention for solving the problem). Because most, if not all, inventions today are improvements of some kind, a practitioner must comprehend the state of the art and what was happening in accessing and identifying patentable subject matter.

D. How Is the Problem Solved?

A third task is the resulting point, i.e., how exactly did the inventors solve the problem that they faced. Ultimately, this is the most important aspect that a practitioner will focus on in understanding and developing the patentable subject matter for a patent application. The eventual patent application needs to adequately describe the invention and how the invention is both implemented and reached.

E. Prior Art

A fourth and final beginning task for a practitioner in receiving and reviewing disclosure documents is to take note of any prior art. After many years of drafting and prosecuting patent applications, a practitioner will likely become familiar with various types of subject matter in an industry. A practitioner should be aware of patents, articles, papers, books, etc., in a particular field of technology. In initially assessing patentable subject matter of a new disclosure, a practitioner should be reflecting on this knowledge of prior art in determining patentable subject matter. When drafting a new patent application, a practitioner should apply such knowledge so he can more fully articulate the novel features of the disclosure materials.

F. Disclosure Meeting vs. Disclosure Materials Alone

A disclosure meeting with one or more of the inventors allows a practitioner the opportunity to discuss a number of issues regarding potential patentability: the features of the invention, the development of the invention, and the process of prosecution and options available. If possible, a disclosure meeting, whether face-to-face or via some teleconferencing, is a preferred manner for interaction between a practitioner and inventors. Such a meeting may be the only time to resolve issues, and it is more effective than through some form of delayed two-way conversation, such as email.

However, a patent application also can be drafted solely from disclosure materials, Some companies utilize a disclosure template for inventors to fill out as part of submission of disclosure materials for assessing whether to proceed with a patent application. Such a template may be detailed enough to address many, if not all, questions that a practitioner might have for inventors during a disclosure meeting. As such, if an inventor's schedule is limited or too valuable to spend on multiple sessions, the crafting of a template may be ideal and act as the disclosure meeting for a company. Use of purely disclosure documents to draft a patent application without a conference or meeting with the inventor is regular practice when a language barrier may be present between a practitioner and inventors such as when, for example, Japanese speaking inventors and English speaking practitioners are working to obtain a patent application.

G. Assessing Statutory Bars to Even Determine Proceeding

Because the preparation of a patent application can be expensive, whether based upon time or money spent on resources, recognizing statutory bars that could prevent validity of a patent or that could preclude issuance of a patent is an important feature of pre-drafting preparation. As previously described, there are a number of statutory bars that may interfere with obtaining and/or enforcing a patent. All of these potential barring events should be questioned and considered when assessing patentability and/or enforcement. Although many types of potential statutory bars exist to securing a patent, the most common include:

- public use and/or knowledge of invention,[1]
- invention publicly and/or privately offered for sale for more than a year,[2]
- invention already patented,[3] including more than a year,[4] and
- invention already in a publicly-accessible printed publication,[5] including for more than a year.[6]

H. Preliminary Questions for Inventors

Given the effect of statutory barring events and the expense involved in preparation and prosecution of a patent application, a practitioner should know as much about the events, if any, as possible. At a minimum, a practitioner should confirm that no such statutory barring events have occurred. Preliminary questions, whether addressed during a disclosure meeting and/or within a disclosure template form for the inventors to fill

1. 35 U.S.C. §§102(a) and 102(b).
2. 35 U.S.C. §102(b).
3. 35 U.S.C. §102(a).
4. 35 U.S.C. §102(b).
5. 35 U.S.C. §102(a).
6. 35 U.S.C. §102(b).

out, are one manner for identifying and confirming potentially limiting actions by the inventors, the company, and/or other individuals.

Practitioners should ask any and all inventors, as well as others involved in the preparation process, whether there were any disclosures relating to a product covered by the invention and/or documents describing the invention. If the invention was ever disclosed to anyone, a practitioner should identify what was disclosed, to whom it was disclosed, when it was disclosed, how it was disclosed, and why it was disclosed. Such information is needed to evaluate any effect of the disclosures, as some disclosures are permitted. For example, working with someone under a non-disclosure agreement is not a public disclosure. It is important to identify all of the circumstances of the disclosure. A disclosure through theft is different from a disclosure resulting from a leak by a company, a company offering to sell a product that included the invention, or the inventor lecturing at a conference on the subject matter of the invention. All of this information should be ascertained and is potentially relevant.

I. Conducting a Prior Art Search

A prior art search, whether conducted independently by an outside entity or done internally, is an investigation into potentially relevant references about the subject matter of an invention. A company might have any of a number of reasons for conducting a prior art search. Some companies want to search for the closest prior art so they will know whether to proceed with a patent application and how best to draft the patent application. Other companies do not want to conduct prior art searches and prefer to prepare a patent application centered solely on the subject matter of the invention. Because prior art references are not limited to U.S. and foreign patents, searches for prior art are rarely all-inclusive. A practitioner should expect that other prior art references will remain unknown, even after a prior art search is conducted. A prior art search may include a third party searching for relevant material to maintain some separation between the prior art and the interests of the practitioner and/or the company. Use of third party searchers may provide cost savings as well.

J. Finding Applicable Prior Art and Drafting Around It

Finding the most applicable prior art as part of a search is often important for drafting a patent application. Knowing the closest state of the art helps one understand claim scope (what the claim covers). Because the claims dictate the scope of the invention, a practitioner is often required to prepare claims that are close to the prior art in the industry but that have novel features to allow for patentability of the subject matter.

K. Knowing That Unpublished Applications and Other Art Not Found May Still Be Out There

However, practitioners need to appreciate that no matter the amount of searching that is performed for prior art, whether conducted by the practitioner or through a prior art searching company, there may still be prior art that could be later uncovered and used against claims of a patent application. Because applications for a utility patent are not published for 18 months after filing, and applications for a design patent are not published until issuance, there may be prior art in the proverbial hopper that may never be accessible until long after preparation and filing of the patent application.

II. DRAFTING A PROVISIONAL APPLICATION

A provisional application is one that will never be examined.[7] It is a placeholder for an inventor to file an application for a patent at a later time. A provisional application allows an inventor and/or company to reserve rights for a later time and still evaluate the need for protection through the patent process. It serves as a mechanism for claiming priority. A provisional application may come in many forms and has few procedural requirements for filing with the U.S. Patent & Trademark Office. The benefit of a provisional application is that the cost can be inexpensive and the filing can be very quick, if necessary. The option of filing a provisional application does not exist for design patents.

A. Legal Effect, Rights Acquired

A provisional application alone provides few rights to an owner. The legal effect of the filing of a provisional application is that an applicant provisionally has met her burden of reducing her invention to practice so long as certain requirements for filing are met and the inventor files a non-provisional application within a year. An applicant has the benefit of filing a non-provisional application and/or a foreign application within one year of the provisional application while still claiming priority. It is as if the applicant filed the non-provisional and/or the foreign application on the date she filed the provisional application.

7. 35 U.S.C. §111(b).

A provisional application also legally protects the term of any corresponding patent from the claim of priority. Because patents today carry a term of 20 years from the filing date of the non-provisional application, an applicant may have a priority date established by the date of filing the provisional application to which it claims priority, with a filing date for patent term calculation purposes being established by the date the non-provisional was filed.

B. Requirements for Filing

Compared to a non-provisional application, there are few procedural and substantive requirements for the filing of a provisional application in the U.S. Patent & Trademark Office (USPTO). The requirements for filing a provisional application include a specification/description of the subject matter of the invention, applicable drawings, identification of the inventors of the subject matter of the invention described, a provisional patent application cover sheet, and an associated government fee. There is no requirement that a provisional application be filed in English. Effectively any document describing the invention will satisfy the requirement of the submission of a specification/description for a provisional application.

Substantively, it is important that a provisional application still meet the requirements for patentability under sections 101 and 112 of Title 35. Because a provisional application must support the claimed subject matter of a later filed non-provisional application, an applicant must meet the statutory requirements of 35 U.S.C. §§101 and 112 in a provisional application. Meeting these requirements allows a later-filed provisional application to properly have a filing date that is the same as the date of filing of the provisional application. Similarly, any drawings that are necessary for describing the subject matter of the invention are required as part of the original filing of a provisional application. Many practitioners will draft a provisional patent application as closely as possible to the form of a non-provisional application (time and money allowing) taking care to include details and features likely to be relied upon should a subsequent non-provisional application need or desire support from the provisional application filing.

Although inventorship for a non-provisional application is defined by the claims, for a provisional application, inventorship is defined by the conception and reduction to practice of any subject matter included in the provisional application that describes the invention. As such, a provisional application will always have at least as many inventors as a later-filed non-provisional application and may include more inventors than a later-filed non-provisional application. If a provisional application describes four features of subject matter for an invention that was invented by two individuals, then a later-filed non-provisional, which claims two features of the four described in the provisional, may include one or both of the same inventors, depending on who conceived of the two features, but not other individuals.

A provisional patent application must include a cover sheet identifying the application as a provisional type application. The cover sheet may take the form of an Application Data Sheet or may be a cover letter. Be forewarned that the failure of a practitioner to include a cover sheet identifying the application as a provisional type application will result in the application being treated as if filed as a non-provisional application.

A government fee is needed to ensure that the provisional application is not abandoned. This is a recurring theme that is pervasive through all filing requirements and prosecution of a patent application.

C. Claims

A patent claim, as required under 35 U.S.C. § 112, is not required for a provisional application. Because a provisional application is never examined by the U.S. Patent & Trademark Office, there is no requirement to include a claim defining the scope of the sought after invention. However, as applicable for conversion processes, including one or more claims in a provisional application may be desirable, as a claim is a requirement for filing a non-provisional application.

D. Priority

A provisional application cannot claim priority to an earlier filed application of any kind.[8] Including a claim of priority will not change the priority date of a later filed non-provisional application. In addition, the filing date of the provisional will remain the date on which the provisional application itself was filed.

E. Conversion to Non-provisional

A provisional application may be converted to a non-provisional application so long as the provisional application is pending before the USPTO.[9]

8. 35 U.S.C §111(b)(7).
9. 37 C.F.R. §1.53(c)(3).

Applicable requirements for filing of a non-provisional must occur, including corresponding fees, and oaths/declarations. In particular, a practitioner must ensure that there is at least one claim, as prescribed by 35 U.S.C. §112. If the provisional application already included a claim, the requirement can be fulfilled by that claim. The other applicable requirement for conversion of a provisional application to a non-provisional application is an additional fee for the conversion.

A practitioner should be keenly aware that the conversion of a provisional to a non-provisional application will limit the term of an eventual patent compared to filing a non-provisional that claims priority to the provisional application. When a provisional application has been converted to a non-provisional application, the term of the eventual patent runs from the filing date of that application. If the conversion does not take place for almost a year from the filing of the provisional application, the applicant potentially will have lost almost a year of term of the patent. By filing a non-provisional application that claims priority instead of converting the provisional application to a non-provisional application, the applicant saves a corresponding government fee and maximizes the term of any eventual patent.

F. Assignment

Any inventor may assign rights to a provisional application, in any capacity, to another individual(s) and/or company.[10] Under U.S. practice, an inventor is the first owner of a patent application. In many other countries, an inventor may automatically be the company for which the "inventor(s)" work. Assigned rights dictate ownership. Inventors may also license instead of assigning in whole. Any assigned rights are negative rights, i.e., the right to exclude others. However, because a provisional application grants no eventual patent rights, an assignment for a provisional application often includes a right to any later filed non-provisional and/or continuation-in-part application. A practitioner should ensure that an inventor assigns all current and future associated rights as necessary in the case of a company seeking patent protection on the subject matter of its employees.

Companies and/or universities, may require all employees (and even students) to sign a duty-to-assign document, which is an instrument that basically states that any invention made by that employee is owned by the

10. 35 U.S.C. §261.

entity. It may even cover personal inventions outside of the office and/or not in the scope of employment.

G. Tick-tock—Tracking the One-Year Clock

Upon filing a provisional application, a practitioner should mark the one year anniversary as a statutory deadline so he can consider a number of potential options.[11]

In order to claim priority to the provisional application a corresponding non-provisional application must be filed while the provisional application is pending, i.e., within a year of the filing date of the provisional application. This year is a year to the day, meaning that if a provisional application is filed on October 3, a corresponding non-provisional claiming priority must be filed no later than October 3 of the following year, if not a weekend or a federal holiday. If a weekend or a federal holiday, the non-provisional application would have to be filed no later than the next workday.

Similarly, a corresponding foreign application that claims priority to the provisional application must be filed while the provisional application is pending, i.e., within a year of the filing date of the provisional application. This year time period is a year to the day.

Once the year period of a provisional application has passed, the U.S. Patent & Trademark Office treats the application as abandoned/expired. After this time, claims of priority to the provisional application alone will be considered improper unless a showing of unintentional and/or unavoidable abandonment/expiration of the provisional application has occurred. A claim or priority to a provisional application still may be made after expiration of a provisional application if the claim is through another application, still pending, that properly claims priority back to the provisional application.

III. DRAFTING A NON-PROVISIONAL APPLICATION

A non-provisional application is an application that, when filed, will be examined by the USPTO.[12] A non-provisional application specifies the scope of protection that an applicant desires to receive as part of an issued patent. A non-provisional application is the mechanism by which an applicant seeks to prevent others from practicing an invention as specified by

11. 35 U.S.C. §§119 and 120.
12. 35 U.S.C. §111(a).

the claims. Although the U.S. government examines an application to determine whether an applicant should be granted a patent, enforcement is the responsibility of the owner of the patent, not the U.S. government.

A. Legal Effect, Rights Acquired

The legal effect of filing a non-provisional application is that an applicant has met the burden of reducing his invention to practice as long as certain requirements for filing are met. An applicant has the benefit of filing another non-provisional application and/or a foreign application that claims priority to the non-provisional while the non-provisional is pending before the USPTO.

Another legal effect of a non-provisional application is that the term of any corresponding patent deriving from it is calculated starting from the filing date. Because utility patents today carry a term of 20 years from the filing date of the earliest non-provisional application, an applicant has a filing date for patent term calculation purposes established by the date the earliest non-provisional application was filed.

A patent that issues from a patent application is a grant by the U.S. government of a right to exclude others from practicing, i.e., making, using, selling, offering to sell, and importing, a particular invention for a set period of time. However, a right to practice the invention as claimed is not among those rights.

A patent equates to personal property.[13] It can be assigned, sold, given away, inherited, mortgaged, and licensed. All claims of an issued patent that derive from a non-provisional application may be conveyed to another by the owner separately, together, or in any type of combination of claims.

B. Requirements for Filing

There are a number of procedural and substantive requirements for the filing of a non-provisional application in the U.S. Patent & Trademark Office.[14] Procedurally, the requirements needed for filing a non-provisional application include a specification/description of the subject matter of the invention, at least one claim defining the scope of the invention, applicable drawings, an oath/declaration signed by all named inventors,[15]

13. 35 U.S.C. §261.

14. 35 U.S.C §111(a).

15. The executed oath/declaration is not required at the time of filing and may be submitted within a set time period thereafter along with payment of a late fee.

and an associated government fee.[16] In addition, unlike with a provisional application, a non-provisional application must be filed in English or be accompanied by another government fee and a translation in English, including a statement that the translation is a true and accurate translation.

Since inventorship for a non-provisional application is defined by the claims, a practitioner should ensure that inventorship is properly identified based upon the claims as filed, and later as amended during prosecution. If the specification/description of the non-provisional application describes four features of subject matter for an invention but claims only two features of the four features described, inventorship will be granted to those individuals who conceived of and reduced to practice the claims for those two features. If other individuals contributed only to the conception and reduction to practice of the unclaimed features, those individuals are not inventors since the claims do not reflect their contribution.

Similarly, if during prosecution of the patent application the claims are amended to remove all features attributed to a particular inventor, that individual's name should be removed from the listing of identified inventors. For example, if an individual conceived of and reduced to practice only the features of claim 2 of a patent application, that individual must be removed as an inventor if claim 2 is canceled during prosecution of the patent application.

Substantively, it is important that a non-provisional application meet the requirements for patentability under section 112 of Title 35. Similarly, drawings, when necessary for describing the subject matter of the invention, are required as part of the filing of a non-provisional application. Unlike with a provisional application, the drawings, specification, and claims for a non-provisional application have set requirements in regard to page margins, font sizes, and formats.

A non-provisional application strictly requires that an oath/declaration by each and every inventor be submitted. The oath/declaration is a statement that the inventor believes himself to be the original and first inventor of the subject matter of the non-provisional application as claimed. Although procedures are in place for accounting for inventors who refuse to execute an oath/declaration or cannot be found in order to do so, each and every inventor must be accounted for by way of an oath/declaration. Since an oath/declaration must be in a language that the inventor understands, it may be in a language other than English. If such is the case, a practitioner

16. 37 C.F.R. §1.53(b).

should file a translation of the oath/declaration along with a statement that the translation is a true and accurate copy of the oath/declaration.[17]

Several government fees are associated with filing the patent application. These include a filing fee, a search fee, and an examination fee. All three fees are due at the time of filing or else the applicant will be subject to a surcharge fee. These government fees must be submitted to ensure the application does not go abandoned. When filing the application, a small entity and a large entity will be charged different fees, with most fees for a small entity being half the price of that for a large entity. A practitioner should keep in mind that entity status can change during prosecution. A simple document reflecting the change of entity status, from small to large or large to small, is all that is needed to change the status designation, along with payment of a further government fee.

C. Claims

A patent claim, as required under 35 U.S.C. 112, is required for a non-provisional application. Inclusion of a claim defining the scope of the sought after invention is required as a non-provisional application is examined by the U.S. Patent & Trademark Office. Failure to include a claim will delay the recognition of a filing date for the non-provisional application.

There are four categories of claims, and each provides protection on varied categories of subject matter:

- a process/method of performing something;
- a machine/apparatus/product, which may include multiple distinct parts;
- an article of manufacture/product-by-process, where the article is defined by its process of manufacture;
- a composition of matter, meaning "all compositions of two or more substances and all composite articles, whether they be the results of chemical union, or of mechanical mixture, or whether they be gases, fluids, powders, or solids."

Following the decisions of certain court cases, new subcategories of these main four types of claims have been established and can be utilized

17. The America Invents Act (AIA) modifies the requirements/practice with respect to oaths or declarations. See AIA subsection of *Patent Groundwork Section.*

by practitioners. One such example is a computer software program that is a method for performing an operation on a computer. A practitioner can utilize a computer readable medium (CRM) type claim to apply the steps of a computer-implemented method that are stored on some form of non-transitory computer readable medium.

D. Strategies Based upon Goals

In preparing a non-provisional application, a practitioner should determine the various reasons for the claims of the application. Because the claims of an application define the scope of protection being sought, the reasons for preparing the claims in a certain manner should be understood. Different independent claims may be filed for different reasons as described herein. In one example, a company may desire claims for its non-provisional application to protect the product that it is about to launch. For example, the company may seek protection for a product anticipated to be launched within the next year. As such, claims should be directed to a commercial embodiment of the product. When an eventual patent is issued, the claims may cover one or more commercial embodiments of the product of the company.

In another example, a company may desire claims for its non-provisional application in order to enter into an area of technology where a competitor is getting involved. A company may determine that a competitor is working on a new commercial embodiment of an already successful product. In this example, the company may desire claims directed to areas of improvement on the original commercial embodiment of the product of the competitor. As such, if a patent eventually is issued, the company can enforce its patent to prevent the competitor from making, using, etc., the improvements claimed in the patent.

In still another example, the company may desire claims for its non-provisional application in order to protect improvements developed on an existing product. For example, the company may desire claims directed to improvements made to a successful commercial embodiment of a product. In this example, claims directed to these improvements in an eventual patent may cover new commercial embodiments of the successful product.

E. Expanding the Ideas

When reviewing a disclosure document and talking to inventors about their invention, it should be considered that the inventive features and concepts identified by the inventors may be narrowly fused. A practitioner should strive to expand upon the inventors' ideas and push the inventors to explore features and concepts outside of the specific implementations the inventors intend to use. It is beneficial to get the broadest possible protection via the broadest possible claim scope yet also confine the claim scope to only those features required for novelty.

For example, if an inventor has developed an improvement on transmission of data from a mobile device, a practitioner should ensure that the improvement on transmission could not also be utilized in other devices, such as wireless computers, hand-held electronic devices, and in vehicle global positioning system satellite navigation systems. As such, a new invention may have advantages and uses an inventor fails to initially highlight. A practitioner should ensure the inventor fully shares these aspects so they may be included in a patent application if they could enhance the protection sought in a patent.

F. Include Examples

One tool that a practitioner may use when preparing a non-provisional patent application is to include one or more illustrations detailing the implementation of the method of the invention and/or the components of an apparatus of the invention. Such a tool can be advantageous both during prosecution and eventual litigation.

Illustrative examples of implementation of the invention may be used by the practitioner during prosecution of the patent application before the USPTO. These examples may be used to help the examiner understand the use of the invention and/or benefits and goals of the invention. Although the examination of the patent application will be dictated by the claims, the use of examples for discussion purposes with the examiner can be extremely helpful in reaching a better understanding of the claims and use of the invention, and for determining claim language that distinguishes over the prior art.

For litigation purposes, the use of examples of the invention in the specification may be helpful in allowing a judge and/or eventual jury better appreciate the technology and benefits of the invention. For patents that are highly technical and that require specialists who have an advanced degree, such as a Ph.D, a judge who presides over litigation of the patent might not have the technical background necessary to appreciate every feature of the novelty of the claims. Similarly, a jury pool deciding the litigation likely would be composed of individuals who also may not have the technical background to appreciate the invention strictly by the claims. The use of examples within the specification, if tied to the claims, may help these individuals better understand the invention by at least following the illustrative examples.

G. Conversion to Provisional

A non-provisional application may be converted to a provisional application.[18] A practitioner needs to submit a request for conversion and an additional fee for the conversion. The request and fee must be submitted prior to the earlier of the abandonment of the non-provisional application, the payment of an issue fee on the non-provisional application, the expiration of 12 months after the filing date of the non-provisional application, or the filing of a request for statutory invention registration.

H. Assignment

Any inventor may assign one or more rights of a non-provisional application, in any capacity, to another individual(s) and/or company.[19] As such, an inventor may assign some claims but not all claims, may assign some claims and license others, or may license all claims but retain a right to practice the claims herself. Under U.S. practice, an inventor is the initial owner of a patent application. In many other countries, an applicant may be the company that the "inventor(s)" works for. This company is the initial owner of the patent. Assigned rights dictate ownership. Inventors may also license instead of assigning in whole. Any assigned rights are negative rights, i.e., the right to exclude others. Care should be taken to ensure that an inventor fully assigns all current and future associated rights as necessary in the case of a company seeking patent protection on the subject matter of its employees.

I. Layout of a Standard Non-provisional Application[20]

1. Priority Claim[21]

A priority claim is a statement at the beginning of the patent application that defines whether the present application claims subject matter within an earlier filed application for support. There are several different types of priority claims.

18. 37 C.F.R. §1.53(c)(2).
19. 35 U.S.C. §261.
20. 37 C.F.R. §1.77.
21. 35 U.S.C. §§119 and 120.

A non-provisional application may claim priority to one or more provisional applications as long as filed within one year of the filing date of the provisional applications.

A non-provisional application may claim priority to one or more earlier filed non-provisional applications as a continuation of the earlier filed non-provisional applications. A continuation application is one that includes the same specification and figures of the earlier non-provisional application, except for the inclusion of different claims that cover a different scope of protection. Such claims are fully supported by the earlier non-provisional application.

A non-provisional application may claim priority to one or more earlier filed non-provisional applications as a divisional application of the earlier filed non-provisional application. A divisional application is one that includes the same specification and figures of the earlier non-provisional application but for the inclusion of different claims that cover a different scope of protection. A divisional application is a type of continuation application wherein an applicant pursues non-elected claims from a restriction requirement that issued in an earlier non-provisional application. As such, for a divisional application, the claims have been filed in an earlier application but have not yet been examined.

A non-provisional application may claim priority to one or more earlier filed non-provisional applications as a continuation-in-part of the earlier filed non-provisional applications. A continuation-in-part application is often referred to as a CIP. A CIP application is one that includes the same specification and figures of the earlier non-provisional application in addition to new subject matter, which may include new figures and description. For a CIP, at least one claim includes one or more features described in the new subject matter. As such, a CIP may include claims that are fully supported in an earlier filed application but must include at least one feature that contains the new subject matter. For example, an earlier filed non-provisional application may describe features A, B, and C. A later filed CIP further may describe feature D. The later filed CIP may include claims directed to any of features A, B, and/or C, but must include at least one claim directed to feature D. This is stipulated because, if the CIP only includes claims directed to features A, B, and/or C, then the CIP is actually a continuation application since all claims are fully supported by the earlier non-provisional application. Although the new subject matter described in the application is not supported in the earlier non-provisional, none of the claims is directed to the new subject matter.

Claims for priority may be included within the specification and/or an Application Data Sheet (ADS). However, it is recommended that claims for priority be included within both items at the time of filing. For example, if the identification of one or more of the earlier applications is in error in the ADS, then the specification of the patent application, correctly identifying the priority claim, may be used to support correction of the ADS or official application infomration that may be in error.

On a final note, a practitioner is always encouraged to include a claim of priority in the specification even, if that could be done in an ADS. In filing a claim of priority to an earlier application, the claim of priority should include language specifying that the contents of the earlier application is included by reference in its entirety. This language ensures that anything and everything from the earlier filed application may be applied to prosecution of the later filed application. The language also may help if the specification of the later filed application inadvertently fails to include everything included in the earlier filed application and the omitted material is needed for support or clarity. If a practitioner desires to include language only in the earlier filed application, inclusion of a comprehensive reference covering the earlier application's contents allows the practitioner to later amend the specification of the later filed application to include the desired language.

2. Statement of Related Applications

In this portion of a specification, a practitioner may identify one or more applications that are related in some manner to the present application. Such a use may be desired in a situation where a number of applications have been filed with respect to a product. Each application may be directed to different parts of the product that need not necessarily interact. If all are filed on the same day, a practitioner may include a statement identifying each of the related applications within this section.

3. Background

The background section is designed to allow a practitioner to identify the technology of the invention and the problem that the invention is looking to address. Ideally, in this section, practitioners should give only a general description. A practitioner does not want to have the description in the background used against the owner during litigation of the patent. A practitioner should understand that if any description should be given of the problem to be solved, just a general description is best.

4. Summary

The summary section is intended to be a brief description of the claimed invention. Each and every feature of an invention need not be included in the summary. The summary should be as broad as possible and should not include language that could limit the scope of the invention. Similar to the background section, the summary section should be very general as to the features of the invention.

5. Brief Description of the Drawings

The brief description of the drawings section of a patent application is meant to do exactly that, briefly identify and describe the figures in the application. If Figure 1 of a patent application is a flowchart of a method, then a brief description of Figure 1 should identify it as such. Similarly, if Figure 2 is a network of computers, the brief description of Figure 2 should identify the figure as a block diagram of a system of computers. This section of a patent application is intended to be a quick reference for what the figures are supposed to show.

6. Detailed Description

The detailed description section is often the longest section of a patent application. This section describes all of the features of the subject matter of the invention. For any figure directed to the features of the invention, the detailed description describes them so that one of ordinary skill in the art at the time of the invention can make or use the invention.

7. Claims

A patent claim is a specific recitation of language to define the scope of patent protection sought by the inventor(s). A patent claim may be compared to a title for land. A title for land defines the exact parameters of the land, including its size, location, orientation, and boundaries. Similarly, a patent claim defines the size, location, orientation, and boundaries of the scope of the invention.

A patent claim is required under 35 U.S.C. §112, 2nd paragraph, in order to receive a patent in a non-provisional application. Thus, one is required to submit at least one patent claim defining the scope of the sought after invention. While a non-provisional application may include hundreds of patent claims, it must include at least one.

Patent claims fall into one of two possible categories. A patent claim is either independent or dependent as specified in 35 U.S.C. §112, 3rd paragraph. An independent claim is a claim that does not contain a reference to a previous claim but rather is read alone to define the scope of protection sought. A dependent claim is a claim that includes a reference to a previous claim along with a further limitation of the subject matter claimed. Dependent claims are specified in 35 U.S.C. §112, 4th paragraph.

The reference to a previous claim in a dependent claim may be reference to either another dependent claim or to an independent claim. As such, a dependent claim includes every limitation of the subject matter that was referred to in the previous claim, as well as the further limitation(s) specifically recited in the dependent claim. Therefore, a dependent claim is always narrower than a claim to which it refers.

A special type of dependent claim is a multiple dependent claim, as specified in 35 U.S.C. §112, 5th paragraph. A multiple dependent claim is one that contains a reference, in the alternative, to more than one claim in addition to the further limitation specifically recited in the multiple dependent claim itself. A multiple dependent claim is therefore construed to incorporate by reference all the limitations of the particular claim in relation to which it is being considered. A multiple dependent claim cannot refer to another multiple dependent claim. Multiple dependent claims are not used as frequently in U.S. patent applications as they may be in certain foreign countries. In the U.S., a multiple dependent claim is treated as several dependent claims that refer back to only one previous claim. Applicable fees treat multiple dependent claims for each possible alternative claim scope. Thus, if a multiple dependent claim refers to two previous claims, then the multiple dependent claim is treated as two dependent claims.

Another type of claim specified by 35 U.S.C. §112, 6th paragraph, is a means-plus-function claim. A means-plus-function claim is a claim that has at least one limitation expressed as a means or step for performing a specified function without the recital of structure, material, or acts for performing such. However, means-plus-function claims are construed to cover the corresponding structure, materials, and acts described in the specification of the non-provisional application and equivalents thereof. As such, if a claim recites a "means for fastening" and the specification of the non-provisional application recites three types of fasteners—soldered connections, staples, and tape—the claim limitation for a means for fastening is construed only to cover soldered connections, staples, tape, and equivalents thereof.

A non-provisional application may include up to three separate independent claims and 20 total claims without incurring any additional claim fees. Although more than three independent and/or 20 total claims may be included in a patent application, the corresponding fees for inclusion of more claims can increase very quickly.

8. Abstract

The abstract of a patent application is designed to be similar to the summary. With a 150-word limit, the abstract seeks a brief description of the features and scope of the invention. In practice, the abstract is intended to permit searchers, practitioners, and examiners to quickly identify what subject matter the patent application covers and describes. A practitioner should ensure that the abstract is not narrower than the claims of the application. The goal is quite simple—keep it broad and keep it brief.

J. Claiming Priority

As noted before, a provisional application cannot properly claim priority to an earlier filed application of any kind. Likewise, inclusion of a claim of priority to a provisional application will not change the priority date of a later filed non-provisional application claiming priority to the provisional application. As such, a later filed non-provisional application will have the priority date of the provisional to which it claims priority, but will have a filing date as the date on which the earliest non-provisional application was filed.

The manner of claiming priority also is important. A mere reference to priority establishes a date of invention, but it does not empower the practitioner to rely on the description of the earlier filed application. Should a later filed application fail to include all features described in an earlier filed application, a simple claim of priority to the earlier filed application will not allow the features only described in the earlier filed application to be claimed in the later filed application. A preferred manner of claiming priority involves a priority claim that includes statement that the content of the earlier filed application is incorporated herein by reference in its entirety. Thus, should subject matter found only in the earlier filed application be needed to perfect a priority claim, a practitioner may utilize the description in the earlier filed application for support in amending the claims.

A claim for priority may include a claim of priority to a foreign application. When the foreign application is not in English, both a copy of the foreign application and an English translation must be submitted as a requirement.

K. Inventor Review

For a non-provisional application, each and every inventor on the application must review the application. A practitioner should ensure that the inventors have received the non-provisional application that will be or has been filed. The review of the specification and figures are required by the inventors since each inventor is required to execute a declaration to the fact that she is an inventor on the application identified in the declaration. Fraudulently executing a declaration, as noted below, is subject to criminal prosecution. Therefore, every effort should be made to ensure that the inventors have reviewed the application and figures and/or are at least provided them prior to execution of the declaration.

Aside from the declaration requirement, inventor review is helpful for a practitioner to have confirmation as to the accuracy of the specification and figures. An inventor likely is the best individual to appreciate both the invention and the description of the invention in the specification. Inventor review may assist a practitioner to clear up any descriptions that are vague, inaccurate, or incomplete.

L. Executed formal papers[22]

Although not required at the time of filing a specification and figures, one requirement that must be met in perfecting the filing of a non-provisional application is an oath or declaration by each of the inventors. All inventors must execute an oath or declaration for a non-provisional application to receive a filing date. Once again, all inventors must execute an oath or declaration. An oath or declaration is a statement by the inventor that he believes he is an inventor or co-inventor of the non-provisional application and that he developed the subject matter of the non-provisional application himself or with the other inventors.

22. 35 U.S.C. §§25 and 115.

The oath or declaration must include the proper identification of the patent application. Any of a number of different forms of identification may be provided including a title, a list of the inventors, a client or attorney docket number associated with the patent application, or, in the case of submission of an oath or declaration after the patent application has already been filed, the serial number and filing date of the patent application.

A practitioner should send the oath or declaration to the inventors for execution along with a final copy of the specification and figures for the non-provisional that will be filed. If an inventor signs a declaration and then the specification or figures are changed before filing, the declaration may be deemed to be improper, thus potentially affecting the validity of any patent issued from the non-provisional application.

Situations may arise when all the inventors cannot execute an oath or declaration. Alternatives exist to having all inventors sign when an inventor has died, becomes incompetent, cannot be found, or even refuses to sign. A practitioner should understand that a non-provisional application still may be filed without all inventors executing an oath or declaration. Evidence of the inability of all inventors to sign must be submitted along with the executed oaths or declarations of the other inventors. An application may also be filed without an oath or declaration and the oath or declaration can be submitted at a later time in response to a Notice to File Missing Parts.

Another type of formal paper that is often requested of inventors for execution at the time of executing an oath or declaration is an assignment. An assignment is a grant of some or all rights associated with the non-provisional application that the inventor has. Under U.S. law, an inventor is the first owner of any issued patent unless an assignment to another person or entity exists. The assignment transfers any or all rights to the entity. Many companies that have inventors as employees will have these employee-inventors execute an assignment at the same time as the oath or declaration. The goal of these assignment documents is to demonstrate a clear chain of transfer of rights.

M. Application Data Sheet (ADS)[23]

An application data sheet (ADS) is a form that specifies a majority of information, from a formalities standpoint, for an application. An ADS is not required for filing a non-provisional application, but it is often

23. 37 C.F.R. §1.76.

used and very effective for specifying details on identifying inventors, identifying assignees, providing details on number of drawing sheets, and establishing a title. Perhaps the most important feature of an ADS is that it allows an applicant to specify one or more applications for priority purposes. If the priority was not included in the application, which it should have been, the claim for priority may still be included in the ADS.

N. Non-publication Request[24]

Under U.S. patent practice, an applicant may request that her application is not published. Utility applications are customarily published by the USPTO after an initial 18-month period. However, publication can be prevented if an applicant files a non-publication request.

A non-publication request must be filed at the same time the application is filed. If a non-publication request is submitted after the filing of the application, it will be deemed improper by the USPTO and the application will still be published in 18 months. Therefore, care should be taken to ensure a non-publication request is timely and properly filed, since it cannot be corrected after filing.

The mechanism for filing a non-publication request is simple. A letter requesting non-publication of the application may be filed. However, a more common method is to simply check a single box included in the ADS provided by the USPTO.

Non-publication of an application often is desired in situations where an applicant does not want the application to become publicly accessible before the application issues into a patent. The application may be directed to technology that is a critical aspect of the future business or current development of a company. As such, this company may not want to permit competitors to see what it is developing. The filing of a non-publication request ensures that the application will not be published until a patent is issued on the application. Should the application never issue into a patent, the application will never publish. However, there is a drawback to filing a non-publication request.

The filing of a non-publication request is also an acknowledgment that the applicant will not file any corresponding foreign applications with the same subject matter. If an application is filed with a non-publication request, an applicant may still file one or more foreign counterpart applications; however, the non-publication request must be rescinded.

24. 35 U.S.C. § 122.

If the request is not rescinded, the application technically becomes abandoned. Therefore it is important to check on whether a U.S. application included a non-publication request before filing a counterpart foreign application.

O. Petition to Make Special[25]

Examination of an application may be requested such that the application is treated as special and moved up in line to be examined. The process for requesting examination of a patent application ahead of other pending applications is done by filing a petition to make special. Generally, a patent application is examined by the USPTO based upon when it was filed. The earlier an application was filed in comparison to other pending applications in a technical art, the more likely it will be examined before those other pending applications. However, there are a number of bases on which early examination of a patent application can be sought. Some require a fee for filing of the petition, while others do not.

The USPTO grants petitions to make special when the application is deemed to be of particular importance to some branch of the public service and the head of a department of the U.S. Government requests the immediate action. If an inventor is 65 years of age or older, or the health of the inventor is such that she may not be able to assist in prosecution, a petition to make special may be granted. Other petitions may be granted if a patent on the invention will enable manufacturing of a product covered by the eventual patent, or if a showing is made that the claims of the application are currently being infringed.

Still other reasons for grant of a petition to make special is when the application is deemed to materially enhance the quality of the environment with respect to basic life-sustaining natural resources. For example, if the application materially contributes to:

(A) the discovery or development of energy resources (such as fossil fuel and hydrogen fuel technologies, nuclear energy, solar energy), or

(B) the more efficient utilization and conservation of energy resources, such as the reduction of energy consumption in combustion systems, industrial equipment, household appliances, etc.

Additional reasons for grant of a petition to make special include applications concerning recombinant DNA research, cancer and HIV/

25. 37 C.F.R. §1.102.

AIDS cures and treatments, superconductivity technologies, and technologies for countering terrorism.

Finally, even if the technology of a patent application does not fall within one of the noted reasons by the USPTO, a request for expediting examination of an application may still be granted. A statement must be submitted that indicates that a pre-examination search was conducted and the results of the search must be submitted along with a detailed discussion of the references, including reasons for patentability. However, practitioners should be aware that discussion of the prior art references will be part of the prosecution history of the patent and may be utilized later against the patentee in claim interpretation in potential future litigation.

P. Duty of Candor and Good Faith[26]

The USPTO places a requirement on all those involved in the prosecution of an application to disclose any information material to the patentability of the application. This duty covers not only the inventors but also the practitioner preparing the application for filing. Although a practitioner has no duty to search for art that may be material to patentability, a practitioner must disclose any such known or uncovered art. Materiality is not a term with a hard and clear definition. Simply put, if an art is known or has been reviewed for application preparation purposes, a practitioner should as a course of best practice simply file the art or inform the USPTO about the art. Failure to adhere to the duty of candor and good faith not only may invalidate any issued patent on the application due to inequitable conduct, it also may find the practitioner facing a review board before his state bar.

On a final note, practitioners and inventors should remember that the duty of candor and good faith runs throughout the life of the application to issuance. If a practitioner or inventor becomes aware of material art after the application has been filed, he still needs to submit the art to the USPTO in an information disclosure statement.

Q. Information Disclosure Statement (IDS)[27]

An information disclosure statement (IDS) is a form utilized for presentation and submission of art that may be material to patentability of the application. When a practitioner, inventor, or other individual involved in the prosecution of the application believes that a reference may be

26. 37 C.F.R. §1.56.
27. 37 C.F.R. §1.56.

material for patentability or may even just be sufficiently related to the technology of the application, the reference must be identified for the USPTO. An IDS allows for input of the relevant data for identification of the art for consideration by the USPTO. Should the art be something other than a U.S. patent or a U.S. published application, a copy of the art must be submitted as well.

References or other information that may be material to patentability may have a priority date after the filing date of the application. For example, the prosecution history of a child application may be material to a parent application. Assume a parent application is filed with a claim directed to features A, B, and C, and a child application is filed six months later with a claim directed to features A, B, and D. If a practitioner in prosecution of the child application makes a statement on the prosecution record about feature A, that statement may be material to patentability of the parent application.

R. Fees

Among the many things associated with filing and prosecuting a patent application, there are associated fees. The USPTO requires payment of governmental fees for varied government actions during prosecution before the USPTO. These fees include filing fees, search fees, and examination fees. There are also fees for claims that exceed 20 total claims and fees for each independent claim in excess of three. There are fees for submission of assignment records. Certain petitions and other filings, such as an IDS in some circumstances, also carry filing fees.

An important type of fee for a practitioner to remember is the fee for an extension of time. Although many submissions may be delayed, the delay requires payment of a fee. The USPTO allows for extensions of time for different types of filings, with each month of extension carrying an increasing cost for the extension.

S. Electronic Signatures

The USPTO allows a practitioner to sign documents requiring the practitioner's electronic signature, which is a type set entry of the name of the signing practitioner between slashes, e.g., /Full Signatory Name/. The slash marks identify the type set entry as an electronic signature. Such a signature is treated by the USPTO as a handwritten signature of the signing practitioner.

An electronic signature must be directly entered by the practitioner. A practitioner may not proxy someone to electronically sign a document for him. Since the signature is treated as and has the same purpose and effect as a handwritten signature by the signing practitioner, the signing practitioner must personally enter the electronic signature.

T. Ready for Filing

Once all requisite USPTO forms and patent application papers have been prepared and accounted for, a non-provisional patent application may be filed at the USPTO.[28] There are a number of different manners for submission of a patent application. One of the most commonly utilized manners for application submission is electronic submission via the USPTO's e-filing system. The USPTO allows a practitioner to file documents associated with a new application electronically as PDF type attachments. The system also allows a practitioner to submit fees associated with the filing to also be submitted electronically. This manner of filing or submission provides confirmation of receipt of the filing immediately and allows applicants to view uploaded files before actual submission of the documents.

Another manner for submission is by direct hand carry to a physical drop off window at the USPTO. There is a drop off window at the USPTO that allows for hand carry submission each day up to midnight. The application will be treated as filed on the day it is received at the window.

Yet another manner for submission of a new application is by Express Mail. A practitioner may mail application documents via express mail with an express mail number. Express Mail allows for tracking of the documents to arrival at the USPTO. Although received days later, an application mailed via Express Mail is treated as having been filed at the USPTO on the day the application was mailed.

An immediate effect of filing a non-provisional patent application is the starting of a clock. If there is no priority claim associated with the non-provisional application, a one-year clock starts from the date on which the non-provisional application is filed. Any foreign counterpart application that seeks to claim priority back to the non-provisional application must be filed no later than one year from that filing date. For a design patent, this period is six months.

---

28. Forms often used in various aspects of the application process are available on the USPTO website. http://www.uspto.gov/forms/.

IV. ASPECTS OF PATENT PROSECUTION ONCE FILED

A. *Filed Executed vs. Filed Unexecuted*

Prior to any substantive examination of the application, there may be some procedural hurdles to overcome after filing a new application. The first hurdle would occur if the application were filed without a declaration by all of the inventors. When the application is filed with the declaration properly executed by all of the inventors identified on the application, the application is said to be filed "executed" and no type of formalities notice is expected from the USPTO for a lack of declaration. However, if the application is filed without a declaration, without all inventors having executed a declaration, or because of a problem with the declaration, the application is said to be filed "unexecuted" and a practitioner will receive a Notice to File Missing Parts from the USPTO.

B. *Notice to File Missing Parts*

A Notice to File Missing Parts (NTFMP) is a formalities notice mailed by the USPTO in response to one or more problems with the initial filing of an application. A practitioner may receive a Notice to File Missing Parts for a number of reasons, although the most common reasons include the need for a declaration by all of the inventors and outstanding fees owed to the USPTO for the filing and/or examination of the application.

C. *Declaration of the Inventors*[29]

When a Notice to File Missing Parts is mailed due to failure to submit a declaration by all inventors, a proper response includes an oath or declaration executed by all the inventors. An oath or declaration is a statement by the inventor that he believes he is an inventor or co-inventor of the application and that he developed the subject matter of the application himself or with the other inventors.

The oath or declaration must include the proper identification of the patent application. Any of a number of different forms of identification may be provided including a title, a list of the inventors, a client or attorney docket number associated with the patent application, or, the serial number and filing date of the patent application.

29. 35 U.S.C. §§25 and 115.

While a practitioner must have all inventors execute an oath or declaration for the application that will be filed, situations may arise when all the inventors cannot execute an oath or declaration. Alternatives exist to having all inventors sign when an inventor has died, becomes incompetent, cannot be found, or even refuses to sign.[30] A response to a Notice to File Missing Parts still may be filed without all inventors executing an oath or declaration. Evidence of the inability of all inventors to sign must be submitted along with the executed oaths or declarations of the other inventors.

D. Payment of Fees

Among the many things associated with filing and prosecuting a patent application, there are fees. The USPTO requires payment of fees when filing a response to Notice to File Missing Parts. If not paid at the time of filing the application, the fees may include the filing fee, the search fee, and the examination fee. In addition, because the application was not filed with all fees paid, a surcharge fee will be due.

Although many submissions may be delayed, the delay requires payment of a fee. The USPTO allows for extensions of time for filing a response to a Notice to File Missing Parts, with each month of extension carrying an increasing cost.

E. Other Issues (No Claim, No Drawings, No Specification)

Although the fees and declaration/oath due are the two most common reasons for issuance of a Notice to File Missing Parts by the USPTO, one could receive a Notice to File Missing Parts for other reasons. For example, mailing of a Notice to File Missing Parts could be for the omission of a specification, a claim, or necessary drawings, or if the submitted application is too informal. Illustrative examples of an application being too informal include papers filed with writing on both sides of the paper, and where the application is not permanent, legible, or reproducible.

30. The America Invents Act (AIA) makes changes to the requirements of filing an oath/declaration to facilitate satisfaction of the requirement and/or submission of a substitute statement to satisfy the requirement.

F. Response to Notice to File Missing Parts

Upon the mailing date of a Notice to File Missing Parts, a two-month clock starts for the filing of a response. Escalating extensions of time are available when more time is need in preparing and/or filing such a response.

G. Executed Declaration

For a Notice to File Missing Parts based upon the failure to include an oath or declaration from all inventors, the response needs to include a properly executed declaration. Only oaths or declarations of inventors who did not previously execute formal papers need to be filed. Therefore, if the application included two inventors and the practitioner was able to get a declaration signed by one of the inventors and filed with the application, then the response to the Notice to File Missing Parts needs only to include an executed oath or declaration by the other inventor who has not filed an oath or declaration. The inventor who previously signed need not sign another oath or declaration for responding. In addition, because a Notice to File Missing Parts was mailed, the practitioner also needs to ensure that the late surcharge fee is paid or authorized as.

H. Payment of All Fees

For a Notice to File Missing Parts based upon the failure to pay all applicable government fees, a payment and/or authorization for payment must be submitted with the response. Again, because a Notice to File Missing Parts was mailed, the practitioner also needs to ensure that the surcharge fee is paid or authorized.

I. Formalities Notice

The Office of Initial Patent Examination performs a review of among other things, the drawings submitted with a patent application. If there is some issue with the drawings, a notice may be sent out reflecting the problem. Examples of issues that may warrant a notice include mislabeled drawings, such as two drawings labeled as the same figure number (e.g., Figure 3); drawings containing color; drawings containing excessive text so as to hinder reproduction; and drawings with improper margins. In these instances practitioners should prepare the appropriate corrections to the drawings without adding new matter.

The USPTO also reviews specifications for procedural problems. If a specification is not legible, not reproducible, or not formatted correctly, such as for margins or page numbering, a notice requiring correction may be mailed by the USPTO. Once again, a practitioner needs to be diligent to correct any issue as soon as possible since major problems might result in the corrections being treated as new subject matter, and thus a new filing/priority date for the application.

J. Filing Receipt

A filing receipt is mailed upon the filing of any new patent application in the USPTO. There are two types of filing receipts: an official filing receipt and an immediate filing receipt for electronic filings.

Any application filed in the USPTO, whether electronically, by Express Mail through the U.S. Postal Service, or by manual drop off at the USPTO, receives an official filing receipt. An official filing receipt is a recordation of the documents and descriptive information received by the USPTO with respect to a new application. The official filing receipt is mailed by the USPTO to an address of record for the application. Information in the official filing receipt includes the title provided, the name of the inventor(s) provided, the filing date of the application, any priority data associated with the application, and other data.

When a new application is filed electronically, an immediate filing receipt is generated by the USPTO to identify the documents used in general terms. The immediate filing receipt can act as a confirmation of filing of the new application as the immediate filing receipt includes an application serial number assigned to the newly filed application.

The official filing receipt can be corrected if it contains inaccurate information. Irrespective of the entity at fault, be it the USPTO, the inventor, and/or the agent/attorney filing the application, correction of the official filing receipt may be requested with the filing of a miscellaneous letter describing the inaccuracy.

Any inaccuracy in an immediate filing receipt can be corrected upon receipt of the official filing receipt.

K. Status Inquiries

A status inquiry is a request to have the USPTO provide a time table for an application to be examined or some action to be taken. A practitioner may submit a status inquiry as a miscellaneous letter to the USPTO. The goal of submitting a status request is to be accorded an amount of time until an action is mailed by the USPTO. In most instances, a status inquiry is filed after the initial filing of the application but before substantive examination of the application has occurred. That said, a practitioner still may file a status inquiry even after examination of the application has begun.

There are two manners for inquiring about the status of an application. As stated above, a practitioner may submit a status inquiry as a miscellaneous letter to the USPTO. A response, in due time, will provide an estimated time for a next action by the USPTO to occur. Alternatively, a practitioner may access an on-line estimation of the time until examination. In addition, a practitioner may obtain a hardcopy printout if needed for presentation to a client or for notation to a file. The on-line version may be accessed through the USPTO's private access portal to applications in which the practitioner is associated. Another benefit of the on-line version is immediate determination of an estimated time. Filing a paper document of a status inquiry will take time to be received and inputted by the USPTO and then processed to provide a written estimation.[31]

L. Restriction Requirement[32]

A restriction requirement is a position taken by the examiner who is reviewing an application that the application, as claimed, includes two or more patentably distinct inventions. The examiner is requiring the practitioner to choose from the different inventions identified by the examiner, by groups of claims, before examination of the application can occur. Were applicants not restricted to one invention per application, examiners would have greatly increased burdens in examining applications. Additionally, the fee structure is formed assuming that only one invention will be pursued in each application.

For example, an application may be filed describing five different and distinct features. One claim in the application may be directed to features one and two, while another claim in the application may be directed to features four and five. An examiner assigned to the application may find that the two claims are patentably distinct and confine the examination of the application to the first claim or the second claim.

31. An examiner may be telephoned to informally check on the status of an application as well. This may be useful in certain instances with deadlines looming for which decisions as to how to proceed need to be made.

32. 35 U.S.C. §121.

A restriction requirement may not be limited to independent claims. An examiner may make a restriction across dependent claims as well. Such a situation may occur when an examiner believes that a genus may have multiple species (subgroups) that are patentably distinct from each other. Thus, it is possible that a restriction requirement could be issued across independent claims as well as dependent claims. Furthermore, a restriction requirement may apply to three, four, or more patentably distinct inventions and may be multi-level. For example, an examiner may restrict between independent claims and then may further restrict between dependent species in dependent claims that depend from the same independent claim.

A restriction requirement may be issued at any time during prosecution of an application. A restriction requirement most commonly is issued as a first action on an application. In assessing the claims as filed, an examiner is more likely to issue a restriction at a first action rather than after examination of claims has begun. However, a restriction requirement may occur even after substantive examination has begun.

A restriction requirement often is issued in instances where the claims of the application are directed to two different patentably distinct inventions found in groups of claims. For example, an application directed to a communication system may have some claims directed to a transmitter unit, some claims directed to a receiver unit, and some claims directed to a satellite unit operating between the other two units. In assessing the claims, the examiner may issue a restriction to one of three groups: Group I to the claims of the transmitter unit, Group II to the claims of the receiver unit, and Group III to the claims of the satellite unit. In essence, the examiner is indicating that each unit is a separate invention. However, there may be instances where an examiner issues restrictions among various species of claims.

Taking the same example of the transmitter, receiver, and satellite units, the examiner may also determine that among the claims directed to the satellite unit, there are multiple patentably distinct inventions. Several embodiments may be shown in the drawings and the examiner may restrict prosection to a particular embodiment. For example, the satellite unit may be shown in a first embodiment in a drawing with a communication feature C. In a second embodiment in a different drawing, the satellite unit may be shown with a communication feature C', which is a slightly different feature from communication feature C. In restricting the application to a particular species, the examiner is indicating that the examination of the claims will be limited to a particular species (one of communication feature C or communication feature C').

Two options exist in responding to a restriction requirement. Regardless of which option is chosen, an applicant must elect (choose) the group or species that will be examined in response to the restriction requirement.

The first option for a response is to elect a claim group/species and to traverse the restriction requirement. This course of action would be a situation in which the applicant does not believe that the restriction is proper. However, traversing a restriction requirement is considered an acknowledgment of the prosecution history of the application that the applicant does not believe the claims at issue in the application are patentably distinct inventions.[33] In arguing that the restriction requirement is improper or unnecessary, the applicant must provide support to show that the burden of examination for all claims is not "undue" on an examiner and/or that the groups of claims are not patentably distinct from each other. Even if a practitioner attempts to traverse a restriction requirement, she *must* still elect a particular group/species that is required by the restriction. Election while traversing the restriction requirement does not acquiesce any position against the restriction requirement.

The second option is to elect a claim group/species without traversing the restriction requirement. In such a situation, a practitioner is agreeing with the decision of the examiner that the application includes multiple patentably distinct claim groups/species. In responding, an applicant will elect the group of claims/species that she wants to have examined. At any time, up to and including the day a patent issues on the application, the non-elected claims/species, those claims/species not chosen for examination, may be filed and pursued in a related application referred to as a divisional application described in more detail herein.

A difference in a species restriction requirement should be noted. Different species of claims share a common genus or generic claim. For example, in the previous example of a satellite unit, the satellite unit as a whole may be a genus claim while two different versions of the communication feature, C and C', may be different species that are restricted by an examiner. The independent claim directed to the genus may recite a satellite while two different dependent claims, directed to species C and C', may recite the satellite operating by communication feature C and the satellite operating by communication feature C', respectively. Be-

33. Some practitioners, even if they disagree with the restriction set forth by the USPTO, will not attempt to traverse the restriction requirement so as to limit the prosecution history created by further arguments made in trying to traverse the rejection.

cause the two species claims share a generic or genus claim, when electing claims, an applicant may choose one of the species, such as communication feature C, and maintain the genus claim in the application. Examination of the application will entail the examiner searching for relevant art where the communication feature is C.

For such a situation, an applicant need not cancel the non-elected species claims directed to communication feature C'. A practitioner should withdraw the non-elected claims in the species. A withdrawn claim is a claim that is still present in the application but is not being examined or reviewed by the examiner. The reason to withdraw the claims of the non-elected species is simple. If the application is eventually allowed because it is not based solely upon the species features of the elected claims, e.g., not based solely upon communication feature C, a practitioner can request that the withdrawn claims (claims with communication feature C') be rejoined. Rejoining the non-elected claims is allowed if the genus claim is patentable over the art of record without reliance on a particular species for patentability.

A notable point in ultimately electing a claim group/species for prosecution is that the subject matter of any amendments, including new claims, must be confined to the elected group/species. New claims added during prosecution that are directed to the subject matter of the non-elected claims in the restriction requirement typically will be identified as improper amendments in light of the previous election.

Another notable effect of election during prosecution is that issuance of a double patenting rejection in a subsequent application directed to the non-elected claims/species is improper. If a practitioner should receive an action in a subsequent divisional application directed to the non-elected claims that includes a double patenting rejection over the elected claims, a response can be filed indicating the improper rejection. Because the original restriction requirement is an acknowledgment that patentably distinct claims/species exist, those patentably distinct claim groups/species cannot be used against each other in a double patenting rejection—an assertion that the claims are not patentably distinct.

In order to expedite prosecution, an examiner often will contact a practitioner of record in order to attempt to get an oral election responsive to a restriction requirement. There is no requirement to elect orally, and a practitioner may wish to see the entire restriction requirement in order to confirm/discuss with a client. However, an oral election might shorten prosecution time, and it might also serve as a courtesy to the examiner leading to a favorable outcome on the patentability of the application.

Once a claim group/species has been elected, a question may arise about the non-elected claim groups/species. Assuming that the restriction requirement was not traversed or the traversal was not successful, an applicant has the option to file one or more divisional applications directed to the non-elected claim groups/species. A divisional application, as described below, has the same specification and drawings and same priority date as the original application. The only difference is that the claims are directed to a non-elected claim group/species. Prosecution of the divisional application is treated separately from prosecution of the original application. In essence, the two applications share everything in common but for the scope of the claims.

However, as previously noted for a species restriction, a practitioner may have the option to withdraw non-elected claims directed to a species and later rejoin those claims upon allowance of the genus or generic claim. It should be noted that the non-elected claims directed to the species that are rejoined have not been examined on the merits, i.e., the USPTO has not examined the particular claim scope of the non-elected claims directed to the species. Ultimately these non-elected claims directed to the species may be rejoined based on their dependency on an allowed genus or generic claim.

M. Non-final Office Action[34]

A non-final office action is often the first office action or examination report regarding the invention claimed in the application by the USPTO. Based upon the original specification and figures, the examiner has searched prior art references and examined the application for any reason to reject the pending claims in the application. If a non-final office action is mailed, it typically means that the examiner has found at least one pending claim that is not allowed to be issued in its current form.

A non-final office action with a determination that at least one claim is not allowable does not mean that the claim, as pending, cannot be issued without amendment. Any of a number of reasons for rejecting claims may be included in a non-final office action, and each type of rejection includes multiple ways to respond.

One type of rejection is a double patenting rejection, for which there are two types: statutory double patenting and obviousness type double

34. 37 C.F.R. §1.104.

patenting. A double patenting rejection means that the examiner believes that another patent or pending application includes claims directed to the same claim scope. A statutory double patenting rejection is one in which a claim of the current application is identical to the claim of another application of the same inventor(s). Such a situation is not very common and may occur when the same exact claim is inadvertently filed in two applications. As described below, addressing this type of double patenting rejection can be difficult. An obviousness type double patenting rejection is one in which a claim of the current application is an obvious variation of the claim of another application of the same inventor(s). This type of double patenting rejection occurs more frequently and may be addressed more easily, as noted below.

Another type of rejection is a failure of a claim to be patentable subject matter under 35 U.S.C. §101. This is referred to as a non-statutory subject matter rejection. A rejection under 35 U.S.C. §101 occurs when the examiner believes that the claim is not directed to patent eligible subject matter. Examples of patent ineligible subject matter include scientific principles, such as gravity; discoveries that occur within nature without the assistance of mankind, such as the element carbon on the periodic table; and natural phenomena, such as the Northern Lights. Patent eligible subject matter is any new and useful process, machine, manufacture, or composition of matter, or any new and useful improvement thereof.

A third type of rejection falls under 35 U.S.C. §112. Some of the more common §112 rejections include a rejection under 35 U.S.C. §112, 1st paragraph, and 35 U.S.C. §112, 2nd paragraph.

A rejection under 35 U.S.C. §112, 1st paragraph, is a contention by the examiner that the claim is not allowable because the claim is not enabled by or adequately described in the specification and drawings. A specification must enable one of ordinary skill in the art to make or use the claimed invention. A claim cannot properly recite a feature if one of ordinary skill in the art, when reading the specification and drawings, cannot make or use the feature. A specification also must adequately describe the claimed invention—what is commonly referred to as the written description requirement. A claim cannot properly recite a feature if the feature is not adequately described in the specification and/or drawings.

A rejection under 35 U.S.C. §112, 2nd paragraph, is a contention by the examiner that the claim is not sufficiently clear in that it does not particularly point out and distinctly claim the invention. Common occurrences for such as rejection occur when a claim recites the same feature in two different terms. For example, a claim may recite a "satellite component" in a first instance and then later recite the same claim feature as the "satellite unit." Interchangeable use of component and unit is not allowable and will warrant the issuance of a rejection under 35 U.S.C. §112, 2nd paragraph.

A fourth type of rejection is a rejection under 35 U.S.C. §102. In essence, a rejection under 35 U.S.C. §102 is a contention by the examiner that a single action or reference renders the claim as anticipated. Occurrences of such a rejection include a prior art reference (such as a patent or publication) that describes each and every feature of a claim, evidence of a commercial embodiment that includes the claimed invention being on sale for more than a year before the filing date of the application, and evidence that the claimed invention was abandoned, suppressed, or concealed.

A fifth type of rejection is a rejection under 35 U.S.C. §103. In essence, a rejection under 35 U.S.C. §103 is a contention by the examiner that an "obvious" combination of particular actions or references finds the claim to be unpatentable. Occurrences of such a rejection include a combination of two or more prior art references that together describe each and every feature of a claim and evidence that the differences between a claim and one or more prior art references would have been an obvious difference to one of ordinary skill in the art when filing the application. The most common occurrence for an obviousness rejection under §103 is an examiner relying on a primary reference for the majority of features of a claim and then utilizing one or more additional prior art references for the features not found in the primary reference.

When responding to a non-final office action, an applicant has an absolute right to amend one or more pending claims so long as the amendments are within the original elected subject matter if previously restricted. If an applicant should attempt to include non-elected claims that were restricted out of the application following an earlier response to a restriction requirement, the applicant may well receive a response from the USPTO indicating that the amendment is improper for being directed to non-elected claims. Absent such a circumstance, an applicant may amend any and all claims, including deleting claims, adding claims, and amending claims.

Upon the mailing of a non-final office action, a clock has effectively started and an applicant is obligated to take some form of action. A response to the outstanding non-final office, whether amending claims or not, must be filed no later than six months from the mailing date of the non-final office action. Ideally a response should be filed no later than three months from the mailing date of the action, because such filing will not incur a government extension fee. After three months form the mailing date of the action, each extension fee for an additional month carries a government fee and the fee quickly escalates in each further month of extension.

A first government extension fee, for one month of extension of time, is due if a response is not filed until after the three-month deadline. A second government extension fee, for yet another one month of extension of time, is due if a response is not filed until after the four-month deadline. A third government extension fee, for yet one more month of extension of time, is due if a response is not filed until after the five-month deadline. However, the extensions available are not endless. After six months from the mailing date of the action, if a response has not been filed at the USPTO, the application becomes abandoned. For example, a non-final office action that is mailed on January 21 will become abandoned on July 22 if an applicant has not filed a response (along with any required extension fees). Although, as described herein, an unintentionally abandoned application may potentially be revived, the government cost is significant and this practice is not desired.

At this point in the prosecution of an application, an applicant has a few options in addressing a non-final office action. Ultimately there are four options that exist although additional actions may still be required.

First, although not ideal and often not performed, an applicant can abandon the continued prosecution of the application. In situations in which the rejection of a claim is sound and supported and there is no claim amendment that can be made to overcome the rejection, an applicant may determine that abandonment of the application is in its best interest.

Second, an amendment to one or more of the pending claims may be filed. In amending a claim, an applicant is voluntarily choosing to change the scope of the claimed invention. Such a response often occurs after incurring a prior art rejection under 35 U.S.C. §102 and/or 35 U.S.C. §103. The single prior art reference or combination of references may teach or suggest each and every feature of the claim. As such, an applicant may choose to amend the claim to include an additional feature or to tweak the scope of the features recited that is not found in the art of record. As previously stated, an applicant has an absolute right to amend one or more claims so long as the amendment is within the original elected subject matter if the application was subject to a restriction requirement. An applicant may include an argument to distinguish the amended claim over the current rejection. If this route is taken, to file an amendment to the claims, the clock stops and the next course of action must be taken by the USPTO.

Third, a practitioner can file a request for reconsideration of the rejection where there are no amendments to the pending claims. In not amending a claim, an applicant is voluntarily choosing to retain the scope of the claimed invention as previously examined. A request for reconsideration often occurs in response to a rejection that an applicant believes is not proper or is deficient. The single prior art reference or combination of reference(s) may fail to teach or suggest each and every feature of the claim. As such, an applicant may choose to retain the claim un-amended and argue the differences between the relied upon prior art reference(s) and the claimed invention. As previously stated, an applicant has an absolute right to argue differences between prior art of record and the claimed invention. If this route is taken to file arguments to distinguish the claims, the clock stops and the next course of action must be taken by the USPTO.

Finally, an applicant can request and conduct an examiner interview. An examiner interview is non-adversarial and conducted on the telephone or in a face-to-face meeting to discuss any of a number of items, including the prior art relied on for a rejection. An examiner interview often is conducted between a practitioner and the examiner. Other parties, such as an inventor, an examiner's supervisor, and/or an owner of the application, may participate in the interview.

The interview is conducted on the telephone or in person at the USPTO. A practitioner often is granted between 30 minutes and an hour, although an examiner may allow more time depending on the circumstances. An examiner interview is designed to clarify the differences between the practitioner and the examiner. Because any discussion is merely summarized at the conclusion of the interview in an interview summary document issued by the USPTO, a frank discussion between the examiner and a practitioner can take place. In the case of a non-final office action, an applicant has an absolute right to receive an examiner interview. Such a tool may be helpful to an applicant/practitioner in gaining approval of an application more quickly.

If the decision is made to conduct an examiner interview, the clock has not stopped and the next course of action still must be taken by the applicant or else there is a risk that the examiner may not remove the rejection after the discussion. If the interview summary document mailed by the USPTO indicates that an agreement was reached between the examiner and the practitioner that the claimed invention is patentable over the art of record, the burden does not shift to the USPTO to take the next action. The burden remains with the applicant. Ultimately, in responding, an applicant will need to file an amendment to one or more of the claims, file a request for reconsideration of the rejections of the pending claims, or abandon the matter entirely.

N. Final Office Action[35]

A final office action is an examination report substantially similar to a non-final office action, as previously described, except it typically occurs later in the prosecution process after an applicant has had a chance to respond to at least an initial non-final office action.

The same reasons for rejection of claims in a non-final office action may be present in a final office action. The most significant difference between a non-final office action and a final office action is that an applicant does not have an absolute right to amend one or more pending claims. A practitioner may attempt to amend any and all claims, including deleting claims, adding claims, and amending claims, but none of these changes have to be admitted. Accordingly, it is this limitation on available actions for applicants in response to a final office action that provides the rationale behind the term "final." This office action provides a final step in this particular phase of prosecution and requires a specific number of actions by the applicant to proceed to a next phase of prosecution.

Upon the mailing of a final office action, it should be remembered that a clock has started. The applicant has the responsibility to take some form of action. Similar to a non-final office action, a response to the outstanding final office must be filed no later than six months from the mailing date of the final office action. A response ideally should be filed no later than three months from the mailing date of the action, as such a filing will not incur a government extension fee. After three months from the mailing date of the action, each extension fee for an additional month carries a government fee, and the fee quickly escalates as the extension time gets longer.

Just as was the case with non-final office actions, a first government extension fee, for one month of extension of time, is due if a response is not filed until after the three-month deadline for final office actions. A second government extension fee, for yet another one month of exten-

35. 37 C.F.R. §1.113.

sion of time, is due if a response is not filed until after the four-month deadline. A third government extension fee, for yet one more month of extension of time, is due if a response is not filed until after the five-month deadline. However, the extensions are once again not endless. After six months from the mailing date of the action, if a response has not been filed at the USPTO, the application becomes abandoned.

An applicant has limited options in addressing a final office action, although one of four things must occur: abandonment, appeal, reopening of prosecution, or allowance.

First, a practitioner can abandon the prosecution of the application. In situations in which the rejection of a claim is sound and supported and there is no claim amendment that can be made to overcome the rejection, an applicant may determine that abandonment of the application is in its best interest.

Second, an applicant can file an amendment to one or more of the pending claims. In amending a claim, an applicant is voluntarily choosing to change the scope of the claimed invention. As previously stated, however, an applicant does not have an absolute right to amend one or more claims. An applicant may only attempt to amend one or more claims and may submit an argument along with amendments to the claim(s) to distinguish the amended claim over the current rejection. If this route is taken, to file an amendment to the claims, the clock has not stopped and the next course of action still must be taken by an applicant although the examiner will address the amendment filed. As such, if the response does not overcome the rejection to have prosecution reopened, the clock continues to run and extension fees continue to exist as does the risk of abandonment.

Third, an applicant can file a request for reconsideration of the rejection where there are no amendments to the pending claims. In not amending a claim, the applicant is voluntarily choosing to retain the scope of the claimed invention as previously examined. An applicant has a right to argue differences between prior art of record and the claimed invention. However, if the practitioner elects to file arguments to distinguish the claims, the clock has not stopped, and he must then take the next course of action unless the arguments lead to an allowance before the end of the time period.

Finally, a practitioner can request and conduct an examiner interview. An examiner interview, as previously described, is non-adversarial and conducted on the telephone or in a face-to-face meeting to discuss any of a number of items, including the prior art used for a rejection. An examiner interview often is conducted between a practitioner and the examiner. Other parties, such as an inventor, an examiner's supervisor, and/or an owner of the application, may participate in the interview.

The interview is conducted by telephone or even in person at a USPTO facility. A practitioner often is granted between 30 minutes and an hour, although an examiner may allow more time depending on the circumstances. An examiner interview is designed to clarify the differences between the practitioner and the examiner. In the case of a final office action, a practitioner does not have an absolute right to receive an examiner interview; however, examiners may be receptive to conducting one if prosecution is likely to be advanced. Such a tool may help a practitioner gain approval on an application more quickly. If an examiner interview is held, the clock has not stopped and the next course of action still must be taken by the applicant or else there is still a risk that the examiner may not remove the rejection even after the discussion.

For a practitioner to stop the clock and shift the burden for prosecution back to the USPTO, one of the following events occurs:

- A practitioner may amend one or more claims, and the amended claims are found to be allowable by the examiner over the art of record. In such a case, the examiner will issue a new non-final office action or a notice of allowance indicating that the pending claims are allowed to issue into a patent.
- A practitioner may file a request for reconsideration, and the pending claims are found to be allowable by the examiner over the art of record. In such a case, the examiner will issue a new non-final office action or a notice of allowance indicating that the pending claims are allowed to issue into a patent.
- A practitioner may appeal the final office action to the Board of Appeals at the USPTO. Further appeals are described below.
- A practitioner may file a Request for Continued Examination (RCE). As described in more detail below, an RCE allows a practitioner to restart the examination process as if the application had just been filed.

O. Request for Continued Examination (RCE)[36]

A Request for Continued Examination (RCE), is a request by an applicant for the examination of the current application to continue. This

36. 37 C.F.R. §1.114.

measure effectively resets the examination process and the same examiner will continue to examine the application claims through one more iteration. There are specific requirements for filing an RCE, but as long as these are complied with, an applicant can continue to prosecute an application before the USPTO despite having already received their allotted opportunities for review. An RCE starts the examination process anew as long as there is a reason for continued prosecution, either an amendment to the claims requiring further review or a new reference to consider in an Information Disclosure Statement (IDS).

As previously stated, the filing of a proper RCE will stop the clock and the next action is the responsibility of the USPTO. This is important since, upon receipt of a final office action, substantive claim amendments typically can be entered only by the filing of an RCE. For examination purposes, the filing of an RCE is treated as a new filing, except that the assigned serial number, filing and priority dates, and examiner remain the same. In addition, the time until the next action by the USPTO is greatly reduced when compared to the filing of a new application. While a new application can take well over a year to be acted upon by an examiner, an RCE will often take four months or less to be acted upon by the examiner. The same examiner also continues the review of the application. This consistency is sometimes beneficial to applicants in advancing the prosecution, since the same examiner does not have to learn about the invention and prior art or record all over again.

Upon the filing of a RCE, the USPTO will respond in one of four ways. The examiner may review the claim amendments and arguments made in the RCE and determine that that claims are in condition for allowance. This is the ideal situation for an applicant. If this is the outcome, an applicant should receive a Notice of Allowance or Notice of Allowability as described herein.

In a second possible outcome, the examiner may find that the amendments to the claims require issuance of a restriction requirement. The RCE may have added new claims or claim amendments that result in what the examiner believes are patentably distinct claims to varied subject matter within the claim set. In response, a practitioner may receive a restriction requirement and will need to respond accordingly as described herein.

In a third outcome, the examiner may review the amendments and/or arguments and issue a new non-final office action. Whether the examiner maintains the previous rejections issued in the earlier final office action or the examiner cites new art references for rejecting the claims, a new non-final office action allows the applicant the opportunity to respond as described herein, including an absolute right to amend the claims, file a request for reconsideration without amending the claims, and/or requesting an examiner interview to discuss the rejections.

In a fourth outcome, the examiner may review the amendments and/or arguments and issue a new final office action. This issuance of another final office action in response to an RCE filing is uncommon, as most examiners at the USPTO will issue a non-final office action response after the filing of an RCE, even if the same rejections are maintained. A final office action is allowed by the examiner if the claim amendments do not overcome the current rejections, but many examiners allow an applicant the opportunity to further amend the claims, i.e., receive a non-final office action. Whether the examiner maintains the previous rejections issued in the earlier final office action or the examiner cites new art references for rejecting the claims, a new final office action allows the practitioner the opportunity to respond as described herein but without an absolute right to amend the claims.

In filing an RCE, a practitioner must follow a few requirements. If one or more of these requirements is not met, the RCE likely will be found improper and additional fees may be necessary to correct the RCE filing.

First, an RCE form must be filled out and executed by the applicant/practitioner. The form is a standard template offered by the USPTO and serves as the formal request for continued examination of the application. Failure to include the RCE form may result in the mailing of a notice of improper reply and the correction will require time and expenses.

Second, a practitioner will have to either amend the claims in some manner, other than deletion of a claim, or file an IDS with at least one reference for consideration. The purpose of an RCE is to request further examination because of a need to address something that has not yet been taken into account. An amendment to one or more claims, other than deletion of a claim, would require an examiner to search and examine prior art, and also factor in the amendment. Thus, such an amendment would be consistent with the reasoning behind an RCE. An amendment to cancel a claim is not proper because cancellation of a claim does not create a reason for an additional search and examination to occur. If anything, cancellation of a claim creates less of a burden on the examiner. Alternatively, a new art reference in an IDS may be material to patentability and may be a key consideration in the claims. As such, even if the claims are not amended as part of the RCE, the filing of an IDS with at least one new reference for consideration is a valid reason for filing an RCE.

Third, a practitioner must respond to the rejections made in the previous final office action as part of the RCE filing. Similar to a response to a non-final office action, a request for reconsideration, or a response to a final office action, a practitioner must argue the patentability of the claims, whether amended or not, over the rejections currently of record. Once again, failure to include a response may result in the RCE being found improper.

The final requirement for filing of an RCE is payment of the government fee. Like many other filings before the USPTO, a government fee must be submitted with the filing. Because the RCE is an attempt to have examination start anew, government fees for the new search and examination must be paid.

P. Appeal[37]

An appeal is a formal review of the latest examination of a patent application and may be initiated after at least two office actions. Ultimately, an appeal can be thought of as a request to have another party, beyond just the examiner and/or the supervisor of the examiner, review the grounds for rejection of claims in the application. The appeals process can take some time, as long as a couple years, and such a course of action will have a longer wait time for an outcome in comparison to pure prosecution before an examiner. However, in instances where a practitioner believes that one or more rejections are improper, an appeal may be the proper course of action to overturn an examiner's decision.

During the appeal the applicant and the examiner present their arguments for patentability over the art of record and in support of rejection of the claims as being proper, respectively. An appeal may only be initiated by an applicant. An examiner cannot appeal a matter to the Board of Patent Appeals and Interferences (BPAI) (hereafter "Board of Appeals") at the USPTO.[38] Whether argued on the briefs alone, meaning by filed papers, or also argued as part of an oral hearing before the Board of Appeals, an applicant eventually will receive a decision made by the Board of Appeals and, in some circumstances described herein, by Pre-

37. 37 C.F.R. §1.191.

38. The BPAI will be replaced by the Patent Trial and Appeals Board (PTAB) under the AIA.

Appeal Conference Panel. If favorable to a practitioner, the decision by the Board of Appeals is binding on the examiner. If favorable to the examiner, the decision by the Board of Appeals may still be appealed to one or more federal courts if the applicant wishes to further pursue an appeal of the decision.

The filing of a Notice of Appeal requires only a few items. Only a Notice of Appeal form needs to be filed and a government fee for the Notice of Appeal has to be paid to stop the clock for required action by the applicant. The form for the Notice of Appeal is a template identifying the application and an executed statement that the applicant desires to initiate an appeal of the rejections of the claims of the application. Upon filing of the Notice of Appeal, a two-month clock starts for the preparation and filing of an accompanying Appeal Brief, as described herein, presenting the arguments in support of the practitioner for the appeal. This two-month period of time may be extended by paying escalating government fees.

One optional action that can be taken along with the filing of a Notice of Appeal is the filing of a Request for Pre-Appeal Brief Conference. A Request for Pre-Appeal Brief Conference is a formal request by an applicant to have the examiner, the examiner's supervisor, and another examiner review the reasons for rejection and a brief argument by the practitioner once more before proceeding to the Board of Appeals. The goal of the pre-appeal conference is to prevent appeals that could or should have been settled between the examiner and the practitioner. Because the process for appeal through the Board of Appeals can take years, the pre-appeal conference allows for a quick response and potential reconciliation of the differences between the examiner and the applicant. The Request for Pre-Appeal Brief Conference seeks to have clear factual and legal errors by the examiner addressed immediately. For example, an examiner may reject a claim based upon a prior art reference that does not have a priority date before the pending application, and, as such, is not a proper prior art reference. Such a clear error may be successfully addressed in a Request for Pre-Appeal Brief Conference.

A conference between the examiners is conducted and a decision by the Pre-Appeal Conference panel is made. The Pre-Appeal Brief Conference results in the re-opening prosecution of the application where the USPTO has to issue a new office action, the allowance of the application, or the rejection of the claims in the previous office action and the appeal process through the Board of Appeals continues. The decision by the Pre-Appeal Conference panel is mailed, and an applicant may be given additional time to decide the next course of action.

The requirements for a Request for Pre-Appeal Brief Conference are fairly limited, but the time table for submission is very specific. A practitioner should appreciate that a Request for Pre-Appeal Brief Conference must be submitted concurrent with the filing of a Notice of Appeal. Thus, a Request for Pre-Appeal Brief Conference cannot be submitted before or after the filing of a Notice of Appeal.

The request itself must present arguments evidencing the clear factual and/or legal errors made by the examiner in the previous office action. Questions of interpretation are not considered clear legal or factual errors and will often result in the rejection being sustained by the Pre-Appeal Brief Conference panel. Failure of the examiner to address specific claim features, failure to apply proper prior art references, and/or failure to apply the proper legal standard for a rejection are some of the bases for filing of a Pre-Appeal Brief Conference request.

The Request for Pre-Appeal Brief Conference must not exceed five total pages. Because the goal is to quickly review any appeal before going to the Board of Appeals in an attempt to correct blatant outstanding issues, the five-page limit is designed to force an applicant/practitioner to immediately present the issue to be addressed, rather than to re-present any and all arguments for overcoming any and all rejections of the claims. A practitioner most likely will need to focus on one or two issues to present in the request due to the five-page limit.

A positive aspect of the filing of a request is that no government fee is associated with the filing. Although the filing must be concurrent with the filing of a Notice of Appeal, which does carry a government fee, there is no separate fee for the submission of the Request for Pre-Appeal Brief Conference review. This may be one of the few instances of a special substantive paper not requiring an accompanying government fee. As such, the Pre-Appeal Brief Conference request is a useful tool for a practitioner to make one more argument before appealing an application to the Board of Appeals.

The decision of the Pre-Appeal Brief Conference panel has one of two common outcomes from the list of possible outcomes. If one or more of the rejections are withdrawn, the conference panel may reopen prosecution of the application where the USPTO will issue a new office action or allowance. In such a situation, an applicant need only wait for a new action from the USPTO. Alternatively, if the rejection of the claims in the previous office action is maintained, the appeal process through the Board of Appeals may continue or the applicant may file an RCE. The decision by the Pre-Appeal Brief Conference panel is mailed and an applicant may be given additional time in which to decide the next course of action. The time in which an applicant may respond is the longer of one month from the mailing date of the panel decision or two months from the mailing date of the Notice of Appeal. Therefore, a practitioner always has a minimum of one month from the mailing date of the panel decision to continue appeal through the Board of Appeals or to file an RCE.

1. Appeal Brief[39]

An appeal brief is a formal paper by the applicant outlining the reasons why the rejections of the claims are improper and evidentiary support for the same. An appeal brief is a written record that will be reviewed by a panel of Board of Appeals judges at the USPTO. There are specific requirements as to the format and content of the appeal brief.

Upon the filing of a Notice of Appeal or mailing date of a decision of the Pre-Appeal Brief Conference panel, a clock has started for the filing of an appeal brief. At this point, the applicant has responsibility to take some form of action. An appeal brief must be filed no later than five months from the filing of a Notice of Appeal. Ideally, an applicant should file an appeal brief no later than two months from the filing of the Notice of Appeal or one month from the mailing of a decision of the pre-appeal conference, whichever is longer, so that the filing will not incur a government extension fee. After this time, each extension fee for an additional month carries a government fee and the fee quickly escalates the longer the time for extension.

A first government extension fee, for one month of extension of time, is due if an appeal brief is not filed until after the non-government fee deadline. A second government extension fee is due for yet another one month of extension of time if an appeal brief is not filed until after the three-month deadline. A third government extension fee, for yet one more month of extension of time, is due if an appeal brief is not filed until after the five-month deadline. However, the extensions are not endless. After five months from the filing of the Notice of Appeal, if an appeal brief has not been filed at the USPTO, the application becomes abandoned.

There are a number of specific items that must be included in an Appeal Brief.[40]

The appeal brief must identify the real party or parties in interest. Specifically, the USPTO requires identification of the owners of the

39. 37 C.F.R. §41.37.
40. 37 C.F.R. §41.37(c)(1).

application that is being appealed. The brief also must identify any related appeals or interferences to the present application on appeal. For example, if the present application has a divisional application that is also on appeal or involved in an interference proceeding, the identification of the related appeal or interference proceeding must be identified for the USPTO in the brief.

The brief further must contain the status of all of the claims from a rejection, objection, and/or allowance standpoint and the status of the claims as to current amendments. The brief should recite the status of all the rejections and include a listing of the current pending claims.

The brief should also include a summary of the claimed subject matter, specifically an identification of the support in the original specification and figures for the pending claims involved in the appeal. An applicant should identify as many of the specific portions of the specification and/or drawings for support of the claim terms and features as illustrative examples. Next, the brief should identify the grounds for rejection to be reviewed by the Board on Appeals. This portion of the appeal brief should identify the specific rejections and claims involved, which the practitioner wants the appeal board to review. A practitioner would not need any allowed claims reviewed and, for that reason, would not include those claims in this section.

The argument section follows where the applicant presents all arguments in support for the position that the rejections of the claims under review are not proper. The arguments section should include all arguments to independent claims as well as to dependent claims. This may be the one and only time that an applicant can present arguments for consideration by the Board of Appeals. Since most appeals before the Board of Appeals are decided purely on the briefs (no oral hearing is held), the appeal brief argument section is an important section to ensure that all arguments are presented to the Board.

Finally, appendices are included in the brief. A listing of the current claims in the application is provided in a claims appendix and any needed accompanying evidence is included in an evidence appendix. Documents of related proceedings, such as related appeals or interference proceedings, are included in a related proceedings appendix. Even if there is no accompanying evidence to provide or related appeals or interference proceedings to identify, these appendix section headers must be filled out and left blank to indicate that there is no evidence. Failure to submit such a statement will result in a notice of non-compliant appeal brief from the USPTO, and the applicant will have to resubmit the appeal brief with the appendices included.

A government fee must be paid with the filing of an appeal brief. Although a fee was submitted for the Notice of Appeal, an additional fee is due for the submission of the appeal brief. This fee is due at the time of filing of the appeal brief and a failure to do so will result in a notice of non-compliant appeal brief being mailed by the USPTO.

2. Request for Oral Hearing[41]

As part of the appeal process, a practitioner may seek to orally argue the rejections before the board of appeals. A request for oral argument allows an applicant typically by way of a practitioner representative to have the ability to meet with the Board of Appeals panel prior to a final decision, in order to argue the rejections before them. An oral argument is an optional step in the appeal process and the appeal may proceed through simply on the written briefs.

During the oral hearing before the Board of Appeals panel, the practitioner is allowed to argue her reasons for patentability over the art or record beyond the written briefs. A practitioner is allotted a 15 minutes to present her argument to the board. The members of the board of appeals may ask questions of the practitioner as well. A benefit of an oral argument is that a practitioner may present her case beyond just the written briefs. There may be instances in which an oral explanation is needed or is important in clearly or properly articulating a point of distinction over an art rejection that may be difficult to achieve on the written record alone.

One impact that an oral argument proceeding does have on the application file is that a full transcript of the hearing is made of record. All statements by the Board and by the practitioner during the oral hearing will become part of the prosecution history of the application. As such, any and all statements might have an impact on scope of protection of any subsequent claims. A practitioner should be mindful of this point in an instance in which an oral hearing is pursued on an appeal.

The process for requesting an oral hearing is fairly simple. A practitioner need only submit an official request for oral hearing, which may be done using a form template provided by the USPTO. Following the submission of the request, a date and time for the oral hearing will be established and provided by the USPTO. In addition, a government fee is due for the request. The government fee is due at the time of filing of the request for oral hearing.

41. 37 C.F.R. §41.47.

3. Examiner's Answer[42]

An examiner's answer is a formal response to the appeal brief outlining the reasons why the rejections of the claims should be maintained and evidentiary support for the same. The examiner's answer is mailed by the USPTO to the applicant. It is a written record that addresses responses to the various sections of the appeal brief and will be reviewed by the panel of Board of Appeals judges at the USPTO.

In the examiner's answer the examiner argues his reasons for rejecting the claims over the art or record. The examiner's answer confirms or traverses formalities that are included within the practitioner's appeal brief. For example, the examiner's answer will confirm the reasons for rejection and the current status of the claims including amendments. In addition, the examiner's argument presents the examiner's reply to the arguments made by the practitioner as to why the rejections of the claims are improper. The examiner's answer is a document reflecting the position of the examiner with respect to the rejection of the claims and rebutting the practitioner's arguments in the appeal brief.

4. Reply Brief[43]

A reply brief is a formal response by the practitioner outlining supplementary reasons for refuting the examiner's answer and evidentiary support for the same. A reply brief is an optional written record that will be reviewed by the panel of Board of Appeals judges at the USPTO. There is no requirement to file a reply brief. Reply briefs are often filed if a new argument is presented in the examiner's answer and the practitioner desires to make a response on the record to address the examiner's additional argument.

Upon the mailing of an examiner's answer, a practitioner should remember that a clock has started for the filing of a reply brief, should the filing of a reply brief be desired. A reply brief must be filed no later than two months from the mailing of an examiner's answer. The two-month time period is not extendible and a reply brief may be filed after this time only because of exceptional circumstances.

The subject matter of the reply brief is to be confined to addressing the arguments made by the examiner in the examiner's answer. As such, a reply brief often is only utilized for new grounds for rejection. The

42. 37 C.F.R. §41.39.
43. 37 C.F.R. §41.41.

argument section presents all arguments to overcome the position that the examiner has taken in the examiner's answer that was not previously addressed in the appeal brief. A government fee is not necessary for the filing of a reply brief.

5. Decision of the Board of Appeals[44]

The decision of the Board of Appeals has one of five common outcomes. If the Board chooses to reverse the rejection of one or more claims, e.g., the appeal was ultimately successful in some manner, prosecution of the application is reopened and the USPTO will issue a new office action or allowance. In such a situation, a practitioner need only wait for a new action from the USPTO.

Alternatively, if the rejections of the claims in the previous office action are maintained, an applicant is left with four other options.

First, the appeal process may continue. An applicant may appeal a decision by the Board of Appeals to a U.S. District Court. The decision by the Board is mailed and an applicant is given a specified amount of time in which to appeal the decision. An appeal to a U.S. District Court will take additional time, but a review by a court may allow for a different outcome through reversal of the Board of Appeals decision. Any decision of the U.S. District Court may be appealed to the U.S. Court of Appeals for the Federal Circuit and ultimately the U.S. Supreme Court.

Second, the appeal process may continue, but through the U.S. Court of Appeals for the Federal Circuit. All patent cases ultimately are appealed through the U.S. Court of Appeals for the Federal Circuit. As such, in this circumstance, an immediate appeal without any appeal through a U.S. District Court may be made to the U.S. Court of Appeals for the Federal Circuit. Any decision of the U.S. Court of Appeals for the Federal Circuit may be appealed to the U.S. Supreme Court.

Third, a practitioner can abandon the application. In situations in which the decision of the Board of Appeals or a federal court is not likely to be overcome by additional appeal and where there is no claim amendment that can be made to overcome the rejection, an applicant may determine that abandonment of the application is in the best interest of the client.

Fourth, even after all appeals, a practitioner may file an RCE, as described herein, to effectively reset the examination process to have the same examiner further review the claims of the application

44. 37 C.F.R. §41.50.

Q. Interference[45, 46]

An interference proceeding is a formal review process by the Board of Patent Appeals and Interferences to ascertain priority between an application and another application or a patent. Ultimately an interference proceeding is a situation in which two different applications, or an application and an issued patent, have the same claim scope and a determination of priority, who invented first, needs to be made.

An interference proceeding may be suggested by a practitioner or an examiner reviewing the application. A practitioner may amend a claim in a pending application so it becomes identical to a claim in another pending application or issued patent to invoke an interference. The practitioner may in essence request an interference proceeding between the parties involved. Similarly, an examiner may determine that a claim of a pending application is identical to another application or issued patent and may suggest an interference proceeding.

An administrative patent judge declares the interference and the Board of Appeals administers the contest. A panel of members of the Board of Appeals ultimately enters a final judgment on questions of priority and patentability arising in the interference.

R. Notice of Allowance[47]

A notice of allowance is a formal paper issued by the USPTO acknowledging that the pending application is in condition for allowance. The notice of allowance includes a Notice of Allowability, a summary of the claims that are allowed, and often includes a statement of reasons for allowance. A statement of reasons for allowance is one or more paragraphs containing the reasons that the examiner identifies for why the claims are being allowed. For example, a statement may identify the closest prior art reference as determined by the examiner and then the deficiencies of that prior art reference with respect to the independent claims in the application.

Upon receipt of a notice of allowance, the pending claims are deemed to be allowable over all art that is of record. As such, the claims are said to be novel and non-obvious over any combination of references submitted in any information disclosure statement or cited by the examiner

---

45. Under the AIA, interferences are eliminated and in essence are replaced by a post grant review proceeding. See *AIA Section*.

46. 37 C.F.R. §41.202.

47. 37 C.F.R. §1.311.

during prosecution. The prosecution of the application officially is closed on the merits. Additional substantive amendments to the claims and/or arguments by a practitioner are not allowed. If further amendments to the claims and/or substantive arguments are needed for the application, an RCE can be filed to continue substantive prosecution.

Upon submission of the issue fee form and accompanying government payment, a patent will issue once the publication department at the USPTO is prepared to publish. All allowed claims and the specification and drawings will be included in the issued patent.

Upon receipt of a Notice of Allowance, a practitioner has a few options in responding. The first and most common option is to fill out an issue fee transmittal form, which is a template form from the USPTO. The form is an acknowledgment of the notice of allowance and indicates a desire by the practitioner for issuance of the patent. A government fee for issuance of the patent must be accompanied with the issue fee form. The issue fee form and payment of the associated government fees must be submitted no later than three months from the mailing date of the notice of allowance. Upon expiration of the three-month deadline, failure to have submitted the issue fee form and payment will result in abandonment of the application.

An additional form may be submitted prior to or concurrent with the issue fee payment form and associated fee. An amendment under 37 C.F.R. § 1.312 may be submitted. Commonly referred to as a 312 Amendment, it allows a practitioner to correct minor or non-substantive mistakes made either by the practitioner or by the USPTO during prosecution. Common examples include correction of a misspelling of a word in a claim, the specification, a drawing, or even the inventor's name. So long as the correction is minor and does not add new subject matter, the 312 amendment should be considered proper and approved. A 312 amendment may delay eventual issuance of the patent since the examiner will have to review and approve the request for amendment; however, a practitioner ideally should correct mistakes prior to actual issuance of the patent.

S. *Ex parte Quayle*[48]

An Ex Parte Quayle action is very similar to a Notice of Allowance. It is a formal paper issued by the USPTO acknowledging that the pending application is in condition for allowance but for one or more formalities

48. *Ex parte* Quayle, 25 USPQ 74, 1935 C.D. 11; 453 O.G. 213 (Comm'r pat. 1935).

that are not deemed substantive in nature. The USPTO is indicating that the application is allowed but that correction of the formalities is needed in order for the application to proceed to issuance. Such actions are seen frequently in design applications. An example could involve a situation where one drawing in a design application is inconsistent with the other drawings in the design application. Because the drawings in a design application constitute the claimed invention, correction of the drawing discrepancy is required to proceed to allowance.

The effect of an Ex Parte Quayle action is very similar to a notice of allowance. Upon receipt of an Ex Parte Quayle action, the pending claim(s) are deemed to be allowable over all art that is of record but for correction of the formalities. As such, the claim(s) are said to be novel and non-obvious over any reference or combination of references submitted in any information disclosure statement or cited by the examiner during prosecution. The prosecution of the claim(s) officially is closed on the merits. Additional substantive amendments to the claim(s) and/or arguments by a practitioner are not allowed. If further substantive amendments to the claim(s) and/or substantive arguments are needed for the application, an applicant may file an RCE, to continue substantive prosecution. Upon correction of the formalities, a Notice of Allowance will be mailed out by the USPTO.

T. Abandonment[49]

Abandonment of an application, whether intentional, unintentional, or unavoidable, is a relinquishment of all rights (current or future) affiliated with that application. Abandonment obviously should be avoided and accepted only upon a thorough understanding of the consequences. Abandonment may occur at any time during prosecution of the patent application when deadlines for some action by an applicant are due and the deadline passes without any action being taken.

U. Options for Correcting Abandonment[50]

Depending upon the reasons for the abandonment, an applicant is left with a few possibilities for attempting to correct the abandonment of the application. In a situation in which the abandonment of the application was "unintentional," an applicant can attempt to correct the abandon-

49. 37 C.F.R. §1.135.
50. 37 C.F.R. §1.137.

ment. An example of an unintentional abandonment could involve a situation where a practitioner was not able to contact the owner of the patent application during prosecution and the deadline for taking action passed before she could reach the owner, or where the USPTO mailed an office action to a wrong address and the applicant or practitioner did not receive it until after the statutory deadline to take action passed. In such examples, an applicant or practitioner can file a petition to revive the application for unintentional abandonment. The petition would have to include evidence of the unintentional abandonment. In addition, a substantial government fee must be paid with the filing of the petition. The petition must be filed in a reasonable amount of time upon learning of the need to correct the abandonment.

Similar to a petition to revive for unintentional abandonment, an applicant can attempt to correct an abandonment that was "unavoidable." An example of an unavoidable abandonment could involve a situation where a practitioner was not able to contact the owner of the patent application during prosecution and the deadline for taking action passed because the owner was in a coma during that statutory time period. As such, an argument could be made by a practitioner that the failure to take an action to respond was unavoidable. In such examples, a practitioner can file a petition to revive the application for unavoidable abandonment. The petition will have to include evidence of the unavoidable abandonment. In addition, a government fee, which will be less than the fee for an unintentional abandonment, must be paid with the filing of the petition. The petition must be filed in a reasonable amount of time upon learning of the need to correct the abandonment.

However, if an abandonment was voluntary—the owner chose to abandon the patent application—the revival of the patent application is not allowed. A practitioner should not attempt to revive such a patent application when she knows the abandonment was voluntary. Docketing mistakes, forgetting to submit a response, or other errors or misunderstanding fall short of being considered voluntary abandonment and the application should be revivable in such instances.

V. Patent Term Adjustment/Extension[51]

The patent term of an issued patent may be adjusted or extended for a period of time due to delays during prosecution of the application that are the fault of the USPTO. Patent term extension may be available for

51. 37 C.F.R. §§1.701 and 1.702.

patents that have a priority date between June 6, 1995, and May 28, 2000. Since fewer of these applications are pending every day, a practitioner likely will not have to address patent term extension. Patents that issue from application filed on or after May 29, 2000, may be eligible for patent term adjustment. Patent terms may be adjusted due to the failure of the USPTO to take certain actions within specified time periods. However, the delays by the USPTO are also offset by delays by a practitioner during prosecution of the application. For example, the time period for an appeal may be added to the end of a patent term if the practitioner was successful on appeal. However, this adjusted period of time may be offset if the practitioner took extensions of time for replying to various actions during prosecution. The total sum of delays by the USPTO and practitioner are taken into account during the prosecution to determine the period of adjustment. A patent term will never be adjusted by taking away a number of days. If the delays of a practitioner during prosecution exceed the delays by the USPTO, the patent term adjustment will simply be zero days—no adjustment.

The USPTO calculates the period of adjustment and includes it as part of the Notice of Allowance. The practitioner is responsible for ensuring that the calculation of the patent term adjustment, if any, is correct. The effect of the patent term extension or adjustment is that the enforcement period of the issued patent will be longer by the number of days calculated for the extension or adjustment.

W. Notice of Issuance[52]

A notice of issuance (sometimes called an "issue notification") is a formal paper from the USPTO stating the date that a patent will issue on the application. The notice also includes the patent number that will be assigned to the issued patent. As such, a practitioner can inform a client about the date so that client can begin the process for marking products/methods covered by the soon to be issued patent.

X. Issuance[53]

The date of issuance of a patent is the date on which legal rights associated with the patent become enforceable. All patents in the U.S. issue on Tuesdays. The patent is immediately enforceable on the day of issuance, and this day becomes a reference point for other procedural actions. The

52. 37 C.F.R. §1.311.
53. 37 C.F.R. §1.314.

day of issuance of a patent is the last day that a practitioner can file an application claiming priority to the issued patent for co-pendency. Any continuation, continuation-in-part, or divisional application that immediately claims priority to the issued patent must be filed no later than the same day the patent issues. Failure to file such an application during pendency of the application/issued patent, both being co-pendent, cannot be corrected.

V. ASPECTS OF PATENT PROSECUTION AFTER FILING UP TO THE DAY OF ISSUANCE

Just because an applicant files an application does not mean that she cannot pursue additional subsequent applications that claim priority to the one application. The following types of applications can be pursued with respect to a co-pending application. The following three types of patent applications, must be filed no later than the day of issuance of the parent application.

A. Continuation Application[54]

The first type of application that claims priority to a parent application is a continuation application. A continuation application is a child application to an earlier filed parent application. The continuation application includes the same specification and drawings as the parent application, but it has different claims. As the name implies, a continuation application is an application to continue seeking claimed inventions on the subject matter included in the original parent application.

New subject matter in the form of drawings and descriptions theoretically may be included as well, although the claims of a continuation application must be fully supported in the original parent application. Inclusion of claims directed to the new subject matter would result in the application being a continuation-in-part application rather than a continuation application. Additional corrections for formalities and typographical errors in the patent application may be corrected in a continuation application.

A continuation application includes many of the same filing requirements as a new non-provisional application described herein. The application must meet the same substantive and formalities requirements. An additional requirement is the inclusion of a claim of priority to the parent

54. 37 C.F.R. §1.53(b)(1).

application. The priority statement may be included at the beginning of the specification of the application and/or in an Application Data Sheet (ADS). A claim of priority must be included for a continuation application to obtain the same priority date as the parent application. Another requirement is that any claim in the continuation must be fully supported in the original parent application. If a claim is directed to new subject matter added to the specification and/or drawings, then the claim is treated as part of a continuation-in-part (CIP) application, as described herein, and has a priority date of the date of filing of the CIP application.

Aside from the new claims being fully supported and the claim of priority, a continuation application must be filed no later than the day of issuance of the parent application to which it claims priority. The parent application/patent and the continuation application must be co-pending before the USPTO. Co-pendency for a patent ends the day after the patent issues. Thus, a continuation application must be filed no later than the issue date of the parent application. After the issue date, the parent application is no longer co-pending and a continuation application cannot claim priority to it.

The filing of a continuation application effectively establishes a priority date for the continuation application that is the exact same date as the priority date for the parent application. Thus, if the parent application was a non-provisional application that claimed priority to an earlier filed provisional application, a properly claimed continuation application will have the same priority date, i.e., the filing date of the provisional application, as the parent non-provisional application. The enforcement period for the continuation application will end the same date as that of the parent application. Therefore, any issued patent on the continuation application will be enforceable for 20 years from the earliest priority date of the parent application.

Continuation applications can be used to round out the scope of protection sought or allowed in the parent application. A continuation application may be directed to features described in the original specification and drawings that were never claimed in the parent application. Furthermore, the parent application may be directed to one component or another component of a system while the claims in a continuation application may be directed to the entire system as a whole. In yet other instances, a continuation application may be directed to claims that could have been filed in the parent application, but were subsequently canceled or amended during prosecution. An applicant even may seek to go after claims that were originally filed but were never issued in the parent application. Accordingly, practitioners may recommend to clients to cancel rejected claims in an application when allowable claims are identified by the USPTO so that allowable claims can proceed to issuance more expeditiously. The rejected claims can then be pursued in a continuation application rather than holding up issuance of the recognized allowable claims while prosecution continues regarding the rejected claims.

B. Continuation-In-Part Application/CIP[55]

The second type of application that can be filed that claims priority to a parent application is a continuation-in-part application (CIP), which is a child application to an earlier filed parent application. A CIP application includes the same specification and drawings as the parent application and some additional new subject matter that is not supported in the parent application. A CIP includes at least one claim directed to the new subject matter. The new subject matter that is added may be any type of new drawing and/or description. At least one claim must be directed to the new subject matter because, if all claims were fully supported by the parent application, i.e., were not directed to new subject matter, then the application would be a continuation application as described herein. Additional corrections for formalities and typographical errors in the parent application may be corrected in a CIP application.

A CIP application includes many of the same filing requirements as a new non-provisional application or continuation application described herein. The CIP application must meet the same substantive and formalities requirements. One additional requirement is the inclusion of a claim of priority to the parent application. In order for certain claims of a CIP application to obtain the same priority date as the parent application, an claim of priority must be included. The priority statement may be included at the beginning of the specification of the application and/or in an Application Data Sheet (ADS). Another additional requirement is that at least one claim in the CIP must not be fully supported in the original parent application and must be directed to the newly added subject matter in the drawings and/or specification. If no claim is directed to new subject matter added to the specification and/or drawings, then the application is treated as a continuation application, as described herein, and has a priority date for all claims that is the same as the priority date of the parent application.

55. 37 C.F.R. §1.53(b)(2).

Aside from at least one new claim being directed to the new subject matter and the claim of priority, a CIP application must be filed no later than the day of issuance of the parent application to which it claims priority. The parent application/patent and the CIP application must be co-pending before the USPTO. Co-pendency for a patent ends the day after the patent issues. Thus, a CIP application must be filed no later than the issue date of the parent application. After the issue date of the parent application, the parent application is no longer co-pending and a CIP application cannot claim priority to it.

The filing of a CIP application effectively establishes a priority date for claims directed to the new subject matter that is the same date that the CIP application was filed, while claims that are fully supported in the parent application have a priority date that is the same as the priority date for the parent application. The enforcement period for the CIP application will remain the same as it is measured from the filing date or priority date of the parent application. Thus, any issued patent on the CIP application will be enforceable for 20 years from the earliest priority date of the parent application.

CIP applications can be used to round out the scope of protection sought or allowed in the parent application. A CIP application may be directed to features described in the original specification and drawings that were never claimed in the parent application just as is done with continuation applications. Furthermore, the parent application may be directed to one component or another component of a system while the claims in a CIP application may be directed to the entire system together. In yet other instances, a CIP application, may be directed to claims that could have been filed in the parent application, but were subsequently canceled or amended during prosecution. An applicant even may seek to go after claims that were originally filed but were never issued in the parent application. However, unlike a continuation in which all the claims must be supported in the parent application, a CIP application can be used to pursue claims on developments or improvements that took place after the original filing of the parent application. It is these instances for which CIP applications are most often utilized.

C. Divisional Application[56]

The third type of application that can be filed that claims priority to a parent application is a divisional application. A divisional application is

56. 37 C.F.R. §1.53(b)(1).

similar to a continuation application and is a child application to an earlier filed parent application. Divisional applications include the same specification and drawings as its parent application, but include claims from the parent application that were not elected in response to a restriction requirement. As the name implies, a divisional application is an application to claims divided out due to the restriction requirement in the parent application. For example, a parent application, as originally filed, might have included two sets of claims, one set directed to a receiver and one set directed to a transmitter. During prosecution of the parent application, a restriction requirement was mailed to restrict the examination to one of the two sets of claims. If the practitioner elected the claims directed to the receiver, the non-elected claims, directed to the transmitter, may be pursued in a divisional application.

New subject matter in the form of drawings and description may be included as well. Although a divisional application may include such new subject matter, the claims of a divisional application must be fully supported in the original parent application. If claims are directed to new subject matter, the application then would be properly referred to as a continuation-in-part application as described herein. Additional corrections for formalities and typographical errors in the parent application may be corrected in a divisional application.

A divisional application includes many of the same filing requirements as a new non-provisional application or continuation application, as described herein. The divisional application must meet the same substantive and formalities requirements. One additional requirement is the inclusion of a claim of priority to the parent application. The priority statement may be included at the beginning of the specification of the application and/or in an Application Data Sheet (ADS). A claim of priority must be included for a divisional application to obtain the same priority date as the parent application. Another requirement is that the claims in the divisional are directed to the non-elected claim scope in the original parent application. If a claim is directed to new subject matter added to the specification and/or drawings, then the application is treated as a CIP application, as described herein, and that claim has a priority date as of the filing of the CIP application.

Aside from the new claims being directed to the non-elected claim scope in the original parent application and the claim of priority, a divisional application must be filed no later than the day of issuance of the parent application to which it claims priority. The parent application/patent and the divisional application must be co-pending before the USPTO. Co-pendency for a patent ends the day after the patent issues. Thus, a divisional application must be filed no later than the issue date of the parent application. After the issue date, the parent application is no longer co-pending and a divisional application cannot claim priority to it.

The filing of a divisional application effectively establishes a priority date for the divisional application that is the same as the priority date for the parent application. Thus, if the parent application was a non-provisional application that claimed priority to an earlier filed provisional application, a properly claimed divisional application will have the same priority date, i.e., the filing date of the provisional application, as the parent non-provisional application. The enforcement period for the divisional application thus will remain the same as the filing date or priority date of the parent application. Thus, the enforcement period for the divisional application will end the same date as that of the parent application. Divisional applications are frequently used to round out the scope of protection not elected in the parent application.

VI. ASPECTS OF PATENT PROSECUTION AFTER ISSUANCE

Even after issuance of a patent, there are some aspects of prosecution that a practitioner should continue to monitor and consider. The issuance of a patent does not end the duties that an applicant and/or practitioner may have with respect to the patent.

A. *Patent Marking*[57]

Patent marking is the marking of the issued patent number on any product or documentation associated with any product or method that the patent covers. Often a company seeks to protect a commercial product it has or is going to launch with a patent. Assuming one or more claims of the patent covers the commercial product after issuance, the issued patent number should be marked on the product. Patent marking carries many useful effects. First, the public is put on notice that a patent exists with respect to a particular product. The "public" includes potential customers, but also includes competitors. The marking of the patent number on a product may constitute a notice to a potential infringer that the product is protected by a patent.

57. 35 C.F.R. §297(a).

Although a patent may be utilized to prevent an infringer from making a claimed invention covered in the patent even when the infringer did not know of the existence of the patent, when enforcing the patent in federal courts, damages may be increased if the product is marked with the patent number. In addition, a willfulness argument may be made if a product is properly marked and treble damages may be recoverable. A practitioner should keep in mind that upon issuance of a patent, any and all products covered by the issued patent should be marked with the patent number.

B. Maintenance Fees[58]

Utility patents require an owner to pay maintenance fees throughout the term of the patent in order to maintain the ability to enforce the issued patent. However, design patents have no maintenance fee for the entire 14 year period of enforcement. The USPTO requires the payment of an escalating maintenance fee during the term of the utility patent. After the passage of certain periods of time, a series of one year windows open for payment of maintenance fees. At 3.5 years, 7.5 years, and 11.5 years after the issue date of a patent one year windows open for payment of the 4th, 8th, and 12th year maintenance fees respectively.

Payment of a maintenance fee is nothing more than a payment made to the USPTO to keep a patent going. Payments may be made in a number of ways. Many companies and practitioners often utilize an outside company that specializes in docketing due dates and in payment of fees. Failure to pay a maintenance fee has serious consequences to an issued patent. Once the period of time in which payment of a maintenance fee is due ends, an issued patent becomes an abandoned patent if no maintenance fee was paid. Although there are mechanisms in place to revive an unintentionally or unavoidably abandoned patent, certain rights may be lost and there is no guarantee that the USPTO will allow the abandoned issued patent to be revived.

Any of a number of reasons may exist for not paying a maintenance fee. First, the technology that the patent covers or the underlying technology that the patent utilizes for implementation may become irrelevant after a certain amount of time, such as 10 years after the issuance. As such, a company may determine that payment of the 12th year maintenance fee is not needed or that the cost is not worth the potential benefit. In other scenarios, all claims of the issued patent may be found invalid during a

58. 37 C.F.R. §1.362.

reexamination proceeding or a litigation proceeding. Unless the patent owner is in a process of appealing such a decision, additional maintenance fees have no reason to be paid. In contrast, some industries tend to have maintenance fees paid for the entirety of the patent. For patents in the pharmaceutical and chemical industries, maintenance fees frequently are paid out for the entire term of the patent since patents in these technologies tend to retain value even at the end of their term of life.

C. *Certificate of Correction*[59]

A certificate of correction is a mechanism by which an applicant may correct an issued patent that has some type of non-substantive error. There are times in which an issued patent has a problem associated with the publication of the issued patent. The fault for the error may be the fault of the practitioner or the fault of the USPTO. The manner in which correction of an issued patent is sought is the same regardless of who is at fault. The only difference is that an error caused by the applicant triggers a fee due for correction of the issued patent. If the fault is entirely that of the USPTO, there is no fee for the correction of the issued patent. However, in both scenarios, the patent owner must initiate the action. Most important, the issued patent could one day be found to be invalid based upon the error even if the error was entirely the fault of the USPTO. As such, patentee has a duty to review an issued patent to ensure that all aspects of the issued patent are accurate.

Therefore, practitioners should review issued patent thoroughly including the specification and drawings, the claims, the claim of priority, any art of record, the inventor names, the title, etc. Should any error be noted, a certificate of correction is typically the mechanism to fix the error. The issued patent will not be changed by the USPTO per se, but an addendum including the correction, will be added to the back of the issued patent.

The requirements for the filing of a certificate of correction include the use of a template form provided by the USPTO. In essence, a patentee files a paper to explain the error and, if the fault of the USPTO, to identify evidence showing that the error was the fault of the USPTO. For example, upon reviewing an issued patent, a pantentee may find that a drawing was omitted from the issued patent. In such an example, the patentee may file a certificate of correction to note that the specific drawing is missing and that the original filing included the missing drawing. In

59. 37 C.F.R. §§1.322 and 1.323.

response, assuming a favorable outcome for the patentee, the USPTO will issue a certificate that is added to the back of the issued patent that would include the missing drawing.

D. Reissue[60]

A reissue of a patent is a mechanism to change the scope of protection of claims in an issued patent, including the addition of claims to the issued patent. A reissue patent is an original patent that has been resubmitted to the USPTO in order to have one or more claims evaluated for patentability. Only an owner of a patent (not just inventors unless the inventor(s) are still the owner) can file a reissue application of a patent since the scope of the patent rights are sought to be changed.

The rationale behind the filing of a reissue patent application is the desire of the patent owner to have a reevaluation of the patent claims against enumerated errors. The enumerated errors must be errors without deceptive intent. This standard is similar to the standard associated with an original filing of an application in that the individuals filing the reissue cannot attempt to deceive the USPTO in the submission of the reissue application. In many cases, the bases for the enumerated errors simply may be a failure to capture all possible scopes of protection during prosecution of the original patent. For example, an original application may have described five distinct features but only claimed four of them for the patent. The fifth feature, which has never been claimed, may be patentable as well. Assuming that a continuation application was not filed during pendency of the original application, a reissue application of the issued patent allows the practitioner the ability to seek patent protection on the fifth feature in additional claims. In submitting the reissue application, the practitioner can add new claims, whether in independent and/or dependent form, directed to the fifth feature that was never previously claimed. Similarly, if the original patented claims were method claims, assuming support exists in the original application, a reissue application of the patent may be used to obtain apparatus, system, or computer readable medium type claims.

Technically speaking, a reissue application is a surrendering of the patent to the USPTO for further prosecution. Although the patent is still enforceable during prosecution of the reissue application, any changes to the claim scope carries potential consequences to the patent owner. A form of defense to patent infringement of a reissue patent is intervening rights.

60. 37 C.F.R. §1.171.

Intervening rights are those rights acquired by a defendant in developing a method or apparatus that infringes a claim modified during the reissue process. If the defendant developed the method or apparatus prior to the filing of the reissue application, the later issuing reissued claims cannot be asserted against the defendant. The rights are "intervening" since they were acquired between issuance of the original patent and issuance of the reissue patent. If a continuation application with the modified claims had simply been filed during pendency of the original patent application, intervening rights would not exist as a defense for the defendant.

Modified claims, whether added or amended, that broaden the scope of protection of the claims carry a special requirement. A broadening reissue application must be filed no later than two years after issuance of the original patent. After two years, only narrowing reissue applications, i.e., reissue applications that include claims that narrow the scope or have the same scope of protection, may be filed on a patent. A practitioner should note the two year date of the issuance of the patent application since this date is the final day to file a broadening reissue application. However, if the reissue application is a narrowing reissue, the application may be filed any time during the term of the original patent. The rationale for the time limit on broadening reissue applications is to provide certainty to the public within a certain time period that the patent rights are no broader than published in the issued patents. As such, others can continue to innovate outside these bounds with some level of certainty.

Continuations and divisionals from a reissue application may be filed during pendency of the reissue application. As such, if a reissue application is subjected to a restriction requirement during prosecution, a divisional reissue application to non-elected claims may be filed during pendency of the reissue application. The same procedures for a restriction in an original application apply to a reissue application.

The requirements for submission of a reissue application are fairly straightforward. A patentee must submit the patent along with the modified claims and other amendments, such as to the specification or drawings, if any. In addition, a statement from the patent owner allowing for the submission of the reissue is needed as well as a declaration from the inventor(s) of the modified claims that the reissue application is being submitted for specific enumerated errors without deceptive intent on the part of the inventor(s). An example of deceptive intent would be a situation in which an inventor knows a claim included in the reissue application to be unpatentable, whether because of known material prior art or an on-sale bar. In such a case, submission of the claim in a reissue application would have deceptive intent. And, like many other filings at the USPTO, a government fee is associated with the submission.

Certain limitations in the modification of the claims exist. First, any modification of the claims must be fully supported by the original specification and/or figures of the issued patent. No new subject matter may be added during prosecution of a reissue application. New aspects fully supported in the original specification and figures may be claimed, but subject matter not supported may not be added and/or claimed.

Second, subject matter that was conceded to the public during prosecution of the original patent application cannot be recaptured. The recapture rule, as it is often referred to, ensures that an applicant cannot reacquire subject matter surrendered to the public during previous prosecution. There are two common situations in which this might arise. First, any non-elected subject matter from a restriction requirement issued in the original application is surrendered to the public upon issuance of the original patent application if a divisional application was not filed during pendency of the original patent application. As such, a reissue application, even if filed within two years of the issuance of the original patent, cannot include claims directed to the non-elected subject matter. Failure to file a divisional application to the non-elected claims amounts to dedications of those claims to the public upon issuance of the original patent. A second common situation in which the recapture rule may take effect is when a claim of a reissue application seeks to circumvent a statement made on the record during prosecution of the original patent. For example, if during prosecution of the original patent a practitioner makes a comment to define a term a specific way, a reissue claim including the same term cannot attempt to include scope beyond the defined term. If the term were "at least one satellite" and an argument during prosecution limited the term to be "three satellites," a claim in the reissue application that included "at least one satellite" could not attempt to limit the term to "one satellite," "two satellites," or "more than three satellites." Such an attempt would seek to recapture the conceded scope of the term during prosecution of the original patent.

The effect for claims that are substantively changed is different than for claims that are not substantively changed. Intervening rights exist for potential defendants in claims that are substantively changed. However, any claims that are not substantively changed, including those that are not changed at all, are not affected by an intervening rights defense by a potential patent infringement defendant. As such, the importance of filing a continuation application while a patent is pending in comparison to utilizing a reissue application should be noted. A continuation application and a broadening reissue patent may have the same claims with identical claim scopes; however, the effect and coverage is much different. Intervening rights exist for a potential defendant that has an infringing method or apparatus that was developed prior to the filing of the reissue application. The intervening rights are a defense to the infringement and a patent owner of the reissue patent is barred from enforcing those claims against that defendant. However, for the same claims in a continuation application that issues into a patent, there is no defense of intervening rights for a defendant and the claims can be enforced against such a defendant.

A reissue patent carries the same term as the original patent and all maintenance fees must be accounted for even during pendency of the reissue application. As such, absent patent term extension, adjustment, or filing of a terminal disclaimer, a reissue patent will expire twenty years from the earliest filing date of the original patent. Because a non-obviousness type double patenting rejection may be issued during prosecution of a reissue application, a terminal disclaimer may be needed to overcome such a rejection. Should this occur, the term of the reissue patent may be shortened to the term of the patent included in the terminal disclaimer. The consequences of seeking claims subject to a terminal disclaimer during prosecution of a reissue patent application should be recognized.

E. Reexamination[61, 62]

A reexamination of a patent is a mechanism for one or more claims in an issued patent to be evaluated again by the USPTO. The reexamination of one or more of the claims is an evaluation of such claims against a potential anticipation and/or obviousness type rejection. The basis for the filing of a reexamination patent is the desire of someone, whether the patent owner or another party, to have the reevaluation of the one or more claims of the patent. The USPTO is the only entity that may reexamine the one or more claims of the patent. As described herein there are differences in reexamination of a patent by the USPTO and a determination of validity or invalidity by a judge or jury in a civil patent infringement action.

61. The AIA modifies reexamination before the USPTO. For example, inter partes reexamination is phased out giving way to inter partes review. See AIA section.

62. 37 C.F.R. §1.510.

Examination of claims by the USPTO in a reexamination proceeding ultimately may produce the same claims as in the patent under review and/or amended claims as an outcome. However, if amended, the claims must be narrower in comparison to the original claims. A reexamination of a patent cannot result in a patent with claims that are broader in scope of protection in comparison to the original claims of the patent. If a patentee seeks to broaden the scope of protection of an issued patent, the pantentee should look to file a reissue of the original patent.

As previously stated, reexamination of a patent may be sought by anyone. The patent owner may seek reexamination of the patent. A defendant in an alleged patent infringement action may seek reexamination of the patent in the action. Other third parties, such as a competitor that has not been issued a cease and desist letter or an action alleging infringement of a patent, may seek reexamination of the patent by the USPTO. Finally, even the USPTO may seek reexamination of a patent. For each of these parties, reexamination of a patent may be sought for a number of reasons.

The patent owner may seek reexamination upon coming across a prior art reference after issuance of the original patent. The patent owner may seek reexamination of the patent in order to have the claims be found allowable by the USPTO over the new prior art reference. If the original claims remain unamended after reexamination, the claims are stronger in having been found novel and nonobvious over the new prior art reference. The patent is strengthened.

A third party, whether a defendant in an alleged infringement action, the USPTO, or anyone else, may seek reexamination of a patent when that entity questions the validity and/or scope of the claims of the patent. A defendant may or may not seek reexamination of a patent based upon prior art that may be utilized as a defense testing validity of the patent. If the claims resulting from the reexamination are unchanged, the use of the prior art in an invalidity defense may be thought of as weakened since the USPTO found the claims allowed over the prior art reference and the USPTO's determination over considered art is given deference.

The USPTO does not frequently initiate reexamination of patents, but the situation may arise. Reexamination of a patent by the USPTO often occurs quickly after issuance of the patent and often involves patent claims that were highly questioned immediately upon issuance. One such example is U.S. Pat. 6,368,227, entitled "Method of swinging on a swing," that issued on April 9, 2002, a copy of the cover page of which is shown below in Figure 2-1. The patent claimed a method for swinging on a swing. Less than two months after issuance of the patent, the director of the USPTO filed a request seeking a reexamination proceeding. The petition was granted and all claims were subsequently rejected. After failure of the owner to appeal the decision, a reexamination certificate was issued canceling all the claims.

Figure 2-1

Cover Page of U.S. Pat. 6,368,227

US006368227B1

(12) **United States Patent**
Olson

(10) **Patent No.:** **US 6,368,227 B1**
(45) **Date of Patent:** **Apr. 9, 2002**

(54) **METHOD OF SWINGING ON A SWING**

(76) Inventor: **Steven Olson**, 337 Otis Ave., St. Paul, MN (US) 55104

(*) Notice: Subject to any disclaimer, the term of this patent is extended or adjusted under 35 U.S.C. 154(b) by 0 days.

(21) Appl. No.: **09/715,198**

(22) Filed: **Nov. 17, 2000**

(51) **Int. Cl.**[7] **A63G 9/00**
(52) **U.S. Cl.** **472/118**
(58) **Field of Search** 472/118, 119, 472/120, 121, 122, 123, 125

(56) **References Cited**

U.S. PATENT DOCUMENTS

242,601 A * 6/1881 Clement 472/118
5,413,298 A * 5/1995 Perreault 248/228

* cited by examiner

Primary Examiner—Kien T. Nguyen
(74) *Attorney, Agent, or Firm*—Peter Lowell Olson

(57) **ABSTRACT**

A method of swing on a swing is disclosed, in which a user positioned on a standard swing suspended by two chains from a substantially horizontal tree branch induces side to side motion by pulling alternately on one chain and then the other.

4 Claims, 3 Drawing Sheets

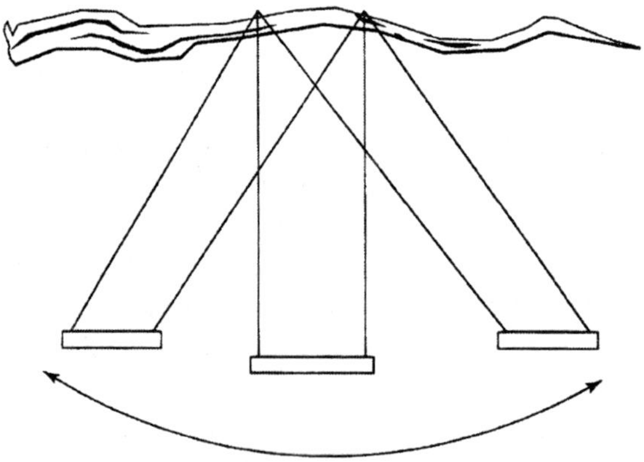

A request for reexamination of a patent does not guarantee reexamimation of the patent will be performed by the USPTO. A request for reexamination may be denied. The requirements for requesting reexamination of a patent include a filing of the request and presentation of a new reason or reasons why the patent claims are invalid. And, like other filings at the USPTO, a government fee is associated with the submission.

Similar to prosecution of a new patent application, any amendment of the claims must be fully supported by the original specification and/or figures of the issued patent. No new subject matter may be added during a reexamination proceeding. New aspects fully supported in the original specification and figures may be claimed, but subject matter not supported may not be added and/or claimed.

Second, a practitioner cannot attempt to recapture subject matter that was conceded to the public during prosecution of the original patent application. There are two common situations in which this might arise. First, because claims resulting from a reexamination proceeding must be either unchanged or narrowed, any non-elected subject matter from a restriction requirement issued in the original application may not be sought in the reexamination proceeding. A second common situation in which the recapture rule may take effect is when a claim during a reexamination proceeding seeks to circumvent a statement made on the record during prosecution of the original patent.

The effect for claims that are substantively changed is different than for claims that are not substantively changed. Rights may exist for potential defendants in claims that are substantively changed. However, any claims that are not substantively changed, including those that are not changed at all, are not affected by the reexamination proceeding.

A patent from reexamination carries the same term as the original patent and all maintenance fees must be accounted for even during pendency of the reexamination proceeding. As such, absent patent term extension, adjustment, or filing of a terminal disclaimer, a patent surviving reexamination will expire 20 years from the earliest filing date of the original patent. Because a non-obviousness type double patenting rejection could be issued during reexamination of the patent, a terminal disclaimer may be needed to overcome such a rejection. Should this occur, the term of the patent may be shortened to the term of the patent included in the terminal disclaimer. Once again, a patentee should understand this fact and appreciate the consequences of seeking claims subject to a terminal disclaimer during reexamination of the patent.

F. Revival of Patent[63]

Abandonment, whether intentional, unintentional, or unavoidable, of a patent is a relinquishment of all rights, whether current or future, affiliated with that patent. Abandonment obviously should be avoided and only be acquiesced to or expressly done upon a thorough understanding of the consequences. Abandonment may occur at any time during the term of the patent when a maintenance fee becomes due and the deadline for payment passes without any action being taken.

Based upon the reasons for the abandonment, a practitioner is left with a few possibilities to attempt to correct the abandonment of the patent. In a situation in which the abandonment of the patent was unintentional, a practitioner can attempt to correct the abandonment. An example of an unintentional abandonment may be a situation where a practitioner was not able to get into contact with the owner of the patent and the deadline for taking action passed before being able to reach the owner. In such examples, a practitioner can file a petition to revive the patent for unintentional abandonment. The petition will have to include evidence of the unintentional abandonment. In addition, a substantial government fee must be paid with the filing of the petition. The petition must be filed in a reasonable amount of time upon being able to correct the abandonment.

Similar to a petition to revive for unintentional abandonment, a practitioner can attempt to correct an abandonment that was unavoidable. An example of an unavoidable abandonment may be a situation where a practitioner was not able to get into contact with the owner of the patent application and the deadline for taking action passed because the owner was in a coma. As such, an argument may be made by a practitioner that the failure to take an action to respond was unavoidable. In such examples, a practitioner can file a petition to revive the patent for unavoidable abandonment. The petition will have to include evidence of the unavoidable abandonment. In addition, a government fee, somewhat less than the fee for an unintentional abandonment, must be paid with the filing of the petition. The petition must be filed in a reasonable amount of time upon being able to correct the abandonment.

However, if an abandonment was voluntary, i.e., the owner actively chose to not pay the maintenance fee and to abandon the patent, the revival of the patent will not be allowed. A practitioner should not attempt to revive such a patent when she knows the abandonment was voluntary.

63. 37 C.F.R. §1.137.

PART 3

Patent Litigation

I have been so constantly under the necessity of watching the movements of the most unprincipled set of pirates I have ever known, that all my time has been occupied in defense, in putting evidence into something like legal shape that I am the inventor of the Electro-Magnetic Telegraph.

—Samuel F. B. Morse
(inventor of the telegraph and Morse code)
Samuel F. B. Morse, His Letters and Journals (1914), vol. 2, 283
(Extract from a letter to his brother describing the challenge of defending his patents on the telegraph, April 19, 1848)

Patent litigation does not just happen. Prior to any courtroom, any deposition, any review of documents, or even any complaint, the process for determining whether to litigate a patent begins with issuance of the patent, or maybe even before. A practitioner involved in the process of litigating a patent should appreciate several things before determining that legal action in a U.S. District Court is the best course of action.

I. REQUIREMENTS FOR AN OWNER OF PATENT IN SEEKING AN INFRINGEMENT ACTION

A patent infringement action in a U.S. District Court is a very costly endeavor. Litigating a patent can cost in excess of $3 million and take at least two years. Also, the appeal process can cost as much as another $2 million and take at least another year of time. Prior to counseling a client on whether to proceed or not, a practitioner should assist a client in understanding the time and resource commitments that a patent litigation, whether offensive or defensive, will require. Given the significant average costof litigation, the estimated costs need to be addressed immediately. If the best case scenario is a judgment of less than $1 million, then litigation may not be in the best interest of a client, or at least a client should be aware that the litigation itself likely will cost more than any payment received in a judgment.

Proper prosecution of the patent during examination before the U.S. Patent & Trademark Office (USPTO) is critical to later litigation. It dictates whether a patent is worth litigating, how well it will hold up to attacks during litigation, and even whether it can be litigated. Fundamental issues during prosecution of a patent, whether substantive or procedural, can be used to invalidate the patent before an owner can even attempt to assert an action against another party.

In addressing the validity and strength of the issued patent, certain details associated with the patent need to be considered. In the U.S., ownership of a patent is defined initially by the determination of inventorship, i.e., the determination of that individual or those individuals who conceived of and reduced to practice the invention. A patentee cannot hope that identification of inventorship during the original prosecution of the patent before the USPTO was proper. An effort should be made to reevaluate the determination of inventors to ensure that proper inventorship is in place. Improper inventorship of an issued U.S. patent can be corrected if the error was without deceptive intent. As such, a practitioner should address the determination of inventorship immediately and certainly before embarking on a litigation.

Another determination to be made before bringing a litigation action is ownership. Just because the face of a U.S. patent indicates that a particular entity is the assignee does not mean that the ownership claim by that assignee is proper. Public records should be reviewed to ensure that the chain of title of ownership is proper. In situations in which the assignee is a company, the chain of title must start with a transfer of rights from the inventor(s). In the U.S., the inventor(s) of a patent are the owners of the patent unless an assignment of rights in the patent has been made by the inventor(s). In addition, it is incumbent on patentees to confirm that no other assignment records exist by any individual or entity in the chain of ownership that deviates from the public record. Confirmation that the inventors did not assign rights prior to any publicly recorded assignment is essential. A practitioner may face sanctions in filing an infringement action against another entity if it can be shown that the alleged owner is not in fact a proper owner to bring the legal action. In addition to the determination of inventorship, a practitioner should look into retaining the inventors as a consultant or witness. Otherwise, a patentee may be left in a difficult position in bringing a litigation action against a defendant that then retains one or more of the inventors.

Still another important factor regarding the validity of a patent that needs to be considered and/or rectified prior to bringing a legal action of infringement against a defendant is the confirmation of payment of the maintenance fees. Maintenance fees for a U.S. utility patent must be paid at certain intervals following issuance of the patent. Failure to timely pay maintenance fees results in automatic abandonment of the patent. Yet again, a practitioner may face sanctions before a court in the event that an infringement action on a patent is brought when the patent is, in fact, no longer enforceable due to abandonment. Maintenance fees must be paid every four years, eight years, and twelve years following issuance of the patent.[1] If the patent is abandoned for failure to pay the maintenance fees, revival of the patent may be sought in order to still bring a legal action against another party so long as the proper paperwork is filed and the abandonment is shown to have been unavoidable or unintentional.

Although not required, a study of the validity of the patent may be made before bringing an action, particularly if the state of the art was unknown to the applicant during prosecution or there is reason to think the most pertinent art may not have been identified and considered by the examiner.[2] A practitioner may search various databases for prior art that is not of record, i.e., was not presented before the USPTO during exami-

1. One year windows for payment of maintenance fees open at 3.5, 7.5 and 11.5 years respectively.

2. Confidence in the strength of a patent can be greatly increased if the state of the relevant art is known by the applicant, inventors or practitioner or if a patentability or clearance search is performed prior to filing a patent application. As such, time and money spent during the prosecution process to

nation of the patent. Alternatively or additionally, an independent search may be conducted. Many search firms will review different patent databases for different countries in addition to publicly accessible databases and subscription databases to search for potential relevant prior art. Practitioners frequently look to this option, since an independent eye may be a good source for evaluating the validity of the issued patent.

Should some prior art be found that is of particular relevance or noteworthiness, reexamination of the patent in light of the reference may be sought.[3] Seeking reexamination of the issued patent may allow for the examination of the patent against the newly found reference. Thus, any claims surviving the reexamination proceeding will be found allowable over that additional reference as well. Such a ruling may be useful if a particular piece of prior art is thought to be the best prior art against the claims of the patent. Although the reexamination process can take some time, the resulting claims from the reexamination proceeding will be stronger against the art of record.

Should a patent believed to be or found to be adequately enforceable to an owner, infringement contentions need to be established against the defendant prior to filing any infringement action. Infringement contentions are assertions based on some form of documentation to show the basis for an owner to assert that another party is infringing a claim of an issued patent. A practitioner should be aware that she may face sanctions from a court in the event that an infringement action is brought against a party without reasonable infringement contentions in place.

The basis or support for the infringement contention is a showing of how a party manufactures, imports, uses, sells, or offers to sell the technology covered by the patent. If all features of a claim of a patent are found in the party's product, the claim reads on the party's product as a contention of infringement. However, if a single feature from the claim is absent from the party's product, the claim does not literally read on the party's product and the product does not infringe the patent with respect to that claim. The basis for infringement may be based upon published documentation by the party, a product made by the party, or even comments about the operation of some current or future product of the party. However, a reasonable basis for infringement contention must exist prior to filing an infringement action.

---

secure strong and well drafted patents may save the patentee time and money and even patent rights down the road should the patent need to be enforced.

3. 37 C.F.R. §1.510.

Two types of infringement contentions should be addressed in initially creating a basis for infringement contentions. The first is direct infringement, i.e., a party directly manufactures, imports, uses, sells, or offers for sale the patented invention in the U.S. without permission. This is the most common type of infringement contention. Direct infringement need not require the accused party know of the patented invention. A party can be a direct infringer without having any knowledge of the existence of the patented invention.

The other type of infringement contention is indirect infringement, i.e., a party does something less than directly manufacturing, importing, using, selling, or offering for sale the patented invention in the U.S. without permission. Indirect infringement contentions are more difficult to show, since a single party is not performing each and every feature of the claim. There are two forms of indirect infringement contentions that a practitioner can assert should direct infringement not be an available option.

First, a contributory infringement contention can be asserted, i.e., that a party assisted another party in the other party's effort to infringe by manufacturing, importing, using, selling, or offering for sale without permission one or more components of the patented invention in the U.S. However, to be a contributory infringer, the component(s) must have no other substantial use but for being used within the patented invention, i.e., the component(s) of the party cannot be utilized for anything more than an eventual infringing use.

Second, an inducing infringement contention can be asserted, i.e., that a party actively aided another party in infringing the patented invention. The party may not make, import, use, sell, or offer for sale any component at all, but it is actively involved in having at least one other party infringe. A practitioner should appreciate that finding a party to be an inducing infringer is more difficult since active involvement is required for proof.

Should it be determined that a change in claim scope of an issued patent may assist in bringing an infringement action, a practitioner may consider filing a reissue of the patent before the USPTO.[4] If done within two years of issuance of the patent, the owner may seek broader scopes of protection.[5]

---

4. 37 C.F.R. §1.171.
5. *See Patent Prosecution Section.*

II. LOCAL RULES[6]

For whichever jurisdiction is selected for pursuit of a patent litigation, the local rules and their effect on the handling of the patent litigation proceedings should be understood. Although the Federal Rules of Civil Procedure (FRCP) take precedence, the local rules of a district court can have an immense impact on how a litigation proceeding must be handled. Local rules of a district court often are in place to delineate rules of the court when the FRCP do not specifically cover a specific issue related to patent litigation and can be drafted so as to encourage negotiation and settlement and also to reduce the number of issues in dispute prior to trial.

III. REQUIREMENTS FOR A COMPLAINT BY THE PATENT OWNER

After assessing all possible effects of bringing an infringement action, including determining whether a cease and desist letter should be sent to a believed infringer, a practitioner may decide to pursue an infringement action.[7] Patents are solely under the jurisdiction of the federal courts. Thus, a practitioner can bring a patent infringement action only against another party in a U.S. district court.[8] For an initial complaint, the owner of the patent must assert the reasons that the party is alleged to have infringed the patented invention, including the specific claims of the patent that have been infringed and the basis for that contention, such as the products of the party that allegedly infringe, and whether the infringement is direct and/or indirect. A copy of the complaint that is filed with the U.S. district court also must be submitted to the known address of the alleged infringing party. In the instance of a corporate entity, an

---

6. Many U.S. District Courts currently have local rules in place for patent cases. Some of the more well-known jurisdictions include: Eastern, Northern, & Southern Districts of Texas; Northern & Southern Districts of California; Southern District of Indiana; Northern District of Illinois; Eastern District of Virginia; Southern District of Ohio; Northern District of Georgia; District of Massachusetts; District of Minnesota; District of New Jersey; Eastern District of North Carolina; Western District of Pennsylvania; Southern District of Ohio; Eastern District of Missouri; and Western District of Washington.

7. Fed. R. Civ. P. R. 3.

8. The filing of a patent infringement action in a state court will be thrown out by the state court immediately as lacking subject matter jurisdiction.

address of the headquarters or of legal correspondence often is readily available. The complaint need not include every detail for alleged infringement, since the discovery process, as described below, may require amendment to the complaint.

IV. REQUIREMENTS FOR ANSWER BY THE ACCUSED INFRINGER

Once a patent infringement complaint has been received by an entity or individual(s), a clock starts for the alleged infringer to respond. An alleged infringer has 21 days to respond to the complaint and must admit or deny each allegation in the complaint or must specify that the party has insufficient knowledge to form a belief as to the truth of the allegation.[9, 10] Twenty-one days is not a great deal of time for an alleged infringer to answer; thus a practitioner for an alleged infringer needs to investigate and prepare its response very quickly.

There are some procedural defenses that may or must, depending on the particular defense, be filed either before or at the same time as an answer. A defendant may effectively seek to dismiss a case by filing a motion to dismiss for some type of procedural problem with the complaint. Examples these defenses include lack of subject matter jurisdiction, lack of personal jurisdiction, improper venue, insufficiency of process, insufficiency of service of process, failure to state a claim upon which relief can be granted, and failure to join a party needed for just adjudication.[11] In many instances, because of the 21-day time period for an answer, a party will respond with these procedural motions concurrent with the filing of an answer to the complaint.

As part of the process of affirming, denying, or specifying insufficient knowledge to form a belief as to the truth of the allegation, an affirmation is an admission. Admitting an allegation that the defendant is incorporated in the state of Delaware may be an innocuous admission. However, a practitioner should keep in mind that an affirmation of an allegation can be used against the defendant and an inadvertent admission on a key issue or allegation could lose or seriously undermine a litigant's case.

In answering the allegations of a complaint, it is important to note that statutory defenses, including non-infringement, invalidity, and

9. FED. R. CIV. P. R. 12(a).
10. FED. R. CIV. P. R. 8(b).
11. FED. R. CIV. P. R. 12(b).

unenforceability of the patented invention are waived if not plead in answering the complaint. As such, a practitioner should consider all reasonable bases for contending non-infringement, invalidity, and unenforceability. In addition, compulsory counterclaims (i.e., counterclaims that arise out of the transaction or occurrence that is the subject matter of the party of the complaint) by the defendant against the patent owner must be addressed at the time of filing the answer.[12] Although an answer, like a complaint, may be amended after the initial filing, most amendments will require a leave of court. Thus, a practitioner should seek to prepare an all-encompassing answer, just as an all-encompassing complaint should be prepared by the party alleging infringement.

In general, the most common assertions in responding to an allegation of patent infringement are the following:

First, the alleged infringer may assert that she was not performing any infringing act within the U.S. To infringe, the act of infringement must occur within the U.S. or its territories, i.e., a non-infringement position.

Second, the alleged infringer may assert that she was not practicing the patent invention at all, i.e., a non-infringement position. She may assert and show that at least one claim feature of the asserted claim is not present in that which is being alleged as manufactured, imported, used, sold, or offered for sale.

Third, the alleged infringer may assert that the patent has expired, whether due to the term of the patent lapsing or abandonment of the patent, i.e., an unenforceable patent position. This person may assert and show that the patent cannot be asserted by anyone against the accused or anyone else.

Fourth, the alleged infringer may assert that the entire patent, or at least the claims alleged to be infringed, are not valid, i.e., an invalidity position. This person may assert and show that the patent does not meet the requirements for patentability, such as the patent being anticipated by or rendered obvious over prior art references or that the patent includes some formal defect.

Fifth, the alleged infringer may assert that the entire patent, or the claims alleged to be infringed, are not enforceable, i.e., an unenforceable patent position. This person may assert and show that the patent is unenforceable, such as a situation where the patent owner has no right to

---

12. The America Invents Act (AIA) modifies the requirements for parties to bring counterclaims in patent litigations. *See Patent Groundwork Section.*

assert the patent infringement action against the accused. An example may be a situation in which misconduct was perpetrated at the USPTO while the patent application was being prosecuted/examined.

Finally, the alleged infringer may assert that she has obtained a license under the patent, i.e., an unenforceable patent position. She may assert and show that the patent owner has no right to assert an infringement action against her, as she is excused from infringement as she has a license.

V. SETTLEMENT CONSIDERATIONS[13]

Whether or not required by the district court, litigants should initially and periodically assess the value or need for settlement. Due to the large expense and time involved in a litigation proceeding, a patent owner may not want to pursue a litigation proceeding through trial. A practitioner is obligated to take a formal settlement offer provided to her as representative of the client to the client for review, even if the practitioner does not believe the offer should be accepted. However, a patent owner is of course not obligated to accept any pre-trial settlement offer from an opposing party. Settlement of a patent litigation before getting heavily involved in the proceedings carries many advantages to both sides of the litigation. For a patent owner, settlement may preserve the strength of the patent without allowing questions as to the validity or unenforceability to be decided in the district court. In addition, a settlement at an early stage may avoid incurring a large portion of the expenses associated with the infringement action. Similar savings on expenses may be an advantage for a defendant as well. In addition, most pre-trial settlements allow for a defendant to steer clear of any admission of infringement and maintain the terms of the settlement as confidential. Such an arrangement may be advantageous in the public eye as to how the alleged infringer is perceived following the settlement.

In situations in which a settlement conference is required (often by local rules), a practitioner is required to meet with the opposing counsel to confer on potential settlement of the action without the need for a trial. In some jurisdictions, one or more mandatory court facilitated settlement conferences are required. The required settlement conferences are

13. Settlement discussions may be a requirement imposed by local rules in certain U.S. District Courts.

designed to force the two sides to discuss settlement at a time when the facts and circumstances are most favorable to reaching a settlement.

VI. CONFERENCE OF PARTIES ON LITIGATION SCHEDULE[14]

A conference of the parties also is held as part of the proceedings to create a litigation schedule for which the parties will be bound to adhere. This usually occurs early in the process and the presiding judge meets with counsel for both parties to discuss the litigation schedule that he would like to occur. The litigation schedule is dictated by the Federal Rules of Civil Procedure, but may also be based upon the local rules of the U.S. district court. Certain procedural rules, including due dates and additional conferences or filings, may be part of the litigation schedule. This meeting is designed to allow all parties to understand the framework that the litigation will adhere to. Often there are instances requiring a change to the schedule that is created. However, the finalized litigation schedule can be modified only upon a finding of the judge to do so or at the judge's discretion. A practitioner should approach a conference regarding the litigation schedule with a desired time frame for proceeding, including time frames for presenting issues of discovery and issues of filings.

VII. COMPLETE INFRINGEMENT CONTENTIONS[15]

Following review of the answer by a defendant, a patent owner often must finalize or complete the infringement contentions. A denial of an allegation by a defendant may result in an infringement contention that is no longer valid or perhaps is no longer desirable to pursue. In response, the infringement contentions may be amended ot removed if they are either invalid or undesired. Most amendments to the initial infringement contentions require leave of the U.S. district court; however, there is often leniency in allowing the patent owner the opportunity to present a clearer representation of the infringement contentions, especially in light of documentation and/or information that was not readily available to the patent owner when filing the complaint. For example, discovery as discussed in more detail later will often provide further details regarding

14. Fed. R. Civ. P. R. 16.
15. Fed. R. Civ. P. R. 15.

the actions for which the allegations of infringement are based. However, until discovery is performed it may be impossible for a patentee to fully obtain all of the information that is relevant to the allegation of infringement.

VIII. INITIAL DISCLOSURE REQUIREMENTS[16]

The initial disclosure requirements of the Federal Rules of Civil Procedure are designed to "accelerate the exchange of basic information about the case and to eliminate the paper work involved in requesting such information." There is a duty to disclose, without awaiting formal discovery requests, certain basic information that is needed in most cases to prepare for trial or make an informal decision about settlement. In general, the parties must disclose certain types of information.

First, the name and known contact information of each individual likely to have discoverable information, along with the subjects of that information, must be provided. Therefore a practitioner should appreciate that witnesses in the action, including inventors, prosecuting attorneys, and other individuals with a working knowledge of the development and prosecution of the patented invention, will need to be identified as part of the initial disclosure.

Second, a copy or identification of all documents; electronically stored information; and tangible things that the disclosing party has in its possession, custody, or control, and may use to support its claims or defenses, must be provided.

Third, a computation of each category of damages claimed by the disclosing party must be provided. Evidentiary material, on which each computation is based, may need to be provided as well.

Finally, an insurance agreement, under which an insurance business may be liable to satisfy all or part of a possible judgment in the action or to indemnify or reimburse for payments made to satisfy the judgment, must be provided.

IX. INVALIDITY CONTENTIONS

A defendant will likely prepare invalidity contentions with respect to the claims of the patent being asserted against her client. Invalidity contentions are documents and other evidence that allege that a claim asserted

16. FED. R. CIV. P. R. 26(a)(1).

against the defendant in the litigation proceeding is invalid. Invalidity contentions often are embodied in charts that compare asserted claims against patentability requirements under 35 U.S.C. §§101, 102, 103, and 112.

Invalidity contentions are one mechanism for contesting the validity of the asserted claims. Whether with respect to a previously occurring event and/or a prior art reference, such as a patent or printed publication, invalidity contentions form the basis for a defendant to demonstrate that the patent, regardless of whether infringed or enforceable, is not valid and cannot be asserted against the defendant. Invalidity is an analysis of patentability of the claims based upon U.S. patent law. Potential issues of unpatentability under 35 U.S.C. §§101 and 112 can often be addressed prior to initiation of a litigation proceeding with a certificate of correction, a reexamination proceeding, or a reissue of the patent. However, invalidity contentions that arise under 35 U.S.C. §§102 and 103 may not be as foreseeable, since the prior art references may not be known to the practitioner or applicant. In these cases, such contentions are reviewed and analyzed as soon as possible, since the prior art references may be used to support an application for a reexamination proceeding in order to have the art be made of record. It is a somewhat common defense tactic for an accused defendant to file a request for reexamination, and if successful, to request a stay of the litigation proceeding. Should the patent claims survive reexamination without substantive amendment over the noted prior art references, the invalidity contention is weakened, at least with regard to the arguments and references considered during reexamination.

X. DEFENSES[17]

The most common defense to a patent infringement allegation is non-infringement. Even if the patent is valid or enforceable, a patent claim cannot be directly infringed if the alleged infringing product or process does not perform each and every feature of the asserted claim. The most clearly valid and enforceable patent cannot successfully pursue an infringement cause of action if the defendant's product is missing a claimed component in an apparatus claim or does not perform a claimed step in a method claim.

A defense of non-infringement must specify the reason the defendant's

17. Fed. R. Civ. P. R. 8 & 12.

product or process does not infringe the claimed invention. With respect to a claim, a defendant may offer multiple reasons as to why a finding of non-infringement is appropriate—e.g., the accused product or process does not have multiple claimed components or the defendant did not perform multiple claimed steps. Each and every reason needs to be identified and specified. Should one of the reasons not persuade a judge or jury, one of the others still might, and a defendant needs to successfully persuade the court of only one non-infringement contention per asserted claim to win the case.

Another defense to patent infringement allegations is the showing of an absence of liability. Even if a defendant is directly infringing an asserted claim of a patent, the defendant may be free from an infringement allegation due to the absence of liability. A number of different factual scenarios can exist in which a defendant can assert an absence of liability.

First, a defendant may assert that a license exists from the patent owner to the defendant that allows for practice of the claimed invention. The defendant may assert that a license was expressed: i.e., a written or oral agreement was made between the defendant and the patent owner, and/or that the license was implied, i.e., the defendant was authorized by an unwritten understanding in light of the circumstances to infringe the claimed invention. Because many entities cross-license technologies and associated intellectual property rights, a practitioner should be aware of all licenses of the represented client with the opposing party.

Second, a defendant may claim to have had prior use of the claimed invention. The contention is that the defendant secretly, or unknowingly to the public, used the invention prior to the invention by the patentee This defense allows a defendant that has been operating the claimed invention as a trade secret to continue to infringe the claimed invention due to prior use before the patent owner.

Third, a defendant may contend that it is allowed to infringe the claimed invention under the "experimental use" exception or "safe harbor" exemption. One of the more common uses of the exemption allows generic manufacturers to prepare generic drugs of a patented drug for regulatory approval before the patent expires. Research can be submitted to the Food and Drug Administration (FDA) in anticipation of eventual expiration of the patent; however, the defendant cannot sell the generic version of the patented drug until the patent has expired.

Fourth, a defendant may contend that the time period for asserting damages has expired, i.e., the patent term has expired or the patent has become abandoned. Once a patent has expired, damages for current infringement cannot be sought against an alleged infringer.[18]

Fifth, a defendant may contend that the patent owner is barred by laches, i.e., that the patent owner took an unreasonable delay pursuing the infringement action in a way that now prejudices the defendant. Although a utility patent owner has the term of the patent, often times 20 years from the earliest filing date, to assert infringement actions against a party, if the patent owner knows of potential infringement and does not timely act on the infringement or if the patent owner takes no action until a change of circumstances for the defendant makes the damages much more severe, the patent owner may be barred by a laches defense to asserting the allegation of infringement. Additionally, infringement of a patent claim is actionable only for actions going back six years from the date of filing of the suit.

Finally, a defendant may contend that the patent owner is equitably estopped from asserting patent infringement. A practitioner should appreciate that the patent owner is barred if facts of the case have been misrepresented to, or concealed from, the defendant or the court. Another reason for barring a patent owner by equitable estoppel includes a finding that fraudulent intent was used to procure either the patent or litigation of the patent. The passage of too much time can be yet another reason for estoppel.

XI. UNENFORCEABLE

A valid and infringed patent may be found unenforceable by a district court. A practitioner that is asserting an infringement action should appreciate the possibility of a contention by the defendant of the patent being deemed unenforceable. Aside from the previous contentions that the moving party is not actually the rightful patent owner to bring the infringement allegation, that the patent has expired or is abandoned, or that the alleged infringer has a license to infringe the patented invention, there are two other common contention that can be made that the patented invention is unenforceable.

First, an accused defendant may assert that the patented invention is unenforceable due to inequitable conduct during prosecution of the patent before the U.S. Patent & Trademark Office (USPTO). Inequitable con-

18. Patentees may bring causes of action for actions and damages going back up to 6 years.

duct occurs when the duty of candor and good faith to the USPTO has been breached. Such a breach may include the failure to submit material prior art known by the applicant; the failure to explain references in a foreign language or submit pre-existing full or partial translations of the references; misstatements of fact, including misstatements in affidavits concerning patentability; and incorrect inventorship with intent to deceive. The party asking the court to find the patent unenforceable, most often the defendant, bears the burden of proving inequitable conduct. The defendant must show by "clear and convincing" evidence that the patent owner/applicant intentionally withheld or misrepresented information, and that the information was "material to patentability."

Second, an alleged infringer may contend that the patent owner has engaged in patent misuse, and thus the owner should be barred from enforcing the patent. A patent misuse defense arises when a defendant alleges that enforcement of the patent is in violation of antitrust laws, i.e., the patent owner is exhibiting a prohibitive and anti-competitive behavior. A patent misuse defense also may arise when a defendant alleges that the patent owner is seeking an improper expansion of the scope or term of the patent. Such a condition may exist where a patent owner seeks royalties beyond the scope or term of the patent. The burden for proving these reasons for unenforceability falls on the party alleging misuse, which is most often the defendant.

XII. REMEDIES

In utility patent infringement actions, there are two main remedies that a patent owner may seek for infringement of a valid and enforceable patent. A patent owner may seek an injunction to prevent further infringement of the claimed invention. Injunctions are considered a type of equitable remedy. Injunctions are designed to provide relief where money damages are insufficient. The patent owner may seek a preliminary injunction, a permanent injunction, or both during a litigation proceeding. A preliminary injunction is an injunction requesting a preliminary order of a court that a person or entity refrain from certain activities or take certain actions until completed. A preliminary injunction asks the court to issue the injunction pending the outcome of a lawsuit or petition asking for a permanent injunction. A permanent injunction is an injunction requesting a final order of a court that a person or entity refrain from certain activities permanently. Once a final ruling has been made, a preliminary injunction may be replaced with a permanent injunction. Historically, upon a finding of infringement, courts in essence automatically issued permanent injunctions against future infringing activities by the infringer. However, after the fairly recent *eBay* decision by the Supreme Court, district courts must perform the balance of hardship test in issuing an injunction. As such, while injunctions are still regularly issued against future infringing activity once infringement of a valid and enforceable patent is found, injunctions are no longer granted automatically.[19]

A patent owner also may seek damages from the defendant. Upon finding for the patent owner, a court shall award the patent owner damages adequate to compensate for the infringement, but in no event less than a reasonable royalty for the use made of the invention by the infringer, together with interest and costs as fixed by the court. When the damages are not found by a jury, the court shall assess them. In either event, the court may enhance damages with an increase of the damages amount up to three times the amount found by a judge or jury. Increased damages may be due to a finding of willful infringement of the claimed invention by the defendant. An allegation of willful infringement by a patent owner increases the potential damages that an alleged infringer may be responsible for if the outcome of the case is not favorable for the defendant. The court may receive expert testimony as an aid to help determine damages or what royalty would be reasonable under the circumstances.

Depending upon the type of case, compensatory damages may be established based upon profits lost by the patent owner due to the infringement by the alleged infringer, sales of a single multifaceted device, e.g., a personal computer that incorporates a patented feature together with unpatented features, or a reasonable royalty. Section 284 of Title 35 provides that a patentee is entitled to damages adequate to compensate for any infringement, and that compensation cannot be less than a reasonable royalty for the use made of the invention by the infringer.[20] The minimum amount that the patent owner can recover is the royalty that it and the alleged infringer would have agreed upon had there been no infringement suit.

In exceptional cases, a practitioner may also seek a remedy of attorney fees of a client. Judges do not commonly provide for the required payment of attorneys' fees by the losing party, but, notwithstanding, a party may seek to have its attorneys' fees paid by the losing party.

19. eBay Inc. v. MercExchange, L.L.C, 547 U.S. 388 (2006).
20. 35 U.S.C. § 284.

In still other cases, issues of patent marking of an item covered by the patent or a document that accompanies a patented process or device would not extend to an alleged infringer of the current dispute taking place between the two parties. A patent owner may be unable to collect past damages for patent infringement if there were a failure to perform the seemingly simple task of properly marking its patented products with patent numbers. Patent marking provides notice to an alleged infringer that the product or method is already subject to an eventual patent litigation proceeding.[21]

XIII. PROTECTIVE ORDERS[22]

Rule 26(c) of the Federal Rules of Civil Procedure provides for the use of a protective order, which is an agreement by the opposing parties to certain rules in governing disclosure of certain materials and documents during the proceedings. Upon motion by a party or by the person from whom discovery is sought, accompanied by a certification that the movant (party initiating the motion) has in good faith conferred or attempted to confer with other affected parties to resolve the dispute without court action, and for good cause shown, the court in which the action is pending or alternatively, on matters relating to a deposition, the court in the district where the deposition is to be taken, may make any order that justice requires to protect a party or person from annoyance, embarrassment, oppression, or undue burden or expense.

Such an order may include provisions that the disclosure or discovery not be had; that the disclosure or discovery may be had only on specified terms and conditions, including a designation of the time or place; that the discovery may be had only by a method of discovery other than that selected by the party seeking discovery; that certain matters not be inquired into, or that the scope of the disclosure or discovery be limited to certain matters; that discovery be conducted with no one present except persons designated by the court; that a deposition, after being sealed, be opened only by order of the court; that a trade secret or other confidential research, development, or commercial information not be revealed or be revealed only in a designated way; and that the parties simultaneously file specified documents or information enclosed in sealed envelopes to be opened as directed by the court. If the motion for a

21. The AIA modifies the requirements of for marking and also sets forth for virtual marking. See Patent Groundwork section.

22. FED. R. CIV. P. R. 26(c).

protective order is denied in whole or in part, the court may, on such terms and conditions as are just, order that any party or other person provide or permit discovery.

It is now common practice and the norm for patent infringement cases to be pursued with a protective order of some kind in place for the protection of the parties' respective interests. A patent litigant should thoroughly explore use of a protective order and take care to ensure the provisions of the protective order are prudent to protect the party's interest. Additionally, practitioners as representatives of the parties are often to some degree obligated to certain actions or inactions as a result of the protective order and as such practitioners should also take care to thoroughly consider the provisions as it is possible the provisions could have a restrictive effect on their ability to do certain types of work or represent certain clients in the future.

XIV. DISCOVERY[23]

Discovery is a procedural mechanism through which opposing parties are required to disclose information that the party knows or possesses and which is requested and may be important for the preparation of the requesting party's arguments for trial. Discovery occurs prior to the trial and for a specific time period as defined by the judge in the case schedule. Although the time period may be modified, all necessary aspects of discovery should be scheduled during the time period provided by the judge as part of the scheduling order.

Unless otherwise limited by court order, parties may obtain discovery regarding any non-privileged matter that is relevant to any party's claim or defense. The request for initiating some type of discovery is contingent upon that party's reasonable belief that she has a good cause of action or defense. A court may order discovery of any matter relevant to the subject matter involved in the patent proceeding. There are a number of different manners for conducting the discovery of material information, with some of the more common manners being: the use of depositions, interrogatories, requests for the production and inspection of writings and other materials, and requests for admission of facts. The FRCP set general limits on the number of each form of discovery a party is entitled to use in the discovery process, although the judge in the case

23. Fed. R. Civ. P. R. 26.

may modify these numbers or the parties could reach agreement on a varied number of a type of discovery.

A. Depositions[24]

A deposition is an oral pretrial examination of a witness who is under oath to respond truthfully to the questions asked of him. A notice of examination by deposition is provided and must identify the particular matters sought to be discovered in the deposition. For example, a list of topics is typically attached to the notice of deposition identifying the topics that will be covered. These topics may be broadly or specifically or defined in the notice of deposition. In response, questioning of the witness is usually restricted to these particular matters. Yet, ultimately the court holds the discretion to specify the scope and extent of the examination. In some jurisdictions, a deponent may be requested or required to bring along documents to refresh his memory and facilitate his testimony. A practitioner should bear in mind that there is a limited number of depositions that a party may seek in a patent proceeding without leave of court.

Many different individuals affiliated in some manner with a patent proceeding may be deposed. Some individuals, experts for the opposing party for example, should always be deposed. Depositions of experts are based upon the initial expert brief and/or rebuttal expert brief prepared and executed (signed) by the expert. Expert witnesses for a deposition differ from factual witnesses because they may opine and provide opinion type testimony in a deposition. In contrast, factual witnesses are limited in their testimony to specific facts to which the witness is personally aware. For common litigation proceedings, a practitioner should appreciate that factual witnesses in the case will undoubtedly include the original inventor(s) of the claimed invention, the individuals involved in the prosecution of the patent through the USPTO, and possibly third-party witnesses.

Finally, another common witness is a Rule 30(b)(6) witness under the Federal Rules of Civil Procedure. If an opposing party is not an individual, the party itself may be named as the deponent. The named entity, for example an opposing party that is a corporation or another organization rather than an individual, must then designate one or more

---

24. Fed. R. Civ. P. R. 27.

officers, directors, or managing agents, or designate other persons who consent to testify on its behalf, and it may set out the matters on which each person designated will testify.

In some instances the testimony of a person or entity may need to be requested using a writ by the court referred to as a subpoena. Attorneys as officers of the court can issue subpoenas ordering witnesses to testify in deposition. In instances where the witness is a 30(b)(6) witness, a subpoena must advise an entity of its duty to make a 30(b)(6) designation. The persons designated by the organization must testify about information known or reasonably available to the organization. The person testifying in a 30(b)(6) deposition is answering questions on behalf of the entity that designated him or her, rather than in their personal capacity. As such, it may be possible that a witness participates twice as a witness, once as a 30(b)(6) witness and once in his or her individual capacity.

B. Interrogatories[25]

Interrogatories are a formal set of specific written questions submitted by a party, pursuant to a discovery order, to an adversary who must respond under oath and in writing, in order to clarify matters of fact and help to determine in advance what facts will be presented at any trial in the case. Similar to as with depositions, there are a limited number of interrogatories that can be provided to another party for answering. An interrogatory should be drafted so as to state the question in a precise manner so as to prompt and require an answer that is pertinent to the issues being litigated. If not, a crafty opposing counsel may be able to properly answer the interrogatory without providing the information the interrogatory was crafted with the hope of obtaining.

C. Production of Documents[26]

Generally a party is entitled to the production and inspection of relevant documents in the possession or control of an opposing party pursuant to discovery. The requesting party must have a reasonable belief that information in the documents is relevant to the issues of the case if discovery is to be granted. A party may serve on any other party a request to produce a number of items in its possession, custody, or control and to

25. Fed. R. Civ. P. R. 33.
26. Fed. R. Civ. P. R. 26.

permit the requesting party to inspect, copy, test, or sample these items. Any designated documents or electronically stored information, including writings, drawings, graphs, charts, photographs, sound recordings, images, and other data or data compilations, stored in any medium from which information can be obtained either directly or, if necessary, after translation by the opposing party into a reasonably usable form may be requested. Any designated tangible things may be requested. A request may be made to permit entry onto designated land or other property possessed or controlled by the opposing party, so that the requesting party may inspect, measure, survey, photograph, test, or sample the property or any designated object or operation on it.

D. Admissions of Facts

Another manner of performing discovery is a request for an admission of facts. A party may ask an opposing party to admit material facts or the authenticity of a document that is to be presented as evidence during the trial. Requests for admission of facts facilitate the administration of the patent proceeding by minimizing the time and expense incurred in proving issues that are not in dispute between the two parties. Facts alone, not matters or conclusions of law or opinions, can be admitted when there is no disagreement between the parties. A response to such a request should admit or deny the request or explain in detail the reason for refusing to comply. Failure to make a response within the specified time results in the matter being admitted, precluding the party from challenging its admission during the trial.

Discovery is not limited to corporate executives, experts, and inventors. Discovery may be sought from third parties that may have no idea as to the importance of the patent proceeding and may not have a vested interest in the outcome. Discovery from third parties may be sought for a number of reasons, such as evidence of products a third party was manufacturing that an allege infringer believes may be prior art to the claimed invention. A moving party may seek to depose the third party in order to gain details into the operation of the third party's product, the sales date of the third party's product, and/or the first public disclosure of the third party's product. Information from third parties may also be useful or persuasive in relation to the damages aspect of the patent litigation, for example, in demonstrating the availability or lack thereof of other entities that could serve as substitutes to the patented product or process. This information may be useful in determining a reasonable royalty for damages purposes.

XV. CLAIM CONSTRUCTION

Every aspect of a patent litigation can be important. Various arguments or positions should be explored for depositions, during trial, while drafting a complaint, and while working with expert and third-party witnesses. However, claim construction may very well be the most influential component in determining the outcome of a litigation proceeding. Though a judge will ultimately decide claim construction disputes, many judges utilize the positions of each side to guide how claim terms should be construed when determining the final claim construction. As such, a practitioner can significantly influence judge's ruling as to how disputed claim terms should be construed. Claim construction can be determinative of two significant positions in a patent proceeding:(1) whether the patent owner has a valid claim, and (2) whether the alleged infringer did in fact infringe the claimed invention. A skilled practitioner representing a patent owner will advocate for a claim construction that reads on the accused infringer's product/method (infringement) and yet does not read on any prior art (valid). Alternatively, a skilled practitioner for an accused infringer will advocate for a claim construction that does not read on the accused infringer's product/method (non-infringement) and/or reads on any prior art (invalid).

If two individuals are given a patent claim to read and interpret, it is not uncommon for the two interpretations of those individuals to be different. For example, one individual may interpret "connected to" as requiring a physical link between two things, while a second individual may interpret the exact same term in the exact same context as merely an operational link, which may be but need not be a physical link, between two things. Due to the technical terms involved and the format of the claim itself, claim construction disputes may arise over both the definition of the technical terms and the semantic interpretation. As part of the process of attempting to resolve or at least narrow the disputes in claim construction, opposing parties are required to exchange a list of disputed claim terms. Any interpretation that is not the "plain and ordinary meaning" may be a disputed claim term.

At a point during the patent litigation the parties will have to submit their respective lists of claim terms that they assert require construction. In generating the list of disputed claim terms, a practitioner should seek to identify both those claim terms that may be identified by the opposing party as needing a claim construction as well as those claim terms that the practitioner's party may need to have construed. An opposing party will seek to have terms construed in a manner to create a strong non-infringement and/or invalidity position, while the patent owner will seek to have terms construed to create a strong infringement and/or validity position. There is a fixed time frame and a fixed number of terms that the court will typically allow to be construed.

Having exchanged the respective list of disputed claim terms, a party must establish a claim construction position for each claim term for construction in its own list, as well as the list from the opposing party. Frequently, claim terms are construed and displayed in claim construction charts. A comprehensive documentation of claim construction positions is created where each disputed term is then construed. A party's expert may be involved in this part of the claim construction process. Claim construction positions are the interpretation that the party seeks the court to adopt with respect to the claim term in dispute. Support for the interpretation also is provided. This support often is based upon the patent itself as well as the prosecution history of the patent and any estoppel that may be relevant. However, a claim construction position for a disputed term may simply be a statement that the party seeks the plain and ordinary meaning of the term and that no other construction of the term is thus needed. At some point in time, the opposing parties will exchange their respective claim construction positions for all disputed terms.

Now, the proposed claim construction positions of the opposing party and corresponding support should be reviewed thoroughly. As previously noted, claim construction positions will often identify how an alleged infringer is going to argue its non-infringement position and/or its invalidity. As such, a thorough review of the claim construction positions of the opposing party is critical.

Following the exchange of the claim construction positions, the parties may be required to provide a joint claim construction statement. A joint claim construction statement is a listing of all disputed terms, with the construction by both sides included therein along with their respective support (citations etc.) for the construction. A joint claim construction statement also may include a listing of previously disputed claim terms that have been resolved. In the exchange of claim construction positions, it may be determined that both parties share the same construction or that the construction proposed by the opposing party does not conflict. Practically this will most often occur as a result of the proposed construction for these terms to be deemed as being non-problematic for each of the respective parties' positions on validity and infringement.

The goal of the listing of disputed claim terms and positions is to be able to provide a specific list of disputed terms with corresponding support for the judge to ultimately rule on in a Markman proceeding.

A. Markman Briefs

Markman briefs are briefs that address the claim constructions that the parties seeks the court to construe in their favor following a Markman hearing.[27] A practitioner preparing an opening Markman brief should provide all facts, evidence, and arguments of the claim construction terms that the parties could not agree about in the construction sought after by the client. The Markman brief is designed to assist the court in resolving the differences in opinion as to the claim construction on one or more terms of the patent. A practitioner should seek to provide the claim construction defined by each party and argue that the claim construction it has proposed is proper, while the claim construction the opposing party has proposed is improper based on the evidence of record. The evidence presented as part of the Markman brief may be based upon the intrinsic record (i.e., the prosecution record of the patent, any admissions by the patent owner, inventors, or others during the trial proceeding) and/or extrinsic evidence (i.e., evidence from expert witnesses, where the evidence itself is not in the record, such as by an expert in the field of technology).

Conversely, a reply Markman brief seeks to provide a proper construction factoring in the construction provided by the other party. A reply Markman brief seeks to clarify errors by the other party in its Markman brief and/or to seek construction of a term or phrase only included by the opposing counsel in its opening Markman brief.

B. Markman Hearing

Based upon the Markman briefs, a Markman hearing will be held. A Markman hearing is a pretrial hearing in a U.S. District Court during which the judge examines evidence from all parties on the appropriate meanings of words and/or phrases used in a patent claim. The Markman hearing is commonly referred to as a claim construction hearing.

27. Markman hearings and associated briefs are so referenced because of the Supreme Court case finding that claim construction is an issue of law rather than an issue of fact. Markman v. Westview Instruments, Inc., 517 U,S. 370 (1996).

The need and ruling of a Markman hearing is rather simple. The language of a patent claim is a matter of law for a judge to decide, not a matter of fact for a jury to decide. As such, a judge must determine the eventual construction of the claims and may take into account the Markman briefs of the parties, evidence provided during the Markman hearing, and recommendations of a special master appointed by the judge. A special master is an individual, often an experienced patent litigator, who will oversee some aspects of the litigation on behalf of the judge and will make recommendations to the judge. A special master may be in charge of overseeing the Markman hearing and making a proposed final determination of claim construction. A special master may have more knowledge of the technical subject matter involved and often may be agreed upon or selected in advance by the opposing parties.

The court's ruling in patent infringement cases is often driven by the interpretation of the claims. Therefore, a Markman hearing, and/or the claim construction that results, may encourage settlement, since the claim construction finding of the judge may indicate or predict a likely outcome for the patent infringement case as a whole. Markman hearings are conducted before a judge, and generally take place before the trial. A Markman hearing may occur before the close of discovery or at the end of discovery. A Markman hearing also may be held after the trial begins, but before jury selection.

The evidence considered in a Markman hearing falls into two categories: intrinsic and extrinsic evidence. Intrinsic evidence consists of the patent documentation and any prosecution history of the patent. It is said to be the evidence internal to the record, i.e., the documents associated with the prosecution of the patent. Extrinsic evidence is testimony, expert opinion, or other unwritten sources beyond the patent itself. Extrinsic evidence may not contradict intrinsic evidence, but it may elaborate into more detail or provide additional examples for someone to understand the extrinsic evidence.

XVI. EXPERT DISCOVERY[28]

Many believe that the findings and testimony of an expert ultimately will determine, or at least carry significant weight with regard to, the outcome of a patent litigation. Patent matters are highly technical in nature. The underlying technology that the claimed invention covers may re-

28. Fed. R. Civ. P. R. 26.

quire significant education and technical expertise to appreciate and elaborate on the nuances. Traipsing through the muck of technical jargon and flow diagrams, an expert witness can be the key component in assisting others (especially a judge or jury) in understanding the technology, appreciating the invention, and identifying the existing prior art and the impact it has, if any, on the claimed invention. The findings and testimony of expert witnesses may be the major basis on which a judge or jury will decide the outcome of a case.

An expert witness is retained by a party during a litigation to provide her opinion on matters based upon her educational background, experience, and other factors. Standard witnesses in a litigation proceeding can only provide factual testimony. Expert witnesses are different in that they may provide both factual testimony and opinion testimony. A practitioner should appreciate that the designation of expert to a witness requires more than just a title by a party. An expert must be "qualified" before a court will recognize any of his testimony in the litigation proceeding. To qualify that someone is an expert, a practitioner needs to establish the educational background of the expert with respect to the claimed invention, the experiences of the expert with respect to the claimed invention, and the basis upon which the witness should be recognized by the court as an expert.

A party may utilize more than one expert in a litigation proceeding. Different experts may be utilized for opinions on infringement or non-infringement, validity or invalidity, enforceability or unenforceability, and damages. Expertise in one area, the technology of the claimed invention, may not be suited to also provide expert opinion on the calculation of the amount of damages to which a patent owner may be entitled.

One of the major contributions that an expert will make in a litigation proceeding is an initial expert report. Unless otherwise stipulated or ordered by the court, for any testimony that may be used or relied upon in the trial proceeding, an expert must prepare a written report that the expert prepares and signs. The report must contain a number of items: a complete statement of all opinions the witness will express and the basis and reasons for them; the facts or data considered by the witness in forming them; any exhibits that will be used to summarize or support them; the witness's qualifications, including a list of all publications authored in the previous ten years; a list of all other cases in which, during the previous four years; that the witness testified as an expert at trial or by deposition; and a statement of the compensation to be paid for the study and testimony in the case.

With respect to the expert report, it should be ensured that all the requirements are met and that a clear basis for all testimony that the expert may provide can be tied to a portion or portions of the expert report for support in testifying on the same. An expert cannot give an opinion during trial that is not supported in detail in an expert report. An initial expert report often will be very lengthy and will require some time to prepare and refine before filing in the court and providing a copy to the opposing party. The preparation of an expert report will take significant time and effort.

An expert's initial report will be based upon the outcome of the Markman hearing and the determination of claim constructions for the asserted claims as the expert will utilize the claim construction of the court in opining on issues of validity and infringement. An expert is bound by the claim construction that the court issues in response to the Markman briefs and hearing. For any claim terms that the court does not construe, the expert can provide her opinion as to the ordinary meaning or understood meaning of the claim term.

Should the opposing party have an expert provide an initial expert report, there is an opportunity to prepare and file a rebuttal expert report. The rebuttal expert report is restricted to rebut the testimony and opinions that the initial expert report from the opposing party provided. A rebuttal expert report cannot include a new argument that had not been addressed in the initial report of the opposing party's expert. The idea of the rebuttal expert report is to allow each party a last opportunity to clarify any issues and counter the arguments or positions that the opposing party's expert has concerning any subject matter raised in the opposing party's initial expert report.

XVII. PRIVILEGE LOG[29]

A privilege log is a legal mechanism for describing documents or other items that a party stipulates is being withheld from production in a civil lawsuit under claims of attorney-client privilege, work product doctrine, or trade secrets. Generally, the burden falls on the withholding party to provide sufficient information on the privilege log to allow the opposing party or court to review and potentially test the claim of privilege. In situations in which an opposing party seeks leave of the district court to test the claim of privilege to one or more documents or items, the presid-

29. FED. R. CIV. P. R. 26.

ing judge may seek in camera review of the contested documents or items to decide whether the claim of privilege is proper or whether the opposing party should have access to the documents or items.

XVIII. MOTIONS IN LIMINE

Another tool that may be utilized during a trial proceeding is motions in limine, which are requests for a court to decide whether specific evidence may or may not be presented to a jury at a trial. Such a motion may address issues that would be prejudicial for the jury to hear in court, even if the opposing side makes a timely objection that is sustained, and the judge instructs the jury to disregard the evidence. If a motion in limine to deny entry of evidence is granted, then the evidence could not be presented in front of the jury, without first approaching the judge outside of the hearing range of the jury and obtaining the proper permission to present. In another case, if a motion in limine to allow entry of evidence is granted, then the evidence could be presented in front of the jury. A violation of a motion in limine order by the judge can result in the court declaring a mistrial.

There are three types of motions in limine: an inclusionary motion in limine seeks the court to have something included in the trial; an exclusionary motion in limine seeks the court to have something excluded in the trial, e.g., excluded as the court has ultimately determined inadmissibility; and a preclusionary motion in limine seeks the court to have something precluded in the trial, e.g., excluded until the court has ultimately determined admissibility. A practitioner should remember that both sides may file opposing motions in limine on the same evidentiary topic and that every piece of evidence may be subject to a motion in limine request by the opposing party.

XIX. *DAUBERT* MOTIONS

A *Daubert* motion is a specific type of motion in limine. A *Daubert* motion may be filed before or during trial to exclude the presentation of unqualified evidence to a jury. A *Daubert* motion is used to exclude the testimony of an expert witness who does not possess the requisite level of expertise or used questionable methods to obtain data. Rule 702 of the Federal Rules of Civil Procedure was amended to include additional provisions that state that a witness may only testify if the testimony is based upon sufficient facts or data, the testimony is the product of reliable principles and methods, and the witness has applied the principles and methods reliably to the facts of the case.

XX. SUMMARY JUDGMENT MOTIONS[30]

Summary judgment motions are motions by either party requesting the court to summarily enter judgment for one party and against the other party, i.e., without a full trial. Summary judgment motions are based upon the available evidence taken in the light most favorable to the non-moving party. A motion for summary judgment contends that in such situations, a ruling in favor of the moving party is supported. In most jurisdictions, for summary judgment to be granted, no genuine issue of material fact can be in dispute between the parties, and the moving party must be entitled to judgment as a matter of law.

XXI. FINAL PRETRIAL CONFERENCE[31]

Rule 16(e) of the Federal Rules of Civil Procedure specifies the requirement for a final pretrial conference. The court may hold a final pretrial conference to formulate a trial plan, including a plan to facilitate the admission of evidence. The conference must be held as close to the start of trial as is reasonable, and must be attended by at least one attorney who will conduct the trial for each party and by any unrepresented party. The court may modify the order issued after a final pretrial conference only to prevent manifest injustice.

XXII. PRETRIAL DISCLOSURES[32]

Pretrial disclosure requirements are requirements of the Federal Rules of Civil Procedure to provide to the court and the opposing party certain information regarding the evidence that it may present at trial. In general, the parties must disclose the following information.

First, the name and, if not previously provided, the address and telephone number of each witness, separately identifying those whom the party expects to present and those whom the party may call if the need arises must be provided.

30. Fed. R. Civ. P. R. 56.
31. Fed. R. Civ. P. R. 16(e).
32. Fed. R. Civ. P. R. 26(a)(3).

Second, the designation of those witnesses whose testimony is expected to be presented by means of a deposition and, if not taken stenographically, a transcript of the pertinent portions of the deposition testimony must be provided.

Finally, an appropriate identification of each document or other exhibit, including summaries of other evidence, separately identifying those which the party expects to offer and those which the party may offer if the need arises must be provided.

XXIII. TRIAL[33]

The vast majority of patent proceedings that are filed in court never result in a civil trial. Whether due to the anticipated cost of the trial or the final claim construction determinations made by the court, parties in a patent proceeding more likely than not will settle prior to trial. However, patent litigation trials do occur. Civil trials follow a rigid process of events when attempting to reach a verdict. Following the pre-trial discovery period and a continued inability of the opposing parties to reach a settlement, the parties will be afforded their opportunities to present their contentions before a judge (or judge and jury) in a civil trial.

In a patent litigation, a jury, in a jury trial, may make a decision or make findings of fact which are then applied by a judge. In a bench trial, a judge makes all the decisions. Should a jury trial be requested, the jury selection process must be commenced to determine the men and women who will hear the case. The jury selection process is often conducted under voir dire, i.e., the process by which prospective jurors are questioned about their backgrounds and potential biases before being chosen to sit for a jury trial.

It is important to understand the difference in issues of law and issues of fact in patent litigations and who makes decisions regarding them. In a bench trial, the judge will make all determinations on issues of fact and issues of law. However, for a jury trial, the process is different. An issue of law must be addressed by applying relevant legal principles, i.e., by an interpretation of the law. This is distinct from an issue of fact, which must be addressed by reference to facts and evidence, and inferences arising from those facts. Issues of law generally are addressed in terms of broad legal principles, and they are capable of being applied to many situations, rather than being dependent on particular circumstances or factual situations. Issues of fact are resolved by a trier of fact. There-

33. Fed. R. Civ. P. Title VI.

fore, in a jury trial, the jury will address all issues of fact, and the judge will address all issues of law. Whether a bench trial or a jury trial, a judge always addresses issues of law.

In the context of a patent proceeding, claim construction is an issue of law and thus is ultimately determined by a judge. Alternatively, a determination whether a prior art reference anticipates a claimed invention or a determination whether a defendant's product infringes a claimed invention is an issue of fact, and therefore ruling is made by a judge in a bench trial and a jury in a jury trial.

The sequence of events that may occur in a patent trial can vary, but certain events are among the more common events. Following any pretrial evidentiary rulings, the parties will give their respective opening statements. The plaintiff, patent owner, will lead with the opening statement to frame the case of infringement that the plaintiff alleges the defendant has and/or is committing patent infringement. The defendant may follow with its own opening statement.

Following the opening statements, the plaintiff will present its contentions and supporting evidence against the defendant. The plaintiff presents its case in accordance with the final claim construction determination made by the court. A plaintiff often will utilize one or more of its experts. As part of the presentation of the case for the plaintiff, the plaintiff may utilize direct examination of witnesses to support its contentions of infringement of the claimed invention. In response, the defendant may utilize cross-examination of the same witnesses to attempt to poke holes in the contentions or positions of the plaintiff.

Following the conclusion of the presentation of evidence by the plaintiff, and prior to initiating the presentation of evidence by the defendant, dismissal motions, often by both parties, are presented to the court. A plaintiff may seek to have the court rule to dismiss the defendant's motion for summary judgment while a defendant may seek to have the court rule to dismiss plaintiff's case all together.

Following these motions, the defendant will be provided the opportunity to present its contentions and evidence supporting the same. Like the plaintiff, a defendant presents its case in accordance with the final claim construction determination made by the court. As part of the presentation of its case, the defendant may utilize direct examination of witnesses to support its contentions of non-infringement and/or invalidity of the claimed invention. In response, the plaintiff may utilize cross-examination of the same witnesses to attempt to poke holes in the contentions or positions of the defendant.

Upon conclusion of the presentation of evidence by the defendant, a plaintiff is afforded the opportunity to rebut certain contentions made by the defendants in its presentation of evidence. Specifically, those contentions that were first raised by the defendants may be rebutted by the plaintiffs. This most often occurs in the context of rebutting a contention that the plaintiff's patent is invalid. The plaintiff may present an expert on the subject matter of the alleged invalidity to bolster evidence as to the validity of the patent.

Following the conclusion of the rebuttal by the plaintiff, and prior to closing argument, more dismissal motions, often by both parties, are presented to the court. This is followed by the closing arguments by the defendant and by the plaintiff. A closing argument often sums up the evidence presented and asks the trier of fact to render a decision as to infringement/non-infringement or a defense in that party's favor. Some experienced litigators will suggest that effective case presentations tell the story of the case, as such, the opening and closing statements will serve as the introduction and the conclusion respectively of that story. Jury instructions follow and then the case is sent to the jury, or in the case of a bench trial, the judge. Finally, the trier of fact will make a determination as to the allegations of the plaintiff and the contentions and defenses of the defendant, thus rendering a final outcome.

XXIV. POST-TRIAL MOTIONS[34]

Aside from the appeal process, there are several post-trial motions that a practitioner should be aware, especially following the conclusion of a trial at a district court. These post-trial motions may need to be filed to preserve rights for appeal or to seek special requests.

One such post-trial motion that may be sought is a motion for a new trial. The moving party may file a motion for a new trial due to the expected outcome of the trial and due to one or more circumstances that, in its opinion, affected the viable outcome of the trial.

Another post-trial motion is a renewed motion for judgment as a matter of law (JMOL). If a party has been fully heard on an issue during a jury trial and the court finds that a reasonable jury would not have a legally sufficient evidentiary basis to find for the party on that issue, the court may resolve the issue against the party, and grant a motion for judgment as a matter of law against the party on a claim or defense that, under the controlling law, can be maintained or defeated only with a

34. Fed. R. Civ. P. Title VII.

favorable finding on that issue. A motion for judgment as a matter of law may be made at any time before the case is submitted to the jury. The motion must specify the judgment sought and the law and facts that entitle the movant to the judgment.

If the court does not grant a motion for judgment as a matter of law, the court is considered to have submitted the action to the jury subject to the court's later deciding the legal questions raised by the motion. The movant may file a renewed motion for judgment as a matter of law and may include an alternative or joint request for a new trial. In ruling on the renewed motion, the court may allow judgment on the verdict, if the jury returned a verdict, order a new trial, or direct the entry of judgment as a matter of law.

Finally, a motion for attorneys' fees pursuant to 35 U.S.C. §285 may be sought. The awarding of attorney's fees is only found in exceptional cases.

XXV. APPEAL

Following a final decision of a U.S. district court in a patent proceeding, appeals to the U.S. Court of Appeals for the Federal Circuit[35] are an automatic right assuming all procedural requirements are satisfied. Since passage of the Federal Courts Improvement Act of 1982, the U.S. Court of Appeals for the Federal Circuit handles all patent appeals from all U.S. district courts.[36] Any decision not in favor of a party may be appealed to the U.S. Court of Appeals for the Federal Circuit. Thus, some issues may be appealed by the patent owner while other issues may be appealed by the accused defendant. The vast majority of patent cases that are appealed have final decisions rendered by the U.S. Court of Appeals for the Federal Circuit as the last decisions.

Following the appeal through the U.S. Court of Appeals for the Federal Circuit, appeals to the U.S. Supreme Court may be sought, but the right of appeal is not automatic. The U.S. Supreme Court has the right to pick and choose the cases it reviews. As such, a would-be appellant seeking appeal of a matter before the U.S. Supreme Court must file a writ of certiorari. A petition for certiorari seeks Supreme Court review not as a matter of right, but as a matter of judicial discretion. Should a patent case reach the Supreme Court, any decision of the Court is final.

---

35. http://www.cafc.uscourts.gov/.

36. 28 U.S.C. §1295 (http://www.federalcircuithistoricalsociety.org/historyofcourt.html).

Section 3

Trademarks, Trade Dress, Unfair Competition, and Trade Secrets

PART 1

Trademarks Groundwork

In real life, unlike in Shakespeare, the sweetness of the rose depends upon the name it bears. Things are not only what they are. They are, in very important respects, what they seem to be.

—Hubert H. Humphrey
Vice President of the United States (1965–1969)

I. BACKGROUND AND RATIONALE

Trademarks are generally grouped with patents and copyrights to form the "big three" types of intellectual property. Since patent and copyright laws in the United States emanate from Article I, Section 8, clause 8 of the Constitution, it may be surprising that the constitutional basis for trademarks and related forms of intellectual property is Article I, Section 8, clause 3, or the "Commerce Clause" as it is more commonly known, a provision distinct from the provision from which patent and copyright protections are derived. The Commerce Clause gives Congress the power "to regulate commerce with foreign nations, and among the several states, and with the Indian tribes." This distinct constitutional basis for trademark protection as compared to patent and copyright protection contributes to the variations in the rights associated with these varied forms of intellectual property, the motivation behind these intellectual property rights, and the implementation of these protections.

First, the motivation and rationale behind trademarks and related intellectual property is not "promotion of progress in science and the useful arts" but rather *regulation of commerce*. To this end, the focus of trademarks is ensuring that commerce is carried out in a manner desired by the Congress of the United States. This preferred manner can theoretically change over time and from Congress to Congress. The general purposes and goals of the trademark system are often described as a *quality control* function that helps consumers have confidence in their purchases. A merchant's seal or mark is her authentic seal by which she vouches for the goods that bear it. It carries her name for good or ill. If another borrows that seal, he borrows the owner's reputation whose quality no longer lies within her control. Buyers can rely on that seal as an indicator of the quality of the goods that bear that mark. In practical terms, if a company makes sporting goods that are known for their innovative technology, durability, and quality, consumers come to look for goods made by that company. As such, trademarks serve as simple and reliable way to facilitate consumer purchases such that consumers can trust in purchases based upon the marks and companies for which they represent. If others were permitted to "take" or "imitate" the mark, then purchasers would not be able to make purchases with the same level of confidence and commerce may be stifled to the detriment of the economy.

Second, trademark and related rights may extend on in seeming perpetuity. While the constitutional clause that gives rise to patent and copyright laws (Art. I §8 cl. 8) explicitly sets forth that these rights be for only "Limited Times," the Commerce Clause has no such language. Theoretically, it would not violate the Constitution should trademark rights (or any other right based in the Commerce Clause) continue on into general perpetuity. The trademark rights of some very valuable trademarks, such as Coca-Cola®, have been in existence for long periods of time and can continue in existence for seemingly as long as they are not abandoned or otherwise relinquished. However, patents and copyrights have specific "limited" terms of duration.

A third distinction between patent and copyrights as compared to trademarks is the existence of state laws that governed trademarks and related intellectual property in addition to the federal system of protection. Patents and copyrights are solely protected under a federal system, but trademarks may be protected under federal law as well as state law/common law. While the corporate entity Burger King is now well known throughout the U.S., the corporate entity was not the most senior owner of the mark nationwide. A family-owned burger stand (Hoots family) was the senior user of the name Burger King in Mattoon, Illinois, and registered the name with the state of Illinois prior to corporate Burger

King's federal registration. After the federal registration by the corporate entity, the Hootses began opening more Illinois locations, and eventually corporate Burger King and the Hoots Burger King met head-on. It was held that while the Hootses retained rights in the Burger King trademark immediately surrounding the initial location, corporate Burger King, with its federal registration, owned rights virtually everywhere else in the nation, including parts of Illinois outside the area surrounding the Hootses' original location. While entities may acquire state/common-law trademark rights, federal trademark rights under the Lanham Act and vested by federal registration provide significantly more comprehensive coverage across the country.[1]

Despite various distinctions between patents and trademarks, the United States Patent and Trademark Office, a bureau of the U.S. Department of Commerce, is given administrative responsibility relating to the procurement of federal trademarks and patents. The Copyright Office is the exception in this "group of three," as it is a department of the Library of Congress—an assisting agency to the U.S. Congress.[2]

II. TYPES OF MARKS

It is not uncommon for the term "trademark" to be used in everyday vernacular, and even in intellectual property discussions, to refer generally to any of the various types of marks described in further detail below. For example, marks that are more properly classified as "service marks" will frequently be called "trademarks." While use of the term "trademark" to generally refer to all marks is not a grievous error, using proper terminology when discussing various marks will promote a better understanding of the protection associated with the marks and will also provide enhanced credibility to the practitioner and her arguments in representation.

A. *Trademarks*

A trademark is any word, name, symbol, or design, or any combination thereof, used (or intended to be used) in commerce to identify and distinguish the *goods* of one manufacturer or seller from those of another and to indicate the source of the *goods*.[3] Examples of trademarks that are

1. Burger King of Florida, Inc. v. Hoots, 403 F.2d 904 (7th Cir. 1968).
2. http://www.copyright.gov/circs/circ1a.html.
3. 15 U.S.C. §1127.

familiar to many include NIKE® for athletic shoes, GAP® for clothing, and FERRARI® for automobiles.

B. Service Marks

A service mark is any word, name, symbol, or device, or any combination thereof, used (or intended to be used) in commerce to identify and distinguish the *services* of one service provider from those of another and to indicate the source of the *services*. UNITED® for an airline and FEDEX® for delivery services are examples of service marks.

C. Collective Marks

A collective mark is any trademark or service mark used (or intended to be used) in commerce by the *members of a cooperative, an association, or other collective group or organization*, and includes marks indicating membership in a union, an association, or other organization. Examples of collective marks or collective trademarks include UNITED AUTO WORKERS (UAW), GIRL SCOUTS OF AMERICA, FLORISTS' TRANSWORLD DELIVERY (FTD), and AMERICAN FEDERATION OF LABOR AND CONGRESS OF INDUSTRIAL ORGANIZATIONS (AFL-CIO).

D. Certification Marks

A certification mark is any word, name, symbol, or device, or any combination thereof, used (or intended to be used) to *certify the regional or other origin, material, mode of manufacture, quality, accuracy, or other characteristics* of the goods or services or that the work or labor on the goods or services was performed by members of a union or other organization. Certification marks includes UNDERWRITERS LABORATORIES and GOOD HOUSEKEEPING SEAL OF APPROVAL.

E Trade Dress

Trade dress is a term of art referring generally to the visual appearance of a product, packaging, or the like that signifies the source of the product to consumers. Trade dress may include features such as size, shape, color or color combinations, texture, graphics, or even particular sales techniques.[4] It may be helpful to remember that the visual

4. John J. Harland Co. v. Clarke Checks, Inc., 711 F.2d 966, 980 (11th Cir. 1983).

impression created by trade dress functions in the same manner as other marks, including word marks. Trade dress may be characterized as the "clothing of the product or service," and accordingly its visual impression creates a commercial impression associated with the source of origin. Among the examples of items considered to be trade dress have been furniture, automobile, and bottle shapes; colors and shapes of pill capsules; the colors of insulation; the shapes of buildings; and even restaurant décor/motif. Two issues—functionality and distinctiveness—are frequently important in resolution of most trade dress matters, especially if the owner of the trade dress wishes to register or enforce the purported trade dress as a mark.

Functionality: Only nonfunctional designs and products are eligible for federal or common-law trade dress protection. A product or its respective shape or configuration will be considered functional if it is essential to the use or purpose of the product/design, if it affects the cost or quality of the product/design, or if it puts competitors at a significant disadvantage beyond the competitive advantage associated with corporate good will, trademarks, and corporate recognition. For example, if a product must be shaped a certain way because that is the only way it can be shaped to serve the functional purpose for which it is designed, the shape of that product is unlikely to be protectable as a mark under trade dress law, since the product's shape will likely be deemed to be functional. Evidence of a utility patent covering the product and its functional features can in many cases be strong evidence undermining an application for trade dress protection.[5] Even evidence on a company's website touting various functional features of a product for which trade dress protection is desired can often destroy a claim for trade dress protection.

Distinctiveness: To be eligible for federal statutory or common-law protection, a purported trade dress must be considered "distinctive." The purported trade dress must serve as a source indicator to consumers. In certain instances the shape or configuration of a product itself can create an association between that product, shape, or configuration and a source in the mind of the consumer, and therefore these features will be considered trade dress. While product packaging in some instances can be deemed "inherently distinctive" and thus eligible for protection as trade dress from its very initial use in commerce, shape or configuration of the

5. Trademark examining attorneys will search for these patents and or request them from an applicant.

product itself must have *acquired* a certain further level of distinctiveness known as "secondary meaning" so as to be associated in the public's mind with the producer or source of the product in order to be protectable as a mark. A product shape or configuration will have acquired "secondary meaning" if the product shape or configuration is so well known or recognized that the consumers link the product shape or configuration with its source. In order for a product shape or configuration to acquire secondary meaning practically, the product will typically have a significant presence in the market including presence for an extended period of time and/or in large volumes. This distinction between trade dress protection for "product packaging" and "product shape or configuration" represents a nuance of trade dress law in which the varied forms of trade dress will require varied eligibility requirements for protection and eventual enforcement.

III. USE (AND INTENDED USE) IN COMMERCE

Federal trademark laws originate from the Commerce Clause; therefore, use or intended use in interstate commerce is a critical aspect of federal trademark jurisdiction. Without actions relating to interstate commerce, federal rights in the mark would not be established. Additionally, use in commerce is also required for a cause of action to exist against an accused infringer or accused wrongdoer.

Use in Commerce: Use in commerce of the mark must be a bona fide use of the mark in the ordinary course of trade and not made merely to reserve the rights in the mark.[6] With respect to the federal trademark

6. 15 U.S.C. §1127 ("The term 'use in commerce' means the bona fide use of a mark in the ordinary course of trade, and not made merely to reserve a right in a mark. For purposes of this chapter, a mark shall be deemed to be in use in commerce—

(1) on goods when—

(A) it is placed in any manner on the goods or their containers or the displays associated therewith or on the tags or labels affixed thereto, or if the nature of the goods makes such placement impracticable, then on documents associated with the goods or their sale, and

(B) the goods are sold or transported in commerce, and

(2) on services when it is used or displayed in the sale or advertising of services and the services are rendered in commerce, or the services are rendered in more than one State or in the United States and a foreign country and the person rendering the services is engaged in commerce in connection with the services.").

system, "use in commerce" and thus congressional regulation in the form of the federal trademark laws requires either interstate commerce (between two or more states) or commerce between the United States (e.g., any state) and another country. Intrastate commerce—actions wholly within a single state—may not give rise to federal jurisdiction. However, these actions may give rise to state or common-law trademark jurisdiction, rights, and causes of action in that state. A mark will be "used in commerce" for goods if the mark is apparent on the goods, the container for the goods, or displays associated with the goods. Similarly, for services, the mark will be "used in commerce" if the mark is used or displayed in the sale or advertising of the services. Again, these goods must also be sold or transported "in commerce" and the services likewise must be provided "in commerce."

Intent-to-Use: While actual use in commerce is the requisite action for federal trademark rights to vest, an intent-to-use application may be filed with the USPTO based upon bona fide or "good faith" intent to use the mark in commerce. Therefore, mechanisms exist for beginning the process of establishing trademark rights before the trademark is actually used in commerce. In essence, the applicant intends to use the mark in commerce after applying for federal registration. Depending on when the trademark is used in commerce, certain actions to amend the application or certify the registration may be taken during prosecution of an application for federal registration of a mark. See *Trademark Prosecution Section.*

IV. FORMS OF MARKS

While there are various types of marks (e.g., trademark or service mark) as described above, these may come in a variety of forms. Below are listed various forms of marks as well as examples of these forms.

Words, Letters, or Numbers: JENGA, G.E., 7-UP
Slogans: JUST DO IT for Nike; WHERE DO YOU WANT TO GO TODAY? for Microsoft
Designs: MR. PEANUT; MONOPOLY man
Color: ROBIN EGG BLUE for Tiffany & Co boxes; PINK for Owens-Corning; BROWN for United Parcel Service (UPS)
Product Shapes: GAMEBOY game console
Product Container Shapes: MRS. BUTTERWORTH bottle; COCA-COLA bottle

Building Appearance: McDONALD'S restaurant; FLATIRON BUILDING in New York City
Sounds: NBC chimes, MONDAY NIGHT FOOTBALL song, HARLEY-DAVIDSON engine
Fragrances: specific CHERRY SCENT[7] and BUBBLE GUM SCENT[8]

It is important to remember that trademarks and other marks should be considered in relation to the goods, products, and/or services associated with those marks. As such, an owner of trademark rights owns rights in a mark for certain categories of goods or services. For example, a car maker may own a mark that relates to a model of automobiles but may not own rights in use of the same or similar mark with arguably unrelated goods, such as chocolate candies. Generally, trademark rights are tied to particular categories of goods and services and other related goods and services for which there would likely be confusion caused by use of the mark. However, certain marks may be so recognizable and pervasive that use of that mark with virtually any other good may be impermissible. Even if the use does not directly infringe the mark, use of the same mark may be impermissible because it would "dilute" the mark. Discussions of dilution, famous marks, and trademark infringement are described in further detail in later sections.

V. SPECTRUM OF DISTINCTIVENESS

Not all marks are created equal. While the strength or value of trademarks are not static and certainly are not forever tied to the initial distinctiveness of the mark, trademarks may be categorized in one of five legally recognized categories of distinctiveness based upon the mark and its relation to the goods or services for which it serves as a mark. The more distinctive a mark, the easier it is to demonstrate it is deserving of protection as a mark. Likewise, the less distinctive a mark, the harder it is to demonstrate it is deserving of protection as a mark.

There are five generally recognized categories of marks listed below in order of decreasing distinctiveness: (1) fanciful or coined, (2) arbi-

7. Reg. No. 2,463,044—"cherry scent" for "synthetic lubricants for high performance racing and recreational vehicles."

8. Reg. No. 2,560,618—"bubble gum scent" for "oil based metal cutting fluid and oil based removal fluid for industrial metal working."

trary, (3) suggestive, (4) descriptive, and (5) generic.[9] Specific categorization involves a somewhat subjective analysis. Also, it is imperative to remember that the distinctiveness of the mark may vary significantly according to the good or service for which the mark is being used. While the mark SALTY brand pretzels might be categorized as a "descriptive" mark, SALTY brand computers may be seen as significantly more distinctive and characterized as an "arbitrary" mark.

Figure 3-1
Spectrum of Distinctiveness

(most distinctive/strongest)	**Fanciful/Coined** **Arbitrary** **Suggestive**	Inherently Distinctive
↓	**Descriptive** (must acquire "secondary meaning") **Generic** (not protectable as a mark)	NOT Inherently Distinctive
(least distinctive/weakest)		

A. *Fanciful/Coined*

Fanciful or coined marks involve terms with no independent meaning and may be coined for the sole purpose of functioning as a mark. Fanciful or coined marks are new or made up words, acronyms, or images. KODAK® is an example of a fanciful or coined mark, as prior to its use in association with film and photography-related products of the company bearing the mark, KODAK had no meaning to someone hearing or reading the term. When considering the policy of trademarks, the more distinctive the mark, the more protection it is afforded. Therefore, it makes sense that marks that have no other meaning other than as a trademark (fanciful/coined marks) are inherently the strongest or most protectable type of mark. XEROX® is yet another example of a fanciful/coined mark, which is discussed further below.

9. Trademark-inherent distinctiveness classifications for trademark were originally set forth by Judge Friendly in *Abercrombie & Fitch Co. v. Hunting World, Inc.*, 537 F.2d 4, 9 (2d Cir. 1976); *see also* TMEP §1209.01.

B. Arbitrary

Arbitrary marks involve terms with a common meaning, but this meaning is unrelated to the goods or services for which the terms serve as a mark. A classic example of this type of trademark is APPLE® for computers. Forrest Gump provided a memorable illustration to facilitate understanding of arbitrary marks when he states, "Lieutenant Dan got me invested in some kind of fruit company." Forrest is, of course, referring to APPLE® computers—a computer and electronics company that most certainly is not a fruit company. The term "apple" had a common meaning prior to the computer company's use, and thus use of the apple for computers provides an arbitrary mark, since apples had no relation to computers prior to use as a mark for a company.

C. Suggestive

Suggestive marks involve terms that impart some quality, feature, characteristic, or purpose of the product or service for which the mark is used. Such a mark may also be described as "allusive." Suggestive marks require some imagination, thought, and perspective to reach a conclusion as to the nature of the goods. The consumer or observer is required to make at least a subtle leap in thought. Stated another way, suggestive marks "suggest" something about the goods or services being offered, but they do not come right out and describe the services. Examples of suggestive marks include COPPERTONE® for sunscreen and lotion, GREYHOUND® for transportation service, and PLAYBOY® for a magazine.

D. Descriptive

Descriptive marks involve terms that immediately describe some quality, feature, characteristic, or purpose of the product or service for which the mark is used. Unlike fanciful/coined, arbitrary, and suggestive marks, descriptive marks are not deemed to be inherently distinctive and require a showing that the mark has "acquired distinctiveness" in order for it to be eligible for protection. Rationale for this requirement is rooted in concerns that permitting entities to exclusively protect marks that merely describe the characteristics of the goods and/or services provided would unduly inhibit competition. Practically, these types of marks often also are not initially viewed as source indicators by the public, and cannot function as a trademark. Examples of marks deemed descriptive but that have acquired secondary meaning so as to receive federal registration include AMERICA ONLINE® for an Internet service provider, RAISIN BRAN® for a cereal, or BANK OF TEXAS® for a bank in Texas.

From a practical perspective, the line between descriptive and suggestive marks may be fuzzy at best. However, from a legal perspective, the categorization of these marks may be the critical issue between a company possessing a valid trademark that is being infringed and not having a trademark at all. This is because marks that are deemed descriptive *require* a showing that the mark has acquired "secondary meaning" as compared to suggestive marks, which are inherently distinctive and protectable as a mark from their initial use in commerce without any showing of having acquired "secondary meaning." As such, the categorization of the mark may seem like semantics in the business world, but it may be critical for protection of the mark from a legal perspective. Entities familiar with trademark law, when considering new marks that could be deemed descriptive or suggestive, may take preemptive action to nudge a mark into the suggestive category whenever possible to increase the chances the mark will be protectable without having to show "secondary meaning," a showing that can sometimes be difficult and costly during enforcement actions.

E. Generic

Generic marks involve terms that name a category of product or service and thus cannot properly function as a trademark. One rationale explaining why marks deemed generic should not be protected as marks is the belief that no manufacturer or service provider should have an exclusive right to use words that generically identify a product or service. The public is best served by these terms remaining in the public domain and available for free and public use. For example, a new airline could not protect the term AIRLINE as its mark. It is easy to predict the confusion consumers would likely encounter as well as the difficulty other airlines would encounter in doing business if one airline were to have exclusive rights to use of the term AIRLINE. It would be difficult to impossible for a generic term to serve as a source indicator and thus trademark protections is not afforded such terms.

Unlike descriptive marks, generic terms may not become protectable as trademarks even if one could show the mark has acquired "secondary meaning." As such, even if it could be shown that the term AIRLINE has acquired "secondary meaning" by showing that the term was so intertwined with one particular airline service provider that consumers almost universally associated AIRLINE with only that particular airline, this mark could not be protected because it is "generic." However, if the same mark were to be deemed a descriptive mark rather than a generic mark, then the mark could be protectable if it were shown that "secondary meaning" was acquired.

Generally, marks that become pervasive in society are extremely strong. Sometimes marks that become too pervasive in essence become too much of a good thing. If marks are misused by the public and become synonymous with a good, they may cease to serve as a brand and be regarded as the name of a category of products. This process of a trademark or service mark or the like becoming generic is referred to as *genericide*. Classic examples of terms that have fallen victim to genericide are ASPIRIN and CELLOPHANE. Aspirin was registered as a trademark by Bayer on March 6, 1899. Over time, Bayer (and a purchaser of the trademark Sterling Drug) was unable to prevent competitors from copying the formula for aspirin (acetylsalicyclic acid) and using the name in a variety of manners. The public no longer recognized a single manufacturer for aspirin. In 1921, with the market flooded, a U.S. federal court ruled ASPIRIN to be a genericized trademark.[10]

Some companies have looked to the Aspirin story and have taken steps to prevent their brands from suffering the same fate as Aspirin when the public begins misusing their marks. Brands that are often cited as examples, having come close to becoming generic due to the public's misuse of the brand's name, include XEROX, KLEENEX, Q-TIP, and WAVERUNNER. Companies such as Kleenex and Xerox have taken active steps through advertising to remind the public that XEROX is a brand of copy machine and that KLEENEX is a brand of tissue, and neither is a product in itself. These actions help ensure that the brands do not become generic. Among other steps that can be taken to prevent a mark from becoming genericized is to use the mark as an adjective with the generic name of the product or service and never use the mark as a noun. Additionally, the mark may be capitalized, set in boldface type, and used with SM (service mark), TM (trademark), or ® if federally registered. Finally, owners of the mark can police misuse and take active steps to educate the public about the proper use of their mark.

10. Bayer Co. v. United Drug. Co., 272 F. 505 (S.D.N.Y. 1921).

VI. MATERIAL NOT ELIGIBLE TO BE PROTECTED AS A MARK

Material that is not eligible to be protected as a federally registered mark is described below, while the particulars of the prosecution and procurement of federal registration is described in further detail in the *Trademark Prosecution Section*. Eligibility for protection as a mark is a distinct issue from an entity's right or practical ability to use a term or like subject matter along with its goods or services. Continued use of marks not eligible for protection or that may have already been rejected in an application for registration can be frequently observed. These words, logos, phrases, and other subject matter are not eligible for protection as a mark, and entities may sometimes continue to use them as marks despite the entities' inability to prevent others from freely using similar or even the exact same words, logos, or phrases.[11] Entities that continue to utilize unprotectable marks risk any good will associated with subject matter used as a mark, and their "mark" may be easily and freely taken by other entities mimicking or even purely coincidentally using it. An illustrative listing of subject matter not eligible for federal protection as a mark is provided below.

A. Confusingly Similar Marks

Consistent with the purposes and goals of the trademark system in preventing consumer confusion, the federal trademark system includes provisions that prohibit registration of certain types of marks that are likely to create confusion between the owners' goods or services and already registered marks. Somewhat akin to the rejection of patent applications in view of already existing similar technology, the USPTO will reject applications for marks deemed "confusingly similar" to existing marks.[12] Thus any mark too similar to an already registered mark will not qualify for federal protection as a mark. *See Trademark Prosecution Section.*

---

11. While an entity is not prohibited from using a mark merely because it fails to qualify for federal protection, continued use of the mark must also not violate other entities' rights under trademark, unfair competition, and other laws.

12. 15 U.S.C. §1052(d) ("[n]o trademark . . . shall be refused registration on the principal register on account of its nature unless it . . . [c]onsists of or comprises a mark which so resembles a mark registered in the Patent and Trademark Office, or a mark or trade name previously used in the United States by another and not abandoned, as to be likely, when used on or in connection with the goods of the applicant, to cause confusion, or to cause mistake, or to deceive.").

B. Marks Not Eligible for Protection Based on Content and/or Subject Matter

Marks may also be excluded from eligibility for federal protection based on the specific nature or subject matter of the content. Section 1052 of Title 15 of the U.S. Code (also referred to as §2 of the Lanham Act) explicitly states that "[n]o trademark . . . shall be refused registration . . . on account of its nature *unless* it . . ." has certain prohibited content, which includes the categories of content listed below.[13] Accordingly, marks composed of the following subject matter are excluded from eligibility for protection as a mark:

1. *Immoral or Scandalous Matter*[14]—Courts have defined "scandalous" under §2(a) to mean, among other things, "shocking to the sense of propriety, offensive to the conscience or moral feelings or calling out for condemnation," and the determination of whether a mark is immoral or scandalous must be made in the context of "contemporary attitudes" and the "relevant marketplace." For example, the graphic design of a dog defecating that was placed on shirts was held to be scandalous in light of the broad audience that may view the mark in almost all public places.
2. *Deceptive Matter*[15]—Deceptive marks, among other things, may be a single deceptive term, a deceptive term within a composite mark that includes nondeceptive aspects, or phonetic or foreign equivalents of a deceptive term that alludes to a deceptive quality, characteristic, function, composition, or use. The determination as to whether a mark is deceptive asks whether the term of character, quality, function, composition, or use is misdescriptive, whether prospective purchasers are likely to believe that the misdescription actually describes the goods or services, and whether the misdescription likely affects a significant portion of the relevant consumers' decision to purchase, all of which would be answered affirmatively when a mark is deemed deceptive.[16] A mark of ORGANIC ASPIRIN for a dietary supplement that does not include aspirin is an example of a mark found to be deceptive.

---

13. 15 U.S.C. §1052.
14. 15 U.S.C. §1052(a); *see also* TMEP §1203.01.
15. 15 U.S.C. §1052(a)and (e)(1); *see also* TMEP §1203.02.
16. *In re* Spirits Int'l, N.V., 563 F.3d 1347, 90 USPQ2d 1589 (Fed. Cir. 2009).

3. *May Disparage, Falsely Suggests a Connection, or Brings Into Contempt or Disrepute*[17]—The right to privacy protects a party's control over the use of its identity or "persona," and under §2(a) of the Lanham Act, a party also acquires a protectable interest in a name or equivalent designation when the name or designation is associated with the party's personality or "persona." As such, disparaging marks or marks that falsely suggest a connection, or bring into contempt or disrepute a party's name or identity, would violate this right to privacy as codified in §2(a) of the Lanham Act.

   Disparaging Matter, Brings into Contempt or Disrepute[18]—SQUAW ONE was found disparaging when used in connection with clothing in light of term "Squaw," meaning an American Indian woman or wife, that Native Americans would consider offensive; KHORAN used as a mark for wines was found disparaging, as alcohol is viewed as a prohibited substance in Islam.

   Falsely Suggest a Connection[19]—SHINNECOCK BRAND LIGHTS mark for cigarettes was found to falsely suggest connection with the Shinnecock Indian Nation; BO BALL mark for oblong-shaped leather ball found to falsely suggest a connection to dual-sport athlete Bo Jackson.
4. *Flags and Government Insignia*[20]—§2(b) of the Lanham Act explicitly prevents protection of marks consisting of or comprising the flag or coat of arms or other insignia of any nation including the U.S., or any U.S. state or municipality, as well as any "simulation" of these items. Obviously the U.S. flag may not be protected as a mark, and neither can the seal of the President of the United States. However, marks may be protected if a significant change is made to the flag or government insignia, such as when the flag forms another design or is obscured by words or designs.[21]

17. 15 U.S.C. §1052(a); TMEP §1203.03.
18. TMEP §1202.03(c–d).
19. TMEP §1202.03(e).
20. 15 U.S.C. §1052 (b); TMEP §1204.
21. The depicted examples are illustratively selected from among the examples provided by the USPTO in TMEP § 1204.01(b).

5. *Names, Portraits, and Signatures*[22]—Marks consisting of or comprising a name, portrait, or signature identifying a particular living individual except by his written consent, or the name, signature, or portrait of a deceased President of the United States during the life of his widow, if any, except by the written consent of the widow, are not protectable.[23] This provision protects rights of privacy and publicity that living people have in their identifying designations. Interestingly, once a person is deceased, their name may theoretically be used as a mark (except for Presidents) for purposes of U.S. trademark law. (E.g., THOMAS EDISON LIFE INSURANCE, FRANKLIN TEMPLETON INVESTMENTS, and the design that is shown below[24] all have a mark that involves well-known deceased, non-presidential historical figures.)

22. TMEP §1206.

23. 15 U.S.C. §1052(c).

24. https://www.ftinstitutional.com/inst/jsp_cm/global_nav/help/frk_trademarks.jsp.

6. *Geographic Terms*[25]—Marks with geographic terms may not be protectable as a mark in several scenarios. First, a mark that is "primarily geographically descriptive" cannot be federally protected unless it has acquired "secondary meaning." Policy concerns weigh against a single entity having exclusive rights for primarily geographically descriptive matter except for specific instances. Protection of such marks without requiring a showing of acquired distinctiveness could lead to others being unable to describe their products. Second, "geographically misdescriptive marks"—marks that include geographic designations that are not accurate for the product for which the mark is being used and for which the misrepresentation is material to purchasing decisions—cannot be protected as marks. Policy concerns dictate that protection of "geographically misdescriptive marks" would increase rather than reduce consumer confusion in direct conflict with the purposes of federal trademark law. Bordeaux is a region of France well known for its beloved wine. If a vineyard in New Jersey grew grapes and sold its wine from those grapes under a name that included BORDEAUX, the mark would not be protectable under federal trademark law, since the wine was not from a vineyard in Bourdeaux, France. Marks for wines and spirits are also explicitly identified as marks that cannot be protected if they consist of or comprise deceptive matter or a geographical indication which, when used with wines or spirits, identifies a place other than the origin of the goods.[26]
7. *Surnames*[27]—Marks that are "primarily merely a surname" cannot be protected.[28] The Lanham Act §2(e)(4) requires a showing of acquired distinctiveness under §2(f) in order to protect a surname as a mark. As such, U.S. federal trademark law continues the common-law belief that the exclusive right in a surname per se cannot be established without evidence of long and exclusive use that changes the mark's significance to the public from that of merely a surname to that of a mark identifying particular goods or services.[29] Common law also recognizes that multiple individuals may share a common surname, each of whom may

25. 15 U.S.C. §1052(a) and (e); *see also* TMEP §1210.
26. 15 U.S.C. §1052(a).
27. TMEP §1211.
28. 15 U.S.C. §1052(e)(4).
29. TMEP §1211.

have an interest in using his surname in business. Therefore, by requiring evidence of acquired distinctiveness (secondary meaning), the law effectively delays appropriation of the exclusive rights in the name.

8. *Functional Marks*—Functional matter cannot be protected as a mark.[30] Matter is deemed functional if it is "essential to the use or purpose of the product or if it affects the cost or quality of the device."[31] From a policy perspective, it is advisable to prevent a single entity from receiving exclusivity through trademark protection on functional aspects of a product so that others may use those aspects of the product. This doctrine preserves the balance between patent and trademark law, as utility patents are deemed the proper mechanism for protection of functional aspects of products.[32] A classic example of an alleged mark being deemed functional is the shape of a guitar. The unique body shape of the particular guitar sought to be protected was found to provide acoustical advantages in terms of the sounds the guitar made, and thus the shape was deemed functional and could not be protected as a mark.[33]

VII. TRADEMARKS, E-MEDIA, AND THE INTERNET

A. *Jurisdiction*

"Use in commerce" is required to establish federal trademark rights and to establish violation (aka infringement) of a registrant's federal trademark rights. Prior to the Internet, e-media, and other electronic communication means, "use in commerce" was often brick-and-mortar sales of products or services. In most instances, a physical product was sold, offered for sale, and/or transported across state lines, thereby establishing the requisite "use in commerce." Infringement was often by physical means, in which products or services that were deemed to cause a "likelihood of confusion" with a registrant's products or services when sold, offered for sale, and/or transported from state to state. However, with the

30. 15 U.S.C. §1052(e)(5); TMEP §1202.02(a).

31. TrafFix Devices, Inc. v. Marketing Displays, Inc., 532 U.S. 23, 33, 58 USPQ2d 1001, 1006 (2001).

32. TMEP §1202.02(a)(ii).

33. *In re* Gibson Guitar Corp., 61 USPQ 2d 1948 (TTAB 2001) .

proliferation of the Internet and related technologies, e-transactions are occurring with increased frequency and in continually evolving formats. Whether actions over the Internet or other digital activities constitute "use in commerce" is a factually specific inquiry. Activities over the Internet that more closely correlate to traditional activities deemed "use in commerce," including sales and offers for sale, will typically be deemed use in commerce or trademark purposes and will support federal registration of a mark. Activities more passive in nature, such as using a mark in uploaded content without sales or offers for sale, are less likely to be deemed "use in commerce."

With respect to enforcement of federal trademarks, an entity generally can be sued only in a jurisdiction in which the entity is present, conducts business, or has some other minimum contacts with or in the jurisdiction. The Internet is pervasive, and its content is accessible in all 50 states. Theoretically, an argument could be made that any use of the Internet or action by an entity on the entity gives rise to jurisdiction in any state. Courts have taken a fact-specific approach to resolving this jurisdictional question based upon the nature and content of the activity by a would-be defendant with active and competing sales in a jurisdiction over the Internet often giving rise to jurisdiction in that location, while a minimal upload or download may not give rise to jurisdiction outside of the entity's physical location. An extensive spectrum of factual scenarios exist that will be resolved based upon the particulars of the matter.

B. Domain Names and Cybersquatting

A domain name is a name consisting of an alphabetical or alphanumerical sequence followed by a suffix indicating the top-level domain (e.g., .com, .edu, .gov) and is used as an Internet address to identify the location of a particular web page on the Internet. This name corresponds to one or more numeric IP addresses used to identify a particular web page or set of web pages on the Internet.[34] Following a precedent established in the early days of domain name registration, registrars of domain names now accredited through ICANN continue to assign names on a first-come, first-served basis and do not check before assigning a

34. *See* Random House Dictionary, Random House Inc. (2011); *see also* Collins English Dictionary—Complete & Unabridged 10th Ed. (2009).

new domain name.[35] Domain names are addresses but also may serve as trademarks. As with other trademarks, a domain name will not be eligible for federal registration unless the mark is being used to identify goods or services of an entity, as compared to merely identifying the location where the applicant's website is located on the Internet. The domain name would not constitute being a mark, just as the address 1060 W. Addison would not constitute being a mark, unless it were found to identify particular goods or services of an entity. Amazon.com® and hotels.com® are examples of domain names that serve as sources of identity of the providers of goods or services and have been federally registered.

"Cybersquatting" is a term that was coined to describe the bad-faith registration and use of another party's trademark as a domain name, with the intent to profit somehow from the good will of that trademark. Akin to "squatters" in derelict buildings, cybersquatters "sit" on unregistered or non-utilized domain names. An even more recent practice related to cybersquatting is known as "typosquatting." "Typosquatting" is the registering of a common misspelling of a trademark as a domain name so that web users are directed to the typosquatter's site when they misspell the domain name of the known website. In the early 1990s it was not uncommon for cybersquatters to register domain names with names of various known companies with an intent to later sell these domain names to the companies for significant profits. For example, mcdonalds.com, candyland.com, and peta.org were all at one point registered and/or used by entities distinct from those entities associated with the marks forming the domain name. At the infancy of the web, a reporter from *Wired* magazine registered the mcdonalds.com domain as part a story on the value of domain names and potential pitfalls ahead. The reporter is rumored to have gone so far as to email (in jest) McDonalds executives from ronald@mcdonalds.com. Candyland is a childrens game from Hasbro, but candyland.com was at one point the domain name for an adult entertainment site. Lastly, the group PETA (People for the Ethical Treatment

35. Internet Corporation for Assigned Names and Numbers (ICANN) is the organization charged with overseeing domain names on the Internet and delegates through domain name registrars. Registration of second-level domain names with top-level domains (.com, .gov, .edu, .mil, .org, .net, and .int). Registration of domain name using these first-level domains is not tied to ownership of trademark rights, which became a mechanism of manipulation for cybersquatters as described below.

of Animals) was likely very upset when an organization entitled "People Eating Tasty Animals" obtained the peta.org domain name.

In 1999 the Anticybersquatting Consumer Protection Act (ACPA) was passed with the hope of preventing cyberpiracy, as it is called in the act. Prior to the ACPA, disgruntled trademark owners attempted to bring suits under trademark and other related causes of action with varying degrees of success. Some trademark owners simply paid large sums of money to purchase the domain name(s) from the cybersquatters. Under the ACPA, anyone who registers, traffics in, or uses a domain name that is identical or confusingly similar to another party's distinctive trademark, with a bad-faith intent to profit from that mark, is civilly liable.[36] Additionally, enhanced domain name dispute policies and procedures have been developed by the organizations that assign domain names. For example, the Uniform Domain Name Dispute Resolution policy, created by ICANN and used by all its accredited registrars, provides for an inexpensive administrative procedure by which a trademark owner can challenge an existing domain name.[37] While cyberpiracy/cybersquatting still exist, improved and expedited mechanisms for trademark owners to obtain domain names that contain their marks now provide trademark owners with more ammunition to fight cybersquatters.

C. Web Commentary

The Internet has increased the ability for individuals to publicly comment on a variety of content. Anyone with an Internet connection and a blog, website, or a twitter account can deliver commentary virtually 24 hours a day, 365 days a week, to varying audiences. In many instances, commentary sites will reference companies, including reference to or display of their trademarks. Referencing a company may require, at a minimum, mention of a word mark that is part of the company's name in order to clearly indicate the entity being referred to by the speaker or writer. While the First Amendment and Fair Use can provide a defense to traditional trademark infringement, as described in the *Trademark Litigation Section*, in some instances online users may wish to avoid using trademarks of other entities whenever possible. Use of trademarks or confusingly similar terms in a domain name could also give rise to a cause of action by the owner of the mark.

36. Antcybersquatting Consumer Protection Act (ACPA), 15 U.S.C. §1125(d).

37. http://www.icann.org/en/udrp/udrp.htm.

An often referenced case relating to commentary sites is the "Bally Sucks" commentary website.[38] An individual (Faber) created a web page titled "Bally sucks" to comment in a negative fashion on Bally's Health Clubs. Bally's Health Clubs brought suit against Faber for a number of causes of action, including trademark infringement, trademark dilution, and unfair competition. The court in this case found in favor of Faber and did not hold him liable for his commentary site. The website was deemed a noncommercial form of protected speech, and the court also found that use of the word "sucks" in the title made the site one in which consumers were unlikely to be confused into thinking the site was owned or affiliated with Bally's Health Clubs. No consumer confusion was believed to be likely, and the site was deemed to be clearly distinguished from Bally's trademarks. While the outcome was positive for Faber, this case illustrates how a commentary site might give rise to liability under trademark laws, or how it could spark issues inflammatory enough to thrust an individual or company into expensive litigation that was neither expected nor desired.

Therefore, when utilizing the Internet and the web, individual and corporate users should be cautious and try to reduce their risks for liability. Steps that may be taken to reduce risks include making efforts to: (1) avoid using someone else's trademark, even if just for commentary; (2) avoid or limit linking to other websites unless you receive permission; (3) refrain from posting information about another company or person, and take care that any information that is posted is accurate to avoid liability for defamation, tarnishment, and other causes of action; and (4) understand that activities over the Internet may give rise to jurisdiction in any state, so you could be forced to defend against a suit brought in another jurisdiction. While many commentary-focused sites operate without incident and without having claims brought against the sites, it is advisable to know the risks that exist so that one can minimize liability risks whenever possible.

D. Trademarks in Virtual Worlds

New e-technologies continue to become pervasive in our everyday world with increasing speed and regularity. Twitter® and Facebook® did not even exist a few years ago. The development of new technologies also has created new intellectual property issues. Wrapped in these new intel-

38. Bally Total Fitness Holding Corp. v. Faber, 29 F. Supp. 2d 1161 (C..D. Cal. 1998).

lectual property issues is also a learning curve of how existing intellectual property can and will be applied to these new technologies and their implementations. This process is currently being played out in "virtual worlds" and may become an increasingly critical issue—especially for trademark owners.

For example, Second Life®, launched in 2003, is an online virtual world developed by Linden Lab.[39] Second Life® users, called "residents," interact with each other and the world through avatars. Virtually anything that a person does in the real world, his avatar can do in this virtual world. As Second Life® has progressed, more and more companies have opened up virtual retail stores. Residents of Second Life® can buy virtual customized shoes from Nike®, Reebok®, or Adidas®; buy virtual furniture from Herman Miller®; get news reported from Reuters®; and contact a law firm with a presence in Second Life®. Accordingly, it's not surprising that legal issues likely will arise that increasingly mimic those in the real world. In particular, property rights (especially intellectual property rights) in Second Life® may be protected, litigated, and enforced with similar conviction as in the brick-and-mortar world.

With the presence and business dealings of corporations known in the real world now also interacting with avatars for currency tied to real dollars, it is likely that trademark and other intellectual property rights will be explored and enforced with increasing regularity. Just as an established athletic company might be inclined to bring suit against a company infringing its mark on products in a sporting goods store in Virginia, the same athletic company may also take steps to enforce its trademark rights if violated in a particular location in a virtual world such as Second Life·® One might expect these issues to be solved in a virtual court in the virtual world; however, it is more likely that IP issues in virtual worlds like Second Life® will be solved in the real world, especially in light of virtual-world ties to real-world payment of U.S. currency for certain actions and purchases. To the extent virtual dealings create a difficult intellectual property result, Congress could even step in at some point and legislate an application of current IP laws and practices to the virtual world, or perhaps it could pass sui generis legislation tailored to the particulars of virtual worlds. In the meantime, trailblazers in Second Life® and other worlds will likely explore the breadth of their trademark rights, or any lack thereof, to the greatest extent possible. Only time will tell how trademark rights are best protected and enforced in virtual worlds.

39. www.lindenlab.com.

PART 2

Trademark/Trade Dress Prosecution

It is a pretty recognizable brand name. Originally it was "Jerry's Guide to the World Wide Web," but we settled on "Yahoo!"

—Jerry Yang (co-founder of Yahoo!®)

While the prosecution of trademark applications differs in many ways from the prosecution of patent applications, there are also many similarities, or at least synergies, with the prosecution of patent applications, particularly with respect to some of the formalities and the handling of examination and procedural matters. The similarities in some of the procedural operations and processing may not be overly surprising given that the same bureau of the United States Government, the U.S. Patent and Trademark Office (USPTO), is charged with the authority and responsibility to handle these administrative agency matters. To avoid duplicate discussion that may arise because of the similarities, some of the common procedural handlings of the USPTO may be covered more completely in the *Patent Prosecution Section*.[1] Also, in many instances, the particulars about office procedure may have distinct nuances, but the concepts and general handling will be the same. Applicants and representatives should reference the *Trademark Manual of Examining Procedures* (TMEP) (or the *Manual of Patent Examining Procedure* (MPEP) in patent matters) as well as the

1. For example, the concept of a "Certificate Mailing" and its use and effect is substantially similar in the spheres of trademark practice and patent practice.

relevant provisions of the United States Code and Code of Federal Regulations when practicing before the USPTO. While there might be an almost infinite number of factual circumstances and considerations that trademark applicants could encounter or consider during the procurement process, this section will provide insight on many of the more regularly encountered matters relating to trademark prosecution.

I. COMMON-LAW RIGHTS

Trademark protection is purported to date back to at least as early as the 1790s, when Thomas Jefferson sought to protect marks of sailcloth makers. Much later, Congress made its first attempt at establishing a federal regime to protect trademarks that was an extension of the copyright powers under the Constitution, but it was struck down. Later Congress finally enacted trademark laws under the Commerce Clause (Article I, §8, cl. 3) rather than under Article I, §8, cl. 8, which provides for the patent and copyright systems. In 1946, Congress passed the Lanham Act, our current basis for federal trademark. The Lanham Act[2] sets forth provisions for federal protection and registration for trademarks and grants administrative authority to the U.S. Patent and Trademark Office. Because trademarks are derived from a provision of the Constitution distinct from patents and copyrights, state trademark law continues to operate and provide its own protections complementary to that of the federal trademark system.

Trademark rights are tied to commercial use of a mark or marks. Accordingly, trademark rights can be acquired for certain goods or services where the mark or service is commercially used. This commercial use may be embodied in any of a variety of commercial uses. In the United States, an entity or individual acquires "common law" trademark rights, without filing an application or any other request with the federal government, through its commercial use of the mark in relation to goods or services. As will be discussed later, entities may also acquire federal rights throughout the entire United States by applying for and receiving a federal registration from the USPTO.

At common law, the extent of the rights associated with that mark may vary from mark to mark and will relate to how pervasive the use of the mark may be. An entity that is only commercially using a mark in one or a handful of states, or even just a portion of a state, may only have

2. 15 U.S.C. §§1051–1127.

trademark rights for those categories of goods or services in that single state, handful of states, or portion of the states. These common-law rights also will be tied only to certain types of goods or services and like goods or services. It is not difficult to imagine scenarios in which several entities use the same or similar marks or related or similar goods in various geographic regions.[3] These entities can theoretically own the same or similar marks or similar goods in various distinct regions across the country. However, it is extremely likely in today's global economy that successful marks will grow and expand geographically and with respect to product and service coverage. A conflict will then necessarily arise between similar or like marks even if they began in geographically disparate and separate areas of the United States. However, federal registration provides trademark rights and coverage throughout the United States, and it is generally preferable to relying on common-law trademark rights.

II. FEDERAL REGISTRATION OF TRADEMARK

A. Benefits

Like other forms of intellectual property, registration provides for a give-and-take in which the applicant will provide information to the public through the USPTO in exchange for certain rights or benefits. As such, trademark owners are enticed to register their marks with the USPTO, and in exchange they receive various benefits, including the following:

1. *Nationwide priority*—By registering its mark, a trademark owner receives nationwide rights. This complete coverage often exceeds the coverage area it would otherwise receive under common-law rights. As such, registration of marks is often recommended to

---

3. The mark "Burger King" provides an example of just such a scenario. The current well-known Burger King fast-food restaurant (a Florida company) was not the first to commercially use the mark Burger King and not even the first in relation to hamburgers. Instead, as the story goes, a small ice cream and burger stand in Mattoon, Illinois, owned by the Hootses was senior in use to the now large and well-known Florida Burger King fast-food restaurant. However, the later Florida Burger King federally registered its mark. As a result of litigation under the Lanham Act, it was found that the as a result of federal registration, the later Florida Burger King owned rights to the "Burger King" trademark throughout the United States except for the market area of the Mattoon Burger King—a 20-mile radius around the restaurant in Mattoon, Illinois. Burger King of Florida, Inc. v. Hoots, 403 F.2d 904 (7th Cir.).

prevent applicants from running into a situation like that of the Hootses[4] in which a later user of the same or a similar mark acquires nationwide rights to a mark through registration except for a small geographic region in which applicants can demonstrate that they are actually commercially using their mark.

2. *Right to bring action in federal court*—Registered trademarks provide jurisdiction for which a trademark owner can bring suit in federal court. In certain instances a trademark holder may be able to bring suit in federal court *without a federal registration*; however, the trademark owner will have a much greater burden of proving proper federal jurisdiction (i.e., diversity jurisdiction and proper amount in controversy) as compared to the virtually automatic grant of federal jurisdiction associated with a federal trademark registration. Trademark owners generally prefer to be in federal court than in state court because of the believed procedural advantages.
3. *Incontestability*—After five years of using its mark continuously, an owner of a federally registered mark may file an affidavit such that the mark is deemed incontestable. An incontestable mark cannot be challenged as being confusingly similar to another mark, as being functional, or as lacking secondary meaning. Thus, incontestability further strengthens a mark and further limits the manners in which an accused infringer or like party can challenge the validity of the mark.
4. *Ability to recover enhanced monetary damages*—It is possible in certain circumstances to recover treble damages (triple the amount of actual damages) as well as attorney's fees if an entity has willfully infringed your registered mark. The ability to ask for and potentially receive such a damages award may further strengthen a trademark owner's settlement position even if such an award is not likely.
5. *Public notice of your claim of ownership of the mark*—Trademark registrations are listed in the USPTO database and thereby serve as a public notice function. Upon registration, the symbol ® may be used along with a mark to indicate that the mark has been federally registered. This symbol in use with a mark provides constructive notice that the mark is claimed as an exclusive right and is federally protected, and removes the effective

4. *See* note 3 above *re* Burger King of Florida, Inc. v. Hoots.

ability for accused infringers to claim "innocent infringement" so as to avoid monetary damages

6. *Ability to record the registration with the U.S. Customs and Border Protection (CBP) Service to prevent importation of infringing foreign goods*—Registration allows you to register your mark with U.S. Customs so that it may take action on your behalf to prevent importation of counterfeit or "gray market" goods.
7. *Reduced Burdens in Enforcement*—Registration of a mark typically can streamline your enforcement case in court, as trademark registration holders can avoid having to prove validity, ownership, and commercial use in interstate commerce.
8. *Basis for obtaining registration in foreign countries*—A federal registration will provide for a clear priority basis by which trademark protection may be sought in other countries that are parties to relevant treaties recognizing such priority claims.[5] A priority claim may be important in preventing a trademark pirate from effectively registering your mark in other countries and then "sell it back to you," as the priority date will typically predate the date when the trademark pirate may have tried to acquire rights in another country
9. *Tool for protecting domain names*—Similar to the benefit of a priority claim as a result of federal registration, cybersquatters and like misappropriaters of domain names may be stopped or put on hold with a registered trademark or evidence of the existence of a registered trademark for a mark used in domain name.

B. Bars to Registration of Marks

Section 2 of the Lanham Act[6] stipulates that no trademark shall be refused registration on the primary register on the account of its nature unless it:

- consists of or comprises immoral, deceptive, or scandalous matter; or matter that may disparage or falsely suggest a connection with persons, institutions, beliefs, or national symbols, or bring them into contempt or disrepute;
- consists of or comprises the flag or coat of arms or other insignia of the United States, or of any State or municipality, or of any foreign nation, or any simulation thereof;

5. *E.g.*, Paris Convention.
6. 15 U.S.C. §1052.

- consists of or comprises a name, portrait, or signature identifying a particular living individual except with the individual's written consent;
- is primarily geographically deceptively misdescriptive; or comprises matter that, as a whole, is functional.

In contrast to the absolute or nonconditional bars described above, Section 2 of the Lanham Act also stipulates what may be considered "conditional prohibitions" on marks that are deemed too descriptive for registration. In particular, Section 2(e) of the Lanham Act prohibits registration of any mark that is considered: (1) merely descriptive or deceptively misdescriptive; (2) primarily geographically descriptive; or (3) primarily merely a surname. However, per the conditional nomenclature, these types of marks can still be registered if they have acquired "secondary meaning." The rationale behind registration is that by acquiring "secondary meaning," marks that would otherwise have been prohibited from registration on account of their descriptiveness are properly registerable if they are shown to have acquired distinctiveness—"secondary meaning."

Section 2(d) of the Lanham Act prohibits registration of a mark which "so resembles a mark registered in the USPTO, or a mark or trade name previously used in the United States by another and not abandoned, as to be likely . . . to cause confusion, or to cause mistake, or to deceive." Based upon this provision, the USPTO may issue rejections of trademark applications in light of previously registered or used marks. This provision also enables interested parties to challenge registrations of other marks that dilute their marks.

C. Registration Process

1. Pre-filing Considerations

Before pursuing registration of a mark, applicants may have already spent significant time in researching selection of a mark in anticipation of eventually pursuing protection of a mark. If so, very little further pre-filing work may need to be performed, as much of that work may already have been performed at the outset of selection and use of a mark. For those who have not investigated, researched, and carefully considered selection of marks for use in their business, more work may be needed prior to filing. Due-diligence work regarding selection of a mark is preferably done prior to final selection and use of the mark. This preparation will enable the applicant to avoid liability for selecting a mark that may infringe upon someone else's rights, to increase the strength of the potential trademark protection available, and to increase the likelihood that the mark is eligible for federal registration. As a resource to applicants, representatives, and examiners, the USPTO provides a regularly updated *Trademark Manual of Examining Procedure* (TMEP).[7] This resource can be extremely helpful in preparing an application for filing as well as during the later-described prosecution process as it provides administrative guidance on preferred practice and procedure before the USPTO.

As discussed further in the *Trademark Groundwork Section*, not all trademarks are created equal. Distinctiveness is at the core of the U.S. trademark system, and it follows that the more distinctive a mark, the stronger the protection for the mark may be. Marks that are minimally distinctive may have a smaller scope of protection and may not provide rights against other minimally distinctive marks that may later enter the market. They also may not possess sufficient distinctiveness and may be rejected by the USPTO over previously used or registered marks should the trademark owner attempt to federally register the mark. If a mark is selected that falls in one of the prohibited or conditionally prohibited types of marks, the applicant may realize he has an unprotectable mark that he has already started to use and that has gained association with his goods or services. While an entity may select a new mark, significant cost, time, effort, and good will can be lost by having to go back to the drawing board.

In a preferred scenario, entities initiating use of a mark should investigate selection of their mark prior to or at least contemporaneously with beginning use to avoid having to change the mark, including branding after good will is acquired. Selection of a mark may be a counterintuitive process. Descriptive marks are typically the first types of mark that are considered for the ease of association with goods. However, these marks either may not be protectable or may require stronger evidentiary showings and proof of distinctiveness compared to marks that have inherent distinctiveness. Accordingly, trademark attorneys will typically suggest marks that are inherently distinctive (fanciful, arbitrary, or suggestive) to maximize their strength from the outset and ensure they are eligible for federal protection.

It may also be advisable to perform a search of existing marks both for clearance purposes and for validity or registrability. While these concepts may involve review of similar subject matter, the analysis and con-

7. http://tess2.uspto.gov/tmdb/tmep/.

clusions may vary. A clearance search is aimed at reducing the risk that a new user of a mark is incurring liability for its use by infringing or diluting a senior party's trademark rights. A validity search is aimed at reducing the risk that a user is beginning use of a mark that may not be protectable or may have very minimal scope of protection in light of a crowded field or other restrictions.

a. Search

Searches are typically recommend but may not be performed despite recommendations, especially in instances when entities lack funding for searching. Unfortunately, many new entities lack capital for maximization of IP rights at the outset of their business and as a result can encounter difficulties due to their inability to perform due diligence or fully investigate IP landscapes in advance. There are many professional search firms that will perform a search of a word and/or graphic mark with respect to a single class of goods or services for several hundred dollars (e.g., $500). Typically, to perform a more thorough search, several classes of goods and/or services may be recommended for searching to further increase the likelihood that the most relevant art is uncovered. For example searching related classes of goods/services is important, notably it may be important to search for both clothing goods and retails services for clothing when searching a mark to be used or being used for clothing, and both food goods and foods/restaurant services, etc., when searching a mark to be used or being used in the food industry. Various databases, including the USPTO database as well as foreign databases, may be searched. In fact, the USPTO provides the Trademark Electronic Search System (TESS),[8] a free, publicly available database for anyone to search. Practitioners and those experienced in trademark matters will regularly search the database for a "quick look" as to the field out there for a certain mark and to provide a quick answer as to whether a particular mark has already been registered and to what goods and services. Additionally, the databases of state records may also be searched, as there are also state common-law rights to review. This indicates that a search of the USPTO TESS database does not necessarily provide a complete picture of the marks currently being used—just those marks that are federally registered.

Search results from professional searchers in a report format typically identify the most relevant marks for review. Some search firms may also provide weighting or may identify some of the closest marks

8. http://tess2.uspto.gov/bin/gate.exe?f=tess&state=4009:npav4e.1.1.

for highlighted consideration. Typically, the representative entity considering using or already using a mark will need to review the results before any conclusions or firm ideas can be drawn from the results. This is often done by an attorney for the trademark owner or pursuer. Whether a non-infringement clearance search is performed or a validity search is performed, one has a significantly clearer picture of the extent of one's rights or potential rights after reviewing the search results and receiving any coinciding advice from one's attorney or representative.

Searching can provide significant insight into the trademark rights environment for a particular mark. However, no search can provide absolutely certain assurance regarding validity or lack of liability for infringement, as it is impossible to ensure that a search is all-encompassing and error-proof. Practitioners should be careful to ensure that clients—especially less sophisticated entities—are well aware that the searches can be comprehensive and effective, but not perfect. Rather, searches are an effective tool for reducing the risk of mark owners and potential mark owners in taking uninformed actions, and they can bring the vast majority of known marks and uses of those marks to the forefront for consideration. Aside from providing more proven information upon which a mark owner or potential mark owner can make more educated decisions, performing clearance searches can also help protect a mark owner against claims of willful infringement and enhanced damages, particularly when counsel has provided a clearance opinion based upon a reasonable search by professional searchers.

b. Registration Particulars

Once preliminary matters including searching have been handled, applicants will have to decide particulars regarding the particular trademark application they pursue with the USPTO.

i. Type

Potential trademark applicants will consider what type of application to file with the USPTO. Should an application be filed based on use, or should an "intent-to-use" application be filed? Should the mark be for goods or services or both? Should an application claim priority relying on a foreign application or foreign registration? Should an applicant file an application on the word portion of a mark, or the logo or symbol, or a combination of both? The answers to what type of application an applicant should file is typically based on the goals of the trademark applicant along with the particulars relating to the entity, including budget, where the applicant is in the process of using the mark ("have been using for years" compared to "have not used it yet"), and the particulars of the business related to the mark.

One common consideration is whether to file an application directed to a word mark, to a design mark, or to a combination of a word and a design mark. Word marks are directed to the term or terms in the mark being covered. According to TESS, Registration Number 978952 is a registration for the word mark—NIKE—and was filed on January 31, 1972. This registration provides an illustrative example of what may be considered a word mark.

Figure 1

Registration for a word mark

United States Patent Office 978,952
Registered Feb. 19, 1974

PRINCIPAL REGISTER
Trademark

Ser. No. 414,176, filed Jan. 31, 1972

NIKE

BRS, Inc. (Oregon corporation)
[illegible] SW. 112th Ave.
Beverton, Oreg. 97005

For: ATHLETIC SHOES WITH SPIKES AND ATHLETIC UNIFORMS FOR USE WITH SUCH SHOES, in CLASS 22 (INT. CL. 25).

For: ATHLETIC SHOES WITHOUT SPIKES AND ATHLETIC UNIFORMS FOR USE WITH SUCH SHOES, in CLASS 39 (INT. CL. 25).

First use June 18, 1971; in commerce June 18, 1971.

Applications may also be filed directed solely to graphics that serve as trademarks. Registration No. 3,473,652 is a design registration to the graphic of a Nike SWOOSH®. This mark may be considered a design mark.

Figure 2
Design registration

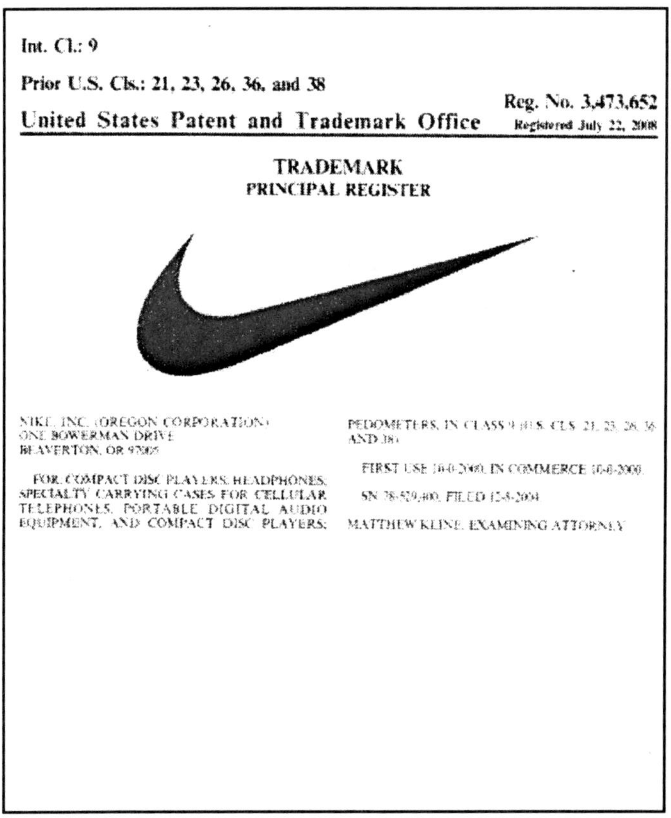

Int. Cl.: 9

Prior U.S. Cls.: 21, 23, 26, 36, and 38

Reg. No. 3,473,652

United States Patent and Trademark Office — Registered July 22, 2008

TRADEMARK
PRINCIPAL REGISTER

NIKE, INC. (OREGON CORPORATION)
ONE BOWERMAN DRIVE
BEAVERTON, OR 97005

FOR: COMPACT DISC PLAYERS; HEADPHONES; SPECIALTY CARRYING CASES FOR CELLULAR TELEPHONES, PORTABLE DIGITAL AUDIO EQUIPMENT, AND COMPACT DISC PLAYERS; PEDOMETERS, IN CLASS 9 (U.S. CLS. 21, 23, 26, 36 AND 38).

FIRST USE 10-0-2000; IN COMMERCE 10-0-2000.

SN 78-529,400, FILED 12-8-2004.

MATTHEW KLINE, EXAMINING ATTORNEY

Combination marks may include words and graphics in combination as a mark. Registration Number 1,325,938 is a registration for a design that includes the word—NIKE—and the SWOOSH logo together. This registration is an illustrative example of what may be considered a combination mark or a word and design mark.

Figure 3

Trademark principal register

Int. Cl.: 25

Prior U.S. Cl.: 39

United States Patent and Trademark Office — **Reg. No. 1,325,938** Registered Mar. 19, 1985

TRADEMARK
Principal Register

NIKE

Nike, Inc. (Oregon corporation)
3900 SW. Murray Blvd.
Beaverton, Oreg. 97005, by merger from
BRS, Inc. (Oregon corporation)
Beaverton, Oreg.

For: FOOTWEAR, in CLASS 25 (U.S. Cl. 39).
First use Jun. 18, 1971; in commerce Jun. 18, 1971.
Owner of U.S. Reg. Nos. 977,190, 1,153,938 and others.

Ser. No. 302,503, filed Mar. 23, 1981.

ERNEST H. LAND, Examining Attorney

As demonstrated above, marks may, among other things, constitute word marks, design marks, or a combination of words and designs. Depending on which of these types of protection is sought, one or more varied applications for registrations may be filed to provide effective protection of the marks. Depending on the factual circumstances, registration of one form of mark may not protect other forms of the mark. Accordingly, selection of the subject matter for registration in each application is an important consideration that requires foresight in prosecution and registrability concerns as well as the eventual enforcement of the mark.

ii. Quantity

Just as the circumstances particular to the applicant and the mark will dictate the type of application to be filed with respect to the mark, the same is true with regard to determining how many trademark applications should be pursued. In some instances, one application may be sufficient to protect a mark. In most instances, multiple applications to different aspects or versions of a mark or marks provide stronger and more focused coverage. As demonstrated above with respect to three registrations to Nike, Inc., applications may be filed to a word mark for a company name, to a symbol or logo used with the company name, or to a combination of both the word and logo. Different color schemes or variations of company logos also may be utilized by companies and thus may require multiple applications to properly protect the trademark rights in each of the variations or color schemes of the logo. For example, it is well publicized that Starbucks®, among other companies, has utilized various logos over the years, many of which have been registered at the USPTO.

Figure 4

Various Starbucks logos

Applicants may also utilize varied trademarks associated with each product line and thus may need to file a trademark application to effectively protect each line. Again, the marks associated with these varied products can be protected in various manners using multiple federal trademark registrations.

iii. Competitor/Infringement Consideration

While it is important to consider the substantive requirements under the Lanham Act as well as the procedural requirements of the USPTO, the mere receipt of a registration may not ensure an entity can effectively protect its marks and good will. Successfully enforcing your registration is also a critical consideration that begins during, and even before, filing of the application for registration. Enforcement and litigation considerations should be woven into a registration strategy. Companies that are most effective in protecting their trademark rights pursue these considerations when deciding which types of marks to pursue, how many applications to pursue, and the particulars of each application. In a sense, skillful prosecution is one of the most effective enforcement tools in providing litigators down the road with a clear, strong, valid registration with which to police would-be infringers. Conversely, a shaky registration or prosecution coverage strategy that is poorly conceived and has a less-than-ideal scope of coverage can undermine the abilities of litigators in later instances.

c. *Principal Register Versus Supplemental Register*

In the United States, the Principal Register is the main or full registry for trademark registrations, and the Supplemental Register is in essence a secondary register. The requirements for registration on the Supplemental Register are less stringent, specifying that the mark be capable of distinguishing goods or service, and not that the mark actually serve that function, as is required for registration on the Principal Registry. Registrations on the Principal Register receive the full benefits of registration, which include the effect of constructive notice, incontestability after five years, and presumption of validity. Conversely, registration on the Supplemental Register does not provide the full benefits of registration and specifically does not provide constructive notice, allow for a claim of incontestability after five years, or provide a presumption of validity. However, it does allow the owners to use and display an official federal registration symbol ® and will act to prevent others from federally registering the same mark that will appear on federal searches, including searches by examining attorneys at the USPTO. After five years, the mark may in essence "graduate" to the Principal Register if a new application is filed for registration on the Principal Register. Applicants may file an application attempting to receive registration on the Principal Register and may select registration on the Supplemental Register if the examining attorney has deemed the mark as not sufficiently distinctive to receive immediate registration on the Principal Register. As such, an applicant may elect to register the mark on the Supplemental Register to give it time to acquire sufficient distinctiveness to permit registration on the Principal Register. Supplemental marks are not eligible for registration with U.S. Customs and Border Protection; however, owners of marks on the Supplemental Register may still sue for trademark infringement. Strategically, one should be aware that there are inherent weaknesses in a claim of trademark infringement brought for a mark that is registered on the Supplemental Register and not on the Principal Register.

2. Initial Filing

Trademark prosecution typically falls somewhere in the middle between patent prosecution and copyright prosecution in considering the extent and amount of activity usually required in prosecution of the registration. Unlike copyright registrations, trademark registration applications are reviewed to ensure that the mark satisfies the requirements set forth in the Lanham Act, as described above. As described, these requirements include several statutory prohibitions against content not eligible for registration as a mark, as well as a prohibition against registration of marks that so resemble previously registered marks as to cause confusion, or to cause mistake, or to deceive as to the owner of the good or service associated with the mark. As such, trademark examining attorneys will review applications to ensure that these requirements under the Lanham Act are met by reviewing the mark itself and the information submitted. Trademark examining attorneys will also, among other things, perform a search for marks that might so resemble the mark applying for registration. Applicants must also identify the class of goods or services for which the mark is being used and must submit specimens in certain instances.

While trademark prosecution typically does not involve office action and amendment practice to the extent of patent prosecution file histories, it is not uncommon for the USPTO to issue a rejection requiring further submission, clarification, or other response from trademark registration applicants. For example, a clarification of a categorization of goods or services may be required or submission of a specimen may be required if not originally submitted. Additionally, a rejection may be issued indicating that the examiner has uncovered a previous mark to which the present mark is confusingly similar. Applicants may argue or submit further evidence to overcome assertions by the examining attorney. However, in many instances, much of the work associated with prosecution of a trademark registration can be performed at or before filing. Accordingly, depending on the particulars, many experienced trademark prosecutors will file applications with minimal rejections or objections by the trademark examiner, except for rejections in light of confusingly similar marks that may be impossible to avoid.

a. *Filing Requirements*

Applicants are encouraged to file trademark applications electronically through the Trademark Electronic Application System (TEAS)[9] as a regular TEAS application or as a TEAS PLUS application. TEAS PLUS applications require submission of a significantly more complete application, submission of an email address, and authorization for communication to be sent by the USPTO by email. In exchange, the TEAS PLUS application is subject to a reduced filing fee compared to a regular application filed through TEAS. Trademark applications can still also be submitted to the USPTO in paper format.

i. Requirements to Receive a Filing Date

The USPTO will grant a filing date to an application under §1 or §44 of the Trademark Act if it is in English and contains all of the following information: (1) the name of the applicant; (2) a name and address for correspondence; (3) a clear drawing of the mark; (4) a listing of the goods or services; and (5) the filing fee for at least one class of goods or services, required by §2.6.[10] Submission of the aforementioned information is the minimum required for receiving a filing date, and applicants that choose to submit only these minimum requirements for receipt of a filing date will typically have to provide supplemental information before the application can be examined further or can issue as a registration. Failure to submit all five of the identified elements will result in the USPTO denying the appli-

9. TEAS is the Trademark Electronic Application System, http://www.uspto.gov/trademarks/teas/index.jsp. Applicants are encouraged to file online for a variety of reasons including the fact that the electronic system walsk applicants and representatives through the steps and requisite materials, In contrast, those that choose to paper file unless they are experienced filers of trademark applicants have a potentially greater risk for inadvertent submissions.

10. 37 C.F.R. §2.21.

cation. The USPTO will return any application papers and refund the fee submitted. While these are the minimum requirements, there are several benefits to submitting a "complete application" rather than just the minimum requirements at the time of initial filing. These benefits can include reduced prosecution time and costs (if represented) and reduced fees if the application is filed using TEAS PLUS.

ii. Requirements for a Complete Application

Further elements are typically required of a trademark application beyond the minimum basic requirements to get a filing date. As enumerated in detail in the Application Checklist in TMEP §818, an application for trademark registration should contain the following elements to be considered complete:

- a clear drawing of the mark;
- a verified statement signed by a person properly authorized to sign on behalf of the applicant;
- a written application, including:

  (a) date on which the application was signed; (b) applicant's name (and doing business as (DBA) designation if appropriate); (c) applicant's legal entity; (d) country of which the applicant is a citizen or the state/country of incorporation or organization; (e) names and citizenship or state/country of incorporation of partners or members (if applicant is a domestic partnership or joint venture); (f) applicant's domicile and post office address; (g) statement forming basis of application per §1(a), §1(b), or §44 of the Lanham Act; (h) identification of the goods/services; (i) class(es) of the goods/services; (j) dates of first use in each class; (k) if applicable, in a §1(a) application—statement that the mark is being used by a related company; (l) if priority is claimed under §44(d)—a benefit claim; (m) a basis for filing (see *basis for application* below); (n) an averment of belief of applicant being owner of the mark by person making the verification; (o) in §1(a) applications, an averment that the mark is in use in commerce; (p) an averment that no other entity has the right to use such mark to the best of verifier's knowledge; (q) a description of the mark if not in standard characters; (r) if the mark includes color, a color claim naming the colors and a separate statement describing where the color(s) appear on the mark; (s) an English translation (if needed); (t) if appropriate, a statement identifying any living individual whose name or likeness the mark comprises and indicating their consent is of record or a statement that the name or portrait does not identify a living individual; (u) claim of ownership of prior registrations of the same or similar marks; and (v) a statement stating "the mark consists of standard characters without claim to any particular font style, size, or color" if the applicant seeks to register the mark in standard characters;[11]

- a filing fee for each class of goods/services;
- in §44(e) applications, a copy of the registration in the applicant's country of origin and a translation if not in English;
- in §1(a) applications, one specimen for each class; and
- if the applicant is not domiciled in the U.S., a designation of a domestic representative is *encouraged.*

Typically, the absence of one or more of the requirements for a complete application will not be fatal to a registration application, and the applicant will regularly be given an opportunity to supplement or fix a deficiency. As mentioned previously, an applicant who files an application based on §1 or §44 may be eligible for payment of a reduced filing fee if the filed application is complete and the applicant uses the USPTO's TEAS PLUS form, agrees to file certain communications through TEAS, and agrees to receive communications concerning the application by email.[12] An applicant may lose the reduced-fee benefit if the application is not complete at filing.[13] However, in many instances an applicant is still given opportunity to supplement applications after filing without losing the benefit of reduced fees of the TEAS PLUS filing as long as a "bona fide effort" was made to file a complete application.

b. Basis for Application

One of the requirements for a proper filing is a basis supporting the filing of a trademark registration application. As you may recall, U.S. trademark law emanates from the Commerce Clause of the U.S. Consti-

11. TMEP §818.
12. TMEP §819.
13. 37 C.F.R. §2.22; TMEP §819.01.

tution, which sets forth that regulation of interstate commerce falls within the powers of the United States Congress. U.S. law thus ties U.S. trademark rights to "use in commerce." In particular, trademark applications may be based upon actual use in commerce, intent to use in commerce, or foreign applications or registrations.

i. Use in Commerce (Section 1(a))

Perhaps the most common basis for filing an application for registration of a trademark is as a result of it being used in interstate commerce. The Trademark Act defines "commerce" as commerce that may lawfully be regulated by Congress, and "use in commerce" is the bona fide use of a mark in the ordinary course of trade.[14] While constitutional scholars have written extensively on the parameters of the Commerce Clause, it is generally recognized that the Commerce Clause has been interpreted by U.S. courts, including the U.S. Supreme Court, to convey a very broad power. Accordingly, only on rare occasions will commercial activity not constitute activity that qualifies as use in commerce, unless the mark is just being explored and has yet to be used or has been used in an isolated instance.[15]

Applicants that base their registration on use in commerce under §1(a) of the Lanham Act will need to include several elements in the application. First, the date of first use of the mark anywhere in connection with goods or services for each class of goods and services should be provided. The date of first use of the mark in connection with the goods or services in commerce (interstate or foreign commerce with the U.S.) for each class of goods or services should also be provided. A submission of one specimen for each class of goods and services should be made. Appropriate specimens for goods may include: labels or packaging for the goods that show the mark; point of sale displays that show the mark and appear where the goods are purchased; instruction manuals shipped with the goods; catalog or Internet displays that show the mark in close proximity to the goods and allow the customer to order the product from the catalog or Internet. Advertisements, brochures, technical specification manuals, and websites where you cannot order the goods are not

14. TMEP §806.01(a).

15. For example, currently the USPTO will reject an application for a mark on medicinal marijuana services for its lack of use in interstate commerce as marijuana use /sale is not lawful under federal law however it is permitted in certain state law such as California.

usually acceptable specimens. Appropriate specimens for services may include advertisements or promotional materials that feature the mark and describe the services. There must be a reference to both the mark and the services. A reference to just the mark is not typically sufficient to qualify as a specimen.

ii. Intent to Use (Section 1(b))

In some instances, an applicant may have selected a mark and is in the process of preparing marketing and advertising materials, placing the mark on products, and making further preparations to use the mark. The mark may not have been used in commerce, but the applicant wishes to establish a date with the USPTO to prevent an instance in which another party may begin using the mark and could jeopardize the applicant's rights in the mark. Under §1(b), applicants may file an application with the USPTO based upon their "intent to use" the mark in commerce. Applicants must include a statement affirming their bona fide intention to use the mark in commerce. No specimen is required. Before the USPTO will issue a registration for the mark, applicants will have to submit an "allegation of use." The allegation of use must include the dates of use for each class and specimen(s). As such, "intent to use" applications can be utilized as a place holders while further work is done prior to actual use of the mark.

An allegation of use may be filed as either an *amendment to allege use* or a *statement of use*—the principal difference being the time of filing.[16] An applicant may file an "amendment to allege use" at any time between the application filing date and the date the examining attorney

16. *See* TMEP §1103 ("The amendment to allege use may be filed after the application filing date but before approval of the mark for publication. 37 C.F.R. §2.76(a); TMEP §1104.03. If the applicant does not file an acceptable amendment to allege use during initial examination, or if an amendment to allege use is filed and withdrawn, and the USPTO issues a notice of allowance under 15 U.S.C. §1063(b)(2) (see TMEP §§1106 *et seq.*), the applicant must file a statement of use within six months of the issuance date of the notice of allowance, or within an extension of time granted for filing of the statement of use. 15 U.S.C. §1051(d). *See* TMEP §§1109 *et seq.* regarding statements of use.

The applicant may not file the allegation of use during the period after approval of the mark for publication and before issuance of the notice of allowance. 37 C.F.R. §§2.76(a) and 2.88(a); TMEP §1104.03. This period is known as the 'blackout period.' *See* TMEP §§1104.03(b) and (c).").

approves the mark for publication. Then, starting with the date the USPTO issues the Notice of Allowance, the applicant has six months to file a "statement of use." This six-month period is extendable upon the applicant filing[17] and a grant of a Request for Extension of Time to file a Statement of Use. Multiple Requests for Extension of Time may be filed to extend the time period beyond six months. However, a mark will not be registered if a statement of use has not been filed within 36 months of the mailing/issue date of the Notice of Allowance.

iii. Foreign Application or Registration (Sections 44(d)&(e))[18]

Section 44 of the Lanham act provides a basis for filing a registration based upon a foreign application for registration (§44(d)) or issued registration of a mark ((§44(e)). Section 44 applications must include a statement of bona fide use of the mark in commerce, and the scope of the goods/services covered by the §44 basis in the U.S. application cannot exceed the scope of the goods/services in the foreign application or registration.

iv. Foreign Application (Section 44(d))

Under §44(d) of the Lanham Act, the filing of a foreign application provides a basis for filing of a registration in the U.S. In order to receive a priority filing date based on the previously filed foreign application, an applicant must: (i) file a claim of priority within six months of the filing date of the foreign application; (ii) specify the filing date, serial number and country of the first regularly filed foreign application;[19] and (iii) verify that the applicant has a bona fide intention to use the mark in commerce on or in connection with the goods and/or services listed in the application.

17. A governmental fee must also be paid.

18. *See also* TMEP Chapter 1000.

19. Instead of specifying the filing date, serial number, and county of the first regularly filed foreign application, it is alternatively acceptable, if appropriate, for the applicant to ". . . state that the application is based upon a subsequent regularly filed application in the same foreign country, and that any prior-filed application has been withdrawn, abandoned, or otherwise disposed of, without having been laid open to public inspection and without having any rights outstanding, and has not served as a basis for claiming a right of priority. . ." TMEP §806.01(c).

v. Foreign Registration (Section 44(e))

Under §44(e) of the Lanham Act, a foreign registration provides a basis for filing a registration application in the U.S. In order to rely on a registration granted by the applicant's country of origin, several requirements must be met.[20] First, the applicant must submit a true copy, a photocopy, a certification, or a certified copy of the registration in the applicant's country of origin as well as a translation of the foreign registration, if applicable. Second, the application must include the applicant's verified statement that it has a bona fide intention to use the mark in commerce on or in connection with the identified goods and/or services. Third, the applicant's country of origin must either be a party to a convention or treaty relating to trademarks to which the United States is also a party, or extend reciprocal registration rights to nationals of the United States by law.

vi. Extension of Protection of International Registration (Section 66(a))[21]

In 2002, the U.S. joined the Madrid Protocol, a treaty administered by the World Intellectual Property Organization (WIPO). The Madrid Protocol Implementing Legislation (MPIA) went into effect on November 2, 2003. The Madrid Protocol is a governing instrument for the International Registration of Marks. Prior to enactment of the MPIA, applicants could file applications based only upon use in commerce, bona fide intent to use in commerce, and ownership of a foreign application or registration as described above. However, section 66(a) of the Lanham Act[22] now provides for "[a] request for extension of protection of an international registration to the United States. . . ." As such, under section 66(a), an application for registration of the mark may be made based off an international application filed with the International Bureau of WIPO in Geneva, Switzerland. The concept is somewhat akin to the filing of a patent application in the U.S. based upon the filing of a Patent Cooperation Treaty (PCT) application. A section 66(a) application will be examined in similar fashion as other trademark applications. However, there are some distinctions. For example, the classification of the goods and services by the International Bureau must be accepted by the U.S. trade-

20. *See, e.g.*, TMEP §§806.01(e) and 1004.
21. *See also* TMEP Chapter 1900.
22. 15 U.S.C. §1141(a).

mark examining attorney, even if it conflicts with the *Manual of Acceptable Identification of Goods and Services*. Also, section 66(a) cannot be amended. However, clarification or amendment to the indicated goods/services within the class may be required. For example, filings under the Madrid Protocol may have much broader identifications then are accepted by the USPTO.[23] There are further filing requirements and nuances associated with trademark applications based upon section 66(a), and these particulars should be reviewed before an applicant files an application based upon an international application to ensure that the relevant requirements are met.[24]

c. *Formalities*

i. Identification of Goods or Services

Since September 1, 1973, the U.S. has used the international classification of goods and services.[25] This international classification applies to any trademark application filed on or after that date. The classification schedule set forth in 37 CFR §6.1 is widely disseminated. Applicants may find the explanatory notes for this classification system particularly helpful in selecting proper classes of goods and services.[26] It is common for trademark owners to file applications in more than one class of goods or services, as businesses often do not operate neatly in only a single class of goods or services.

ii. One Specimen for Each Class

Consistent with U.S. trademark law being based on "use in commerce," a specimen or an actual example of how the mark is being used or will be used in connection with the identified goods and/or services needs to be provided to the USPTO. The specimen must be "substantially exact" to the drawing. Very little leeway is permitted in this requirement, although in certain instances an amendment may be made if it is not deemed a

23. A §66(A) application may come in with and identification of goods or services that includes "computer software." In the USPTO, software is required to specific a particular use or function and in some instances whether it is downloadable reloaded, computer media, or online non-downloadable.

24. *See, e.g.*, TMEP §§806.01(e), 807.12(c), 807.13(b).

25. *Nice Agreement Concerning the International Classification of Goods and Service for the Purposes of the Registrations of Marks.*

26. http://www.uspto.gov/trademarks/notices/international.jsp.

material alternation. Generally this determination regarding the specimen is made by examining attorneys based upon how the mark looked when it was filed which can include position of wording, color (if claimed), etc. As such, it is important to be accurate and consistent and pay attention to details.

A specimen for a mark used on goods demonstrates the mark on the actual goods or packaging for the goods. Among the acceptable submissions for specimens in connection with goods are the following items: tags or labels for the goods, containers for the goods, displays associated with the goods, or photographs of the goods showing the mark on the goods. The actual product itself should not be submitted to the USPTO and will be discarded or destroyed if provided to the USPTO. Typically invoices, announcements, order forms, bills of lading, leaflets, brochures, publicity releases, letterhead, or business cards will not satisfy the specimen requirements for goods.

A specimen for a mark used in connection with services demonstrates the mark used in sale or advertising for the services. Among the acceptable submissions for specimens in connection with services are signs; brochures about the services; advertisements for the services; business cards or stationary showing the mark in connection with the services; or photographs showing the mark as used in rendering or advertising the services.

For electronic applications, an image of the specimen (depicting as much of the label/advertisement as possible) may be submitted in a .jpg format. *For paper applications*, the specimen can be submitted with the application. Physical specimens filed with the application should be flat and 8-1/2 by 11 inches or smaller;[27] however, specimens consisting of videotapes, audiotapes, CDs, or computer diskettes are acceptable for certain types of marks that cannot be "used" in other ways.

The specimen requirements also vary depending upon whether the applicant is filing an application based on "use," "intent to use," or an application based solely on a foreign application or foreign registration. For applications based on "use," one specimen should be submitted for each class of goods/services listed in the original application. For applications based on "intent to use," one specimen for each class of goods/services should be submitted at the same time as the "allegation of use." Applications based solely on a foreign application or foreign registra-

27. If a submission is made that exceeds these dimensions, the USPTO will create a facsimile of the specimen, insert the facsimile in the application file wrapper, and destroy the original submission.

tions are exempt from the specimen requirement and do not need to submit a specimen.

iii. Filing Fee

The total filing fees associated with trademark applications are generally tied to the number of classes of goods and services for which the mark is being registered and also the manner in which the filing is being made (e.g., TEAS PLUS, electronically, paper). The USPTO provides a list of fees on its website, and applicants and representatives may wish to review and confirm the governmental fees on the fee schedule so they can accurately anticipate the costs associated with trademark application(s). At time of publication, the current fee schedule is $275 per class if TEAS PLUS is used,[28] $325 per class if application is filed electronically, and $375 per class if application is filed on paper.[29]

iv. Drawing

Applicants for registration must submit a clear drawing with the original application in order to receive a filing date, but this does not cover applications for registration of a sound, scent, or other nonvisual marks. The drawing submitted in the application should clearly show the mark sought to be registered. The drawing will be reproduced and should be clear so that it may properly serve its notice function. One should note that the submission of a specimen showing how the mark is being used does not satisfy the drawing requirement. Additionally, a drawing submission having two or more drawings displaying materially different marks will not satisfy the drawing requirement and will not receive a filing date because the requirement for a clear drawing of the mark will not have been satisfied. While the TEAS system will facilitate preparation of a proper drawing based upon the information submitted by the applicant, those who actually prepare drawings will want to prepare the drawings on 8½ by 11-inch non-shiny white paper, and the mark itself should be no larger than 3½ by 3½ inches. Additionally, the heading of the drawing should comprise the applicant's name, correspondence address, listing of goods and/or services, and the dates of use (or the wording "Intent to Use"). Drawings submitted may be "standard character" drawings or "stylized or special form" drawings.

---

28. TEAS.
29. http://www.uspto.gov/web/offices/ac/qs/ope/fee092611.htm.

Standard Character Drawings

Standard character drawings[30] comprise only Latin character letters and numbers, Roman or Arabic numerals, and common punctuation or diacritical marks. The mark does not include a design element. A standard character claim must also be filed.[31] The USPTO provides a listing that includes letters, numbers, punctuation, and diacritical marks.[32] An applicant wishing to register a typical company name irrespective of the font of the lettering would file a standard character drawing.

Stylized or Special Form Drawings

If the particular style of lettering is important to the mark or if the mark includes color, a design, or a logo, applicants must utilize a "stylized or special form" drawing. The image should be in black and white unless color is being claimed as a feature of the mark. In the special form, the drawing should be substantially identical to the mark as it appears on the specimen or the foreign registration. Similar size requirements for paper and image size apply as for the standard character drawing.

If color is a feature of the mark for which protection is sought, a color drawing must be submitted. Additionally, a color claim naming the colors that are a feature of the mark and statement describing where the color(s) appear on the mark must be submitted.[33]

v. Description of the Mark

A description of a mark is required if the mark is not in standard characters. Even when the application is in standard characters, the trademark examiner may require submission of a description of the mark.[34] Thus, trademark examiners will have fairly broad discretion as to whether a description is required even if the mark is deemed to be in standard characters. Because applicants are required to file a description if the mark is not in standard characters, a description will be required in any application in which an applicant is claiming a particular font style, size, or color of words, letters, or numbers. A description alsowill be required

30. 37 C.F.R. §.2.52(a).

31. The standard character claim should read, "The mark is presented in standard character format without claim to any particular font style, size or color."

32. http://teas.uspto.gov/standardCharacterSet.html.

33. 37 C.F.R. §2.52(b)(1); TMEP §807.07.

34. 37 C.F.R. §§2.37, 2.52(b)(5).

if the mark contains a design element; includes non-Latin characters or non-Roman or non-Arabic numerals; includes color, motion, or broken lines to show placement; or is 3-D or a configuration of goods or packaging. TMEP §808.01 sets forth further instances in which a description of the mark will be required.

vi. Signature

Obviously an applicant can personally sign the requisite verification for an application. A variety of other people may also sign the verification on behalf of the applicant, and the signatory need not be an attorney, although attorneys are among those who may sign on behalf of the application. A person with legal authority to bind the applicant, a person with firsthand knowledge of the facts and actual or implied authority to act on behalf of the applicant, or an attorney with actual or implied power of attorney may each sign the verification on behalf of the applicant. As with other areas of law, including patent law, electronic submissions require a varied form of signature. As such, in TEAS applications, conventional signatures are not required. Instead, an adopted symbol that acts as your signature serves the same purpose. For example, —/John M. Fleming/— or —/David R. Gerk/— would be a sufficient "signature" for the authors of this book to file a verification in a TEAS application; however, a symbol beyond just a person's name, such as —/Ochocinco85/— or —/King of Pop/— could also be an acceptable signature if it's used as a symbol.

vii. Translation and Transliteration

If an application to register a mark includes non-English wording, an English translation must be included in the application.[35] An English translation is required even if only one of the words or a portion of the words appears to be non-English wording. In some instances, a word or combination of words that might be typically seen as foreign conveys a different commercial impression, and thus a translation may not be required. By way of example, the TMEP provides the mark MAÑANACOMPUTERS as an example of a word that would require a translation of *MAÑANA*, which is a Spanish word meaning "tomorrow," and the English word COMPUTER. However, if the combination of those two words conveys a different commercial impression, a transla-

35. 37 C.F.R. §2.32(a)(9).

tion may be not be required. Similarly, for the mark "felizcity" no translation may be needed, as it is a play on words of the English word "felicity" with the Spanish word "*feliz*," which means "happy" in English.[36] The USPTO, on a case-by-case basis, may judge whether a translation is required, and the examining attorney assigned to the case will likely provide guidance on whether or not a translation is required.

An application that comprises non-Latin characters must include a transliteration (a phonetic spelling) of those characters, and either an English translation or a statement that this portion (non-Latin character portion) has no meaning in a foreign language.[37] Examples of the statements that are provided by the TMEP include:

> The non-Latin characters in the mark transliterate to "Asahi," which means "Rising Sun" in English.
> OR
> The non-Latin characters in the mark transliterate to "Asahi," which has no meaning in a foreign language.[38]

3. Prosecution and Examination

As described, trademark applicants may file their applications either electronically or physically via paper applications, with applicants increasingly utilizing electronic applications. Paper applications can be hand-delivered or mailed to the USPTO; however, applicants should review the particulars regarding paper filings with the USPTO, as an application will typically not be awarded a filing date until the USPTO physically receives the application.[39] Paper applicants can file a Certificate of Express Mail along with the application, in which instance the application will be awarded the "date of deposit" to the U.S. Postal Service if the Express Mail Certificate is properly executed. Applicants can avoid many of these timing concerns by utilizing electronic submission, as a filing receipt is immediately generated, and concerns about delays or even a delivery failure by the U.S. Postal Service can be avoided. Electronic submission is an attractive option for filing of trademark applications.

36. TMEP §809.
37. 37 C.F.R. §2.32(a)(10).
38. TMEP §809.
39. 37 C.F.R. §2.195; TMEP §303.

a. Review for Compliance with Minimum Requirements

When the USPTO receives a trademark application, the application is given a receipt date and then reviewed for compliance with the requirements for granting of a filing date.[40] If it is determined the application does not meet the minimum filing requirements, the receipt date is "cancelled" as of the filing date. The applicant will need to either file a new application through TEAS or file a new paper application, which may include the previously filed application papers along with another filing fee and the additional information or materials needed to satisfy the filing date requirements.

b. Initial Examination

Trademark examination occurs by a FIFO (first-in, first-out) process. Applications are generally examined in the order in which they are received at the USPTO. The same is true for amended applications, remands from the Trademark Trial and Appeal Board (TTAB), and statements of use. There are two procedures by which an applicant can make an application "special" so that initial examination will be considered "expedited." An applicant may file a (1) *Request to Make Special—Registration Inadvertently Cancelled* or (2) *Petition to Make Special.*[41] In the first instance, the application will have to have been inadvertently cancelled or expired under specific sections of Title 15.[42] In the second instance, the application will need to be accompanied by a statement of facts by affidavit or declaration that shows the special action is justified. Most commonly, this "justification" involves the existence of actual or threatened infringement, pending litigation, or a need for registration as a basis for securing a foreign registration.[43] In both mechanisms to make the application special, a petition will need to be filed and a fee may need to be paid among other requirements for granting of the petition.

c. Substantive Examination of Applications

After the USPTO determines that an application has met the minimum filing requirements, an application serial number is assigned and the ap-

40. For applications filed under §66(a), the International Bureau will determine whether the application complies with §66(a) before sending the request for extension of protection of international registration to the USPTO.

41. TMEP §702.02.

42. 15 U.S.C. §§1058, 1059, 1141k.

43. TMEP §1710.

plication is forwarded to an examining attorney. This process may take varying lengths of time, most commonly approximately three months, sometimes less. Trademark examiners are each assigned a certain number of cases that constitute what is often referred to as their "docket." While each examiner has his specific preferred manner of reviewing cases, the examining attorney reviews the application to determine whether it complies with all applicable rules and statutes and includes all required fees. This initial examination of the application must be a "complete examination." The initial examination includes a search for conflicting marks and an examination of the written application. Initial examination also includes review of any preliminary amendment(s) or other documents filed by the applicant before an initial Office action is issued about the drawing and any specimen(s) or foreign registration(s). A determination is made whether the mark is eligible for the type of registration requested, whether amendment is necessary, and whether all required fees have been paid. If upon completion of this "complete examination" the examining attorney finds the application is in condition for publication, he will approve the application for publication for opposition. The USPTO will then send a notice of publication or certificate of registration to the applicant in due course. However, if the application is deemed not to be in condition to be approved, the examining attorney will contact the applicant or the identified representative and inform that person about the reason(s) why the mark may not be registered and about the defect(s) that can be corrected or amended to place the application in condition for approval.

d. Reasons for Refusal

The examining attorney may refuse an application for various reasons, as described in further detail in the *Bars to Registration* section earlier in this chapter. To illustrate, if the examining attorney finds the mark to involve immoral or scandalous matter, to be deceptive, or to be primarily geographically deceptively misdescriptive, to name a few concerns, the examining attorney will refuse the application.[44] Likewise, if the application is found to so resemble a mark previously used by another in the U.S., the examining attorney will refuse the application. The examining attorney may make refusals based on more than one ground, and it is appropriate for the examining attorney to identify all grounds on which

44. *See* TMEP §§1203–1212.

the application should be refused. Citing all the reasons for refusal will assist the applicant in correcting the application in an efficient manner and help advance the prosecution of the application.

e. Attorney's Letter/Action

If the examining attorney determines that the mark that is subject of the application is not entitled to registration or that amendment(s) to the application are required, the examining attorney will provide a written "Office Action" to the applicant informing him as such. In some instances, an examining attorney may telephone, email, or otherwise contact the applicant in advance of issuing an Office Action, depending on the circumstances of the case.

Office Actions will include a summary of the status of the application and acknowledgment of documents that have been filed. The Office Action will also identify the ground or grounds that form the basis for the refusal and obvious remedies, if applicable, that the applicant can take that would make the application allowable. The examining attorney is required to identify the applicable sections of the Trademark Act that support refusals of registration. When the refusal is based on likelihood of confusion with a previously registered mark, this mark will be identified and the registration provided along with a copy of any registrations forming a basis for the refusal. Publications that provide a basis for the refusal will also be identified and a copy provided along with the Office Action.

Applicants will have a six-month statutory period to respond to most Office Actions. This time period runs from the issue date, also referred to as the mail date, of the Office Action. Failure to reply within this six-month period will result in the application becoming abandoned.

f. New Matter Raised After First Action

Generally, under preferred USPTO practice, examining attorneys are prohibited from making a new refusal or issuing a new requirement after the first Office Action that could have been raised in the first Office Action. This practice is to ensure, among other things, that prosecution advances in a timely fashion and that the applicants are aware of all defects in their application from the outset so as to avoid a piecemeal sequence of refusals. In some instances the examining attorney can take action to correct an inadvertent error in a subsequent action. However, examining attorneys are to do so only when the failure to do so would result in "clear error" based upon USPTO administrative guidelines.

A different situation arises when an applicant submits information that raises a new issue. In this case, the applicant's action may have caused the new issue to arise, and thus the examining attorney is more justified in providing new grounds of refusal in light of the action taken by the applicant. Despite examining attorneys being strongly discouraged from issuing new grounds after the first Office Action except for limited instances, the decision to do so is an administrative decision that may be difficult for an applicant to traverse on procedural basis alone. Applicants will typically be better served in attempting to cure the application substantively as compared to attempting to fight the examining attorney on the technicalities of this refusal after the first Office Action. However, in one instance, §66(a) applications, the examining attorney is prohibited from issuing a refusal more than 18 months after the date on which the International Bureau forwards the request for extension of protection to the USPTO.[45]

g. *Examiner's Amendment*

In certain circumstances it may be appropriate for the examining attorney to issue an examiner's amendment to expedite prosecution of an application. An examiner's amendment is an amendment that is initiated by the examining attorney rather than by the applicant. Except for certain specific instances, the examiner's amendment must be authorized by the applicant or the applicant's representative or attorney. It is common for the examining attorney to telephone, email, or otherwise communicate with the applicant or other representative or attorney to discuss the proposed examiner's amendment and request approval. Because examiner's amendments often involve minor amendments or modifications to the application and are not likely to significantly delay the registration process, applicants are typically inclined to authorize examiner's amendments when needed. Examiner's amendments may be used to amend the identification of goods/services, enter a disclaimer, add the state of incorporation, or amend from the Principal Register to the Supplemental Register. Examiner's amendments may not be used to amend the dates of use if verification would be required. Amendments that require either the

45. *See* §68(c) of the Trademark Act, 15 U.S.C. §1141(h); Article 5 of the Madrid Protocol; *see also* TMEP §1904.02(g) and 1904.039(a).

filing of a substitute special form drawing or the submission of a substitute specimen also may not be made by examiner's amendment. Even though applicants often approve an examiner's amendment, applicants are well served to review the examiner's amendment to ensure that it is accurate and appropriate and does not undermine the applicant's trademark rights. An applicant should not file correspondence confirming an examiner's amendment, because this will delay processing of the application. A written response to an examiner's amendment is not required. If the applicant or her representative disagrees with an examiner's amendment, the applicant is well served to object immediately, and preferably by telephone or email, so that the objection is considered before publication or issue.

h. Interview

In instances where a telephonic meeting or so-called "interview" could serve to clarify certain issues and lead to either a better understanding between the examining attorney and the applicant or could otherwise advance prosecution of the application, an applicant may request an interview with the examining attorney. Examining attorneys may also initiate interviews if they feel the interview will expedite prosecution of the application.

In practice, interviews can be especially useful opportunities to clarify issues for which there seems to be a misunderstanding between the applicant and the examining attorney. Complicated or difficult cases are especially benefited by an examiner interview, as are instances in which the applicant does not want certain information or arguments "on the record." Interviews may be performed only by persons with proper authority to act on behalf of the applicant in the case. Also, the substance of an interview must be made of record in the application, and the action of the USPTO is based exclusively on the written record. Accordingly, examiner interviews can provide an opportunity for frank conversation between examining attorneys and applicants in which just the conclusions and agreements are generally recorded on the written record and preserved in the file.

Regardless of whether agreement is reached or not, the examining attorney will typically record issues that were discussed and keep a record as to whether agreement was reached as part of the "Notes to the File" section of the record. Because the interview is not recorded, its content and discussion will not become part of the record of the case, save for the notes or summary memorializing the interview. Any time an interview is performed, an applicant or her attorney or representative should review the notes or record kept by the examining attorney that is to become part of the record of the file. At this time, the involved party should feel free to respectfully request that the examining attorney remove certain language or comments or otherwise add language or comments consistent with what was discussed in the interview that would be most beneficial. Care should be taken to ensure that statements against the applicant's interest are not recorded as part of the record when possible. It is the oral nature of interviews that allows applicants to speak freely with reduced concern that the applicant's or its representative's words will be used or twisted against it in litigation down the road.

i. Priority Action

An Office Action that is issued following a communication between the examining attorney and the applicant or other individual with proper authority to bind the applicant, in which the various issues raised in the application and the actions an applicant must take to put the application in condition for publication or registration, is referred to as a "Priority Action." Priority Actions are issued after the examining attorney contacts a person with proper authority, and the examining attorney or person with proper authority discuss merits of the application. The Priority Action will include a discussion of all refusals and other requirements, including evidence supporting the refusal. Priority Actions will also describe action the applicant may take to put the application in condition for publication or registration.

j. Evidence

Examining attorney actions are to be supported by relevant evidence and proper citation that is to be placed in the record of the file and provided to the applicant. A search is performed, and the record should indicate the libraries and/or files searched and the result of those searches. The examining attorney will also note the documents reviewed for the record, and this information will be provided to the applicant. While examining attorneys may include the entire search in the record, it is sufficient to include only a portion of the search results if the portion included constitutes a representative sample of the entire search.

With the Internet now a mainstream conduit of commerce, evidence pulled from the Internet continues to be increasingly utilized in trademark matters. Significant case law relating to uses of Internet information has continued to develop over the years. This case law can be referenced to better understand when information gathered over the Internet may be used as evidence and what it may be used to show or prove. Evidence's probative value may vary depending on which evidence from the Internet is being presented, as well as the particular source of the information.[46]

As a matter of actual occurrences now, much of the evidence relied upon by examining attorneys in trademark cases is housed or found on the Internet including online dictionaries and various other sources of information. Perhaps the most commonly relied upon evidence by examining attorneys are webpages of various other companies or entities to demonstrate relatedness of goods/services in a confusion refusal or use of a term in the marketplace to demonstrate a term is descriptive, deceptive, a surname, geographic, etc. For example, examining attorneys may utilize databases provided by Lexis Nexis®. The evidence located by the examining attorney will be attached to the office action to support the refusal and then also referenced in the letter.

k. Amendments and Responses to Office Actions

Changes to the trademark itself are not allowed, as trademark rights begin on the day of filing. Consistent with the notice function that the applicant is claiming rights in the very trademark filed in the application, changes cannot be made to the trademark itself. This prohibition on changes prevents an inherent unfairness to the public that is put on notice. Applicants can file a further distinct mark at any point, but that mark will have rights associated beginning only on the date of filing. As such, unlike patents in which the claims that set forth the metes and bounds of the invention and can be amended after filing as long there is support in the originally filed application, changes are not permitted to the trademark for which federal registration is sought in an application unless the changes will not "materially alter" the mark. As such small changes can be made depending on the specific circumstances. Applicants may find themselves in a position to make amendments to trademark applications or to respond to Office Actions, as a variety of issues may arise relating to the use and perception of the mark. For example, applicants may find themselves in a position where they have to convince an examining attorney that the mark is not confusingly similar to an

46. TMEP 710.01(b).

already registered mark. In other instances an applicant may need to provide clarification regarding information in the original application, such as the identification of goods or services. In some instances, argument on behalf of or by the applicant in response to a rejection may be successful. However, such an argument is more likely to be successful if evidence is submitted along with, or in lieu of, mere arguments in response to an Office Action by the trademark examining attorney.

"Likelihood of confusion" refusals

If the examining attorney uncovers a mark filed prior to the applicant's mark and believes the applicant's mark and the previously filed mark are confusingly similar such that there is a "likelihood of confusion" to consumers, then the examining attorney will issue a rejection to the later-filed application for registration. Generally speaking, the examining attorney will need to show the similarity between the two trademarks as well as a correlation between the goods and services. In order to overcome or traverse this type of refusal, the applicant must demonstrate that despite the examining attorney's initial conclusion, there is in fact no "likelihood of confusion" between the two marks. Refusals based on "likelihood of confusion" in relation to a previously filed mark are a type of Office Action that will typically require evidence to be submitted along with arguments in order to overcome the rejection and change the examining attorney's mind.

Among the ways that an applicant can overcome or attack these refusals is to undermine either the similarity between the trademarks, the relationship between the goods and services of the marks, or both. For example, distinctions in the appearance, sound, or meaning or commercial impression of the two marks can be used to attack the examiner's refusal. If the descriptions of the goods and services are unrelated or varied, or if distinct channels of trade are used for the goods or services of the trademarks, these facts may also undermine the refusal. Information relating to consumers, including distinctions in the types of consumers, how they purchase, how much information and expertise they bring to their purchases, and how sales are made, all can be important evidence and can rebut the examining attorney's findings. Facts relating to what type and how many other trademarks are used on similar goods purchased by consumers also can be used to attack a likelihood of a refusal because of trademark confusion.

The particular evidence to be submitted will vary from case to case and may vary in its persuasiveness. In some instances, listings from search engines or online user tracking statistics convincingly show a lack of relationship between certain goods and services. Outside of computer sources, yellow page listings, newspapers, periodicals, and trade journals can be persuasive and reliable evidence traditionally utilized in trademark matters. Additionally, state trademark databases may be used. In instances in which particularized types of evidence are needed, an expert may submit an expert opinion or even an affidavit if needed. In summary, any information or evidence that demonstrates or proves that a consumer may not be confused by the two marks may be submitted as evidence or as part of an argument to overcome a rejection. Additionally, in some circumstances, a consent agreement for registration can be obtained from the owner of the senior registered trademark and may overcome a rejection by the examining attorney.

Generic or descriptiveness rejections
The examining attorney may issue an Office Action refusing registration of the trademark for being "descriptive" or "generic" and thus the examining attorney has deemed the mark that is the subject of the application to lack sufficient distinctiveness to be federally registered as a mark. In an instance where the examining attorney asserts that the mark is "generic," evidence must be presented that demonstrates the mark is not generic in order to overcome the evidence. Significant evidence may be required to effectively overcome the refusal, as the applicant is in essence attempting to demonstrate that the trademark is in fact not generic or the common term for the goods or services provided in associated with the mark. Among the more effective evidence that can be used to demonstrate the trademark is not generic are newspapers, journal articles, and other publications that use the term generically and thus convey that the use of the trademark is not the same as the use of the term in conjunction with the particular goods or services. While initially internet sources were viewed with skepticism, most of these sources are now considered mainstream depending on the particular source and can be effectively relied upon by both examining attorneys and applicants as evidence.

Similarly, it also may be fairly difficult to overcome refusals in which the examining attorney deems the trademark to be "descriptive." Again, applicants can present evidence showing that the trademark is not merely "descriptive" by contrasting general use of the term to use of the trademark in connection with particular goods or services. Applicants may also overcome a refusal of a trademark for being descriptive by demonstrating with substantial evidence that the applicant's goods or services have become known to the public. This can be done through survey evidence or showings of ongoing and sustained advertising throughout the country. The particular type of evidence may vary some based on the specifics of the case.

If the examining attorney cannot be convinced and maintains the rejection of the mark, the applicant can amend the application so it is made for the supplemental register rather than the Principal Register. While the Supplemental Register does not entitle the applicant to all the rights of the trademark being registered on the Principal Register, the trademark will be entitled to a presumption of "acquired distinctiveness" after five years of registration, when the mark may be amended to the Principal Register. In a sense, the passage of time will become evidence of distinctiveness.

Limiting or clarifying your identification of goods and services to overcome refusals

Applicants may continually try to seek as broad coverage as possible. If an applicant provides a broad description of the goods and/or services for which the trademark is being used and the application is refused based upon the previous trademark, the applicant may consider narrowing, limiting, or clarifying the description of goods or services in a manner that may further distinguish the goods and/or services offered by applicant with trademark as compared to the senior trademark, which caused the application to be rejected. For example, if an applicant is a personal trainer in a health club and the applicant's application lists "training services" as part of its description, and the application was rejected in light of a similar mark that appeared in "pet training services," the applicant may consider amending the description of services to be more focused to "personal training services" to further distinguish it from the services of other trademarks.

I. Final Office Actions

Final action is appropriate when a clear issue has been developed between the examining attorney and the applicant, i.e., the examining attorney has previously raised all outstanding issues and the applicant has had an opportunity to respond to them. For a second action to be made final, all requirements or refusals must have been made in the first action. No refusal or requirement may be made final, even if it is a repeated refusal or requirement, unless the entire action is made final.[47] Thus, if the examining attorney makes a new refusal or requirement in a second or subsequent action, a repeated refusal or requirement may not be made final. A first action by an examining attorney may not be a final action, as an applicant is entitled to at least one opportunity to reply to any issue raised by the examining attorney.[48] The TMEP indicates that examining attorneys are to make second Office Actions final whenever possible so as to further efficiency on prosecution.[49] Practically speaking, examining attorneys are required to satisfy certain metrics for having handled and disposed of a certain number of cases in certain time periods, such as a quarter or a year, and thus there is a practical disincentive for examining attorneys to extend prosecution beyond the amount to which the applicant is entitled as a full and fair hearing.

Depending on the type of application, certain particularities may exist with respect to issuance of final actions. In §44(d) type applications, a final action may not be issued by the examining attorney until the applicant submits a copy of the foreign registration; however, once the application is otherwise in a condition for final refusal, the examining attorney will suspend the application pending receipt of a copy of the foreign registration.[50] In §66(a) applications, the examining attorney cannot issue a new refusal more than 18 months after the date on which the International Bureau (IB) forwards the request for extension of prosecution to the USPTO.

m. Applicant Action After Issuance of Final Office Actions

There is a statutory requirement for applicants to respond to a final action within six months of the issuance date of the final action.[51] In most instances, the only response that an applicant can properly file with respect to a final Office Action is one in compliance with an outstanding requirement or a notice of appeal of the decision of the examining attorney.[52] It is

47. TMEP §714.03.
48. TMEP §714.01.
49. TMEP §714.03.
50. *Id.*
51. 15 U.S.C. §1062(b); 37 C.F.R. §2.62(a).
52. 37 C.F.R. §2.64(a) ("On the first or any subsequent reexamination or reconsideration the refusal of the registration or the insistence upon a requirement may be stated to be final, whereupon applicant's response is limited to an appeal, or to a compliance with any requirement, or to a petition to the Director if permitted by §2.63(b)").

noteworthy that merely the notice of appeal, which is a very brief form type document, needs to be filed within the statutory time frame, and further particulars regarding an actual appeal, if pursued, can be filed later in accordance with the applicable time frames. In certain circumstances, a petition[53] to the Director of the USPTO is the third type of proper response to a final Office Action that can be filed.

Despite the above-described limitations on what constitutes a proper response to a final Office Action, an applicant's amendment or argument may be considered and entered after a final Office Action if the amendment or argument places the application in condition for publication or registration, or will put the application in better form for appeal. Placement of an application in letter form for appeal may involve, for example, a reduction in the number of issues on appeal.[54] An applicant can file a request for reconsideration asking the examining attorney to reconsider his decision for a variety of reasons, including arguments presented by the applicant. However, until an examining attorney enters these arguments and withdraws the final rejection, applicants should understand that the six-month clock of the statutory time period for response continues to tick. Thus applicants who hope to successfully traverse a final Office Action through filing a request for reconsideration may need to file a notice of appeal to preserve the right to appeal the case and prevent the application from being abandoned in the event the request for reconsideration is not successful. The notice of appeal need not be filed along with the request for reconsideration, and applicants can wait until they start to approach the six-month time period before filing the notice of appeal to try to avoid the notice of appeal fee if they believe their request for reconsideration may be considered. Furthermore, as the six-month deadline approaches, applicants may be well advised to call or otherwise correspond with the examining

53. The petition must be permitted under 37 C.F.R. §2.63(b)(2) ("b) After reexamination the applicant may respond by filing a timely petition to the Director for relief from a formal requirement if...(2) the examiner's action is made final and such action is limited to subject matter appropriate for petition to the Director. If the petition is denied, the applicant shall have until six months from the date of the Office action which repeated the requirement or made it final or thirty days from the date of the decision on the petition, whichever date is later, to comply with the requirement. A formal requirement which is the subject of a petition decided by the Director may not subsequently be the subject of an appeal to the Trademark Trial and Appeal Board.).

54. TMEP §715.02.

attorney to ensure that he or she acts on the request for reconsideration before the end of the statutory period. By being proactive with the USPTO and the examining attorneys, applicants and representatives can save costs, in many instances in the form of unnecessary government fees for superfluous filings to ensure that applications do not go abandoned.

n. Suspension of Action

Suspension of action in the context of trademark prosecution means suspension of action by the examining attorney. This suspension of action will not toll the six-month statutory time for which applicants are required to respond to Office Actions. The examining attorney has the discretion to suspend the application "for good and sufficient cause."[55] The following are some of the reasons why the examining attorney may suspend an application:[56] (1) applicant's filing of a petition to cancel a cited registration, (2) awaiting submission of a copy of a foreign registration in a §44(d) application when the applicant has indicated the foreign application is still pending, (3) if there are conflicting marks in pending applications, (4) when there is a proceeding relevant to the registerability of the applicant's mark pending before either a court or the Trademark Trial and Appeal Board (TTAB), (5) a pending cancellation or expiration of a cited registration, (6) pending expiration of "insurance" extension request, or (7) a pending correction or limitation to an international registration.

o. Abandonment

An application may become abandoned because the applicant failed to take action within the specified response period, often the six-month statutory period, required for responding to Office Actions or, alternatively, as a result of an express abandonment by the applicant or his or her representative.[57] Express abandonment requires affirmative action. An applicant may expressly abandon an application by filing a written request for abandonment or withdrawal of the application, signed by the applicant, someone with legal authority to bind the applicant (e.g., a corporate officer or general partner of a partnership), or a practitioner qualified to practice.[58] While there may be instances where it may be in

55. 37 C.F.R. §2.67.
56. TMEP §§716.02(a)–(g).
57. TMEP §718.
58. 37 C.F.R. §2.68.

an applicant's interest to expressly abandon an application, such as if it is part of a requirement of a settlement agreement, it is typically preferable to merely let an application go abandoned rather than expressly abandon it. Abandonment before the USPTO has distinct requirements and triggering mechanisms as compared to the legal "abandonment" of a mark, which requires the elements of cessation of use and intent not to resume use. As such, by merely letting an application go abandoned compared to expressly abandoning a mark with a written filing, an applicant will perhaps avoid or limit creation of persuasive evidence regarding abandonment were he later to try to register or enforce the mark.

4. Ownership

a. Establishing Ownership of Applications or Registrations

The original applicant of an application for trademark registration is presumed to be the owner of a trademark application or registration unless there is an assignment.[59] While a recorded assignment is not required in order for an assignee in applications or registrations based on §1 or §44 of the Trademark Act to take action with respect to the application or registration,[60] an assignment or other document affecting title must be recorded with the USPTO in order for an assignee to obtain a certificate of registration in his or her name.[61] When a party other than the owner of record in applications or registrations based on §1 or §44 attempts to take an action, that party must establish ownership of the application or registration by either (1) recording the assignment or other document affecting title with the USPTO and notifying Trademark Operations that the document has been recorded, or (2) submitting other evidence of ownership, such as a document transferring ownership or an affidavit or declaration under 37 CFR §2.20 that a valid transfer of legal title has occurred.[62] Generally speaking, assignments should be registered as a course of practice to ensure the registration is valid against subsequent purchasers, as recordation provides prima facie evidence of execution of the assignment.[63]

59. 37 C.F.R. §3.73(a).
60. 37 C.F.R. §3.73(b).
61. 37 C.F.R. §3.85.
62. 37 C.F.R. §3.73(b)(1).
63. 15 U.S.C. §1060.

b. Assignment of Marks

Assignments of trademarks must be executed in writing.[64] A registered mark or an application to register a mark that has been filed with the USPTO is assignable with the good will of the business in which the mark is used or with that part of the good will of the business connected with the use of and symbolized by the mark.[65] In an intent to use application under §1(b),[66] in order to ensure that a mark can only be assigned along with some business or good will associated with the mark and to prevent "trafficking" in marks, the applicant is prohibited from assigning the application before the applicant files an allegation of use except for assignment to a successor of the applicant's business to which the mark pertains if that business is ongoing and existing.[67] Extension of trademark protection to United States (§66(a)) applications may be assigned, together with the good will associated with the mark, only to a person who is a national of, domiciled in, or has a bona fide and effective industrial or commercial establishment in a country that is a party to the Madrid Protocol.[68] Assignments of extensions of protection to the United States must be recorded at the IB of WIPO, and the IB will notify the USPTO of changes to ownership that are recorded with the IB.

c. Recordation

Just as is the case with recordation of documents with respect to patents, recordation with the USPTO is not a determination by the USPTO regarding the validity or the legal effect of that document. Each application or registration for which a document is recorded requires payment of a recordation fee.[69] The USPTO will generally record whatever documents are submitted for recordation without reviewing the specific contents of those documents. It is understood that to properly record an assignment requires submission of an assignment cover sheet[70] along with a copy of the document, a copy of an extract from the document, or a

64. 15 U.S.C. §1060(a)(3).
65. 15 U.S.C. §1060(a).
66. 15 U.S.C. §1051(b).
67. 15 U.S.C. §1060(a).
68. 15 U.S.C. §1141; TMEP §501.01(b).
69. 37 C.F.R. §§2.6 and 3.41 (the current fee for recordation of a single property is $40).
70. 37 C.F.R. §3.31 sets forth the contents of the trademark assignment recordation cover sheet.

statement signed by both the party conveying the interest and the party receiving the interest that explains how the conveyance affects title. Only the information provided in the cover sheet will be recorded. The USPTO will not record a document that is not in English unless it is accompanied by an English translation signed by the translator.[71]

In some circumstances, recordation of an assignment or change of name document will result in the Trademark Database (TRAM and TARR) being automatically updated.[72] However, in other circumstances applicants will have to notify Trademark Operation that the ownership has changed.[73] While applicants may record physical documents, they preferably should record assignments electronically through the Electronic Trademark Assignment System (ETAS),[74] as electronic submissions receive significantly faster recordation and the system can be used to create a Trademark Assignment Recordation Coversheet with an online form. If for some reason an error occurs on the cover sheet recorded, it can be corrected if it is apparent by comparing the cover sheet to the accompanying document to which it pertains and by submitting a corrected cover sheet along with a copy of the document originally submitted for recording and a recording fee. Trademark assignment records may be publicly searched electronically.[75]

d. Updating of Ownership Information

Recordation of appropriate documentation with the USPTO and notification to the Trademark Operation of an ownership change will not result in an update of the Trademark Database with new owner information unless the owner files a written request to amend the registration pursuant to §7(d) of the Trademark Act or the owner takes action such as filing a §8 affidavit or §9 renewal application. Therefore, if the owner of the registration does not take action, the new owner of the mark must record the assignment document and file a written request that the Trademark Database be updated along with payment of the requisite fee.[76]

71. 37 C.F.R. §§.3.26.
72. TMEP §504.
73. 37 C.F.R. §3.85.
74. http://etas.uspto.gov/.
75. http://assignments.uspto.gov/assignments.
76. TMEP §505.02.

e. Post-examination

After the mark has been examined or registered, there are a number of proceedings that can be initiated to challenge marks or decisions made by the Office regarding registerability of the marks. The Trademark Trial and Appeal Board (TTAB) is an administrative tribunal that is empowered to make determinations only with respect to the right to register a mark, and it is the entity charged with deciding issues regarding registerability. The TTAB is considered to include the Director and Deputy Director of the USPTO, the Commissioner for Patents, the Commissioner for Trademarks, and the administrative trademark judges.[77] The TTAB is not empowered to make determinations regarding the right to use or issues of infringement or unfair competition. Matters not dispositive of the case may be handled by a single interlocutory attorney to whom authority has been delegated,[78] while dispositive matters and decisions on the merits of the case are rendered by a panel of at least three TTAB judges.[79] Certain administrative matters, such as stipulated scheduling motions, may be acted upon by TTAB paralegals or through the Electronic System for Trademark Trials and Appeals (ESTTA).[80] The TTAB, not being a judicial court, also cannot make determinations regarding constitutionality.[81] Generally speaking, the TTAB has jurisdiction over four types of inter partes proceedings (opposition, cancellation, interference, concurrent use) and one ex parte proceeding (ex parte appeal).[82]

f. Inter Partes Proceedings

Inter partes proceedings before the TTAB are fairly similar to litigation before one of the federal district courts; however, proceedings before the TTAB are conducted fairly exclusively in writing, with the TTAB's decisions based upon the written record. For example, the TTAB does not preside over the taking of testimony. As such, testimony is taken akin to depositions in federal district court litigation, and the transcripts and exhibits from the testimony are filed with the TTAB. Typically, parties

77. 15 U.S.C. §1067(b).
78. 37 C.F.R. §2.127(c).
79. 37 C.F.R. §§2.129(a) and 2.142(e)(1).
80. TBMP §102.03.
81. Trademark Trial and Appeal Board Manual of Procedure (TBMP), 3d Ed. (May 2011), §102.01, *available at* http://www.uspto.gov/trademarks/process/appeal/Preface_TBMP.jsp.
82. TBMP §102.02.

to the proceeding never physically come before the TTAB unless the TTAB makes a specific request that the parties meet at the TTAB's office in a pretrial conference[83] or unless an oral hearing is requested. Just as with a federal district court trial proceeding, inter partes proceedings before the TTAB include pleadings, motion practice, conferencing, disclosures, discovery, briefing, trial, oral argument (if requested), and finally a decision.[84]

i. Opposition Proceedings

Opposition proceedings are those in which a party seeks to prevent the issuance of a registration, in whole or in part, of a mark on the Principal Register.[85] "Any person who believes that he would be damaged by the registration of a mark" may file an opposition thereto, but the opposition may be filed only as a timely response to the publication of the mark.[86]

ii. Cancellation Proceedings

Cancellation proceedings are those in which a party seeks to cancel an existing registration, in whole or in part, of a trademark on the Principal Register or the Supplemental Register. Petitions for cancellation can be filed only after the issuance of a registration and may be filed by "any person who believes that he is or will be damaged by the registration" of the mark.

iii. Interference Proceedings

Interference proceedings for trademarks, akin to the former patent interference proceeding,[87] are those in which the Board makes a determination as to which, if any, of the owners of conflicting applications or registrations is entitled to registration. Interferences are initiated by the Office as a result of petition to the Director. A petitioner must show that there are extraordinary circumstances, i.e., that the petitioner would be unduly prejudiced without an interference, in order for the Office to

83. 37 C.F.R. §2.120(i)(2).

84. TBMP §102.03.

85. TBMP §102.02.

86. 15 U.S.C. §10672(a); TBMP §303.

87. The America Invents Act (HR 1249), passed September 16, 2011, amends Title 35 of the U.S. Code to no longer provide for interferences. Instead, section 6 of that act provides for "Post-Grant Review Proceedings" with respect to patents.

initiate an interference.[88] As a matter of practice, if an opposition or cancellation proceeding can be pursued, such availability will prevent a petitioner from being able to demonstrate the requisite undue prejudice in order to initiate an interference proceeding.[89] Until all of the marks that are to be involved in interference proceedings are published in the *Official Gazette* for opposition, even an interference that has been declared by the Director shall not be instituted by the TTAB.

iv. Concurrent Use Proceedings

Concurrent use proceedings are those in which the Board determines whether one or more applicants are entitled to a concurrent registration on the Principal Register. Because this registration would be a concurrent registration, it would have conditions fixed by the TTAB to the manner or place of use of the applicant's mark or with respect to the goods and/or services associated with the mark.[90] Among the more common restrictions is a geographic restriction. Logically, these conditions facilitate "concurrent use" of the mark in differing manners or for differing products or services without violating the rights of the other user(s). Concurrent use proceedings are initiated by filing an application for registration as a lawful concurrent user. The TTAB will institute the proceeding only after each of the involved applications has been published for opposition in the *Official Gazette* and all oppositions have been withdrawn or dismissed.[91]

g. Ex Parte Proceedings (Appeal)

The TTAB also is charged with jurisdiction over ex parte appeals of decisions of final refusal to register a mark by examining attorneys. Consistent with its name, ex parte appeals are appellate in nature and thus are generally more simplified and shorter in nature than inter partes proceedings. Practice in an ex parte appeal before the TTAB consists generally of only the filing of briefs by the applicant and examining attorney along with an oral hearing if requested by the applicant.[92] This type of practice will be recognizable to those familiar with appellate practice in other areas of law.

88. TBMP §102.02; *see also* TBMP §1002.
89. 37 C.F.R. §2.91(a).
90. TBMP §1101.01.
91. TBMP §§1102.01 and 1105.
92. *See e.g.*, TBMP §102.03 and Chapter 1200.

5. Registration and Post-registration Proceedings

a. *Duration, Maintenance, and Renewal*

While trademark rights can be maintained indefinitely, certain actions are required to maintain a federal registration and prevent the Director from cancelling the registration for such reasons as non-use. In the time period between years five and six immediately after registration of a mark, as well as every 10 years dating from registration, the owner of a mark must file an "affidavit of use" pursuant to §8 of the Trademark Act.[93] This §8 affidavit, as it is commonly called, verifies to the USPTO the continued use of the registered mark. Additionally, a renewal application pursuant to §9 of the Trademark Act[94] must be filed every 10 years. In light of the general 10-year alignment of both the §8 affidavit and the §9 renewal application, but for the initial §8 affidavit filing, it is common for trademark owners to file both the §8 affidavit and §9 renewals together. The USPTO does not provide renewal reminders to applicants/registrants. Further, as trademark rights evolve, it may become difficult to re-obtain a trademark registration in light evolution of terminology and the identification of items becoming more crowded and restrictive. As such, care should be taken to avoid abandonment of any unintentional abandonment of a registration for a mark.

b. *Affidavit of Incontestability*

After a mark has been registered on the Principal Register and has been in continuous use for five years or more, the owner may file an affidavit of incontestability (§15 affidavit) pursuant to §15 of the Trademark Act.[95] Under §33(b) of the Trademark Act,[96] if the right to use the mark has become incontestable under §15, then the registration is conclusive evidence of the validity of the registered mark and its registration, of the registrant's ownership of the mark, and of the owner's exclusive right to use the registered mark in commerce, subject to certain defenses and exceptions. Sections 15 and 33(b) apply only to registrations issued on the Principal Register, not the Supplemental Register. Applicants need not file an affidavit of incontestability if they choose not to invoke the benefits of incontestability. The requirements for maintaining and re-

93. 15 U.S.C. §1058; *see also* TMEP §1604.
94. 15 U.S.C. §1059; *see also* TMEP §1606.
95. 15 U.S.C. §1065; *see also* TMEP §1605.
96. 15 U.S.C. §1115(b).

newing a federal registration are not affected.[97] Section 15 affidavits are not "accepted" by the USPTO but rather are reviewed for compliance with the rules and statute; USPTO records are updated to reflect receipt, and the owner is provided acknowledgment of receipt of the affidavit.[98] Acknowledgement of receipt of a §15 affidavit provides a notice function to the public, but this is not a determination by the USPTO that the mark is in fact incontestable.[99] In instances where the affidavit is deemed noncompliant, the owner is notified of the noncompliant affidavit and it is not recorded. In these instances, the applicant can file a new §15 affidavit with a new fee.

c. Surrender

An owner of a registration may voluntarily surrender his or her registration for cancellation.[100] No fee is required. Surrender may be effected as part of a settlement agreement to avoid litigation or as another type of dispute resolution action. Practically speaking, it is uncommon and counterintuitive for registrants to affirmatively surrender a registration unless the surrender is required to avoid litigation or other adverse action. However, the Trademark Act provides such a mechanism for surrender.

d. Amendment and Correction of Registrations

In certain instances, amendments can be made to trademark registrations. Pursuant to §7 of the Trademark Act,[101] a registration based on an application filed under §1 or §44 of the Trademark Act may be amended for "good cause." No amendments that "materially alter" the character of the mark may be made.[102] This standard is also applied during examination of the application for registration. Registered extension of protection of an international registration in the United States cannot be amended.[103] Depending on circumstances, a variety of amendments could potentially be made that conform to this standard, including, for example, amendment of the drawings, amendment to restrict the identification of goods

97. TMEP §1605.
98. TMEP §1605.
99. *See* Arman's Systems, Inc. v. Armand's Subway, Inc., 215 USPQ 1048, 1050 (TTAB 1982).
100. 15 U.S.C. §1057(e).
101. 15 U.S.C. §1057(e).
102. 15 U.S.C. §1057(e).
103. TMEP §1609.02.

that does not require republication, and amendment to disclaim part of a mark. Applicants should closely review the relevant provisions of the Trademark Act and the TMEP before making or attempting to make an amendment to an application or registration.

e. *Division*

Owners of a registration should consider dividing a registration into two or more registrations if ownership has changed with respect to some but not all of the goods or services.[104] To divide the registration, the assignment or document changing title must be recorded with the USPTO, and a fee must be paid in addition to the request made by an authorized person. In an instance when the IB notifies the USPTO that an international registration has been divided as a result of a change in ownership to some but not all the goods/services, the USPTO will treat this notification as a request to divide out the assigned goods/services from the registered extension of protection and will proceed to create a new registration. The owner does not need to file a separate request to divide.

f. *Reinstatement*

In an instance in which an applicant has proof that the application was inadvertently abandoned due to a USPTO error, an applicant may file a "Request for Reinstatement" to reinstate the application rather than filing a "Petition to Revive."[105] A request for reinstatement of an application must be filed within two months of the issuance date of the notice of abandonment or, if the applicant has not received a notice of abandonment, within two months of the date the applicant had actual knowledge that the application was abandoned.[106] In the instance of a cancelled or expired registration, a registrant may file a request to reinstate the cancelled or expired registration if the registrant has proof that a USPTO error caused a registration to be cancelled or expired due to failure to file a §8 affidavit, §71 affidavit, §9 renewal application, or a response to an examiner's Office action refusing to accept an affidavit or renewal application.[107] Regardless

104. 37 C.F.R. §2.171(b).

105. TMEP §1712.01 (illustrative instances in which a Request for Reinstatement may be effective in reinstatement of an application that has gone abandoned are set forth in this section).

106. 37 C.F.R. §2.146(d).

107. TMPE §1712.02 (illustrative instances in which a Request for Reinstatement may be effective in reinstatement of a registration that has gone abandoned are set forth in this section).

of whether a Request for Reinstatement has been filed with respect to an application or a registration, no fee is required. It is important to note that the Director has no authority to waive a statutory requirement such as a §8 affidavit[108] or a proper §9 renewal application.[109] Therefore, if the registrant did not timely file a §8 affidavit, §71 affidavit, or §9 renewal application, a request to reinstate a cancelled or expired registration will be denied, regardless of the reason for the delay.[110]

g. *Revival*

An applicant may file a petition to revive an application abandoned because the applicant did not timely respond to an Office action or notice of allowance.[111] The applicant must file the petition within two months of the mailing date of the notice of abandonment or within two months of having actual knowledge of the abandonment if the applicant did not receive the notice of abandonment and the applicant was diligent in checking the status of the application every six months.[112] In order for a proper petition for revival to be filed, the applicant must submit the petition fee, a statement signed by someone with firsthand knowledge of the facts that the delay in filing the response on or before the due date was unintentional, and the proposed response, unless the applicant is alleging that it did not receive the Office Action. The unintentional-delay standard of revival does not apply to incomplete responses. Instead, incomplete responses are handled by the examining attorney, as the examining attorney has discretion to grant an applicant additional time if the applicant's failure to file a complete response was inadvertent.[113] Registrations that have been abandoned for reasons other than an error by the USPTO cannot be revived with a petition to revive because the Director has no authority to waive a statutory requirement.

6. Protest

A Letter of Protest (LOP) is a mechanism by which a party can alert the USPTO about relevant evidence in determining registrability of an

108. 15 U.S.C. §1058.
109. 15 U.S.C. §1059.
110. TMEP §1712.02(a).
111. 37 C.F.R. §2.66.
112. 37 C.F.R. §2.146(i).
113. 37 C.F.R. §2.65(d).

applicant's mark. In particular, an LOP can initially be filed by an interested party by sending a letter explaining why registration of a mark should not occur or why a particular requirement is necessary with respect to the application. The letter should be accompanied by relevant evidence. The evidence submitted in the LOP may support any reasonable grounds for refusal appropriate in ex parte examination.[114] If the LOP is filed before the application is published for opposition, the USPTO will grant the LOP so long as "the evidence is relevant and supports any reasonable grounds for refusal in ex parte examination."[115] However, if the LOP is filed within 30 days *after* the application has published for opposition, it must be clear error for USPTO not to consider the evidence in order for the LOP to be granted by the USPTO. Granted LOPs are sent to the examining attorney for a determination as to whether the evidence supports a refusal or a requirement.

Practically speaking, the contents of the letter accompanying the evidence is somewhat inconsequential but for the stated reason as to why registerability should be denied or restricted, as the accompanying evidence is the more critical aspect of the submission. To prevail in causing the examining attorney to refuse or restrict a mark, credible third-party objective evidence typically should be submitted. Opinion or pure argument will typically not provide sufficient support for a refusal or restriction. When relevant evidence is submitted in an LOP, the LOP can be an effective tool in preventing issuance of a registration of a mark, as it is estimated that in 2009, in approximately 40 percent of the cases in which a pre-publication LOP was granted, the examining attorney consequentially took some action as a result of the LOP.[116]

---

114. While any ground upon which the USPTO could support a refusal of the registration of a mark may be provided for in a LOP, TMEP §1715.01(a) specifically identifies four illustrative grounds for refusal based upon an LOP: (1) descriptiveness or genericness; (2) likelihood of confusion with prior U.S. trademark application(s); (3) likelihood of confusion with prior U.S. trademark application(s) and the existence of a pending infringement litigation between the trademark owner and the applicant of the applied-for mark; and (4) the trademark owner's registered mark has been included with the description of the goods and services of the applied-for mark.

115. TMEP §1715.02(a).

116. Elizabeth C. Buckingham, *Letters of Protest: An Attractive Alternative to a U.S. Opposition,* INTA Bulletin, Vol. 66 No. 4.

PART 3

Trademark/Trade Dress Litigation

If names are not correct, language will not be in accordance with the truth of things.

—Confucius

I. REQUIREMENTS FOR BRINGING SUIT

A. Infringement and Related Causes of Action

The actions and requirements for bringing a trademark infringement suit in a federal district court do not differ significantly from the requirements for bringing a patent or copyright infringement lawsuit or any other civil lawsuit in a federal district court. Distinctions generally arise merely from the substance of the case. A complaint must be filed along with a cover sheet, a filing fee, and a certification of interested parties. As those familiar with litigation in federal district court are aware, the complaint sets forth the claim or claims against the accused infringer and indicates the corresponding requests or demands. It is imperative to determine identification and claim of proper personal jurisdiction and subject matter jurisdiction, or in other words, jurisdiction over the defendant and a federal question (or diversity jurisdiction), respectively. Additional assertions, such as one of proper venue, should be made and should include proper statutory citation. Trademark plaintiffs should also include any other claims in the complaint, such as violations of various provisions of the Lanham Act,[1] dilution claims, unfair competition claims, claims based in contract law, or supplemental claims, including state law claims to be heard or considered as part of the case. Trademark litigations may be somewhat distinct from patent and copyright claims, as there may be common-law and statutory claims asserted. For example, Section 43 of the Lanham Act (15 U.S.C. §1125) gives rise to many of the key statutory causes of action, including unfair competition, trademark and trade dress infringement, importation to infringing goods, dilution, and cyberpiracy prevention. However, other related and similar common-law causes of action (e.g., common-law unfair competition and trademark infringement) can and should be brought as additional claims in the suit.

Plaintiffs in a trademark infringement case—like plaintiffs in any other federal litigation—will want to reference closely the Federal Rules of Civil Procedure (FRCP) to ensure proper action in initiating and pursuing a claim against an accused infringer. Typically, trademark infringement plaintiffs will want to make certain assertions to satisfy key provisions of the FRCP. For example, in order to ensure compliance with FRCP 8(a), plaintiffs should at least identify the trademark that is being infringed, assert that the plaintiff is the owner of the trademark, assert that the trademark has been registered with the USPTO, and provide allegations describing the infringing activity. Plaintiffs should attach a copy of the active registration, as well as evidence of the infringing activity, if at all possible. This evidence may be copies of advertisements, product catalogs, web pages, photographs, or other materials evidencing the infringing activity. While every instance of infringement need not be included in the complaint, sufficient evidence should be included to support each of the claims made in the complaint. Evidence of registration and infringement should be included in the complaint as an attached exhibit. Along with or soon after filing the complaint, the plaintiff in some instances may file a motion for preliminary injunction to enjoin the defendant from further infringing the plaintiff's mark, and an expedited hearing on this motion may be requested. The judge may grant or deny the motion and/or alter the discovery schedule accordingly.

While the timing of the case schedule is subject to judicial modification, after filing of the complaint, the defendant in a typical scenario will

1. For example, many claims of trademark infringement and like causes of action stem from the Lanham Act. *See, e.g.*, regarding trademark infringement Lanham Act §43(a) [15 U.S.C. §1125(a)] and regarding dilution Lanham Act §43(c) [15 U.S.C. §1125(c)].

have 20 days to file an answer.[2] The answer addresses the claims brought by the plaintiff and should include defenses, counterclaims, and related assertions. Sometime after the filing of the complaint and answer there typically will be a scheduling conference held by the judge that sets forth the time line in which each side serves requests for, and is required to provide responses to, requests for production of documents, written interrogatories, and the holding of depositions.

As experienced litigators will be aware, the FRCP also requires certain mandatory initial disclosures early in the case. Likewise, various motions will be filed throughout the case, ranging from potentially dispositive motions, such as motions for summary judgment, to motions to correct typographical errors in a submission. The most procedurally based and minor motions are often unopposed to facilitate the progression of the case and avoid "tit-for-tat" behavior between litigants. Finally, assuming the case has not been settled, it will go to trial, and the voluminous evidence obtained and exchanged during the case will be subject to some procedural compiling and whittling down to facilitate court review through a narrowing of the issues for trial. In fact, judges will aggressively force opposing parties to try to come to agreement on issues of evidence, assertions, and sometimes even reduction in the claims being brought to reduce the judicial burden and decision making required of the court.[3] Further details of IP litigations, many of which transcend through trademark, copyright, and other IP litigations, are discussed further in the *Patent Litigation Section.*

B. Declaratory Judgment

In certain instances, an entity that fears that a trademark infringement suit (or like suit) may be initiated against it can bring suit as a plaintiff to have a court declare that there is in fact no trademark infringement occurring, and may even ask for the court to award damages for, among other things, false accusation of trademark infringement or invalidity of

---

2. The timing of various filings may differ in state court trademark actions and may vary from state to state.

3. For example, both sides will typically have to create a Joint Appendix of evidence submitted in the case, the contents of which are agreed upon by both sides. Likewise, entire deposition transcripts are typically not included in the Joint Appendix. Instead, select pages and sections are chosen and agreed to by both sides to again limit the amount of evidence utilized and considered at trial.

the trademark registration. Declaratory judgment actions also are described in both the *Patent Infringement* and *Copyright Infringement* sections of the *New Practitioner's Guide*, as the Declaratory Judgment Act authorizing declaratory judgment actions applies broadly to any type of actual controversy and thus is applicable to each area of intellectual property, assuming the requirements of (1) the existence of an actual controversy and (2) the jurisdictional requirements regarding the case being proper for federal court are met. Declaratory judgment actions may be an effective tool for an accused infringer to facilitate selection of a preferred venue for litigation and also to, in essence, call a trademark infringement plaintiff's "bluff" with respect to accusations of trademark infringement. Many of the filing requirements of declaratory judgment action are similar to those filed by a trademark owner, but from the opposing perspective. For example, a declaratory judgment plaintiff will want to identify jurisdiction for the case in the Declaratory Judgment Act in conjunction with 28 USC §1338, which gives rise to trademark infringement claims in federal district court. Instead of evidence of infringement, declaratory judgment plaintiffs should consider including evidence of accusation of infringement, evidence that supports an apprehension of suit, and evidence of non-infringement or other defenses, among other evidence.

II. INFRINGEMENT

In order to succeed on the merits in a trademark infringement action, a plaintiff must establish that: (1) the marks accused of being infringed are valid and legally protectable; (2) the marks are owned by the plaintiff; and (3) the defendant's use of the marks to identify goods or services is likely to create confusion concerning their origin.[4] In particular, the plaintiff must show that the defendant's use of the mark is likely to cause confusion as to the affiliation, connection, or association of defendant with plaintiff, or as to the origin, sponsorship, or approval of defendant's goods, services, or commercial activities by plaintiff.[5] It is this "confusion" that underlies the analysis and determination of trademark infringement, as one will recall that trademark protection stems from the Commerce Clause of the U.S. Constitution, and that trademarks serve to identify the source of origin for goods and services and thus to prevent

4. Opticians Ass'n v. Independent Opticians, 920 F.2d 187, 192 (3d Cir. 1990).

5. 1-800 Contacts, Inc. v. WhenU.com, Inc., 414 F.3d 400 (2d Cir. 2005).

consumer confusion in making purchase decisions. Thus, use of marks that are too close or so similar to marks of other entities that they create a "likelihood of confusion" are deemed improper and an infringement of the senior owner's trademark rights—what is commonly referred to as a trademark infringement.

A. Likelihood of Confusion

In determining whether or not there is "likelihood of confusion" between the plaintiff's mark(s) and the accused infringing mark(s), several factors will be used to help make the determination. While the exact factors will vary from circuit to circuit across the country, these factors are fairly similar. The factors applied by the Second Circuit Court of Appeals, often referred to as the *Polaroid* factors (named after the case in which they were enumerated), to some extent served as a model for the factors applied in various other circuits.[6]

The *Polaroid* factors applied in determining likelihood of confusion are: (1) strength of the plaintiff's mark; (2) the degree of similarity between the plaintiff's and defendant's marks; (3) the proximity of the products or services covered by the marks; (4) the likelihood that the plaintiff will bridge the gap; (5) evidence of actual confusion of consumers; (6) the defendant's good faith in adopting its own mark; (7) the quality of the defendant's product or service; and (8) the sophistication of the consumers. Of course, showing the reverse of some or all of the above factors will weigh in favor of a finding *against* a likelihood of confusion and thus a finding of non-infringement of the mark of the plaintiff by the accused infringing mark of the defendant. For example, if a defendant demonstrates that the plaintiff's (senior owner's) mark is weak, used for goods unrelated to the defendant's goods, and not similar to the mark of the defendant, this will help weigh against or demonstrate that there is not a likelihood of confusion. While these factors (or the like or equivalent factors in the relevant jurisdictions) must be considered in determining likelihood of confusion, they are not all always dispositive. Depending on the facts of the case, certain factors may be discarded as irrelevant or as carrying very little weight. Typically, the first three fac-

6. Polaroid Corp. v. Polarad Elecs. Corp., 287 F.2d 492, 495 (2d Cir. 1961) (". . the strength of his mark, the degree of similarity between the two marks, the proximity of the products, the likelihood that the prior owner will bridge the gap, actual confusion, and the reciprocal of defendant's good faith in adopting its own mark, the quality of defendant's product, and the sophistication of the buyers").

tors relating to the strength of the mark, the relatedness of the goods or services, and the similarity of the marks carry the most weight in the analysis, as they are most directed to the core inquiry being performed. However, strong evidence of actual confusion of the defendant's bad faith in choosing or using a mark may be a controlling factor in the analysis in certain factual scenarios. Each of these *Polaroid* factors is discussed in further detail below. Similar factors are applied in the other judicial circuits across the country and are analyzed in a similar fashion.[7]

Strength (or weakness) of the plaintiff's mark

The strength (or weakness) of the plaintiff's mark is an important factor in determining likelihood of confusion. The stronger the mark, the broader the "coverage scope" of the mark may be and thus the more activity that may be considered to constitute infringement. Strong arbitrary or coined marks are more easily infringed than are weak descriptive marks. Fanciful or coined marks, such as KODAK® and XEROX,® may be easily infringed by any similar marks, especially when they have achieved widespread notoriety and recognition. In other instances the strength of the mark may at least in part be as a result of public notoriety and advertising rather than inherent distinctiveness of the mark. Apple, Inc. has utilized the letter "i" by applying it to many basic product names (iPhone, iPod, iPad) to create a globally recognized branding convention that is readily identifiable in relation to Apple products. As such, sale of personal electronic products or perhaps various other categories of products by another party using the name or brand "i-something" may be deemed as being likely to cause confusion and thus infringement of one or more of Apple's trademark(s).

Degree of similarity between plaintiff's and defendant's mark

The similarity of the mark with respect to appearance, sound, connotation, and commercial impression is another important consideration when the analyzing marks under the likelihood-of-confusion test. While marks need not be identical to infringe, the closer an accused infringing mark is

---

7. For example, while the U.S. Court of Appeals for the Second Circuit applies the Polaroid factors, the U.S. Court of Appeals for the Federal Circuit applies the *DuPont* factors, and the U.S. Court of Appeals for the Ninth Circuit applies the *Sleekcraft* test. The particular factors for each court can be found listed at a number of locations and references including at the following website: http://likelihoodofconfusiontrademark.com/likelihoodofconfusioninternet.html.

to the mark of the plaintiff, the stronger and easier the case for likelihood of confusion, all other things being the same. Varied spelling of terms in some instances may create a noticeable distinction in marks that obviates confusion, while in other instances terms that may clearly vary in spelling still may sound almost identical and thus be deemed likely to cause confusion to the consumer. This factor of similarity between the marks often somewhat overlaps and interplays with the next factor: proximity of the products or services covered by the marks. In some instances, identical marks may be deemed not to infringe because of the distinction of the products or services for which they are utilized by the plaintiff and defendant, while vaguely similar marks may be deemed to infringe because of the identical nature of the products or services for which the marks are used by the plaintiff and defendant. However, generally speaking, more similar marks are more likely to cause confusion and thus more likely to infringe.

Proximity or relatedness of the products or services covered by the mark
Another of the more critical factors in the likelihood-of-confusion analysis is consideration of how similar or dissimilar the products or services covered by the plaintiff's mark are to products or services of the accused infringing party. Marks deemed similar that are also used for interchangeable goods or services more likely will be found to weigh in favor of infringement, as compared to a situation wherein the goods or services of the trademark owner and the party accused of infringing are wholly distinct and unrelated. This particular factor—or a like factor applied in other circuits—may also include a consideration of how the goods or services are sold or traded. If the plaintiff sells products to brick-and-mortar retail consumers while the defendant sells to only distributors online through the Internet, the distinctions in trading channels and manner of sales may be generally deemed to some degree to cut against a finding of likelihood of confusion. The closer the goods are in similarity, the easier and the stronger the likelihood of confusion, other factors being the same.

Likelihood that the plaintiff will bridge the gap
How likely the plaintiff is to expand its product line or service into products or services like those being offered by the defendant accused of infringing the mark also will be a relevant factor. Similarly, potential expansion into varied trade channels is another consideration that relates to this factor or like factors. Furthermore, the likelihood of geographic

expansion can be an important consideration. With the proliferation of the Internet and globalization of markets, it is increasingly easy for a trademark infringement plaintiff to paint a reasonable picture of likely expanding geographic markets and sales.

Evidence of actual confusion of consumers
Actual confusion may be extremely persuasive evidence of a likelihood of confusion; however, unlike some of the other factors that differ from actual confusion, absence of actual confusion will not affirmatively prove a lack of likelihood of confusion. Evidence of actual confusion may be demonstrated through actual letters from consumers who are confused by the source of origin of products or who may have purchased one product thinking it to be another. Additionally, some litigants may consider submitting survey evidence to show actual confusion. Litigants on both sides are advised to be meticulous in preparing survey evidence to show actual confusion or the lack thereof, as attacks on the methodology of the survey for these types of factors are common in litigation.

Defendant's good faith (or lack thereof) in adopting its own mark
Intent plays a role in a determination of likelihood of confusion. A defendant that is deemed to have purposely chosen a mark similar to that of a senior party so as to tread on the good will of the senior party's mark will have a very steep uphill battle in demonstrating a lack of likelihood of confusion. This bad faith in choosing a mark may cause the court to infer a likelihood of confusion, which may be difficult to overcome. Direct evidence of the defendant's intent may be difficult to obtain. As such, circumstantial evidence may be the best indicator of intent to tread on the good will of a senior party. In contrast, if a junior party chose a mark for some logically affiliated reasons, such as basis of its location, relation to its name, or other seemingly "good faith" reasons, this factor may then cut in the defendant's favor. Evidence of a trademark search prior to selecting the mark and the performance of due diligence by the defendant in selecting its mark may also be persuasive evidence of the lack of "bad faith" on the part of the defendant in choosing the accused infringing mark.

Quality of the defendant's product or service
Products bought on impulse and inexpensive products are generally more readily confused than are expensive and well-researched purchases. Trade-

marks associated with gum purchased at a checkout counter of grocery stores may be more readily confused than would trademarks for luxury cars. A purchaser of gum at a checkout counter often decides in an instant to purchase the gum, while the purchase of a $50,000 automobile will typically involve research entailing thorough review and inspection of the product beforehand.

Sophistication of the consumers
A customer's sophistication is often limited to the previous factor of the quality of the defendant's products or services. Consumers with a high degree of sophistication typically are less readily confused about similar marks. A purchaser of jumbo jets for a commercial airline likely will have significant sophistication about the products being reviewed for purchase and probably will not be confused between two aircraft with similar trademarks. However, an ordinary citizen purchasing a soda at the local convenience store may be more easily confused by similar marks on the soda cans. If the typical consumer for the products or services in question is a Ph.D. chemist reviewing chemicals in detail before purchasing them, that person would be significantly more sophisticated than would a high school student quickly viewing pens and pencils for a purchase between classes.

B. Reverse Confusion

In unique situations, infringement of trademark rights may be alleged based on a theory of "reverse confusion." In a reverse confusion fact pattern, a junior user of a mark (defined as a second or *subsequent* user of a mark who may or may not have rights to use that mark) will be using the mark much more expansively, in effect saturating the market with its use such that the public associates the mark with the junior user. While the junior user is not benefiting from the good will acquired by the senior user, the senior user still may have a cause of action against the junior user for the damage being caused by the junior user of a mark. For example, a senior user of the mark "Thirst Aid" for beverages successfully pursued a cause of action against a junior user promoting its beverage using the term as part of a slogan—"Gatorade is Thirst-Aid."[8]

8. Sands, Taylor & Wood Co. v. Quaker Oats Co., 978 F.2d 947 (7th Cir. 1992).

III. DILUTION

In some instances an owner of a valid and enforceable mark may have a cause of action—a claim for "dilution" against a party using a similar mark—even if a "likelihood of confusion" cannot be proven sufficiently to provide for a finding of trademark infringement. Dilution claims may be pursued under the Lanham Act[9] as well as under state law claims. In order to bring a cause of action for dilution, the mark must be sufficiently distinctive or have acquired sufficient distinctiveness to be considered a famous mark.[10]

Dilution claims may trace their roots back at least to an early case in the UK in which Kodak bicycles, while perhaps not likely to be confused with Kodak® cameras, were found to have diluted the famous mark.[11] The theory behind providing for dilution claims is that to limit the cause of action for owners of marks to when they can show likelihood of confusion allows junior users to unjustly tread on the good will of the senior party. Famous marks are those that have been or are so distinctive, either inherently or through their acquired distinctiveness, that their use with virtually any good or service conjures up thought or reference to the senior mark. Given the renown and identification for such a mark, allowing others to use it for goods or services, even if clearly not associated with the owner of the mark, steadily chips away at the good will and brand value of the famous mark. If Kodak is permitted to be used by a another entity as a brand for bicycles and then is permitted to be used as a brand by another company—and so on and so forth—soon the famous KODAK brand will

9. The Trademark Dilution Revision Act of 2006 (H.R. 683) was signed into law on October 6, 2006, and amended the trademark law, especially federal dilution law, in significant part in response to the U.S. Supreme Court decision of *Moseley v. V Secret Catalogue, Inc.*, 537 U.S.418 (2003), which specified the need to show *actual trademark dilution* rather than merely the *likelihood of dilution* in order to succeed on a claim of dilution.

10. 15 U.S.C. §1125(c) ("Subject to the principles of equity, the owner of a famous mark that is distinctive, inherently or through acquired distinctiveness, shall be entitled to an injunction against another person who, at any time after the owner's mark has become famous, commences use of a mark or trade name in commerce that is likely to cause dilution by blurring or dilution by tarnishment of the famous mark, regardless of the presence or absence of actual or likely confusion, of competition, or of actual economic injury.").

11. Eastman Photographic Materials v. Kodak Cycle, 15 R.P.C. 105 (Eng. 1898).

cease to have the strength, recognition, and clear indication of origin that it formerly had. Similar hypothetical scenarios for other marks can be envisioned (e.g., Nike bath and tile cleaner, Microsoft medium roast coffee, Mercedes-Benz software, or IBM cleaning services).

There have been some notable instances where seemingly famous marks continue to be used by other companies for distinct products. These instances often arise where the senior use of a mark is a smaller entity or sold products or services only in specific categories of goods and services, while a junior party came along that sold distinct products or services and grew to become a famous mark. Also, in some instances the common term of the mark may not provide a basis for trademark protection when used alone, but will provde protection when combined with other terms. In this instance, the entities can continue to coexist, and any of the goods and products and services associated with the mark will play a key role in defining the boundary of trademark and related rights.[12]

A. Determining if a Mark Is Famous

In order to make a valid claim for dilution, the mark must first and foremost be deemed "famous." According to the Lanham Act,[13] "a mark is famous if it is widely recognized by the general consuming public of the United States as a designation of source of the goods or services of the mark's owner." The statute also provides that courts may take into account relevant factors in determining whether or not a mark is a famous, including specifically the following: (1) the duration, extent, and geographic reach of advertising and publicity of the mark, whether advertised or publicized by the owner or third parties; (2) the amount, volume, and geographic extent of sales of goods or services offered under the mark; (3) the extent of actual recognition of the mark; and (4) whether the mark was registered.[14] In reviewing these factors, it is somewhat apparent how the relating facts will either weigh in favor or weigh against the mark at issue being properly considered a famous mark. Specific case law can provide more specific and pertinent guidance regarding the delineated factors; however, the factors are described in further detail below.

12. An example of a well-known mark that is used as a mark (or part of a mark) for several companies with varied goods and services is DELTA, for which corporate entities exist for Delta Airlines, Delta Faucet, and Delta Dental.

13. 15 U.S.C. §1125(c)(2).

14. *Id.*

Duration, extent, and geographic reach of advertising and publicity
The longer a trademark has been publicized and advertised in association with goods and/or services, the more pervasive and widely disseminated are the advertisement and publicity across the country, which strongly weighs in favor of the mark being deemed famous. Coca-Cola® is a common example of a mark that has been used extensively, for a very long duration, and with expansive geographic reach in advertising and publicity. Other marks and companies with well-known advertisement and publicity campaigns include Nike, Microsoft, and Target. Largely because of these campaigns, these marks are readily identifiable to virtually the entire population. Such longstanding and widespread recognition from advertising and publicity supports a claim that these marks should be considered "famous marks."

Amount, volume, and geographic extent of sales of goods or services
Logically, the more sales of goods or services associated with the mark, the stronger the claim that the mark is famous, all other factors aside. A trademark, as previously described, serves to identify source of origin and helps consumers in making purchase decisions. The more goods and services sold and provided to the public bearing the mark, the more easily the source of the goods or services is identified or distinguished from the goods and services of others.

The extent of actual recognition of the mark
Regardless of a company's sales figures or marketing budget, marks that are well recognized for whatever reason are more likely to be considered famous. This factor, aimed at actual recognition, is related to the first two factors, but more pointedly gets to the heart of the matter regarding recognition of the mark. In determining the extent of actual recognition of a mark, market survey evidence often helps show the extent of actual recognition.

Whether the mark was registered
Federal registration of a mark prior to bringing a dilution action is extremely important, as the lack of a valid registration for the mark at issue cuts sharply against a plaintiff's claim of dilution. That aside, failure to have registered a mark prior to attempting to enforce the mark also may further burden a claimant's ability to produce evidence proving the requisite elements of the claims against the defendant (i.e., ownership of a valid mark). Failure to register the mark will also undermine arguments regard-

ing the pervasiveness, value, and importance of the mark given that the owner has failed to even go through the trouble of registering the mark.

B. Types of Dilution

Claims of dilution under the Lanham Act are categorized as either "dilution by blurring" or "dilution by tarnishment." State dilution claims also recognize dilution in the varied forms of blurring or tarnishment, but the particulars may vary to some degree from state to state.

1. Blurring

"Dilution by blurring" is defined as an "association arising from the similarity between a mark or trade name and a famous mark that impairs the distinctiveness of the famous mark."[15] In making a determination about whether a mark is likely to cause dilution by blurring, courts consider factors that include: (1) the degree of similarity between the mark or trade name and the famous mark; (2) the degree of inherent or acquired distinctiveness of the famous mark; (3) the extent to which the owner of the famous mark is engaging in substantially exclusive use of the mark; (4) the degree of recognition of the famous mark; (5) whether the user of the mark or trade name intended to create an association with the famous mark; and (6) any actual association between the mark or trade name and the famous mark.[16] An example of a mark found to dilute another mark by blurring is "Perfumebay," which was used for online sales of perfume and deemed to have diluted the mark of well-known online auction site "eBay."[17]

2. Tarnishment

Tarnishment is an "association arising from the similarity between a mark or trade name and a famous mark that harms the reputation of the famous mark."[18] A classic example of dilution by tarnishment involved sale of a poster depicting a bag of the illegal drug cocaine with a slogan "Enjoy Cocaine," which was found to dilute the "Enjoy Coca-Cola" mark owned by Coca-Cola.[19] A more recent and more nuanced example of "dilution

---

15. 15 U.S.C. §1125(c)(2)(B).
16. *Id.*
17. Perfumebay Inc. v. eBay, Inc., 506 F.3d 1165 (9th Cir. 2007).
18. 15 U.S.C. §1125(c)(2)(C).
19. Coca-Cola Co. v. Gemini Rising, Inc., 346 F. Supp. 1183 (E.D.N.Y. 1972).

by tarnishment" involved the "Victor's Secret" mark, which was found to dilute the famous "Victoria's Secret" mark for women's lingerie and clothing.[20]

IV. DEFENSES AND COUNTERCLAIMS

A defendant accused of trademark infringement or dilution of a mark may either demonstrate that there is not infringement or dilution, or prove that despite infringement there is an absence of liability because the use is properly considered a fair use or a parody, or that an equitable defense applies. Many defenses in trademark cases may fall under either the heading of "fair use," including what may sometimes be referred to as "nominative use," or parody. In certain circumstances, if equity dictates, one or more equitable defenses, such as laches, estoppel, acquiescence, or unclean hands, may be applicable. Defendants may also be in a position to bring counterclaims such as trademark infringement against the plaintiff (e.g., claiming to in fact be the senior owner) or misuse of the trademark by the plaintiff.

A. Fair Use

When a descriptive mark is used in good faith for its primary meaning rather than its secondary or trademark meaning, and no consumer confusion is likely to result, a "fair use" defense may be made. For example, use of the term "all bran" in describing a type of cereal or "fish fry" to described a batter for fish are examples where courts have determined that the use of the terms was fair use, as the terms were purely descriptive and did not violate the trademarks' rights of Kellogg's brand "All-Bran" cereal[21] and Zatarain's "Fish-Fri"[22] marks, respectively. The Lanham Act also sets forth specific exclusions when activity that could be considered dilution is not actionable. Not surprisingly, "any fair use, including nomi-

20. V Secret Catalogue, Inc. et al. v. Moseley, 558 F. Supp.734 (W.D. Ky. 2008).

21. Peaceable Planet, Inc. v. Ty Inc., 362 F.3d 986, 988 (7th Cir. 2004) ("An example is 'All Bran.' The name describes the product. If the first firm to produce an all-bran cereal could obtain immediate trademark protection, and thus prevent all other producers of all-bran cereal from describing their product as all bran, it would be difficult for competitors to gain a foothold in the market. They would be as if speechless.").

22. Zatarain's, Inc. v. Oak Grove Smokehouse, Inc., 698 F.2d 786 (5th Cir. 1983).

native or descriptive fair use, or facilitation of such fair use," including use in comparative advertising, or promotion or identification, and parodying, criticism, or commentary on the famous mark owner or goods or services of the famous mark, is not actionable under dilution. "All forms of news and reporting and news commentary" as well as "any noncommercial use of the mark" are not actionable under the federal dilution statute.

A related but varied defense that may be asserted is referred to as a "nominative use" defense. Nominative use involves use of a mark in a fashion that is necessary for purposes of identification of another's product. The policy behind a nominative use defense is that in some instances use of a trademark is necessary to identify and talk about another party's products and services, and there is deemed to be virtually no other way to identify or reference the product or service. To prohibit use of the mark in these instances would stifle speech, and thus this defense protects use of the mark for limited purposes of identification and discussion of another's products and services. Accordingly, a defendant may be successful in asserting that use of trademark is merely a nominative use if (1) the product or service group is not readily identifiable without using the mark, (2) only so much of the mark as reasonably necessary to identify it was used, and (3) there was no suggestion of endorsement or sponsorship by the entity that owns the mark.[23]

B. Parody

Artistic and editorial parodies of trademarks are believed to serve a valuable critical function and are entitled to some degree of First Amendment protection. As such, in certain circumstances, use of trademarks in or as part of a parody function will be protected speech. A critical issue with respect to the defense of parody is the extent to which the use is directly

23. New Kids on the Block v. News America Publishing, Inc., 971 F.2d 302 (9th Cir. 1992) (A successful nominative use defense was pursued in a case involving *USA Today* and the pop group New Kids on the Block. *USA Today* ran a telephone poll in which readers could vote for their favorite member of the group. The New Kids on the Block sued *USA Today* for trademark infringement for use of their mark. The court held that the use of the trademark "New Kids on the Block" was a nominative use because the group was not readily identifiable without using the mark; only so much of the mark was used as was reasonably necessary to identify it; and there was no suggestion of endorsement or sponsorship by the group with regard to use of the mark by the newspaper.).

tied to a commercial use. The more directly an accused infringing mark is tied to a commercial use, the less likely a parody defense will be successful, as the commercial use will undermine the "protected speech" basis of the parody defense. For example, while use of a character resembling a pig named "Spa'am" in a Muppets movie was not found liable for violating Hormel's trademark rights in the "Spam" mark based on the parody defense,[24] use of "Gucchic Goo" on diaper bags, an apparent allusion to the Gucci® brand handbags, was *not protected speech* under the parody defense.[25] Thus, while the parody defense is a well-established defense to trademark infringement that may shield certain use of marks from liability, the specific boundaries of what particular actions may or may not constitute "parody," insulated from liability as free speech as compared to infringement of trademark rights, is an extremely fact-specific analysis that is best made in light of analogous case law precedents.

C. Equitable Defenses

Like other areas of intellectual property, equitable defenses of laches, estoppel, and acquiescence may serve as defenses to trademark infringement. These defenses typically emanate from extended delay on the part of the trademark owner in enforcing its rights and/or certain actions by the trademark owner such that finding the defendant liable for infringement of the mark, even if its actions satisfy the likelihood-of-confusion test for infringement, would now be considered unjust. Likewise, unclean hands—a defense that arises in other areas of law—may also serve as a basis for a defense to trademark infringement. Trademark law also recognizes the defenses of innocent infringement, fraud, and abandonment.

V. REMEDIES

A variety of remedies may be available to a successful trademark infringement or dilution under the Lanham Act. Courts may issue both preliminary and permanent injunctions as they deem reasonable to prevent the violation of any rights of a registrant of a mark and to prevent violation of the Lanham Act specifically, including trademark infringement, importation of infringing goods, or dilution.[26] Additionally, suc-

24. Hormel Foods Corp. v. Jim Henson Prods., 73 F.3d 497 (2d Cir. 1996).

25. Gucci Shops, Inc. v. R.H. Macy & Co., 446 F. Supp. 838 (S.D.N.Y. 1977).

26. 15 U.S.C. §1116(a).

cessful plaintiffs may recover any damages sustained by the plaintiff, infringer's profits, and the costs of the action in a fashion that makes the plaintiff whole consistent with the principles of equity.[27] In exceptional cases,[28] a plaintiff may recover reasonable attorneys' fees.[29] Lastly, the court may order that any infringing article bearing the word, term, name, symbol, or device be destroyed.[30]

27. 15 U.S.C. §1117(a).

28. Federal courts have interpreted the Lanham Act such that malicious, fraudulent, deliberate, or willful trademark.infringement may qualify as "exceptional circumstances" and thus result in attorneys' fees being awarded. *See, e.g.*, United Phosphorus, Ltd. v. Midland Fumigant, Inc., 205 F.3d 1219, 1232 (10th Cir. 2000).

29. 15 U.S.C. §1117(a).

30. 15 U.S.C. §1118 (in a cause of action for dilution a court may order destruction of goods only if dilution is deemed "willful").

PART 4

Unfair Competition

Our life is not really a mutual helpfulness; but rather, it's fair competition cloaked under due laws of war; it's a mutual hostility.

—Thomas Carlyle

I. BACKGROUND AND RATIONALE

Herbert Hoover once stated, "[c]ompetition is not only the basis of protection to the consumer, but is the incentive to progress." Generally speaking *fair competition* provides the greatest benefit to consumers. Benefits to consumers from a system of fair competition are not just theoretical. Fair competition has the tangible effects of, among other things, keeping prices down, increasing output, and encouraging rapid innovation. Laws and regulations for maintaining fair competition or preventing "unfair competition" are related in purpose and function to trademark laws. Not surprisingly, the constitutional basis for these laws and regulations, like federal trademark law, is rooted in Article I, Section 8, Clause 3, the Commerce Clause of the U.S. Constitution. The Commerce Clause gives Congress the power "to regulate commerce with foreign nations, and among the several states, and with the Indian tribes" and federal unfair competition laws have been enacted by Congress to regulate commerce to the desired benefit of consumers and the public. Like trademark law, which also can be considered a form of unfair competition, unfair competition laws at the federal level are rooted in the Commerce Clause. Unfair competition laws, like trademark law, exist at the state/common law level as well. Unfair competition laws can vary significantly from state to state, although many provisions in state unfair competition statues have language similar to federal unfair competition provisions.

Like some other types of intellectual property laws, unfair competition laws are aimed at ensuring commerce is conducted in the "Goldilocks" spectrum of activities. Desirable fair competition is sometimes described as the activities that fall between overly aggressive or overly zealous competitive activities and activities that lack any competitive aspects and undermine competition. While overzealous competitive activities and activities that undermine competition are two ends of a spectrum, each harms consumers. Consumers will either not be able to make informed decisions about products and services due to their inability to separate fact from fiction (unfair competition) or will lack any real choices for providers of products or services due to one or a select few holding power over the market (monopolistic). Accordingly, unfair competition laws and regulation prevent overly zealous competition while antitrust laws and regulation prevent activities that undermine competition.

Figure 8-1

Spectrum of Fair/Unfair Competitive Activities

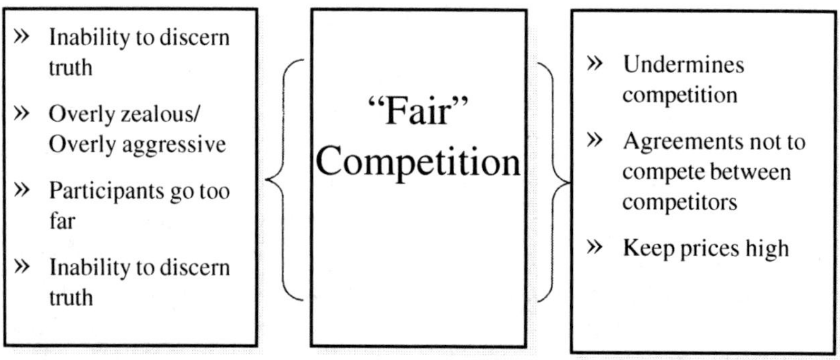

Unfair competition is a larger umbrella of laws under which several particular types of "unfair competition" claims may be brought. Unfair competition laws are often considered catch-all provisions for guarding against unfair, deceitful, and unethical practices in business. As such, these causes of action are often brought in lawsuits with other causes of action, including trademark infringement and trademark dilution under the U.S. Trademark Act. Prior to the existence of federal statutory provisions concerning unfair competition, causes of action had to be brought based upon state/common law. The *Restatement of Unfair Competition*, a treatise summarizing "black letter" law of state/common law causes of action, sets forth a general summary of unfair competition laws that currently exist. In general, the *Restatement* describes the principles of competition in the United States. A person or entity is not liable for commercial harm that occurs to another by engaging in a business or trade *unless* the harm results from acts or practices of an actor that includes (1) deceptive marketing, (2) infringement of trademarks, (3) misappropriation of trade values including trade secrets, or (4) other acts of unfair competition.[1] As described, in the *Restatement*, actors also may be liable if acts or practices of the actors are actionable under federal or state statue, international agreements, or other common law principles. Section 43(a) of the Lanham Act and §5 of The Federal Trade Commission Act (15 U.S.C. §45(a)(1)) are the most commonly encountered federal statutes that regulate "unfair competition" at the federal level.

II. FEDERAL STATUTORY CAUSES OF ACTION

Prior to enactment of federal laws prohibiting unfair competition, actions against these "unfair" practices were brought under common law/

---

1. *Restatement of Law (Third), Unfair Competition,* Chapter One—The Freedom to Compete—§1 General Principles ("*One who causes harm* to the commercial relation of another by engaging in a business tor trade *is not subject to liability to the other for such harm* ***unless***:

> (a) the harm results from acts or practices of the actor actionable by the other under the rules of this Restatement relating to:
>
> (1) *deceptive marketing*, as defined in Chapter Two;
>
> (2) *infringement of trademarks* and other indicia of identification as specified in Chapter Three;
>
> (3) *appropriation of intangible trade values* including *trade secrets* and the *right of publicity*, as specified in Chapter Four, or from other acts or practices of the actor determined to be actionable as an *unfair method of competition*, taking into account the nature of the conduct and its likely effect on both the person seeking relief and the public; or
>
> (b) the acts or practices of the actor are *actionable by the other under federal or state statutes, international agreements, or general principles of common law* apart from those considered in this Restatement.")
>
> (Emphasis added.).

state law. As is common for federal statutes in various areas of law, the federal statutes prohibiting unfair competition include codification of previously existing common law principles developed over time in case law into statutory provisions.

A. §43(a) of the Lanham Act (15 U.S.C. §1125(a))

Section 43(a) of the Lanham Act[2] provides a cause of action against "[a]ny person who, on or in connection with any goods or services, or any container for goods, uses in commerce any word, term, name, symbol, or device, or any combination thereof, or any false designation of origin, false or misleading description of fact, or false or misleading representation of fact which:

(A) is likely to cause confusion, or to cause mistake, or to deceive as to the affiliation, connection, or association of such person with another person, or as to the origin, sponsorship, or approval of his or her goods, services, or commercial activities by another person, or

(B) in commercial advertising or promotion, misrepresents the nature, characteristics, qualities, or geographic origin of his or her or another person's goods, services, or commercial activities, *shall be liable* in a civil action *by any person who believes that he or she is or is likely damaged by such act*." (Emphasis added.)

Two aspects of §43(a) are worth highlighting: (1) who can bring an action under §43(a) and (2) what harm must an entity have suffered in order to be able to bring a claim under §43(a). First, "*any person* who believes he or she is *likely to be damaged*" may bring an action for violation of the Lanham Act under §43(a). As such, not only can competitors bring causes of action but so can any individual consumers or members of the public who were harmed or are likely to be harmed down the road. This leads to the second noteworthy aspect, that a "likelihood of being harmed" is sufficient harm to support a claim under §43(a). While most causes of action require the "actual harm" to have already occurred before a party can bring a claim, §43(a) permits parties that are likely to be harmed to bring a claim even if that harm has not yet occurred.

2. 15 U.S.C. §1125(a).

B. §5 of the Federal Trade Commission Act (FTCA) (15 U.S.C. §45(a)(1))

The Federal Trade Commission (FTC) is headed by five commissioners, each nominated by the President and confirmed by the Senate. Each serves a seven-year term. The President chooses one commissioner to act as the chairman and no more than three of the commissioners can be from the same political party. The FTC was created in 1914 with an original purpose of preventing unfair methods of competition in commerce as part of the battle to "bust the trusts." Since then, the commission has been delegated greater authority, including the power to police anticompetitive practices and prohibitions against unfair and captive practices. The FTC is the only federal agency with both consumer protection and competition jurisdiction in broad sectors of the economy.[3]

Under the Federal Trade Commission Act, the FTC is empowered to: (a) prevent unfair methods of competition and unfair or deceptive acts or practices in or affecting commerce;[4] (b) seek monetary redress and other relief for conduct injurious to consumers; (c) prescribe trade regulation rules defining with specificity acts or practices that are unfair or deceptive and establish requirements designed to prevent such acts or practices; (d) conduct investigations relating to the organization, business, practices, and management of entities engaged in commerce; and (e) make reports and legislative recommendations to Congress.[5] In particular, whenever the commissioners believe or have reason to believe that an entity is using or has used unfair competition or deceptive acts they may hold a hearing and take action to enjoin the actor from continuing the unfair or deceitful practices.[6] In addition, the FTC is well recognized for further regulation of trade as

3. http://www.ftc.gov/ftc/about.shtm.

4. *See, e.g.*, 15 U.S.C. §45(a)(1) ("Unfair methods of competition in or affecting commerce, and unfair or deceptive acts or practices in or affecting commerce, are hereby declared unlawful.").

5. http://www.ftc.gov/ogc/stat1.shtm.

6. *See, e.g.*, 15 U.S.C. §45(b) ("Whenever the Commission shall have reason to believe that any such person, partnership, or corporation has been or is using any unfair method of competition or unfair or deceptive act or practice in or affecting commerce, and if it shall appear to the Commission that a proceeding by it in respect thereof would be to the interest of the public, it shall issue and serve upon such person, partnership, or corporation a complaint stating its charges in that respect and containing a notice of a hearing upon a day and at a place therein fixed at least thirty days after the service of said complaint. The person, partnership, or corporation so complained of shall

the FTC has jurisdiction for review of certain corporate activities in relation to antitrust concerns and claims.

C. Section 337 Investigations before the International Trade Commission (ITC)[7]

The U.S. International Trade Commission (USITC) is a quasi-judicial agency with broad investigative responsibilities on matters of trade.[8] Section 337 of the Tariff Act of 1930 (19 U.S.C. §1337) empowers the commission to conduct investigations into allegations of certain unfair practices in import trade. Section 337 identifies the infringement of various intellectual property rights, including patent infringement, trademark infringement, and copyright infringement, as well as other forms of unfair competition in import trade to be unlawful practices. Forms of unfair competition that may be investigated by the ITC include misappropriation of trade secrets, passing off, false advertising, and antitrust violations.

The ITC's role is to protect against import injury to U.S. industries among which may include importation of items protected by U.S. intellectual property rights. Jurisdiction of the ITC is in rem. Stated another way, jurisdiction is over the article(s) being imported rather than the party or parties. In order for a valid complaint[9] to be filed before the

---

have the right to appear at the place and time so fixed and show cause why an order should not be entered by the Commission requiring such person, partnership, or corporation to cease and desist from the violation of the law so charged in said complaint. Any person, partnership, or corporation may make application, and upon good cause shown may be allowed by the Commission to intervene and appear in said proceeding by counsel or in person. The testimony in any such proceeding shall be reduced to writing and filed in the office of the Commission. If upon such hearing the Commission shall be of the opinion that the method of competition or the act or practice in question is prohibited by this subchapter, it shall make a report in writing in which it shall state its findings as to the facts and shall issue and cause to be served on such person, partnership, or corporation an order requiring such person, partnership, or corporation to cease and desist from using such method of competition or such act or practice. . . .").

7. ITC investigations under 19 U.S.C. §1337 are often referred to as "Section 337" investigations for shorthand.

8. http://www.usitc.gov/press_room/about_usitc.htm.

9. Complainants that desire the ITC to hear a case file a complaint and the ITC will decide whether to initiate an investigation that is delegated to one of the ITC Administrative Law Judge (ALJ).

ITC, there must be: (1) an unfair act, (2) importation, and (3) a domestic industry.[10] The unfair act requirement is satisfied by the unfair intellectual property related actions being complained of, which may include patent or trademark infringement and other intellectual property violations previously delineated. Therefore, if a domestic entity is only infringing a patent by making and selling accused infringing products in the United States, the ITC will not have jurisdiction to begin an investigation. However, if the same product is being imported from a foreign country and sold in the United States, then the importation requirement will be satisfied. Finally, there must be a domestic industry relating to the article being protected. In other words, an entity must be practicing the invention or producing the article. Non-practicing entities (NPEs), or patent trolls as they are sometimes pejoratively called, may not be able to bring a case before the ITC as they often will not be able to demonstrate the domestic industry requirement for initiation of an investigation by the ITC. However, in certain instances licensing related activities may satisfy the requirement. In particular, it has been held that litigation activities such as preparing for and engaging in patent litigation, if connected to the execution of a license could prove a domestic industry.[11]

Litigation, especially patent litigations before the ITC, has been pursued with increasing frequency. While litigation before the ITC is discussed in further detail in the *Patent Litigation Section*, it is worth noting some characteristics of interest relating to ITC investigations. ITC investigations have very fast case schedules (e.g., 12 to 15 months) compared to traditional litigation in other courts. ITC cases are also heard before an administrative law judge (ALJ) and typically permit virtually unlimited discovery. The ITC only has jurisdiction to grant either a limited, or in some instances a general, exclusion order over the product(s). No money damages can be awarded by the ITC. It is common for complainants in an ITC case to concurrently pursue damages in a similar case in district court in which money damages can be awarded.

10. 19 U.S.C. §1337(2) (The requirement of a domestic industry applies only to articles protected under §1337(a)(1)(B-E), which includes articles protected by patent, copyright, trademark, mask work, or design. Other forms of unfair competition under §1337(1)(A) do not require a showing of a domestic industry.).

11. Certain Coaxial Cable Connectors and Components Thereof and Products Containing Same, USITC Inv. No. 337-TA-650, Comm'n Op. at 49-50 (Apr. 14, 2010), EDIS Doc. No. 422832.

III. COMMON FORMS OF UNFAIR COMPETITION

Unfair competition is a broad category of intellectual property that includes numerous statutory rules and common law principles that prevent competitive practices that are deemed to go beyond that which is acceptable and labeled "unfair." Trademark infringement can be considered one form of unfair competition. As described above, in the eyes of the ITC, patent infringement and copyright infringement are also considered to be unfair trade practices. Patent, trademarks, copyright, and trade dress causes of action are typically considered as intellectual property rights and stand-alone issues and causes of action that are covered herein individually in detail. However, several other common forms of unfair competition may arise at common law or through broad statutory regulations, such as the Lanham Act, that typically are not considered as stand-alone IP topics but rather are typically characterized as types of unfair competition. False advertising, product disparagement, passing or palming off, and right of publicity are types of unfair competition for which causes of action may be brought under one or more of the above described federal statutes and/or under state common law.

A. False Advertising

False advertising often involves advertisements that misrepresent the nature, quality, or character of goods or services. These misrepresentations may be made concerning an entity's own goods or services or they may be directed to the goods or services of another entity. Not only are express or literally false statements actionable, but implicitly false representations may give rise to a claim for false advertising. In determining whether a representation constitutes false advertising, a fact finder will often look to whether a substantial number of consumers were under a false impression. Practically, this evidence is introduced by way of survey evidence. Certain promotional statements or exaggerations reasonably expected of a seller relating to the degree of quality of the product or service that cannot be precisely determined will typically not be considered false advertising. These imprecise promotional statements may include statements such as "better," "superior," or "best" and are sometimes referred to as puffery as the seller is puffing her product or service. An example of acceptable puffery language would be Papa John's advertisements that claim "better ingredients, better pizza." In contrast, if a burger restaurant advertised that a "particular competitor" used baby sheep in their hamburger patties when in fact the competitor did not, these advertisements would be an example of impermissible false advertising.

B. Product Disparagement

Product disparagement can be considered a particular type of false advertising and involves discrediting a competitor's product with an intentional and untrue statement about another company or its products or services. The statement above about a burger restaurant using baby sheep in its burger patties would qualify as "product disparagement," assuming the statements were intentional and untrue. Product disparagement has traditionally been a state law claim that was similar to a "trade libel" claim. Common law requirements for actions of product disparagement sometimes included a showing of intent or recklessness on the part of the actor, as well as actual harm. In many instances, product disparagement type actions are now brought under §43(a) of the Lanham Act. As stated before, §43(a) does not require any intent to be attributed to the actor and no actual harm needs to have occurred. Instead, only a likelihood of harm needs to be shown. Thus, §43(a) of the Lanham Act has lowered the threshold for alleged victims of product disparagement cases in order to be able to bring a claim.

C. Passing Off

"Passing off" (or "palming off") is a misrepresentation by a person that his goods or services are the goods and services of another or have some association with the goods of another. Under common law, an entity would have a tort cause of action against another entity for "passing off" its goods or services. Actions previously actionable under passing off common law now also may be brought as violations of the broad provisions of §43(a) of the Lanham Act. "Passing off" may be characterized more specifically as either "regular passing off" or "reverse passing off." Each of these categories may be further labeled as or divided into "express" versus "implied." An entity may perform *express passing off*, *implied passing off*, *express reverse passing off*, or *implied reverse passing off*. These various types of "passing off" are further illustrated below.

- *Express passing off*: Falsely placing another entity's mark on products you are providing. (You sell coffee you brew in your house from beans you grew in your yard and you place a Starbucks logo on the cups.)

- *Implied passing off*: Using a picture, sample, or like device to falsely and impliedly represent that the product being provided is the product of the entity from the picture, sample, or like device. (You sell coffee you brew in your house from beans you grew in your yard and you place a picture of a Starbucks cup of coffee near a window you are selling coffee out of.)
- *Reverse express passing off*: Removing or otherwise obliterating the original mark on a product without the mark owner's permission and rebranding the product. (You buy bags of Starbucks coffee beans, remove any trademarks, add your own mark, and then sell the bags of coffee.)
- *Reverse implied passing off*: Removing or otherwise obliterating the original mark on a product without the mark owner's permission and selling the product in an unbranded state. (You buy bags of Starbucks coffee beans, remove any trademarks on the bags, and resell them unbranded.)

In light of potential liability for passing off, one may wonder when it is acceptable to use, mention. or include another entity's mark. It would seem to be illogically restrictive and counter to that observed in the world to have to ensure another entity's mark is never seen once the product leaves the manufacturer or retailer's control in a first sale. While passing off is prohibited, certain common "collateral uses" of goods are acceptable and will not give rise to causes of action under unfair competition laws if the uses occur in a certain manner. Below are several permissible collateral uses of goods:

- *Rebottled/repackaged goods*: If entity A purchased the original product, it can typically continue to use the original owner's trademark if the label makes entity A's own identity clear, as well as the lack of any affiliation to the original mark on the goods.
- *Repaired/recondition goods*: If entity A purchased the original product, it can typically continue to use the original owner's trademark if the label makes clear entity A's own identity, as well as the lack of any affiliation to the original mark on the goods. Entity A typically should also disclose that the goods are used.
- *Dealerships, service outlets, and replacement parts*: Entity A may use another entity's mark provided it does not falsely represent that it is an "authorized" dealership or service outlet.

- *Comparative advertising*: Comparative advertising including use or display of another entity's marks is acceptable as long as the ads are truthful.

D. Right of Publicity

The right of publicity is the right to control the commercial use of one's own identity. As such, a person's right of publicity is violated by an unauthorized commercial use of a person's *name, image, likeness,*[12] or other personal attributes (e.g. voice, identity, etc.) in a way that causes commercial damage to the plaintiff. Rights of publicity are protected under state/common law. Approximately half of the states have enacted laws recognizing the right of publicity and it is believed that the right of publicity also exists through common law principles in the states that have not enacted right of publicity laws. A state that has a more sizable or influential population of people with images of recognizable value may be more inclined to enact strict laws protecting right of publicity, thus it may be obvious to predict some of the states that have passed right of publicity laws. California and New York, two states known to have a significant number of high profile actors, musicians, broadcasters, entertainers, and other celebrities, each has enacted right of publicity of laws, with New York being the first state to do so in 1903. One rationale behind right of publicity laws is related to the rationale behind the protection of trademarks as the name, image, and likeness of an individual may serve as a source of origin and provide quality assurance information. Additionally, there is an equitable aspect to allowing celebrities and others with personas of value to profit from their personas as these individuals have historically dedicated significant time, effort, and resources to develop their personas and it is only fair that they, not a third party, receive the fruits of those efforts.[13] While the right of publicity varies state to state, some of the more well known cases provide a further understanding of what may be protectable under the right of publicity.

---

12. "Name, image, and likeness" are consistently protected under right of publicity across the states. However, that which is considered part of "name, image, and likeness" varies from state to state.

13. As a legally irrelevant aside, the actions and behavior of today's reality TV stars may effectively undermine this theory based on the rapidity and ease with which anyone who gets an audience is able to reach celebrity status for arguably no reason more than their appearance on a widely disseminated media.

- *Martin Luther King Jr. Center for Social Change v. American Heritage Products*[14]—The Martin Luther King, Jr. Center for Social Change was successful in preventing American Heritage Products from manufacturing busts of Martin Luther King, Jr. as funeral accessories. (MLK Jr. was deceased at the time and the case included Coretta Scott King as administrator as a plaintiff for Mr. King's estate.)
- *Midler v. Ford Motor Company*[15]—Ford's use of another person's voice in its commercials that sounded similar to Bette Midler's voice, after Bette Midler refused to lend her voice to the commercials, violated her right of privacy.
- *Hirsch v. S.C. Johnson & Son*[16]—S.C. Johnson's use of "Crazylegs" (a nickname associated with Elroy "Crazylegs" Hirsch—a running back and receiver for the L.A. Rams and Chicago Rockets professional football teams) on a shaving gel for women violated Hirsch's right of publicity.
- *Hoffman v. Capital Cities/ABC, Inc.*[17]—Dustin Hoffman was awarded $3,270,000 related to violation of his publicity rights for a magazine's use of a digitally manipulated image of his character in "Tootsie" dressed with a Richard Tyler gown and Ralph Lauren shoes, before the case was overturned on First Amendment grounds.

Among other celebrities who have brought actions for violation of the right of privacy or similar causes are Elvis Presley, Groucho Marx, Bela Lugosi, Muhammad Ali, and Arnold Palmer, to name a few.

Even in states in which a right of publicity law or similar law has been enacted, this right may be limited in varying manners. The First Amendment of the U.S. Constitution provides a significant limit to the right of publicity. Because the Constitution is the supreme law of the land and any state or common law right of publicity that encroaches on the First Amendment will be deemed unconstitutional and nullified. As a result, the publication of an unauthorized biography is permitted and would not be deemed a violation of the right of publicity.[18] As is com-

---

14. 296 S.E. 2d.697 (Sup. Ct. Georgia 1982).
15. 849 F.2d 460 (9th Cir. 1989).
16. 90 Wis. 2d 379, 280 N.W.129 (1979).
17. 33 F. Supp. 2d 867 (C.D. Cal. 1999).
18. Depending on the content, the subject of the biography could of course bring other causes of action such as torts or other actions based on the accuracy of that stated in the biography.

monly seen on various news programs, a news organization may show a *portion* of an actor's performance, but not the entire performance, as a showing of the entire performance could undermine the economic ability of the performer to sell tickets to the performance, as well as the economic incentive for the actor to make the investment required to produce a performance of interest to the public.[19] Another limitation on the right of publicity may be the death of the person whose name, image or likeness is being used. The states are somewhat split on whether rights of privacy continue on after the death of a person. Rights of privacy end in New York upon death, however, the right of privacy continues after death such that a person's name, image, or likeness may not be used without permission of his or her heirs in California. More states are moving to the category of states that protect the name, image, and likeness of celebrities post mortem, perhaps as a result with the ease with which new technologies can manipulate images and video.

IV. REMEDIES

The remedies awarded under state and common law unfair competition laws vary by jurisdiction. Unfair competition and trademark infringement violations have the same remedies under the Lanham Act and range from injunctions[20] to monetary damages, including treble damages with costs and fees in certain circumstances.[21] Courts have the discretion to award profits under the Lanham Act if willful infringement is found—i.e., the infringer acted "wantonly and maliciously and in reckless disregard" of the plaintiff's rights. Attorneys' fees can only be awarded if it shown that the accused party intentionally violated the rights of the plaintiff. The Lanham Act is a remedial statute aimed at making a harmed party whole again as if its rights had not been violated. Courts will not grant punitive damages awards and will not award damages for Lanham Act violations when the party has already been awarded the damages under other theories of recovery. It is common for courts to award injunctions in unfair competition cases that are tailored to the harm that the injunction is addressing.

19. *See, e.g.*, Zacchini v. Scripps-Howard Broadcasting, 433 U.S. 562,576 (1977) (a showing of the entire 15-second performance of human cannonball deemed a violation of the right of privacy).

20. 15 U.S.C. §1116.

21. 15 U.S.C. §1117.

PART 5

Trade Secrets

I believe in rules. Sure I do. If there weren't any rules, how could you break them?

—Leo Durocher
Major League Baseball infielder/manager,
Member, Baseball Hall of Fame

I. BACKGROUND AND RATIONALE

A trade secret can be any confidential information that has value to an entity because it provides that entity with a competitive advantage. This confidential information of value can take many forms including a formula, pattern, compilation, program, device, method, technique or process. Not all entities that make valuable commercial advances choose to, or are able to, protect these commercial advances utilizing the patent system. Instead, the entity may prefer to keep the discovery confidential and rely on the protection provided to the innovation as a trade secret. As such, trade secrets provide a varied and desirable mechanism to protect certain developments and information. While most intellectual property laws involve rights tied to already public information, or at least information that becomes public in exchange for the grant of rights such as in patents, trade secret law protects nonpublic or secret information.

While other types of intellectual property are protected under a federal system, trade secret law is generally provided for under a quilt of varied trade secret laws each enacted individually at the state level, many of which are based on the provisions set forth in the Uniform Trade Secrets Act (UTSA). The UTSA codified the basic principles of common law trade secret protection including a cause of action for misappropriation of a trade secret. Misappropriation of trade secrets can take different forms including acquisition of a trade secret by improper means or disclosure of a trade secret without proper consent.

Logically, once information ceases to be confidential or "secret" nothing can be done to effectively make it unknown or a secret again. As the saying goes, once you let the cat out of the bag it is virtually impossible to put it back in the bag. Unlike patent or trademark law wherein injunctions can be issued to prevent future prohibitive conduct that will harm the rights holder, nothing can be done to turn back time so that a disclosed "trade secret" is once again a confidential trade secret. Trade secret laws therefore are aimed at (1) providing mechanisms for rights holders to prospectively reduce the risk the information is disclosed, (2) providing causes of actions against actors that violate trade secret rights, and (3) discouraging misappropriation and/or disclosure of trade secrets.

While various intellectual property laws at the state and federal level may provide some protections, or at least some deterrence for misappropriation of trade secrets, it is incumbent on an entity possessing a trade secret to take active steps to prevent misappropriation or even incidental disclosure of the trade secret. When dealing with outside entities, the most common mechanism for protecting misappropriation of trade secrets is the use of nondisclosure agreements, often referred to as NDAs for short. A trade secret should rarely, if ever, be shared outside an organization if there is a desire to continue to maintain the information as a trade secret. However, if the information must be shared for a business development or other purpose, entering into an NDA should be required of any party that will have access or may learn of the trade secret information. While a trade secret cannot be put back in the bag even if it is caused to be disclosed by a party that signed a NDA, a cause of action will be much easier to bring with an NDA than without one. NDAs are, in essence, contracts and may be drafted as harshly or leniently as desired by the parties. Additionally, a party that enters into an NDA may take more care in protecting another entity's trade secrets as the party does not wish to be liable under the terms of the NDA. As such, an NDA provides further deterrence for misappropriation or even accidental disclosures by others of trade secrets. The regular use of NDAs also may provide evidence that the information covered under the NDA is in fact deemed a "trade secret" by the party that owns it. This evidence could be used to help rebut an entity that attacks the information's status as a trade secret.

II. DEFINITION

While state laws governing and protecting trade secrets may vary significantly from state to state, the definition of what constitutes a trade secret is well recognized. A "trade secret" is any information, including a formula, pattern, compilation, program, device, method, technique, or process, that derives independent economic value, actual or potential, from not being known by others and is the subject of reasonable efforts to maintain its secrecy.[1] Stated another way, any confidential information that has value to an entity because it provides the entity with a competitive advantage may be considered a trade secret. The "trade secret" itself, as identified above, may be any of a wide array of information embodied in countless forms. As such, the particularity of the trade secret actually is of less importance. The dispositive inquiries as to whether nonpublic information can be considered a trade secret is focused on whether (1) the information has economic value to the entity and (2) whether reasonable efforts have been made to maintain its secrecy.

III. PROTECTION OF TRADE SECRETS

A. Uniform Trade Secret Act

In 1979. the National Conference of Commissioners on Uniform State Law, a group of legal scholars, created the Uniform Trade Secrets Act (UTSA) in the hope that each state would adopt like provisions of the act and thereby a uniform body of trade secret law would be created that stretched across the states. Many states have adopted the act, most amending, revising or otherwise tailoring its provisions. Accordingly, trade secret laws in moving from state to state may have a common starting point but may vary significantly in the final provisions.

B. Trade Secrets Act[2]

Federal law does provide nuanced protections of trade secrets and the handling of trade secret information. The Trade Secrets Act (TSA) provides protections with respect to the federal government's handling of information deemed to be a trade secret. Under the TSA, the federal government and its agencies and employees are prohibited from publishing, divulging or disclosing trade secret information unless authorized to

1. Uniform Trade Secret Act.
2. 18 U.S.C. §1905.

do so by law. A violation of this act can result in fines, imprisonment for up to a year, and/or removal from the office or employment. Thus, the Trade Secrets Act sits as a deterrent for federal employees to disseminate private information they may come across in the course of their work.

C. Economic Espionage Act of 1996[3]

Under the Economic Espionage Act of 1996, misappropriation of a trade secret is deemed a federal crime. Whether the intended or known beneficiary is a foreign government, instrumentality, or agent ("economic espionage")[4] or a third party (theft of trade secret),[5] the deceptive obtaining, duplication, receiving, or buying of a trade secret related to or included in a product owned by another is a criminal act subject to fine and/or imprisonment. Under this act it is also a criminal offense to attempt to commit any of the above described acts or to conspire with one or more persons to commit any of the above described acts. "Economic espionage" can result in fines of up to $500,000 ($10 million for organizations) and/or up to 15 years in prison. "Theft of trade secret" can result in imprisonment for up to 10 years and/or fines up to $5 million.

D. The Freedom of Information Act[6]

Under the Freedom of Information Act (FOIA) the federal government, including federal agencies, have a duty to share information with the public if a request for the information is made. The FOIA includes mechanisms and provisions by which the government no longer is obligated to disclose trade secrets and other privileged or confidential information it has obtained. Accordingly, an entity may and should identify trade secret information that it believes should be exempted from public disclosure under the FOIA.

IV. MISAPPROPRIATION

A misappropriation of a trade secret can be established in most jurisdictions if it can be demonstrated that (1) the information incorporates a trade secret; (2) a party took reasonable steps to preserve the secrecy of the trade secret; and (3) the accused defendant misappropriated the secret

3. 18 U.S.C. §1831, *et seq.*
4. "Economic Espionage"—18 U.S.C. §1831.
5. "Theft of trade secrets"—18 U.S.C. §1832.
6. 5 U.S.C. §552.

or used improper means, in breach of a confidential relationship, to acquire the trade secret. Varied parties may be claimed to have misappropriated a trade secret and, depending on who the actor is that is accused of the misappropriation, a misappropriation may have occurred in varied situations.

A. Those with Legitimate Access

Entities with legitimate access typically will need to be shown to have violated a duty of trust or confidence for misappropriation to have occurred. The duty to main the secrecy of the trade secret that was violated may be implicit, such as that deemed to generally fall within general duties of a particular job position. It could also be explicit, such as in expressed terms of an employment contract.

B. Theft by Strangers

If there is misconduct that leads to improper acquisition of a trade secret, such as breaking and entering into a business's office, a misappropriation of trade secret will likely be found. However, reverse engineering that results in information being uncovered by another entity is generally permitted activity. Additionally, if a third party is unaware that information is a trade secret that was misappropriated or improperly obtained, the third party will generally not be liable. As such, use of a stolen trade secret without knowledge it is a misappropriated secret will not create liability.

C. Government Disclosure

Any action against the government or its actors typically stems from the government or its actors improperly disclosing or disseminating, to the harm of the owner, previously received information that was identified as trade secret information.[7]

V. REMEDIES

The remedies available for misappropriation or other conduct relating to trade secret varies from jurisdiction to jurisdiction and from state to federal causes of action. Each of the described federal statutes also has varied ranges of remedies that might be awarded based on the particular

7. See Trade Secrets Act.

facts of each case. Generally, trade secret violations may result in compensatory and/or punitive damages. Additionally, injunctions are also a commonly available remedy.

VI. INTERPLAY OF TRADE SECRETS WITH OTHER FORMS OF INTELLECTUAL PROPERTY

Unlike other forms of intellectual property in which the rights holder must apply for a formal grant of intellectual property rights from the government, trade secret law does not require an application with the government. In fact, it is the inaction in the form of *nondisclosure* of the trade secret information that gives rise to the trade secret rights. In practice, preventing disclosure of trade secrets may be a very active process that may include expensive security systems, surveillance, and internal protocol to keep the information "secret." Because a trade secret may be any of a wide variety of information, an entity wishing to protect important information may need to weigh whether treatment as a "trade secret" is the best tool in its intellectual property tool belt to protect this information as compared to other tools that may include patent or copyright protections for example.

A. *Patents*

Patents may be obtained on methods, processes, and devices and provide the patentee the right to exclude others from making, using, selling, offering for sale, or importing the invention that is patented. In exchange for this right to exclude others, inventors and patent rights owners *publicly disclose* their inventions in the publicly issued patent, which describes how to make and use the patented invention. In light of this public disclosure requirement, it would be impossible to protect the exact same information under both a patent and as a trade secret, so a decision must be made between these two tools in the intellectual property tool belt. Each of these tools has certain advantages.

Compared to patents, keeping information regarding methods, processes, and devices as a trade secret have several recognizable advantages. First, trade secret rights can extend on in perpetuity as long as the trade secret is not disclosed publicly, while a utility patent expires 20 years from filing of the application. Second, information may be kept as a trade secret for minimal costs as compared to the significant costs, including government fees, that are incurred during the patent prosecution process, as well as the requisite payment of maintenance fees. In some instances, the costs to maintain information as a trade secret may require security costs, but, in most instances, trade secret rights can be maintained for comparatively much less than prosecution of one or more patents to protect the rights. In instances when patent protection might be unavailable, limited in scope, or deemed too costly to pursue, maintaining and protecting information as a trade secret provides a valuable intellectual property right. It practically may be impossible for innovators, especially small and medium entities, to patent each and every technological advance. As such, trade secret protection may be utilized to fill the gap in protection that may be created as a result of economic realities. Third, a wider variety of subject matter may be protected as a trade secret compared to patents because trade secret protections lack the statutory requirements for patentability (§101), novelty (§102), non-obviousness (§103), and written description (§112) that may prevent patent rights from being granted.

However, trade secrets are not without disadvantages compared to patents. Among these disadvantages is the inability to protect trade secrets from reverse engineering or independent creation. In contrast, patent rights protect the owner of the rights from any entity making, using, selling, offering for sale, or importing that claimed in the patent regardless of how the subject matter recited in the patent came to fruition. Reverse engineering is not a defense for a patent infringement claim. However an entity that uncovers information held as a trade secret using reverse engineering without misappropriating information will not be liable under trade secret law. Protecting information by keeping the information as a trade secret risks a scenario in which another entity uncovers that information through reverse engineering or other innocent means for which there will be no action available.

An interesting scenario also arises if an entity A decided to protect information—for example the secret method for a popular soft drink—as a trade secret and another entity B somehow later arrives at the trade secret and attempts to patent each of the product and process respectively, believing each to be new. In theory, if entity B sought to patent the product itself, the previous sales of soft drinks with the secret formula by entity A would be an on sale bar under §102(b) that would destroy novelty and prevent any patent from issuing on the product. In a similar scenario, if entity B independently created or reversed engineered the secret process for making the soft drink, entity B could receive a patent as entity A's use of the process was in secret as a trade secret and never publicly disclosed such that it would not give rise to an event that bars patentability. In such an instance, the law now has provisions that would permit entity A to continue to practice the method as a prior user because they were protecting the process as a trade secret.[8]

B. Copyrights

A similar analysis can be performed between copyright and trade secret protection. While copyright has a longer life than patents, it still has a "limited term" compared to a trade secret, which can extend on in perpetuity barring public disclosure. There are prosecution costs associated with the registration of copyrights, but the costs are minimal compared to those that are typically accrued during prosecution of a patent application. There are also some limits on that which can be protected under copyright laws (e.g. ideas and functional aspects cannot be protected) while trade secret can be used to protect virtually any type of information of value. A decision between trade secret and copyright protection may occur in attempting to protect computer codes as copyright protection requires submission of at least a portion of the code to the Copyright Office as a deposit in exchange for registration. Similar to that described with respect to patent protection, this requirement of public disclosure of information in exchange for copyrights places trade secret and copyright protections at odds in certain circumstances. Entities with software and computer code and various other types of information worthy of protection may have to decide whether copyright or trade secret is a preferable tool in the intellectual property tool belt for providing effective protection.

8. The prior user right defense now provided for under the America Invents Act (AIA) provides protections against a later patent for those who commercially use their innovation prior to the filing date of the later patent but had not pursued patent protection. See *Patent Groundwork Section.*

Section 4

Copyrights

PART 1

Copyright Groundwork

The primary objective of copyright is not to reward the labor of authors, but '[t]o promote the Progress of Science and useful Arts.' To this end, copyright assures authors the right to their original expression, but encourages others to build freely upon the ideas and information conveyed by a work. This result is neither unfair nor unfortunate. It is the means by which copyright advances the progress of science and art.

—Justice Sandra Day O'Connor
Feist Publications, Inc. v. Rural Telephone Service Co.
499 US 340, 349 (1991)

I. BACKGROUND AND RATIONALE

At a very high level, copyrights may be considered to be somewhat the converse to patents. Patents are directed to new and non-obvious inventions and generally are directed to an inventive concept that is reduced to practice. Protection may be broadly available for a broad concept. For example, the first person to conceive of a chair, assuming the claims of the patent are broadly written, could theoretically receive broad coverage for any chair regardless of the pattern on the fabric, the shape of the backrest, or the configuration of the legs. Copyright protects the converse, as the first inventor of a chair could not lay claim to "copyrights" to all variations, configurations, and designs of chairs that followed the initial concept of the chair. Rather, copyrights exist to the particular fabric pattern on the seat, the ornate carvings on the arm, or the unique angles and undulations of the legs and armrests. It is the particular expression of the concept that is deemed of value as intellectual property and protectable under copyright laws in the United States.

Copyrights and similar rights internationally have evolved based upon a variety of rationales for providing protection. Many countries, including the U.S., the United Kingdom, Canada, and Australia, root their copyright laws on an "incentive theory," which holds that economic incentive is provided by a bundle of copyrights. The creators of the works covered by the copyrights are eligible for protection. When these creators are compensated financially through sales of works covered by copyright and sale of licenses for copyrighted works, they are further encouraged to continue to create more works, pushing our development forward. While the copyright framework in many countries is based upon an economic incentive, some jurisdictions also provide for protection of copyrights based upon a "natural rights" theory in which the creator of a work is believed to be entitled to certain rights in a work because of having "given life" to the work. These countries may provide such protections as guarding the works from destruction, ensuring proper attribution, and maintaining the integrity of the works. For example, in some jurisdictions it may be a violation of a copyright or a related right to destroy a protected work or to alter or vary the work in a manner that harms its "good name."

Article I, Section 8, Clause 8 of the U.S. Constitution is known as the constitutional source for U.S. copyright laws as well as for U.S. patent laws, as previously described. In contrast to patents and copyrights, trademark law does not find its constitutional basis in Art. I, § 8, cl. 8. Instead, trademark laws are rooted in Congress's broad powers under the Commerce Clause—Article I, Section 8, Clause 3.[1] The Commerce Clause is described further in the *Trademarks & Trade Dress* sections.

> "The Congress shall have Power . . . To promote the Progress of Science and useful Arts, by securing for limited Times to Authors and Inventors the exclusive Right to their respective Writings and Discoveries."
>
> *U.S. Constitution*, Article I, Section 8, clause 8

1. "[The Congress shall have Power] To regulate Commerce with foreign Nations, and among the several States, and with the Indian Tribes." U.S. CONST. art. I, §8, cl. 3.

Because our modern vernacular varies a bit from the language used when the U.S. Constitution was written, one might easily be misled to believe "useful Arts" refers to subject matter covered by copyrights. However, it is understood that when the Framers drafted this provision of the Constitution, the underlined terms related to what is now referred to as copyrights, and the boldface words relate to what is now referred to as patents.

> "The Congress shall have Power . . . To promote the Progress of Science and **useful Arts**, by securing for limited Times to Authors and **Inventors** the exclusive Right to their respective Writings and **Discoveries.**"
> *U.S. Constitution*, Article I, Section 8, clause 8 (Emphasis added)

The terms "Science," "Authors," and "Writings" are understood to have a varied meaning from their common meaning in everyday life today. "Science" was understood to relate to subject matter referred to as "The Arts," including writing, painting, drawing, etc. The terms "Authors" and "Writings" are understood in the context of the U.S. Constitution to be broader in scope than the current use of these words in American vernacular. "Authors" and "Writings" have not been interpreted to relate solely to the written word; instead they have been interpreted to provide a constitutional basis for visual arts, sound recordings, movies, computer code, and varied other forms of "works." Similarly, singers, songwriters, painters, artists, and other artisans are recognized as "Authors" under the constitutional framework.

Consistent with the principles set forth in the U.S. Constitution, the copyright scheme is constructed to strike a balance of intellectual property protection so as to promote progress in the "Sciences." As such, the protection must not be too strong or too weak. If the copyright protections are too strong, then authors will be discouraged from producing new works, as the copyright protections of earlier authors will be overly broad and/or stringent and few non-infringing new works will be possible. Likewise, if the copyright protections are too narrow or too weak, then authors again will be discouraged from producing new works, as they could be easily and readily copied and the original authors would receive little or no compensation for their efforts. Perhaps the best solution is a "Goldilocks" type of protection that encourages new works by providing just the right amount of protection to stimulate the creativity of new works yet still protect the works once finished so that the authors are fairly compensated for their efforts.

II. PREREQUISITES FOR PROTECTION—ORIGINALITY AND FIXATION—17 U.S.C. §102

Section 102(a) of Title 17 of the United States Code sets forth the prerequisites for copyright protection, stating that copyright protections subsist "in original works of authorship fixed in any tangible medium . . . from which they can be perceived, reproduced, or otherwise communicated, either directly or with the aid of a machine or a device."

A. *Originality—17 U.S.C. §102(a)*

In order for a work to be protectable by copyright law, it must be "original." However, the originality requirement is not particularly stringent, especially when compared to the concept of "novelty" as contemplated with respect to U.S. patent law. A classic example illustrating the distinction between the originality requirement for copyrightability and the novelty requirement for copyrightability involves an author who somehow independently creates an exact duplicate of a previous work. In this instance, the second work would be copyrightable because, even though it wasn't "novel," it did "originate" with the second author. Contrast this scenario with an inventor who independently conceives of an invention that somehow is an exact duplicate of a previous invention in the realm of patent law. The second invention is not patentable, as it would not be deemed "novel" even though it was "original." While in theory the author of the second created exact duplicate work would be copyrightable, case law exists that supports a practical implementation of a finding of copyright infringement of the previous work rather than independent creation and copyrightability if the second author had access to the previous work.[2]

The originality requirement for copyrightability of a work is sometimes characterized as comprising two elements—"that the work was independently created by the author (as opposed to copied from other works), and that it possesses at least some minimal degree of creativity."[3] A work will satisfy the independent creation aspects as long as it is not a mere mechanical reproduction of a previously existing work, even if the work is unknowingly created as substantially identical to an existing work.

2. Bright Tunes Music Corp. v. Harrisongs Music, Ltd., 420 F. Supp 177 (1976) (aff'd sub. nom. ABKCO Music, Inc. v. Harrisongs Music, Ltd., 722 F.2d 988 (2d Cir. 1983)).

3. Feist Publications, Inc. v Rural Telephone Service Co., 499 U.S. 340, 358–59 (1991).

The creativity aspect also sets a low threshold, requiring only that work "possess some creative spark, 'no matter how, crude, humble, or obvious it might be.'"[4] Others believe the division of the "originality" threshold into two distinct aspects—the two prongs of "independent creation" and "minimal degree of creativity"—to be merely semantics.[5] Instead, they would suggest that "independent creation" and "minimal degree of creativity" are two sides of the same coin. Regardless, it is well settled that originality is a low threshold for copyrightability.

B. Fixation—17 U.S.C. §101

Copyright protection subsists in original works of authorship "***fixed*** in any tangible medium of expression, now known or later developed, from which they can be perceived, reproduced, or otherwise communicated, either directly or with the aid of a machine or a device."[6] Section 101 of the Copyright Act explicitly defines the term "fixed" for purposes of the Copyright Act:

> A work is "fixed" in a tangible medium of expression when its embodiment in a copy or phonorecord, by or under the authority of the author, is sufficiently permanent or stable to permit it to be perceived, reproduced, or otherwise communicated for a period of more than transitory duration. A work consisting of sounds, images, or both, that are being transmitted, is "fixed" for purposes of this title if a fixation of the work is being made simultaneously with its transmission. 17 U.S.C. §101

Several aspects of fixation are noteworthy. First, fixation can be in any tangible medium, "now known or later developed." As such, fixation on a computer-related technology, such as on memory or a display, satisfies the fixation requirement even though computers were in their infancy when the Copyright Act was written. Additionally, fixation can be performed with the aid of a machine, such as a camera, video camera, cassette tape recorder, and other machines. Also, fixation occurs only if it is done by or under the authority of the author. In works consisting of sounds, images, or both, fixation occurs if it is being transmitted and

4. *Id.* at 349.
5. 1 Nimmer on Copyright §2.01[B], at 2-14 to 2-15 (1999).
6. 17 U.S.C. §102(a) (Emphasis added).

otherwise fixed, such as when someone records a musical performance with a sound-recording device. Fixation can be as simple as writing a poem on a napkin or as complicated as filming a motion picture. The fixation requirement is a logical correlation to copyright's protection of the specific expression of ideas and *not* the ideas themselves.

C. Idea/Expression Dichotomy—§102(b)

The idea/expression dichotomy is the concept in copyright law that "ideas" cannot be protected by copyright, only their specific expression. Section 102(b) of Title 17 of the United States Code codifies what is commonly referred to as the idea/expression dichotomy:

> In no case does copyright protection for an original work of authorship extend to any idea, procedure, process, system, method of operation, concept, principle, or discovery, regardless of the form in which it is described, explained, illustrated, or embodied in such work. 17 U.S.C. §102(b)

In the early days, copyright protected against only literal copying and not a more abstract taking of a copyrighted work. However, as copyright protection moved beyond mere protection of only literal copying, the idea/expression dichotomy developed as a manner of describing subject matter that was eligible for copyright protection and that which is deemed outside its scope. The idea/expression dichotomy is believed to have formally found it origins in the U.S. in 1880 in *Baker v. Seldon*[7]—a case involving copyright claims relating to accounting forms. In *Baker*, the Supreme Court held that there was a distinction between a particular accounting book and the system of accounting taught in the book. The accounting book was protectable by copyright; the system of accounting was not protectable under copyright. Further examples of the manifestation of the idea/expression dichotomy might include: (a) the idea of a skyscraper having a helical shape (not protectable) compared to the architectural plan of a particular helically shaped building (protectable); (b) the idea of a British spy novel (not protectable) compared to a particular James Bond novel (protectable); and (c) the idea of speech recognition and typing software (not protectable) as compared to the specific computer coding/software program that recognizes speech and types into the word processor (protectable). While the idea/expression dichotomy

7. Baker v. Seldon, 101 U.S. 99 (1880).

was codified into U.S. federal law in 1976, it was well rooted in U.S. copyright law before then, and it continues to define a limit of copyright protections to particular expression(s) of an idea compared to the idea itself.

III. TYPES OF PROTECTABLE WORKS

"Authorship" is a bedrock principle for copyright protection reaching back to Article I, Section 8, clause 8, continuing on through the statutes that govern today's copyright laws.[8] U.S. law explicitly provides that copyright protection exists in original "works of authorship" fixed in any tangible medium.[9] Title 17 goes further and provides an *illustrative* list of categories of explicitly recognized "works of authorship" setting forth the following categories:

(1) literary works;
(2) musical works, including any accompanying words;
(3) dramatic works, including any accompanying music;
(4) pantomimes and choreographic works;
(5) pictorial, graphic, and sculptural works;
(6) motion pictures and other audiovisual works;
(7) sound recordings; and
(8) architectural works.[10]

While these categories are merely illustrative and the statute allows for other categories of works of authorships, the above listing of works provides a substantially comprehensive list of categories of "works of authorship" eligible for copyright protection. While an *illustrative* listing of "works of authorship" might suggest that other categories may exist but have not been explored or may someday exist, practical experience likely dictates otherwise, as evidenced by the treatment of computer programs and their continued increase in prevalence. Upon first glance at the above list, one could credibly argue that none of the above eight categories includes computer programs, and thus computer programs either might not be protectable under copyright or might be an example of a "work of authorship" that is protectable but sits outside the eight iden-

8. 17 U.S.C. §101 *et seq.*
9. 17 U.S.C. §102(a).
10. *Id.*

tified categories. However, computer programs, including source code, object code, and other forms, are protectable under copyright as "literary works." Computer programs clearly illustrate that the above categories are typically read fairly broadly, and as such, many forms of creative works can be deemed to fall into one of the eight listed categories.

A. *Literary Works to Architectural Works—17 U.S.C. §102*

While deciding which category of "work of authorship" a particular work falls under may not be critical for determining whether or not the work is protectable under copyright law, proper characterization may be important, as it relates to the specific rights conveyed under copyright regarding that work. By way of example, certain rights may apply to "sound recordings" that do not apply to "literary works." As such, each of the eight categories of "works of authorship" is described in further detail below.

1. Literary Works—§102(a)(1)

"Literary works" are works, other than audiovisual works, expressed in words, numbers, or other verbal or numerical symbols or indicia, regardless of the nature of the material objects, such as books, periodicals, manuscripts, phonorecords, film, tapes, disks, or cards, in which they are embodied.[11] Works of fiction, nonfiction, novels, short stories, poems, articles, speeches, catalogs, biographies, and computer programs, including source code or object code, are all considered literary works. Also, it is noteworthy that both *The Road Not Taken,* by Robert Frost, and a poem about a pony that a six-year-old writes on construction paper could be considered "literary works" under copyright law and thus eligible for protection.

2. Musical Works—§102(a)(2)

"Musical works" include the musical notes and accompanying lyrics in a musical composition that may be in the form of sheet music, CDs, records, cassette tapes, and digital audio or MP3 players. The author of a "musical work" is often a composer and/or song writer. There is a distinction between "musical works," which are the musical notes and any accompanying lyrics, and "sound recording" that is a particular performance,

11. 17 U.S.C. §101.

which may be of a musical work but also of readings, presentations, or lectures. As discussed under the *Sound Recordings Section*, the author of sound recordings is the performer whose performance is fixed in a tangible medium (e.g., recorded).

3. Dramatic Works—§102(a)(3)

Dramatic works may include plays or theatrical performances, treatments, and scripts prepared for cinema, radio, and television. Dramatic works can be works such as plays and either radio or television scripts that are often intended to be performed and often include spoken text, plot, and directions for action.[12] Additionally, if music accompanies a dramatic work, the entire work in some instances may be considered a dramatic work, and the music may be considered an independent musical work. William Shakespeare may be considered the father of theater, and, for illustrative purposes here, his works may be examples of dramatic works.

4. Pantomimes and Choreographic Works—§102(a)(4)

"Choreography is the composition and arrangement of dance movements and patterns usually intended to be accompanied by music. As distinct from choreography, pantomime is the art of imitating or acting out situations, characters, or other events. To be protected by copyright, pantomimes and choreography need not tell a story or be presented before an audience. Each work, however, must be fixed in a tangible medium of expression from which the work can be performed."[13] This fixation in a tangible medium often can be notated on paper or computer, or filmed in the case of choreographic works, and it can be recorded electronically or filmed in the instance of pantomime.

5. Pictorial, Graphic, and Sculptural Works—§102(a)(5)

"Pictorial, graphic, and sculptural works" include two-dimensional and three-dimensional works of fine, graphic, and applied art, photographs, prints and art reproductions, maps, globes, charts, diagrams, models, and technical drawings, including architectural plans. Such works shall include works of artistic craftsmanship insofar as their form but not their mechanical or utilitarian aspects are concerned; the design of a useful

12. http://www.copyright.gov/fls/fl119.html.
13. http://www.copyright.gov/fls/fl119.html.

article, as defined in this section, shall be considered a pictorial, graphic, or sculptural work only if, and only to the extent that, such design incorporates pictorial, graphic, or sculptural features that can be identified separately from, and are capable of existing independently of, the utilitarian aspects of the article.[14] A wide variety of works are encompassed in this category and may include photographs, prints, maps, comics and cartoons, technical drawings, and designs on textiles, apparel, and footwear, to name a few.

6. Motion Pictures and Audiovisual Works—§102(a)(6)

"Motion pictures" are audiovisual works consisting of a series of related images that, when shown in succession, impart an impression of motion, together with accompanying sounds, if any.[15] "Audiovisual works" are works that consist of a series of related images that are intrinsically intended to be shown by the use of machines, or devices such as projectors, viewers, or electronic equipment, together with accompanying sounds, if any, regardless of the nature of the material objects, such as films or tapes, in which the works are embodied.[16] Any Hollywood-style movie, from *Star Wars* and *Gone with the Wind* to *Field of Dreams* and *The Social Network,* serves as a practical example of a work falling within this category. Additionally, less grandiose productions, such as a videotaped production of a staged "Mardi Gras–style" parade or a "Dixieland" musical jam session, also are examples of protectable subject matter under this category of works.[17]

7. Sound Recordings—§102(a)(7)

"Sound recordings" are works that result from the fixation of a series of musical, spoken, or other sounds, but not including the sounds accompanying a motion picture or other audiovisual work, regardless of the nature of the material objects, such as disks, tapes, or other phonorecords, in which they are embodied.[18] Sound recordings are works of specific fixed performances.

---

14. 17 U.S.C. §101.
15. 17 U.S.C. §101.
16. 17 U.S.C. §101.
17. Easter Seal Society v. Playboy Enterprises, 815 F.2d 323 (5th Cir 1987).
18. 17 U.S.C. §101.

It may be important to closely consider the distinctions between "sound recordings" and "musical works," as they may be easily confused. For example, Michael Jackson wrote and composed the song *Billie Jean*. Michael Jackson also sang/performed *Billie Jean*, which was recorded on his well- known album "Thriller" in 1982. As the writer and composer of the underlying notes and lyrics of *Billie Jean*, Michael Jackson was the author of a musical work for *Billie Jean*, and as the singer/performer of the recorded performance of *Billie Jean*, he also is the author of a sound recording of *Billie Jean*. If Usher wanted to perform *Billie Jean* as a tribute to Michael Jackson, he would have to get permission from Michael Jackson's estate[19] so as to not infringe on Michael Jackson's copyright in the musical work to *Billie Jean*. Usher would own and could enforce a copyright in his particular sound recording of *Billie Jean* to prevent others from copying that sound recording. If Bono wants to perform *Billie Jean*, he must obtain permission from Michael Jackson's estate but he would not need to obtain permission from Usher, as Usher merely has rights relating to his "sound recording."

8. Architectural Works—§102(a)(8)

Copyright protection for works considered "architectural works" is a relatively recent category of protectable works recognized in the Architectural Works Copyright Protection Act (AWCPA).[20] Under this provision, "architectural works"[21] created on or after December 1, 1990—the implementing date of the law—are eligible for protection.[22] "An 'architectural work' is the design of a building as embodied in any tangible medium of expression, including a building, architectural plans, or drawings. The work includes the overall form as well as the arrangement and composition of spaces and elements in the design, but does not include individual standard features."[23] In practice, habitable structures such as homes and office buildings, as well as uninhabited structures like museums, churches, pergolas, gazebos, and garden pavilions, are also covered. Structures not covered include bridges, cloverleafs, dams, walkways, tents, recreational vehicles, mobile homes, and boats,[24]

19. Or whoever owns the copyright after Michael Jackson's death.
20. H.R. Rep. No. 735, at 6936 (1990).
21. 17 U.S.C. §102(a)(8).
22. 37 C.F.R. §202.11 (d)(3).
23. 17 U.S.C. §101.
24. 37 C.F.R. §202.11 (d)(1).

as well as standard features in and of themselves, such as windows, doors, and other staple building components.[25]

Prior to the AWCPA, U.S. copyright law provided some protection for monuments, memorials, and other sculptural creations as sculptural works under §102(a)(5). However, homes, office buildings, and other buildings were not eligible for protection and were subject to virtually unlimited copying and imitation without recourse for their creators even though the plans for such buildings were protectable under copyright. With the passage of AWCPA, these buildings themselves are now protectable under U.S. copyright law.

The AWCPA provides protections for "architectural works," whether embodied as a building, architectural plans, or drawings. Copying the building itself or the architectural plans/drawings can each be considered an action of infringement that violates an owner's rights under copyright law. Drafters of the AWCPA and its copyright provisions regarding "architectural works" considered potential effects on the public and third parties, as provisions were also included that preserve the public's ability in "making, distributing or public display of [pictorial representations] of the work, if the building in which the work is embodied is located in or ordinarily visible from a public place."[26] Additionally, the bill leading to the AWCPA was originally drafted with the arguably broader language of "three-dimensional structure[s]," but this phrase was removed to avoid protecting core infrastructure, such as highway bridges, clover leafs, canals, and dams, the protection of which might lead to increased costs in building and maintaining our nation's infrastructure.[27]

B. Items Not Protected by Copyright

Certain materials are generally not eligible for copyright protection.[28] Illustrative examples and categories of items not protectable under federal copyright law are provided below:

---

25. 37 C.F.R. §202.11 (d)(2).

26. 17 U.S.C. §120(a) (In short, anyone is able to photograph, paint, or depict public buildings without fear of liability for infringing copyright law.).

27. John Hoaas, *The Architectural Works Copyright Protection Act: Building on Copyright*, pp. 5–6, http://tlc.usm.maine.edu/cli_admin/journal_pdf/vol_000_issue_000_article_005.pdf .

28. *See generally* U.S. Copyright Office, What Is Not Protected By Copyright?, Copyright Basics, Circular 01, pg. 3. (2011).

Works not fixed in a tangible form are not protectable. Consistent with previously described requirements for a work to be eligible for protection under U.S. copyright law, works that have not been fixed in a tangible medium are not eligible for protection. However, once they are fixed—e.g., once a performance has been recorded—the work and performance thereof may be protected under copyright law.

Ideas, procedures, methods, systems, processes, concepts, principles, discoveries, or devices are not protectable. Many of these terms should conjure up patents and patent protection in the mind of the reader. An instruction manual, illustration, or particular description of one of the above items—a particular fixed tangible expression of those items—may, however, be protectable under copyright.

Simple, short phrases and slogans and familiar symbols or designs are not eligible for protection, as they lack originality. Other items that are not protectable and may be conveniently categorized in this group include titles, names, short phrases, and slogans; variations of typographical ornamentation, letter or coloring; and mere listings of ingredients or contents. However, certain recipes that include or are accompanied by substantial literary expression, including explanation, directions, or otherwise protectable literary expression, may be protectable. Not surprisingly, a particular collection of recipes (e.g., a cookbook) may also be protectable.[29] Even if the individual recipes lack sufficient originality, the collection and arrangement of recipes may satisfy the originality threshold. See the *Compilations and Derivative Works Section.*

Items formed entirely by common property lacking originality are not protectable. Examples may include standard calendars, height and weight charts, tape measures, rulers, and other like items. Facts such as dates or statistics are not eligible for protection, nor are works of the United States government, such as statutes, laws, cases, or white papers.[30] However, a subsequent arrangement or compilation of any of these items may provide sufficient originality to be deemed eligible for protection for that particular arrangement. See the *Compilations and Derivative Works Section.*

C. Compilations and Derivative Works—17 U.S.C. §103

"A 'compilation' is a work formed by the collection and assembling of preexisting materials or of data that are selected, coordinated, or ar-

29. http://www.copyright.gov/help/faq/faq-protect.html.
30. 17 U.S.C. §105.

ranged in such a way that the resulting work as a whole constitutes an original work of authorship. The term 'compilation' includes collective works."[31]

Feist Publications, Inc., v. Rural Telephone Service Co.[32] is a well-known copyright case involving a copyright infringement action over telephone listings in which Feist had duplicated and sold Rural's telephone listings. The compelling evidence was Feist's inclusion of "dummy listings" that had been specifically inserted by Rural in its phone listing to identify copycats. While it was clear that Feist had copied the listing, the Supreme Court found that this particular telephone listing compilation lacked the requisite amount of originality to be protected by copyright. However, had the telephone listing possessed sufficient originality, it may have been protectable as a compilation.

"A 'derivative work' is a work based upon one or more preexisting works, such as a translation, musical arrangement, dramatization, fictionalization, motion picture version, sound recording, art reproduction, abridgment, condensation, or any other form in which a work may be recast, transformed, or adapted. A work consisting of editorial revisions, annotations, elaborations, or other modifications which, as a whole, represent an original work of authorship, is a 'derivative work.'"[33]

Illustrative examples of derivative works may include any movie made from a screenplay, book, or manuscript. The "Batman" movies may be considered derivative works of the *Batman* comic books. The musical "Wicked"—the story of *The Wizard of Oz* told from the point of view of the Wicked Witch of the West—may also be an example of a "derivative work." Additionally, mezzotint engravings of classic paintings[34] or a photograph of a sculpture, such as Michelangelo's *David,* may be considered "derivative works."

The subject matter of copyright, as specified by section 102, includes compilations and derivative works, but protection for a work employing preexisting material in which copyright subsists does not extend to any part of the work in which such material has been used unlawfully.[35] The

---

31. 17 U.S.C. §101; *see also* "collective work." ("A 'collective work' is a work, such as a periodical issue, anthology, or encyclopedia, in which a number of contributions, constituting separate and independent works in themselves, are assembled into a collective whole.").

32. 499 U.S. 340 (1991).

33. 17 U.S.C. §101.

34. Alfred Bell v. Catalda Fine Arts, 191 F.2d 99 (2d Cir. 1951).

35. 17 U.S.C. §103(a).

copyright in a compilation or derivative work extends only to the material contributed by the author of such work, as distinguished from the preexisting material employed in the work, and does not imply any exclusive right in the preexisting material. The copyright in such work is independent of, and does not affect or enlarge the scope, duration, ownership, or subsistence of, any copyright protection in the preexisting material.[36] As discussed further elsewhere in this section, the creation of a derivative work is an exclusive right of the owner of the preexisting copyrighted material.

IV. RIGHTS OF COPYRIGHT OWNERS

A. *Five (Six)[37] Basic Rights*

The owner of a copyright, assuming certain of these rights have not been assigned or otherwise transferred, holds a bundle of exclusive rights under U.S. copyright law.[38] In particular, the owner of copyright has the exclusive right to do and to authorize the following actions:

(1) to *reproduce* the work in copies or phonorecords;
(2) to prepare *derivative works* based upon the copyrighted work;
(3) to *distribute* copies or phonorecords of the copyrighted work by sale or other transfer of ownership, or by rental, lease, or lending;
(4) to *perform* the work publicly;[39]
(5) to *display* the work publicly;[40] and
(6) to *perform* the work publicly by means of *digital audio transmission.*[41]

---

36. 17 U.S.C. §103(b).

37. Traditionally there were considered five basic rights of copyright owners, with the "right to perform the work publicly by means of digital audio transmission" added more recently under 17 U.S.C. §106(6) being considered as a further specification of the right to publicly display certain works.

38. 17 U.S.C. §106.

39. Applies to literary, musical, dramatic, and choreographic works, pantomimes, and motion pictures and other audiovisual works.

40. Applies to literary, musical, dramatic, and choreographic works, and pantomimes, and pictorial, graphic, or sculptural works, including the individual images of a motion picture or other audiovisual works.

41. Applies to sound recordings.

It is illegal to violate any of these rights of the owner of copyright or the rights of attribution and integrity of certain authors[42] ("moral rights" described later). These rights do have certain limitations, most of which have been codified in the Copyright Act of 1976 in 17 U.S.C. §§107–21. Some of these limitations take the form of specified exemptions from copyright liability, discussed in further detail in the *Limitations and Defenses Section.*

***Reproduction*:** Copyright owners' exclusive right to reproduce their works may be the most important and recognizable right under copyright law. Years ago, reproduction was only a simple, straightforward, and often purely physical concept. For example, in the world of paper publishing, if someone wanted to read John F. Kennedy's Pulitzer Prize–winning book *Profiles in Courage,* but rather than purchasing a copy, photocopied a friend's copy, that person would be in violation of John F. Kennedy's "right of reproduction." Likewise, copies of a photograph or painting could not be made without permission of the copyright owner.

With the explosion of the computer, Internet, and other electronics and related technology, violations of copyright owners' rights of reproduction are increasingly easy to perform and difficult to prevent. Copying or downloading copies of music files, graphics, photographs, television programs, movies, videos, or any other subject matter eligible for copyright protection may be a violation of the copyright owners' right of reproduction, even though the copy is made in electronic format over a computer or computing device such as a PDA.

A&M Records, Inc. v. Napster, Inc.[43] was a landmark copyright case involving violation of a copyright owner's right of reproduction of music utilizing digital media. Napster was a peer-to-peer file-sharing service that provided a platform for users to download music files from other users on the site. Napster was found liable[44] under copyright laws and was forced to shut down. The initial popularity of Napster likely was a precursor to web-based music-downloading sites such as iTunes, in which users pay for their music file(s) rather than download them for free. *Napster* can be contrasted with *Sony Corporation of America v. Universal City Studios,*[45] which is a good measure of how copyright law

42. 17 U.S.C. §106A.

43. 239 F.2d 1004 (2001).

44. Napster was held liable for contributory infringement and vicarious copyright infringement.

45. 464 U.S. 417 (1984).

has handled the previous technology leap in reproduction machines: videocassette recorders (VCRs). The Supreme Court in *Sony* held that private, noncommercial taping of television programs was permissible because copying was only for "time shifting," so as to be able to watch programming at a later time.[46] As technology makes content reproduction quicker, easier, and more accessible, copyright owners may continue to face an uphill battle in protecting their works.

***Derivative Works*:** While it is easy to assert that a work is a "derivative work," this term is a term of art, and so a work qualifying as a derivative work must both contain originality and be lawfully created consistent with 17 U.S.C. §103(a). Owners of the copyright in the underlying works will own rights in the derivative works as long as the work that is created based off the underlying work satisfies the originality requirement. Copyright owners also frequently grant permission to others to prepare derivative works—often under a license or other contract. In the absence of other terms, the creator of the derivative work will own the rights to the derivative work. However, the owner of the copyright in the derivative work will only own rights to the subject matter of the derivative work that satisfies the originality requirement, but will not own any rights in the subject matter of the underlying work itself.

For example, if Ian Fleming is the owner of the copyrights to a series of James Bond spy novels and he permits a certain movie production company to make one of the novels into a movie, that movie production company then may own the copyrights to that particular film, but it will not own the rights to the other novels in the series. As such, the movie production company is an owner of the copyright of that particular "derivative work"—the movie—but not to any of the other James Bond works. Accordingly, if this movie production company wants to make another James Bond movie, the movie production company will need to otherwise legally obtain the rights from the copyright owner so it may create another derivative work.

Distribution: The distribution right gives copyright owners the right to make works available to the public in a variety of manners including through sale, rental, lease, or lending. Pursuant to this right, copyright owners can prevent others from distributing unauthorized copies of works

46. Napster tried drawing analogies to the "time shifting" concept but was unsuccessful, as the court in *Napster* distinguished the cases likely because users of Napster were copying content from others that they did not possess or have a right to while users in *Sony* were accessing content they already were legally entitled to view on their TVs.

and to control the first distribution of an authorized copy of a work. However, pursuant to the "first sale doctrine," a copyright owner cannot control distribution of that particular work after a first distribution (e.g., sale). Accordingly, if a reader purchases the book *The Hunger Games* from a bookstore, the copyright owner in the book cannot prevent the reader from reselling, lending, or otherwise distributing that particular copy of *The Hunger Games*. However, the reader would still be in violation of the distribution right if he or she began producing and selling copies of *The Hunger Games* without the copyright owner's permission.

***Public Performance*:** The right to perform, display, and perform by means of digital audio transmission all are rights associated with "public" actions. In the privacy of your own home or at a family gathering, you may sing *Billie Jean* or read aloud *The Road Less Traveled* without fear of violating either Michael Jackson's or Robert Frost's respective public performance rights. However, if you sang *Billie Jean* as part of a live musical concert or read *The Road Less Traveled* before a public audience at Madison Square Garden without permission from the copyright owner, you would likely be in violation of the "right to perform" publicly.

A public performance right, which requires identification and individualized negotiations for each instance of public performance, could stifle, rather than promote, progress in the science and the arts. There are certain specific, limited exemptions to the public performance right so that certain specific actions that might otherwise be deemed a violation of the performance right are not deemed infringements of copyright under U.S. copyright law.[47]

Limitations for Businesses: Business establishments are allowed to play the radio or show television programs according to certain specified provisions.[48] Non–food service or drinking establishments that have less than 2,000 square feet of space or food service establishments that have less than 3,750 square feet are allowed to play radio or television programming without acquiring permission. Furthermore, if the establishment exceeds the above-delineated square-footage requirements, there is a limitation on the number of loudspeakers and televisions—no more than six loudspeakers and/or four televisions, and no television can be bigger than a 55-inch screen. As such, restaurants and businesses may

47. 17 U.S.C. §110.
48. 17 U.S.C. §110(5).

play sporting events and other radio or television broadcasting for customer enjoyment without fear of copyright infringement liability if they are in compliance with this statutory exemption.

Teaching Limitations, Charitable Limitations, and Other Limitations: A variety of additional exceptions or limitations on the exclusive performance right exist. The following instances are not deemed to be infringement of copyright:

- performance or display of a work by instructors or pupils in the course of face-to-face teaching activities of a nonprofit educational institution;[49]
- performance of a nondramatic literary or musical work or of a dramatic-musical work of a religious nature in the course of services at a place of worship or other religious assembly;[50]
- performance of a nondramatic literary or musical work other than in a transmission to the public, without any purpose of direct or indirect commercial advantage and without payment of any fee or other compensation for the performance to any of its performers, promoters, or organizers;[51]
- performance of a nondramatic musical work by a governmental body or a nonprofit agricultural or horticultural organization, in the course of an annual agricultural or horticultural fair or exhibition conducted by such body or organization;[52] and
- performance of a nondramatic musical work by a vending establishment open to the public at large without any direct or indirect admission charge, where the sole purpose of the performance is to promote the retail sale of copies or phonorecords of the work.[53]

Performing Rights Organization (PRO): Since it would be logistically impractical for businesses to attempt to identify each copyright owner and acquire rights from each owner for each work a business or performer wished to perform publicly, entities known as performing rights organizations (PROs) or performing rights societies have formed and serve the role of intermediary between copyright owners in various works

49. 17 U.S.C. §110(1).
50. 17 U.S.C. §110(3).
51. 17 U.S.C. §110(4).
52. 17 U.S.C. §110(6).
53. 17 U.S.C. §110(7).

and businesses, performers, and members of the public who wish to perform those works. Performance rights organizations serve to collect royalties in relation to the performance rights of its members and then distribute these royalties to its members—typically minus its fees or costs. Performance right organizations generally license performance rights only for non-dramatic performances, not the other exclusive rights of copyright holders. The three most known performance rights organizations in the United States are ASCAP, BMI, and SESAC. However, similar organizations can be found in at least forty countries around the world.[54]

Exception for Sound Recordings: The exclusive rights of the owner of a copyright in a sound recording are limited to the rights of reproduction, preparation of derivative works, distribution (already discussed), and performance by digital audio transmission (discussed later).[55] As such, sound recordings are not protected by the fourth (performance) and fifth (display) rights of the "bundle of rights" of copyright owners.

***Public Display*:** Akin to the performance right, copyright owners have an exclusive right to display their works publicly. The "public" aspect of the display right is substantially the same as the public aspect of the performance right, and, accordingly, private or personal display, such as in your home, is unlikely to violate this right. If a copy of a work is legally obtained (e.g., purchased), that particular copy or version of the work may be publicly displayed without liability under copyright. However, further copies cannot be displayed publicly. For example, a painting, poster, or sculpture purchased from the artist or sculptor may be displayed in public, but electronic images (e.g., copies) of the work may not be displayed publicly. Only the work itself may be displayed unless authorization from the copyright owner is otherwise obtained.

The Internet has increased the significance of the public display rights in part because copyright owners can more easily demonstrate "display"[56] of a protected work online, compared to a "distribution" or "performance." While the right of public display was codified prior to the preva-

54. http://www.iamusic.com/articles/performing-rights.html.

55. 17 U.S.C. §114(a) ("The exclusive rights of the owner of copyright in a sound recording are limited to the rights specified by clauses (1), (2), (3) and (6) of section 106, and do not include any right of performance under section 106 (4).").

56. 17 U.S.C. §101 (To "display" a work means to show a copy of it, either directly or by means of a film, slide, television image, or any other device or process or, in the case of a motion picture or other audiovisual work, to show individual images nonsequentially.).

lence of the Internet and computing of today, showing a work over the Internet often falls within the definition of public display.[57]

***Public Performance by Digital Audio Transmission*:** This particular right applies only to "sound recordings" and came into effect in 1996.[58] From a practical perspective, this right generally refers to public performance in particular circumstances—by way of satellite, cable, and webcasts. Performance of sounds recordings over FM and AM radio—for example, playing songs over the radio—is not covered by this provision, as those performances are analog transmissions.[59] As may be apparent, the rights associated with music and performance or duplication of songs, including sound recordings, can be complicated and legally complex to navigate if one is unfamiliar with the applicable statutory provisions and the nuances contained therein.

B. Moral Rights—17 U.S.C. §106A

"Moral rights" is a translation of the French term "*droit moral*" and refers to the ability of authors to control the fate of their works relying on a connection between an author and her creation.[60] Moral rights protect the personal and reputational value of a work to its creator rather a purely monetary value. The creator's rights differ by jurisdiction and culture internationally and may include the right to receive or decline credit for his work, the right to prevent his work from being altered without permission, the right to control ownership of his work, the right to dictate terms and conditions regarding display of his work, and the right of royalties on resale of his work.[61]

---

57. The Google search engine is a well-known search engine that displays images from various websites, including use of thumbnail images, in its search results. Interestingly, courts have held that website framing does directly infringe the public display right and that an image search engine thumbnail is fair use. Perfect 10, Inc. v. Google, Inc., No. 06-55405, 2007 U.S. App. Lexis 11420 (9th Cir. May 16, 2007).

58. The Digital Performance Right in Sound Recordings Act of 1995, P.L. 104-39, effective Feb. 1, 1996.

59. However, permission must still be obtained from the author or composer of the underlying work, which is conventionally done by purchase of a license for particular songs or albums through Performance Rights Organizations/Societies (PRO/PRS), as described under the Public Performance section.

60. Betsy Rosenblatt, Moral Rights Basics (Harvard Law School,1998). http://cyber.law.harvard.edu/property/library/moralprimer. html.

61. *Id.*

Intellectual property in the United States has typically been incentive-focused rather than moral rights-focused. Many European countries recognized "moral rights" of authors in certain works early on. Likewise, European countries typically also provide more protection for moral rights, as a broader range of works qualify for protection.

While "moral rights" may be protected under various trademark, privacy, and defamation statutes in the United States, 17 U.S.C. §106A (the Visual Artists Rights Act of 1990 (VARA)) provides the primary protection for moral rights under U.S. copyright law.[62] As the name suggests, VARA protects the moral rights for works of "visual art," and the moral rights vest automatically in the author(s) of these works. Under this statute, authors of works of visual arts are entitled to the right of *attribution* and the right of *integrity*. The right of attribution enables authors to prevent misattribution of a work, while the right of integrity enables authors to prevent intentional distortion, mutilation, or other modification of a work if that distortion is likely to harm the author's reputation, and to also prevent destruction of works of recognized stature.[63]

Section 101 of Title 17[64] defines, by way of example, works of visual art that qualify for protection under VARA[65] and also defines works that are not works of visual art and thus do not qualify for protection under VARA.[66] Under these provisions, authors of works of visual art,

62. *Id.*
63. 17 U.S.C. §106A(a).
64. 17 U.S.C. §101.
65. A "work of visual art" is—
    (1) a painting, drawing, print, or sculpture, existing in a single copy, in a limited edition of 200 copies or fewer that are signed and consecutively numbered by the author, or, in the case of a sculpture, in multiple cast, carved, or fabricated sculptures of 200 or fewer that are consecutively numbered by the author and bear the signature or other identifying mark of the author; or
    (2) a still photographic image produced for exhibition purposes only, existing in a single copy that is signed by the author, or in a limited edition of 200 copies or fewer that are signed and consecutively numbered by the author.
66. A work of visual art does not include—
    (A)
        (i) any poster, map, globe, chart, technical drawing, diagram, model, applied art, motion picture or other audiovisual work, book, magazine, newspaper, periodical, data base, electronic information service, electronic publication, or similar publication; (ii) any merchandising item or advertising, promotional, descriptive, covering, or packaging material or container;

including paintings, drawings, prints, sculptures, and photographs existing in a single copy or a limited edition of 200 or less signed and numbered copies, automatically will receive the identified rights of attribution and integrity. These moral rights are not available for "works made for hire," cannot be transferred (e.g., assigned), and end with the death of the author. These limitations on "moral rights" are consistent with the historical origination of these moral rights as being based on a connection between the author and his/her creation rather than monetary incentives. Therefore, a sculptor who spends three years of work completing a single sculpture is entitled to "moral rights" under VARA in the sculpture, while a printing shop that prints out a million copies of a single poster in a printing run for sale and distribution would not be entitled to moral rights in the poster under VARA.

C. Limitations and Exceptions to the Rights of Copyright Owners

1. Fair Use

Notwithstanding the previously described rights of copyright owners, the fair use of a copyrighted work, which may include reproduction in copies or phonorecords or other means, may not be infringement of copyright if done for certain purposes, such as criticism, comment, news reporting, teaching, scholarship, or research.[67] Fair use is an often-asserted defense (or perhaps, more properly, exemption) in copyright infringement litigations and requires a four-factor analysis of: (1) the purpose and character of the use, (2) the nature of the copyrighted work, (3) the amount and substantiality of the portion used in relation to the work as a whole, and (4) the effect of the use upon the potential market for or value of the work.[68] Fair use will be discussed further in the *Copyright Infringement Section.*

2. First Sale

As mentioned previously, owners of a particular copy of a work are

---

(iii) any portion or part of any item described in clause (i) or (ii);

(B) any work made for hire; or

(C) any work not subject to copyright protection under this title.

67. 17 U.S.C. §107.

68. *Id.*

entitled to "sell or otherwise dispose of the possession of that copy."[69] Owners of a particular copy may also "display the copy publicly . . . to viewers present at the place where the copy is located."[70] One rationale for the "first sale doctrine" is the equitable concept that once the copyright owner has sold or otherwise parted with a particular copy of a work, his rights in that particular copy are exhausted, as he has already had a chance to bargain for compensation for this particular work—whatever that compensation may be—and no longer should be allowed to retain control over that particular copy of a work.

3. Good Faith

A limited "good faith exception" exists that permits courts to limit damages to $200 for educational institutions, libraries, archives, and public broadcasters provided these entities had a reasonable belief that their alleged infringing activity was "fair use."[71]

4. Compulsory Licensing and Varied Exemptions to Specific Works and Entities

Several provisions of Title 17 provide specific exemptions to the above-described rights.[72] Compulsory licensing provisions relating to certain works and entities are also provided. In the absence of these statutory provisions, copyright owners could use contract law and sell or license rights under any terms they desired or *never sell or license the rights at all*. However, these statutory provisions require licensing for certain works and with certain provisions. These compulsory licensing provisions may be deemed as a step by the U.S. government to prevent copyright owners from holding too strong a right(s), such that innovation and creativity would be stifled. These provisions may be deemed "Goldilocks provisions," which attempt to strike a balance between copyright owners and the rights of the public and public domain, and the opportunity to continued use of these works by the public in creation of further works.

While the particulars of compulsory licensing are unlikely to be encountered except for those working in these areas of copyright law, U.S. copyright law provides for compulsory licensing in varying degrees in the following instances:

---

69. 17 U.S.C. §109(a).
70. 17 U.S.C. §109(c).
71. 17 U.S.C. §504(c)(2).
72. 17 U.S.C. §§108, 110–22.

- retransmission of broadcast signals by cable television companies[73] and satellite companies;[74]
- mechanical licenses, such as rerecording a nondramatic composition after first publication by the author[75] (e.g., anyone can "cover" a song once the composer gives permission to someone to do so);
- use of recorded music in jukebox;[76]
- noncommercial broadcasting of published musical, pictorial, graphical, or sculptural works;[77] and
- secondary transmissions of television superstations and network for home viewing.[78]

Whether it be the jukebox or satellite television, certain innovations may cause the pendulum of incentivized balance of copyright provisions to swing so far in one direction that the rights provided to copyright owners are either too potent or not potent enough. Each instance carries a risk of stifling creativity and progress in the sciences and arts. The U.S. Congress enacted legislation believed to help the pendulum swing back.

V. TERM OF PROTECTION

Arguably the most complicated issue under U.S. copyright law is determining the term of life that a copyright owner enjoys for a particular work, especially for works created prior to 1978. A determination of the term of copyright protection can be a complicated matter, as the term of life may be dependent upon several factors, including the date of creation, the date of publication (if any), and under which U.S. Copyright Act the work was created and/or published.[79]

Works created today or at least on or after January 1, 1978, involve a more straightforward determination of their term of life. Specifically, works created on or after January 1, 1978, are automatically protected from the date of creation through the **author's life plus 70 years**.[80] If

73. 17 U.S.C. §111.
74. 17 U.S.C. §122.
75. 17 U.S.C. §115.
76. 17 U.S.C. §116.
77. 17 U.S.C. §118.
78. 17 U.S.C. §119.
79. *See* 17 U.S.C. §§302–304.
80. 17 U.S.C. §302(a).

there is more than one author of the work, the term of protection is the last surviving author's life plus 70 years.[81] If no natural person is identified as the author of a work, the author is identified under a fictitious name, or the work is a work made for hire, copyright endures for a term of **95 years from first publication, or a term of 120 years from its creation, whichever expires first.**[82] As such, copyright for works that are not works made for hire and that have a known author or author(s) are not necessarily tied to a publication date but rather solely based on "date of creation" and the life of the author.

Works created before January 1, 1978, may require a more complicated analysis to determine when the term of rights expires, as the term of copyright has been extended with passage of laws over time. Works that were in existence and/or in a term of protection may have had their term of life extended based on certain provisions.

(a) *Works created but not published or copyrighted before January 1, 1978,* generally endure for the same term as those provided above with respect to works created after January 1, 1978.[83] However, certain provisions are also set forth to ensure that the work does not expire before December 31, 2002, if it remains unpublished and not before December 31, 2047, if published before December 23, 2002.[84] These provisions attempt to coordinate the terms of unpublished works as of the time of the Copyright Term Extension Act of 1998 (aka Sonny Bono Copyright Extension Act), which was created to promote more consistency with the term of life provisions moving forward.

---

81. 17 U.S.C. §302(b).

82. 17 U.S.C. §302(c).

83. Author's life plus 70 years OR shorter of 95 years from publication or 120 years from creation (for anonymous works, pseudonymous works, works made for hire).

84. 17 U.S.C. §303:

> ("(a) Copyright in a work created before January 1, 1978, but not theretofore in the public domain or copyrighted, subsists from January 1, 1978, and endures for the term provided by section 302. In no case, however, shall the term of copyright in such a work expire before December 31, 2002; and, if the work is published on or before December 31, 2002, the term of copyright shall not expire before December 31, 2047.
> (b) The distribution before January 1, 1978, of a phonorecord shall not for any purpose constitute a publication of the musical work embodied therein.").

(b) *Works with copyright subsisting as of January 1, 1978* (pre-1978 published works still in effect as of January 1, 1978), will vary in their duration depending on their date date of publication and on whether or not they were published with notice or were properly renewed. Section 304 sets forth the detailed provisions regarding these works.[85] Generally, works falling into this category—assuming registration and notice formalities have been met—endure effectively for 95 years from the date of publication.[86]

The most current schedule of extended terms of copyright protection for works is regarded as being a result of successful lobbying to extend copyright protection in certain well-known works. For example, Mickey Mouse made his screen debut in 1928 as "Steamboat Willie," and the copyright on Mickey was set to expire in 2003, with the copyrights on other Disney characters Pluto, Goofy, and Donald Duck set to expire a few years later.[87] As a result of successful lobbying by Disney and other copyright holders—the Copyright Term Extension Act of 1998 was enacted and extends the copyright for these and other similarly situated works, preventing them from entering the public domain until 2019.[88] As time passes and as we approach and pass the 2019 time frame, the duration of rights of copyright owners will continue to become increasingly consistent,[89] assuming no further statutory modifications are made to the current copyright duration provisions.

85. Traditionally under previous U.S. copyright laws, copyright owners were require to renew their copyrights in order to enjoy continued protection. Renewal became effectively automatic in 1992 so that copyright owners no longer needed to take action to receive the copyright extension provided for in the 1976 Copyright Act. As a result, works published before 1965 required active renewal, but works published after 1965 did not require renewal to receive the fullest term of protection available under U.S. law.

86. 17 U.S.C. §304.

87. Chris Sprigman, *The Mouse That Ate the Public Domain: Disney, the Copyright Extension Act, and* Eldred v. Ashcroft (March 5, 2002), http://writ.news.findlaw.com/commentary/20020305_sprigman.html.

88. *Id.*

89. Author's life plus 70 years OR shorter of 95 years from publication or 120 years from creation (for anonymous works, pseudonymous works, works made for hire).

VI. OWNERSHIP

A. Author as Default Owner

Copyright in a protectable work vests initially in the author or authors of the work.[90] When there is more than one author, the work may be described as a "joint work," and the authors are deemed co-owners of copyright in the work.[91] As one may recall, each author is initially the owner of the bundle of five rights (reproduce, prepare derivative works, distribute, perform, display) described in detail earlier in this chapter. These rights are property rights and may be transferred or licensed as a group or individually. Ownership of a copyright is distinct from any material object in which the work is embodied.[92] For example, a reader can purchase a new book from a neighborhood bookstore, read it, and when the reader is done, can resell it without infringing the copyright, as the copyright in the underlying work is distinct from the material object in which the work is embodied (the single copy of the book itself).

B. Works Made for Hire

Although there is a general rule that the person(s) who creates a work is the author(s) of that work, a specific category of works called "works made for hire" is an exception to the rule.[93] In a work made for hire, the employer (or the party who commissioned the work) rather than the employee (or the person that actually created the work) is considered the author. U.S. Copyright law defines a "work made for hire"[94] as:

1. a *work prepared by an employee* within the scope of his or her employment, OR
2. a *work specifically ordered or commissioned* for use as a contribution to a collective work as part of a motion picture or other audiovisual work as a translation, as a supplementary work, as a compilation, as an instructional text, as a test, as answer material for a test, or as an atlas *if the parties expressly agree in a written*

90. 17 U.S.C. §201.

91. *Id.*

92. 17 U.S.C. §202.

93. U.S. Copyright Office, *Works Made for Hire under the 1976 Copyright Act*, Circ. 9, p. 1 (2011).

94. 17 U.S.C. §101.

> *instrument* signed by them that the work shall be considered a work made for hire.

In interpreting whether a work is properly considered a "work made for hire," courts often look to the relationship between the parties. First it must be determined whether the work was prepared by an employee or an independent contractor. If the person preparing the work is deemed an employee, the work is considered a work made for hire under part 1 of the definition. The determination as to whether one preparing a work is an employee frequently may be more complicated than expected, as the definition of employee is an agency law definition in which the factors of (1) control by the employer over the work, (2) control by the employer over the employee, and (3) status and conduct of the employer are among the various issues considered.[95]

If the preparer of the work is not deemed an employee under this analysis, the work must qualify as a work made for hire under part 2 of the statutory definition. In particular, the work must be a work "specifically ordered or commissioned" of the particular types listed in part 2, and the part 2 parties must have expressly agreed in a written instrument that the work shall be considered a work made for hire. The requirement of an express agreement and a written instrument in part 2 of the definition is likely an attempt to limit the number of after-the-fact disputes regarding whether a work was or was not a "work made for hire," as this determination will often be dispositive of who is the owner of the copyright in the work.

C. Transfer/Assignment

Copyright, like other personal property, can be transferred. As such, ownership and authorship are two distinct concepts, as the author is the default owner, but the author of a work and the owner of the copyright in the underlying work may be distinct as a result of subsequent transfer, often in exchange for monetary payment or other compensation. In order for a transfer of an exclusive right of copyright ownership to be valid, the transfer must be in writing and signed by the owner of the rights that are being conveyed.[96] The written instrument of conveyance may be recorded with the Copyright Office, and doing so will provide the receiv-

95. Community for Creative Non-Violence v. Reid, 490 U.S. 730 (1989).
96. 17 U.S.C. §203.

ing party with certain privileges, including constructive notice of the transfer of ownership should ownership later be disputed.[97]

VII. PUBLICATION

"Publication" is the distribution of copies or phonorecords of a work to the public by sale or other transfer of ownership, or by rental, lease, or lending. The offering to distribute copies or phonorecords to a group of persons for purposes of further distribution, public performance, or public display constitutes publication. A public performance or display of a work does not of itself constitute publication.[98]

As previously described, publication is important for works created prior to 1978, as it will affect the duration of copyright protection for these works. Publication date also is determinative of anonymous works, pseudonymous works, and works made for hire. Additionally, publication may be significant for all works, because if a work is registered within three months of first publication, the work receives the benefit of a registration date back to the first publication. Earlier dates of registration may be beneficial during an infringement action, as statutory damages, including attorneys' fees, are available to successful plaintiffs only if the work was registered prior to the act of infringement.

VIII. NOTICE

Until March 1, 1989, when the Berne Convention Implementation Act of 1988 came into effect in the U.S., notice of copyright was a condition of protection under copyright. This act, among other things, did away with certain copyright formalities in the United States, including notice of copyright, and thus copyright notice is no longer required under U.S. law. However, many continue to recommend use of copyright notice, because it informs the public that the work is protected by copyright, identifies the copyright owner, and provides the year that the work was first published. More important, if proper copyright notice appears on a published work that is infringed, it will remove the ability for the alleged infringer to successfully argue that it is an innocent infringer that is entitled to reduced damages.

---

97. 17 U.S.C. §205.

98. 17 U.S.C. §101.

17 U.S.C. §§401–406 set forth notice provisions for various types of works and products containing underlying works. For example, visually perceptible copies notice[99] should have:

1. the symbol © (the letter C in a circle), or the word "Copyright," or the abbreviation "Copr.";
2. the year of first publication of the work;[100] and
3. the name of the owner of copyright in the work, or an abbreviation by which the name can be recognized, or a generally known alternative designation of the owner.

Placing notice on works to the extent possible is encouraged, since inclusion of notice has virtually no downside and may provide advantages to the copyright owner during enforcement of his copyrights.

99. 17 U.S.C. §401.

100. 17 U.S.C. §401(b)(2) also sets forth permissible exceptions for certain products ("in the case of compilations, or derivative works incorporating previously published material, the year date of first publication of the compilation or derivative work is sufficient. The year date may be omitted where a pictorial, graphic, or sculptural work, with accompanying text matter, if any, is reproduced in or on greeting cards, postcards, stationery, jewelry, dolls, toys, or any useful articles.").

PART 2

Copyright Prosecution

To promote public education and creative exchange, [copyright law] invites audiences and subsequent authors to use existing works in every conceivable manner that falls outside the province of the copyright owner's exclusive rights. Copyright law's perennial dilemma is to determine where exclusive rights should end and unrestrained public access should begin.

—Neil Weinstock Netanel
"Copyright and a Democratic Civil Society,"
Yale Law Journal, 1996

I. INITIAL REGISTRATION CONSIDERATION

Throughout the *New Practitioner's Guide,* the term "prosecution" has been broadly used as a heading to categorize the actions involved in obtaining and/or formalizing intellectual property rights. The actions involved in obtaining and/or formalizing patent, trademark, and copyright rights vary significantly. In the United States, patent prosecution involves an application process involving substantive review for novelty, obviousness and written description, and best mode requirements, among others. Conversely, trademark and copyright prosecution are generally registration-type processes, although trademark applications are considered in view of previously registered marks to ensure that a confusingly similar mark has not already been registered. Copyright registration, however, does not involve a review of the subject matter to be registered in view of previous works. Rather, the application is reviewed to ensure that the requisite formalities have been complied with, including any requisite deposits.

The U.S. Copyright Office, which has been a part of the Library of Congress since 1870, is responsible for administering the national copyright registration system and mandatory deposit provisions for published works. The Copyright Office also administers the compulsory and statutory licensing provisions concerning, among other things, satellite and cable transmissions. Each year the Copyright Office acquires hundreds of thousands of books, films, sound recordings, and other creative works of authorship and provides them to the Library of Congress's national collection. While copyright registration does not involve the "substantive review" entailed in patent prosecution, it is beneficial for applicants and their representatives to understand the particulars of the application process to ensure that registrations include the proper subject matter, ownership information, and characterizations so that registration will provide for an enforceable claim should the registered copyright later be infringed.

For example, the copyright registration application involves identification of dates of first publication, ownership information, inquiry as to whether the work was a "work made for hire," and other information that may relate to the duration and ownership of rights associated with the work. Deposit requirements must also be met to formalize the rights associated with a registration. Additionally, because the deposit may be relied on in litigation to determine the particular subject matter covered by the registration and whether an accused infringing work infringes the registered copyright, deposits should be carefully selected and should be pristine in appearance and viewability whenever possible. Some applicants may utilize an enlarged, clearly printed, or enhanced presentation of the work for deposit to ensure that the subject matter of the work is clearly understood and viewed. A characterization or categorization of the type of work is also made when the registration application is submitted.

II. BENEFITS OF REGISTRATION

Registration is not a condition for creation or receipt of copyrights. Unlike patents in which an applicant's rights do not begin until a patent is issued by the USPTO[1] or trademarks in which a mark owner's rights do

1. Certain provisional rights are available under 35 U.S.C. §154(d) starting at a date prior to issuance of a patent, i.e., the date of publication. For example, if a U.S. application publishes and then eventually issues with one or more "substantially identical" claim(s), an applicant may sue for and receive damages dating back beyond the issue date to the date of publication.

not begin until the mark is used in commerce,[2] copyrights subsist upon fixation in a tangible medium. No use, application, or registration is required for copyrights to be established. Copyrights come into existence contemporaneous with creation and fixation of the work. This concept may be captured by a previous logo of the U.S. Copyright Office, which includes a depiction of the nib of a fountain pen a mere moment before or after contact with paper. Copyright is created at the moment in which the nib of the author's pen fixes the original work. As such, this logo was an especially fitting symbol for the U.S. Copyright Office.

While copyright rights vest with or without registration with the U.S. Copyright Office, there are several advantages to registration, and particularly in registering works soon after creation and/or initial publication, with the U.S. Copyright Office.

- *Copyright must be registered (or preregistered) before an infringement suit can be filed.* A work of U.S. origin must be registered (or at least preregistered in certain circumstances) before an infringement suit may be initiated against an accused infringer. As such, early registration avoids delays before bringing suits.
- *Establishes prima facie evidence of validity.* Registration within five years of publication establishes prima facie evidence of validity and the facts stated in the registration certificate.

2. "Intent-to-use" applications may be filed with the USPTO in certain circumstances to preserve an early date until use in commerce is actually made.

- *Early registration may allow collection of increased damages for infringement.* If registration is filed within three months of the publication of the work or prior to infringement of the work, statutory damages and attorney's fees may be available to the owner. Otherwise, only actual damages and lost profits are available.
- *Facilitates in preventing importation of infringing works.* Registration with the U.S. Copyright Office enables registration of the work with the U.S. Customs Service, which assists in preventing importation of infringing works.
- *Registration establishes public record of the copyright.*

In some industries, authors will regularly register works as a protective mechanism in the event the work gains popularity. In doing so, these authors can preserve their ability to receive the benefits above. In some instances, it may be possible to provide some protection to a fairly large number of works with a single registration, such as when an author registers a catalog containing a line of products. Other authors may prefer a wait-and-see approach, saving registration costs and fees by registering only select works once they are deemed to have certain value worth protecting. In doing so, these authors may be limiting the theories of damages, claims, and beneficial presumptions they may otherwise have been able to assert. Varied copyright prosecution strategies may be implemented by copyright owners who have sufficient budgets to achieve their desired copyright goals.

III. PREREGISTRATION

Preregistration is a fairly new procedure in the Copyright Office that may be utilized by certain classes of works that have been determined to have a history of pre-release infringement.[3] Preregistration, somewhat akin in concept to an intent-to-use application in trademark law or a provisional patent application in patent law, serves as a placeholder for such limited purposes as when a copyright owner desires to sue for infringement while a work is still being prepared for commercial release. Preregistration is not a substitute process for registration, but rather a mechanism that enables earlier enforcement proceedings to be brought in certain circumstances.

3. 17 U.S.C. §408(f); 37 C.F.R. §202.16.

Only the following types of works—motion pictures, sound recordings, musical compositions, literary works being prepared for publication in book form, computer programs (including videogames), and advertising or marketing photographs—are eligible for preregistration. Applications for preregistration can be made only online and require only submission of the application, including as full a description of the work as possible and payment of the fee. No copies or phonorecords of the work itself or any part thereof are to be submitted.

In order to preserve the benefits of preregistration, an applicant must proceed to register the work within the earlier of one month after the copyright owner becomes aware of the infringement or three months after the first publication of the work. If registration is not made pursuant to these prescribed time periods, a court may dismiss an action for copyright infringement that was initiated based upon preregistration. As such, timely registration is a requirement to perfect the rights granted pursuant to the preregistration procedure.

IV. REGISTRATION PROCESS

For many years, copyright registrations were submitted to the U.S. Copyright Office in paper format, along with any additionally required materials, including deposit materials and payment for the application. However, the primary means for submission of applications for registrations of copyrights is now by electronic format.[4] The preparation and filing process, regardless of the particular manner in which the application is submitted, is described in further detail below.

A. Preparation and Filing of the Application

Preparation of a copyright application can be a quick and efficient process, assuming the requisite information is known and available to the preparer of the application. The U.S. Copyright Office website, http://www.copyright.gov/, is rich with information, explanations, and tutori-

4. In fact, applicants who utilize online registration and submit their registration through the electronic Copyright Office will pay reduced fees for processing of their application as compared to an applicant requiring filing by paper means. It is still acceptable for applicants who submit their electronic applications via the electronic Copyright Office to submit paper copies of their deposits.

als explaining what materials to provide to the U.S. Copyright Office, which forms to utilize, the fees associated with each type of application, and how many deposits are to be provided. Information relating to the registration is easily identified on the website under the "How to Register a Work" heading, and forms can be found on a website tab labeled as such ("Forms"). Additionally, many of the most common questions relating to the registration process and even to U.S. Copyright questions can be found on the U.S. Copyright Office website, including frequently asked questions.

A basic claim for copyright registration may be made for a (a) single work, (b) multiple unpublished works if they are all by the same author and owned by the same claimant, or (c) multiple published works if they are first published together in the same publication on the same date and owned by the same claimant. In the United States, the *author,*[5] the *copyright claimant,*[6] the *owner*[7] of the exclusive right(s), or the *duly authorized agent* of any of three previously entities listed may submit or file an application form with the U.S. Copyright Office. There are currently three options for filing an application with U.S. Copyright Office: (1) Online Registration, (2) Registration Using Fill-In Form CO, and (3) Registration via Submission of Paper Forms.

1. Online Registration

Online registration is generally the preferred or recommended mechanism for registration and provides for a reduced filing fee, the fastest processing time, online status tracking, secure online payment, and the capability to electronically upload deposit requirements. Literary works, works of visual arts, works of performing arts (such as motion pictures), and sound recordings may be registered via online registration. While the deposit requirements for published works require submission of a physical copy deposit (and thus cannot be done purely electronically), the online registration process may still be used for published works, as

5. An *author* in this context may be the person who actually created the work or the employer or other person for whom the work was prepared in the context of a "work made for hire."

6. A *copyright claimant* may be the author of a work or a person or organization who has obtained by contract the legal title in an application.

7. An *owner* is an owner of ***any*** of the exclusive rights that constitute a copyright. As such, multiple entities could qualify as an "owner," since each of the "bundle of rights" in a copyright could be separately or individually owned.

instructions are provided during the application for subsequent physical submission of the deposit requirement.

2. Registration Using Fill-in Form CO

The next preferred method from the perspective of the Copyright Office, as well as of most applicants, is registration utilizing Fill-in Form CO. This method utilizes a bar code–scanning technology to scan a bar code uniquely provided on each form. An applicant or applicant's representative merely fills in provided fields on Fill-in Form CO on a computer and then may print and mail or otherwise deliver the paper application along with payment (e.g., check or money order) and the associated deposit requirement to the Copyright Office.[8] The Copyright Office warns that Form CO should not be saved and utilized for future application for registration, as the bar code on each form downloaded is unique and intended for unique applications as part of the case-tracking process.

3. Registration with Paper Forms

A third option for registration is utilization of paper forms, as has traditionally been done. Paper forms still exist for literary works (Form TX); visual art works (Form VA); performing arts works such as motion pictures (Form PA); and sound recordings (Form SR). However, these forms are no longer readily available on the Copyright website (consistent with the Copyright Office's desire to encourage applicants to e-file whenever possible), but may be requested from Copyright Office staff and mailed to the requester. Certain types of works and applications must be filed on paper with the proper fee and deposit requirement. Vessel hull designs (Form D-VH), mask works (Form MW), and renewals of copyright claims (Form RE) are among those works that must be filed on paper, and because these specific works and applications must be registered using a paper application, the forms are provided on the U.S. Copyright website. Applicants and representatives should confirm the preferred and required methods of filing prior to filing their application, as the filing parameters may change over time.[9]

---

8. IP practitioners practicing in the greater Washington, D.C. area will often have a courier hand-deliver such a filing to the U.S. Copyright Office located in the Library of Congress to ensure safe arrival and to solidify a registration date without potential delay from postal mailings.

9. http://www.copyright.gov/circs/.

B. Deposit Requirements

U.S. Copyright laws include a specific requirement for applicants to satisfy certain "deposit requirements" in order for the works to be registered with the U.S. Copyright Office and to receive the benefits associated with the registration. The rationales for submission of a deposit include providing clarity as to the subject matter covered in a particular registration. However, the deposit requirement of the U.S. Copyright Office also has had a significant impact on populating the shelves of the U.S. Library of Congress.

The deposit requirements may vary based upon type of work, whether or not a work is published, and/or method of application. Generally, the following deposit requirements apply:

- For unpublished works, one complete copy or phonorecord is to be submitted.
- If the work was first published in the U.S. in 1978 or later, two complete copies or phonorecords of the best edition are to be submitted.
- If the work was first published in the U.S. prior to 1978, two complete copies or phonorecords of the work as first published are to be submitted.
- If the work was first published outside the U.S., one complete copy or phonorecord of the work as first published are to be submitted.

Unfortunately, special deposit requirements do apply even for some of the more commonly registered works. Some of the common special deposit requirements include the following:

- If the work is a *motion picture*, the deposit requirement is one complete copy of the motion picture (published or unpublished) and a separate written description of its contents.
- If the work is a *literary, dramatic, or musical work published only in a phonorecord*, the deposit requirement is one complete phonorecord.
- If the work is a *computer program* (published or unpublished), the deposit requirement is one visually perceptible copy in source code of the first 25 pages and the last 25 pages of the program, or the entire program if the program is less than 50 pages.

- If the work is embodied in *CD-ROM* format, the deposit requirement is one complete copy of the material—e.g., the CD-ROM, the operating software, and any accompanying manuals. If registration is sought for the computer program on the CD-ROM, the deposit should also satisfy the computer program requirement—including the first 25 pages and last 25 pages of source code for the program.

C. Registration

A copyright registration is effective on the date the U.S Copyright Office *receives all the required elements in acceptable format*. It is not uncommon for it to take several months before the U.S. Copyright Office will review an application it has received, as the Office receives more than 600,000 applications each year. Assuming all the information has been provided in the filed forms, the fees are paid, and the deposit requirement has been satisfied, a registration can be issued with an effective date that is the date the application was filed with the U.S. Copyright Office. Copyright applications, unlike patent and trademark applications, are not subject to substantive review to determine if the subject matter is novel or nonduplicative, or even identical to a prior registration. Upon satisfaction of the application, deposit, and fee requirements, a registration is granted. While legally inconsequential, those accustomed to receiving a Grant of Letters Patent with its gold ribbon may be a bit disappointed when receiving a "registered copyright," as its form is simply a copy of the application that was originally submitted to the U.S. Copyright Office, with the further inclusion of a stamp indicating registration. Again, this registration will often have an effective date that is the date the application was received at the U.S. Copyright Office, in contrast to patents, which generally become effective upon the issue date, which can often be years after the USPTO initially received the application.

PART 3

Copyright Litigation

Almost anyone can be an author; the business is to collect money and fame from this state of being.

—A.A. Milne (Author of *Winnie the Pooh*)

I. REQUIREMENTS FOR BRINGING SUIT

A. *Infringement*

The actions and requirements for bringing a copyright suit in federal district court do not differ significantly from the requirements for bringing a patent or trademark infringement lawsuit or any other civil lawsuit in federal district court. Distinctions arise merely from the substance of the case. For example, a complaint must be filed along with a cover sheet, a filing fee, and a certification of interested parties. As those familiar with litigation in federal district court are aware, the complaint sets forth the claim or claims against the accused infringer and the requests or demands. Identification and claim of proper personal jurisdiction and subject matter jurisdiction or, in other words, jurisdiction over the defendant and a federal question (federal copyright law)[1] respec-

1. 28 U.S.C. §1338 ("(a)The district courts shall have original jurisdiction of any civil action arising under any Act of Congress relating to patents, plant variety protection, copyrights and trademarks. Such jurisdiction shall be exclusive of the courts of the states in patent, plant variety protection and copyright cases. . . .").

tively must be identified. Additional assertions, such as an assertion of proper venue, should be made, including statutory citation. Copyright plaintiffs also make any other claims in the complaint, such as violations of the Digital Millennium Copyright Act (DMCA), claims based in contract law, or supplemental claims to be heard or considered as part of the case.

Plaintiffs in a copyright infringement case, just like plaintiffs in any other federal litigation, will want to reference closely the Federal Rules of Civil Procedure (FRCP) to ensure proper action in initiating and pursuing a claim against an accused infringer. Typically, copyright plaintiffs will want to make certain assertions to satisfy key provisions of the FRCP. For example, in order to ensure compliance with FRCP 8(a), plaintiffs should at least identify the copyrighted work that is being infringed, assert that the plaintiff is the owner of the copyrighted work, assert that the copyright for the work has been registered with the U.S. Copyright Office, and provide allegations describing the infringing activity. Plaintiffs should attach evidence of registration with the U.S. Copyright Office, ideally the certificate of registration but at least the registration number, as well as evidence of the infringing activity, if at all possible. Section 411(a) of the Copyright Act indicates that federal registration of the copyright claim is a requirement for initiating suit of a copyright infringement claim and thus it is prudent to include evidence of such a registration.[2] It is also recommend that plaintiffs include copies of infringing works or similar evidence as an exhibit to the complaint. Further particulars not unique to copyright cases and somewhat common to the various types of intellectual property are described in more detail in the *Patent Litigation Section* and to some degree in the *Trademark and Trade Dress Litigation Section.*

B. Declaratory Injunction

In certain instances, an entity that is fearful of a copyright infringement suit being initiated against it can bring suit as a plaintiff to have a court

2. 17 U.S.C. §411(a); *see also* Reed Elsevier v. Muschnick, slip. op., 559 U.S. _____ (March 2, 2010) (Holding that the failure to register a copyright prohibits federal court from hearing the case not for lack of subject matter jurisdiction but rather for failure to meet a claim-processing rule. As such, a motion for failure to state a claim rather than lack of subject matter jurisdiction would likely be the grounds for dismissal of a case in which a copyright plaintiff has failed to register the copyright.).

declare that there is in fact no copyright infringement occurring and can even ask for the court to award damages for, among other things, a false accusation of copyright infringement. Declaratory judgment actions are described also in both the patent and trademark infringement sections as the Declaratory Judgment Act,[3] authorizing that declaratory judgment actions applies broadly to any type of actual controversy and thus is applicable to each area of intellectual property assuming the requirements of (1) there being an actual controversy and (2) the jurisdictional requirements for federal court are met. Declaratory judgment actions may be an effective tool for accused infringers to more effectively select a preferred venue for litigation or to in essence "call a potential copyright plaintiff's bluff" with respect to accusations of copyright infringement. Experienced litigators in other areas will likely be familiar with declaratory judgment actions and their use, purpose, and requirements. Many of the filing requirements of declaratory judgment action are similar to those filed by a copyright owner but just from the reverse or opposing perspective. For example, a declaratory judgment plaintiff will want to identify jurisdiction for the case in the Declaratory Judgment Act in conjunction with the 28 USC §1338, which gives rise to copyright claims in federal court. Instead of evidence of infringement, declaratory judgment plaintiffs should consider including evidence of accusation of infringement and evidence that supports an apprehension of suit so as to demonstrate a proper claim for declaratory judgment. Claims and evidence that support the declaratory judgment plaintiff's assertions relating to claims of invalidity of the copyright registration, non-infringement, applicable defenses, or other relevant evidence as are applicable also should be included in the complaint to the extent possible.

II. INFRINGEMENT

Copyright infringement occurs when one or more of the exclusive rights provided to copyright owners are violated. If a copyrighted work is reproduced, distributed, performed, publicly displayed, or made into a derivative work without the permission of the copyright owner infringement has occurred.[4] To infringe an exclusive right, an accused work must be (1) derived from the copyrighted work and (2) be substantially similar to the

3. 28 U.S.C. §§2201–2202.
4. http://www.copyright.gov/help/faq/faq-definitions.html.

copyright work. Courts will generally apply these two requirements in similar, however nuanced, fashion, varying the specifics or the exact terminology used to investigate these concepts in the factual inquiry.

A. Derivation

Copying is typically proven with indirect or circumstantial evidence as it is very rare in which someone will be able to provide direct evidence of copying. From a policy perspective, because direct evidence often will not exist, requiring direct evidence of copying would likely prove to be a fatal requirement for copyright owners. It is a rare occasion when an accused infringer will be witnessed or when the defendant admits to copying. There is also no requirement that the copying has been done in an intentional or willful manner. Depending on the facts of the case, it may even be concluded that copying has been done subconsciously. One of the more famous copyright infringement cases involved Beatle George Harrison's song entitled "My Sweet Lord" for which he was accused of infringing the plaintiff's prior song "He's So Fine."[5] In that case, the judge concluded that Mr. Harrison subconsciously possessed the melody when it was shown he previously had ample access to it as the previous song was a No. 1 song on the music charts. It was concluded that, in coming up with his song, Mr. Harrison had likely derived subconsciously the accused work from the copyright protected work he was accused of infringing.

Copyright owners have the initial burden of producing evidence and the burden of persuasion in showing copying occurred. This burden can be met through either (1) a showing that the creator of the accused work had access to the copyrighted work and that the accused work is substantially similar to the work under copyright or (2) a showing that these works are "strikingly similar" as, in some particular instances, access to the work can be inferred as a result of the similarity being so close that it is in essence unbelievable that the accused infringer could not have copied the copyrighted work. These initial showings or inferences of copying are rebuttable through proof of independent creation or sometimes

5. Bright Tunes Music Corp. v. Harrisongs Music, Ltd., 420 F. Supp. 177 (S.D.N.Y), *aff'd sub nom.*, ABKCO Music, Inc. v. Harrisongs Music, Ltd., 722 F.2d 988 (2d Cir. 1983).

6. An extreme hypothetical example would be proof that the defendant was stranded on a remote island that does not have electronics or communication with the rest of the world during the time when a copyrighted song was in existence.

proof that the defendant could not have access to the copyrighted work.[6] Copying alone is not sufficient for there to be copyright infringement. The copying also must have been an "improper appropriation" for copyright infringement to be found as liability will be avoided if the derivation or copying was permissible in quantity or kind.

B. Substantial Similarity

The second element of a case for copyright infringement is a showing intended audiences for the two works find "substantial similarity" in the two works. It is important to keep in mind that the substantial similarity analysis is focused on the particular expression of the works, not merely similarity in a general concept, genre, or idea. Merely writing a spy novel about a British spy will not likely infringe the copyright associated with the James Bond series of books or movies. However, a story about a British spy who is popular with the ladies, drives Aston Martin cars, drinks martinis made by shaking and not stirring the ingredients, receives gadgets from an old nutty professor type character, and reports to a boss with a single letter code name—will be much more likely to infringe the copyright related to the James Bond books or movies.

Copyrights provide protection for particular expressions of ideas but not for the ideas themselves and thus a determination as to substantial similarity is made based on the expression of ideas of the protected work as compared to the accused infringing work. While the test as to whether two works are substantially similar has been phrased in a variety of ways, one way to characterize the determination is that it is a determination whether an average observer would recognize the accused work as having been appropriated or taken from the copyrighted work.[7]

III. DEFENSES AND COUNTERCLAIMS

A. Fair Use

Fair use is perhaps the most well known copyright infringement defense and even those with limited legal training or expertise in copyright law will often at least recognize the term "fair use." The fair use defense is codified in Section 107 of Title 17 and provides that it is not an infringement to make "fair use" of a copyrighted work for purposes such as

7. Ideal Toy Corp v. Fab-Lu Ltd., 360 F.2d 1021, 1022 (2d Cir. 1966).
8. 17 U.S.C. §107.

criticism, comment, news reporting, teaching, scholarship, or research.[8] In determining whether the use made of a work in any particular case is a fair use, the factors to be considered shall include (1) the purpose and character of the use, including whether such use is of a commercial nature or is for nonprofit educational purposes; (2) the nature of the copyrighted work; (3) the amount and substantiality of the portion used in relation to the copyrighted work as a whole; and (4) the effect of the use upon the potential market for or value of the copyrighted work.[9]

A fair use type defense may be utilized in a variety of instances and circumstances, however, the focus of the analysis of the asserted defense typically will be an analysis rooted in the four factors delineated above. A use of a copyrighted work that is deemed noncommercial, for educational or social commentary, uses only minimal parts of a work, and has little or no effect on the underlying work will more likely be found a "fair use" as compared to use of the entirety of work as part of a business or for profit with minimal informational, artistic, or educational value, and in a manner that significantly undermines the market for or value of the original work. In practice, the impact on the market for the work will often be weighed more heavily than the other factors to the extent one factor carries the day of the analysis. Under the umbrella of fair use, parody can be considered one nuanced type of fair use and involves "use of some elements of a prior author's composition to create a new one that, at least in part, comments on that author's works."[10] Parody may be a defense more commonly used by news sources, entertainers, and bloggers and protects use by the public of certain copyright protected expression for purposes by commentary and related purposes. A parody defense more likely will be successful if the parody expression is noncommercial, does not substantially hurt or undermine the value of the product, and involves taking only a minimal amount of protected subject matter so as to convey the message of the parody as compared to commercial use of large portions of protected expression that results in the destruction of the market for the original work.

B. OTHER DEFENSES

Depending on the factual circumstances, an accused infringer may assert or use any of the following as defenses to liability for copyright infringement.

9. *Id.*
10. Campbell v. Acuff-Rose Music, 510 U.S. 569, 580 (1944).

1. Invalidity

Invalidity is one of the more common defenses asserted and may materialize in evidence or a showing that the work was not original, lacks subject matter that is eligible for copyright protection, or that someone other than the plaintiff is actually the owner of the copyright. If a work is found to have been in the public domain or if the copyright was not properly registered, then the claim of copyright infringement is improper.

2. Independent Creation

A defendant can successfully defend against allegations of copyright infringement if it can be shown that she had independently created the work she is accused of infringing. Practically speaking, it may be difficult to prove independent creation unless the creator was diligent in memorializing the creation process or unless the creation process was done with witnesses or in a medium that records or memorializes dates. Nowadays, many artists, creators and producers post creative works on blogs, websites, on Facebook® or YouTube.®[11] These postings could serve as evidence of creation dates if one were attempting to prove earlier creation of material.

3. De Minimis Infringement

Even if an accused infringer admits to copying portions of the copyrighted work the accused infringer may not be liable for infringement if it can be shown that the appropriation was "de minimis." In other words, the defendant is asserting that the amount taken was so small that it is irrelevant. Similarly, a defendant might assert that he or she has not taken any of the creative or new subject matter that in essence gives rise to copyright protection but instead has merely taken facts and not the

11. Additionally, Internet technology, such as The Way Back Machine (http://www.archive.org/web/web.php), which uses internet bot technology to capture images of websites and archive these pages, is an ongoing project to archive the Internet. Accordingly, users in essence can go back in time to see certain web pages and content posted months or years earlier. It perhaps could be used to demonstrate independent or earlier creation. Even if not sufficient proof from an evidentiary requirement perspective, it may give insight into a litigant regarding the facts of a case and provide leads regarding obtaining more concrete evidence. This technology is already being used by patent firms to research prior art for patents in litigation.

protected form of expression. Often a "de minimis" type argument is made in conjunction or as part of a "fair use" argument.

4. Scenes *a Faire*

Similar to a "de minimis" infringement defense, an accused infringer may assert that to the extent the subject matter was derived or copied, he or she has merely copied or used "scenes *a faire*" or the standard or common place characteristics or features. Returning to the spy novel example, it is expected that elements such as sports cars, foreign bank accounts, and spy gadgets will be a part of the story as they are common-place in that genre of book. Likewise, in a love story two characters often meet, then date, then have a misunderstanding that results in tension and turmoil, followed by a near break-up and finally the couple reconfirms their love. These concepts are "scenes *a faire*" and generally cannot be protected by copyright. However, specific sequences, compositions, or features can be protected by copyright. Scenes *a faire* is commonly understood with respect to novels or movies but it can also be a defense with respect to subject matter, such as computer source code with respect to something such as the common practice of listing variables at the outset of the program or using certain common abbreviations in the code.

5. Merger Doctrine

Another variation on defenses such as de minimis infringement and scenes *a faire* is what is referred to as the "merger doctrine." In asserting the merger doctrine, the defendant alleges that the underlying copyrighted work is so simple, so common, so trite, that there are only a few ways to express the idea. In essence, the idea and its expression are merged. For example, there are only so many ways to depict a football player—in shoulder pads with cleats and a helmet. This generic idea cannot be protected under copyright. Of course, a specific or particularized expression of the idea will still be protectable.

6. Statutory Limitations

Section 108-122 of the United States Code[12] set forth a number of statutory limitations to the exclusive rights of copyright owners. Among the more notable provisions in these sections is the so-called library excep-

12. 17 U.S.C. §§108-122.

tion,[13] limitations on performance and display,[14] limitations on rights with respect to computer programs,[15] and satellite television limitations.[16] In addition, if three years have expired before the plaintiff brought suit for infringement then the statute of limitation may have expired as copyright claims are subject to the statute of limitations.

7. Safe Harbors

The 1998 Digital Millennium Copyright Act (DMCA) includes in Title II of the act certain safe harbor provisions relating to online content. This title, which is also referred to as the Online Copyright Infringement Liability Limitation Act (OCILLA), provides a safe harbor for many activities performed by telecommunications companies, internet service providers (ISPs), hosts, and related entities for claims of contributory infringement or other copyright liability based upon content that was transmitted, stored, displayed, etc., by the telecom companies and Internet service providers.[17] A rationale behind the safe harbor for ISPs and like entities is that, because ISPs merely provide a platform for use by customers, it is unfair or impracticable for ISPs to have to police the immense amount of content and activity that occurs using their infrastructure and technology. Further, it perhaps would be unfair to hold those entities liable for copyright infringement of users merely because the infringement occurred using the service for access to the Internet. As such, the OCILLA provisions of the DMCA limit liability to ISPs and like entities for activities for infringement of copyright for transmitting, routing, or providing a connection to infringing activity;[18] for intermediate and temporary storage of infringing material on a system or network of the service provider;[19] for storage of infringing material residing on the ISPs system or network;[20] or for "linking" to infringing material at the direction of a user.[21] In order to qualify for the safe harbor, the ISPs have to take certain affirmative actions, including removal of content when they receive notice of alleged infringing activity. The distinction

13. 17 U.S.C. §108.
14. 17 U.S.C. §110.
15. 17 U.S.C. §117.
16. 17 U.S.C. §122.
17. 17 U.S.C. §512.
18. 17 U.S.C. §512(a).
19. 17 U.S.C. §§512(a-b).
20. 17 U.S.C. §512(c).
21. 17 U.S.C. §512(d).

between activities by ISPs that fall within the safe harbor of the DMCA and actions and actors for which the safe harbor does not apply and the actor that is deemed liable for infringement may be somewhat nuanced and may include considerations of other non-infringing activities performed using the technology and the amount of control the entity has over content. Napster was a well-known online site that provided a conduit for peer-to-peer file sharing and was eventually shut down by the courts for its role in the copying and distribution of copyrighted music.[22]

8. Equitable Defenses

Abandonment is one type of equitable defense available to defendants in copyright infringement cases, although it will typically require affirmative action of abandonment, such as an announcement by the copyright owner that he or she is abandoning the copyright of a particular work. Additionally, common equitable defenses, such as estoppel, acquiescence, and unclean hands, are available to copyright infringement defendants depending on the circumstances of the case. Most equitable defense arise as a result of the passage of time or actions by copyright holder that make allowance of a copyright holder to successfully bring an infringement claim to be inequitable.

9. Copyright Misuses

Misuse of a copyright involves using a copyright to secure an exclusive right or limited monopoly beyond those granted by the Copyright Office and contrary to public policy. A finding of copyright misuse will result

---

22. The Napster online peer-to-peer file-sharing service website brought significant attention to online copyright activities in the 1999-2001 timeframe. The Napster service facilitated the exchange of music and other files using the easy-to-use MP3 file medium. The contents of many of these files shared were under copyright and in sharing these files, it was argued, exclusive rights (e.g. distribution, reproduction) of the copyright owners were violated and Napster was liable for direct infringement, contributory infringement, and vicarious infringement of the plaintiff's copyright. This activity was subject to a number of litigations in which individual artists (e.g., Metallica, Dr. Dre, etc.) initiated lawsuits, as did a number of recording companies through the RIAA, which eventually led to the site shutting down in compliance with a court injunction. A&M Records, Inc. v. Napster, Inc., 239 F.3d 1004 (9th Cir. 2001). As such, the Napster litigation(s) provides some further insight into the issues relating to online file sharing and copyright issues.

in the copyright being found to be unenforceable. Copyright misuse does not invalidate the copyright but will render it unenforceable for the period of misuse. In order for actions by copyright owners to rise to the level to be considered misuse, the actions generally will need to rise to the level of an antitrust violation. Misuse in the context of copyright may occur most often with respect to computer software and other situations involving licensed works. Among scenarios in which misuse has been found are situations in which a licensee agreed to not create competing products, a licensee agreed not to use competitors' products, and enforcement of a license that precluded development of new non-infringing works.

IV. REMEDIES

Copyright owners may pursue a variety of remedies and typically will pursue injunctions and damages. Depending on the facts of the case, the evidence available, and other litigations concerns such as the disruptive nature of discovery requests relating to a damages theory (e.g. infringer's profits), copyright owners will want to take time and carefully develop their damages theory for pursuit at trial.

A. Injunctions

Copyright owners may request a preliminary injunction at the outset of the case as well as a permanent injunction once infringement has been found after trial and the conventional four-factor injunction test is used to determine whether or not a court should award an injunction.[23] Under copyright caselaw, irreparable harm is generally presumed when a copyright is found to be infringed,[24] however, the finding of infringement does not result in issuance of an automatic injunction.[25] The court will still need to perform an equitable evaluation of the particulars of the case in light of the four factor injunction test with the finding of infringement—but the finding of copyright infringement begins that evaluation with equities leaning in favor of issuance of an injunction.

---

23. 17 U.S.C. §502.

24. Apple Computers v. Franklin Computer Co., 714F.2d 1240 (3rd. Cir. 1983).

25. The Copyright Act provides that courts may grant injunctive relief on such terms as it may deem reasonable to prevent or restrain infringement of a copyright. 17 U.S.C. §502(a).

B. Impound and Disposal

Courts may order the impounding, destruction, or other reasonable disposition of all copies made in violation of the copyright owner's rights, including all plates, molds, matrices, masters, tapes, film negatives, or other means or reproduction.[26] The court also shall take associated records into custody and will put in place a protective order to protect the confidentiality of these records with respect to discovery and use of the records.[27] From a policy perspective, impoundment and/or disposal of infringing goods and the means to continue infringing activity makes sense as allowing further copies to be made would allow continued violation of copyright owners' rights. Historically, impoundment and disposal have been somewhat drastic acts that were imposed in special circumstances. The provisions of the most recent version of the U.S. Copyright Act, however, give courts discretion to impose this remedy as deemed reasonable.

C. Damages

1. Actual Damages

Under §504 of the Copyright Act, a plaintiff that proves copyright infringement is entitled to damages. If the work that was infringed was registered prior to the first instance of infringement, the plaintiff can recover the actual damages that occurred as a result of the infringement. Actual damage is typically measured in terms of the profits lost by the copyright holder as a result of the infringement. In proving the lost profits it is the initial burden of the copyright holder to come forth with evidence demonstrating lost profits and, upon this showing, the defendant must rebut that showing. In some instances, the plaintiff may assert that actual damages should be calculated in terms of a reasonable royalty for the work. Both lost profits and reasonable royalty assertions are consistent with the understanding that the primary measure of market values is based on the extent to which the market value of the copyrighted work is impaired or harmed by the infringement.

In showing actual damages, such as lost profits, copyright owners will assert, among other things, that sales decline in a particular period is tied to the infringing activity; the infringer and copyright owner have the same customers and the infringing and copyrighted products have the

26. 17 U.S.C. §503.
27. *Id.*

same or similar uses; the infringer and copyright owners are competitors; and the infringing product acts as a substitute for the copyrighted product. In arguing against actual damages, such as lost profits, an accused infringer will highlight various other factors for the sales lost by a copyright owner; differences between infringing product and copyrighted product; distinctions in sales, including geographic distinctions or customer sophistication; the existence of other competitors that would have and could have made sales in place of infringing products; and other market explanations for any decline in sales identified by the copyright owner. Both parties will typically have experts testify regarding the actual damages theories and the court's determination of damages may very well come down to a battle of experts.

2. Infringers' Profits

While actual damages and infringing profits cannot both be collected in overlapping fashion, actual damages and infringer's profits can be collected if they are mutually exclusive such that they are not duplicative and to the extent the two sums are mutually exclusive they may be added together.[28] Plaintiff copyright owners once again will have the initial burden of showing the profits made as a result of the infringing product and the correlation between the sales and the infringement. Financial information, such as sales numbers, will typically be acquired through discovery during litigation from the accused infringer, which can often be extremely disruptive to the business operations of the opposing side. In an instance where the infringing work is an exact or substantially identical copy to the protected work, the correlation between the profits and the infringement more easily will be made than when the product is not identical or substantially identical to the copyrighted product. In such an instance, the copyright owner may point to evidence that demonstrates the criticality of the copied elements, including marketing and advertising for both the protected and infringing products, customer responses, and other evidence indicating key features of both the copyrighted and infringing products. In pursuing infringer's profits in lieu of or in addition to actual damages, plaintiffs also may be able to use the mechanics of litigation in their favor as discovery requests for infringers' profits can tend to be extremely disruptive for defendants (and their organizations) and may apply further pressure on the defendant for a quick settlement.

28. 17 U.S.C. §504(b).

3. Statutory Damages

Rather than actual damages or infringers' profits, copyright owners may elect for statutory damages as a remedy upon a finding of infringement. Pursuant to the Copyright Act, a copyright plaintiff can recover statutory damages in the range of $750 to $30,000 for each work infringed (not each copy of each work).[29] In the case of a finding of willful infringement, copyright plaintiffs may recover up to $150,000 for each infringed work. As such, copyright owners may choose to pursue statutory damages rather than actual damages when statutory damages may give rise to very large statutory damage awards in instances in which proving actual damages may be difficult or burdensome. For example, in one case, a jury awarded $72,000 for each infringing act of the 440 separate infringing acts, which were airings of copyrighted television episodes, for a total damages award of $31.68 million.[30] In order to be eligible for statutory damages, the copyright owner must have registered the copyright either before infringing activity began or within three months of first publication.[31] However, election of statutory damages can be at any time before final judgment. The possibility of statutory damages may prove to be an effective motivator for pre-litigation settlements. As such, prompt registration of a copyright may be one of the most effective ways to improve a litigation position so as to ensure statutory damages are available.

D. *Attorneys' Fees*

If the copyright owner has registered the copyright, either before infringing activity began or within three months of first publication, a claim may be made for attorneys' fees when appropriate.[32] However, if timely registration is not made, a claim for attorneys' fees will not be permitted. Attorneys' fees are available to a prevailing copyright infringement plaintiff and the defendant respectively.

---

29. 17 U.S.C. §504.

30. Feltner v. Columbia Pictures Television, Inc., 523 U.S. 340 (1998). (In this case, C. Elvin Feltner, Jr. owned Krypton International Corporation and operated televisions stations that aired shows licensed from Columbia Pictures, including shows such as *Who's the Boss?*, *Silver Spoons*, *Hart to Hart,* and *T.J. Hooker*. After Columbia revoked the license for these shows over a dispute for delinquent royalty payments, the television stations continued to air the copyrighted shows—effectively without a license. As a result, each airing was deemed a separate instance of infringement.).

31. 17 U.S.C. §412.

E. Criminal Provisions

In certain instances, if infringement activities are deemed to be willful infringement for the purposes of commercial advantage or private financial gain, these activities may rise to the level of criminal prosecution. For example, if the offense consists of reproduction or distribution of at least 10 copies during any 180-day period, which have a total retail value of more than $2,500, imprisonment of up to five years, a fine of up to $250,000 ($500,000 for corporate offenders), or both may be issued as a penalty in the case.[33] Criminal liability also can be brought under a similar provision as copyright infringement without the requirement of there being a demonstrated motive for profit.[34] Under this provision, if an actor reproduces or distributes 10 or more copies of a work with a total value of $2,500 or more, imprisonment for up to three years, a fine of up to $250,000 ($500,000 for corporate offenders), or both may be issued in the case. Under the same provisions, reproduction or distribution of a single work if valued at $1,000 or more can provide a basis for imprisonment of up to one year, a fine of up to $100,000 ($200,000 for corporate actors), or both. Criminal penalties also are available for pre-release distribution of a copyrighted work over a publicly accessible computer network[35] and for circumvention of a copyright protection system in violation of the DMCA.[36] Criminal penalties in copyright cases are prosecuted by the U.S. Department of Justice and thus most civil litigators will not have to worry about criminal remedies or provisions except for alerting the department as to believed criminal activities by an accused infringer or advising an accused defendant of any potential liability under these provisions in infrequent instances.

F. Customs Seizure

If a copyright is registered, a request can be made for involvement of the U.S. Customs and Border Protection (CBP).[37] Use of CBP to prevent importation of infringing works can be an effective way to combat infringement and misappropriation in lieu of or in conjunction with enforcement in federal court.

32. *Id.*
33. 17 U.S.C. §506(a)(1)(A); 18 U.S.C §2319(b).
34. 17 U.S.C. §506(a)(1)(B); 18 U.S.C. §2319(c).
35. 17 U.S.C. §506(a)(1)(C); 18 U.S.C. §2319(d).
36. 17 U.S.C. §1204.
37. 19 C.F.R. §133.31 *et seq.*

Section 5

Conclusion

> *[W]e're going to aggressively protect our intellectual property. Our single greatest asset is the innovation and the ingenuity and creativity of the American people. It is essential to our prosperity and it will only become more so in this century.*
>
> —President Barack Obama, March 11, 2010

We thank you for reading the *New Practitioner's Guide to Intellectual Property* (*NPG*) and hope that it has provided useful insight into practical aspects of intellectual property (IP). Although the *NPG* is comprehensive in coverage of the occurrences a practitioner (or applicant, inventor, or IP owner) may face in handling patents, trademarks, and copyrights, there are still numerous other aspects of intellectual property that may be encountered.

Esteemed practitioners often are able to skillfully handle any of the number of issues that can arise in the world of intellectual property on behalf of their clients in sufficient degree to at least identify the issues so as to be able to seek expertise in that area for further action. Whether your interests, business objects, or legal practice are focused on patents, trademarks, copyrights, or another particular niche of IP, improved understanding of areas outside of your expertise allows a practitioner to better assess and represent client interests. IP protection and enforcement unfortunately does not fit neatly into little boxes. Likewise, practice in IP requires a skilled practitioner to be well versed and multi-faceted in their IP skills and understanding. For example, patent prosecution understanding provides a patent litigator invaluable skills to draw from in litigating patent infringement cases. This same concept holds true for other areas of IP, whether the understanding and experience is obtained in trademarks, copyrights, trade secrets, or unfair competition. Interdisciplinary understanding in IP is critical for effective use of the U.S. intellectual property rights system and its importance only increases as technology and IP rights continue to intertwine in technology sectors from Internet based technologies to biotechnology to automated manufacturing. As playwright and author Anton Chekhov stated, "[k]nowledge is of no value unless you put it into practice."

We are hopeful and optimistic that the *New Practitioner's Guide to Intellectual Property* has provided you with a sizeable chunk of knowledge regarding intellectual property. However, we leave the second half of Mr. Chekov's quote, putting that knowledge into practice, to you.

—Dave & John

Index

B

C

D

E

G

H

I

L

R

T

V

W

About the ABA Section of Intellectual Property Law

From its strength within the American Bar Association, the ABA Section of Intellectual Property Law (ABA-IPL) advances the development and improvement of intellectual property laws and their fair and just administration. The Section furthers the goals of its members by sharing knowledge and balanced insight on the full spectrum of intellectual property law and practice, including patents, trademarks, copyright, industrial design, literary and artistic works, scientific works, and innovation. Providing a forum for rich perspectives and reasoned commentary, ABA-IPL serves as the ABA voice of intellectual property law within the profession, before policy makers, and with the public.